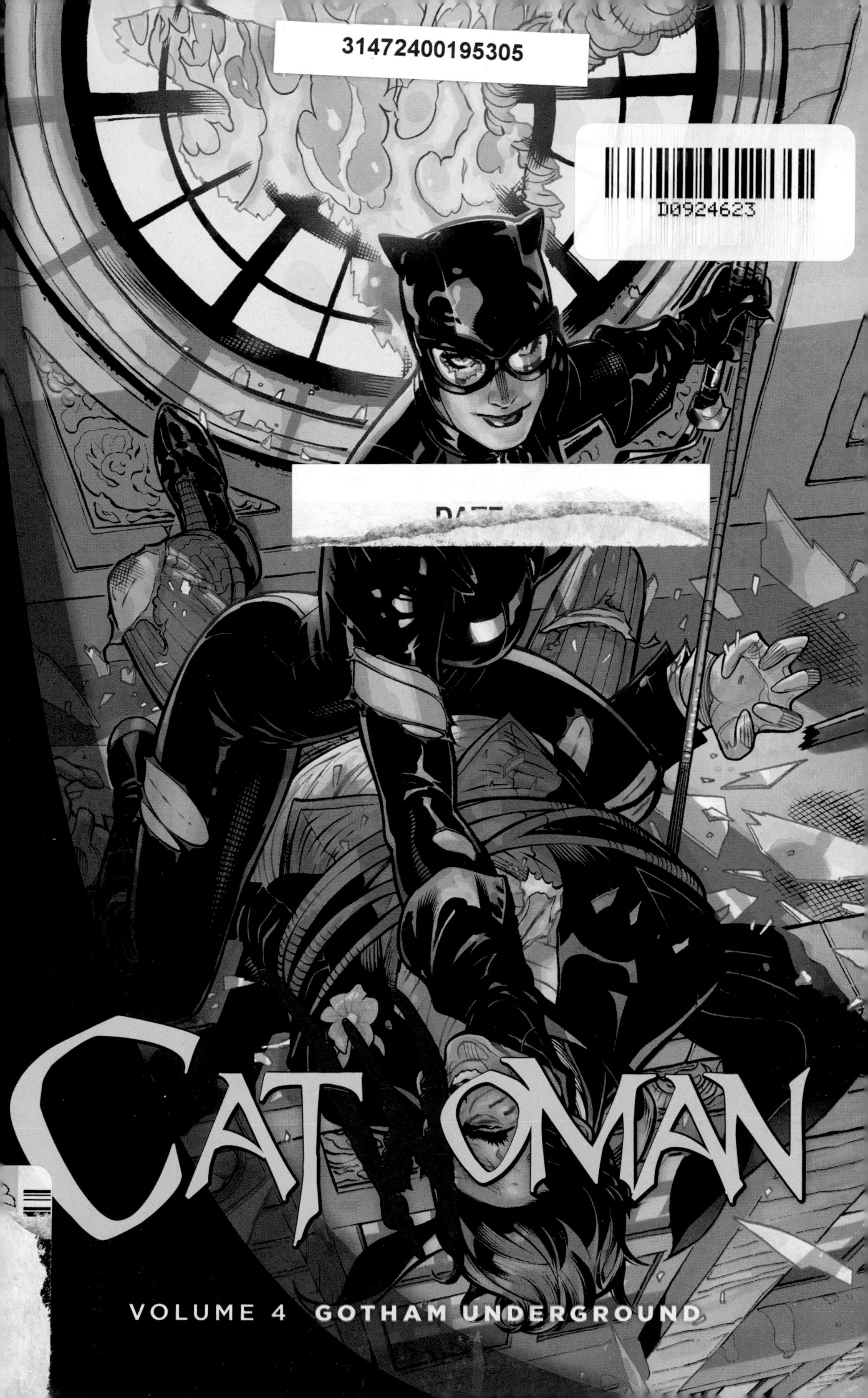

CATWOMAN

VOLUME 4 GOTHAM UNDERGROUND

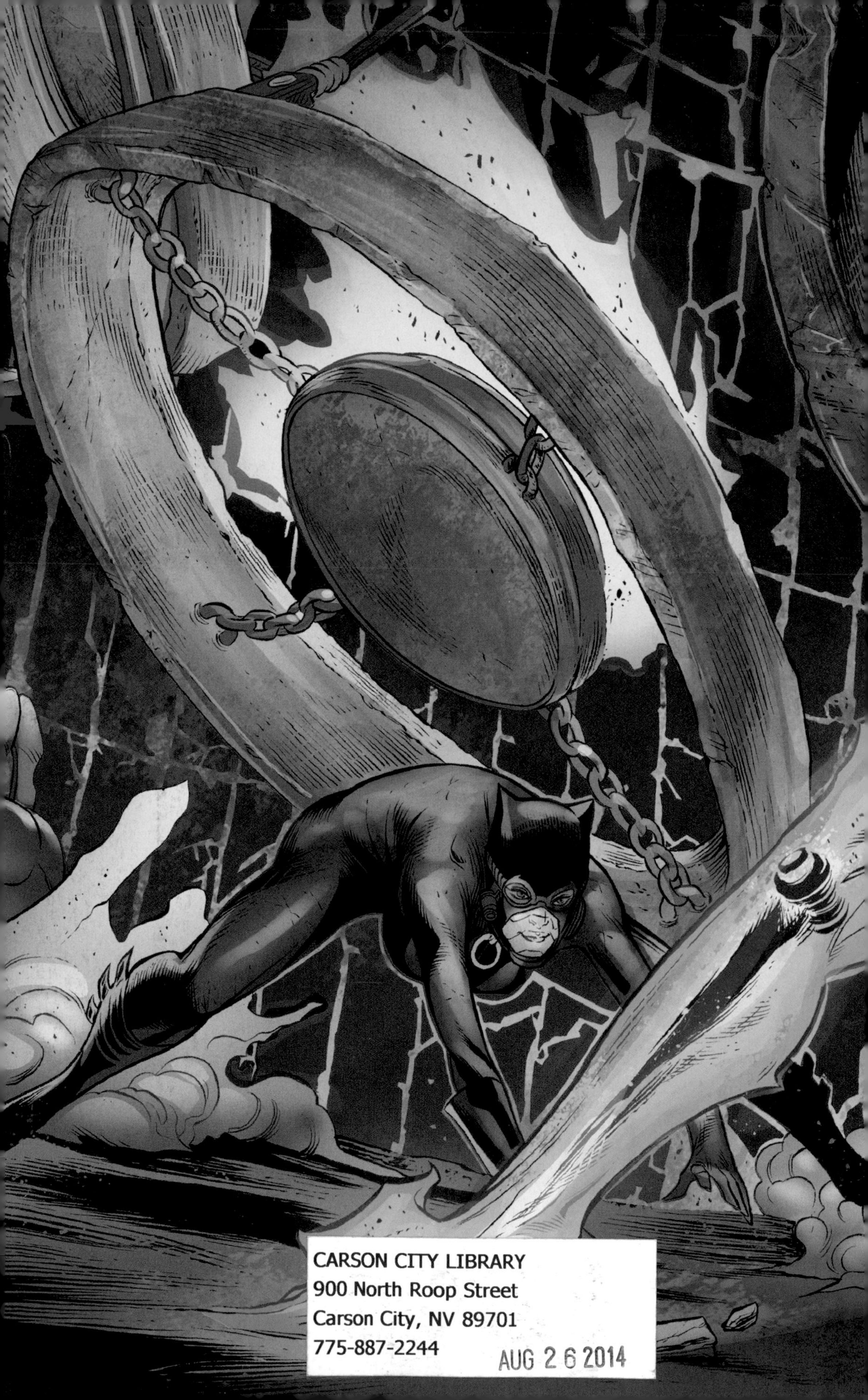

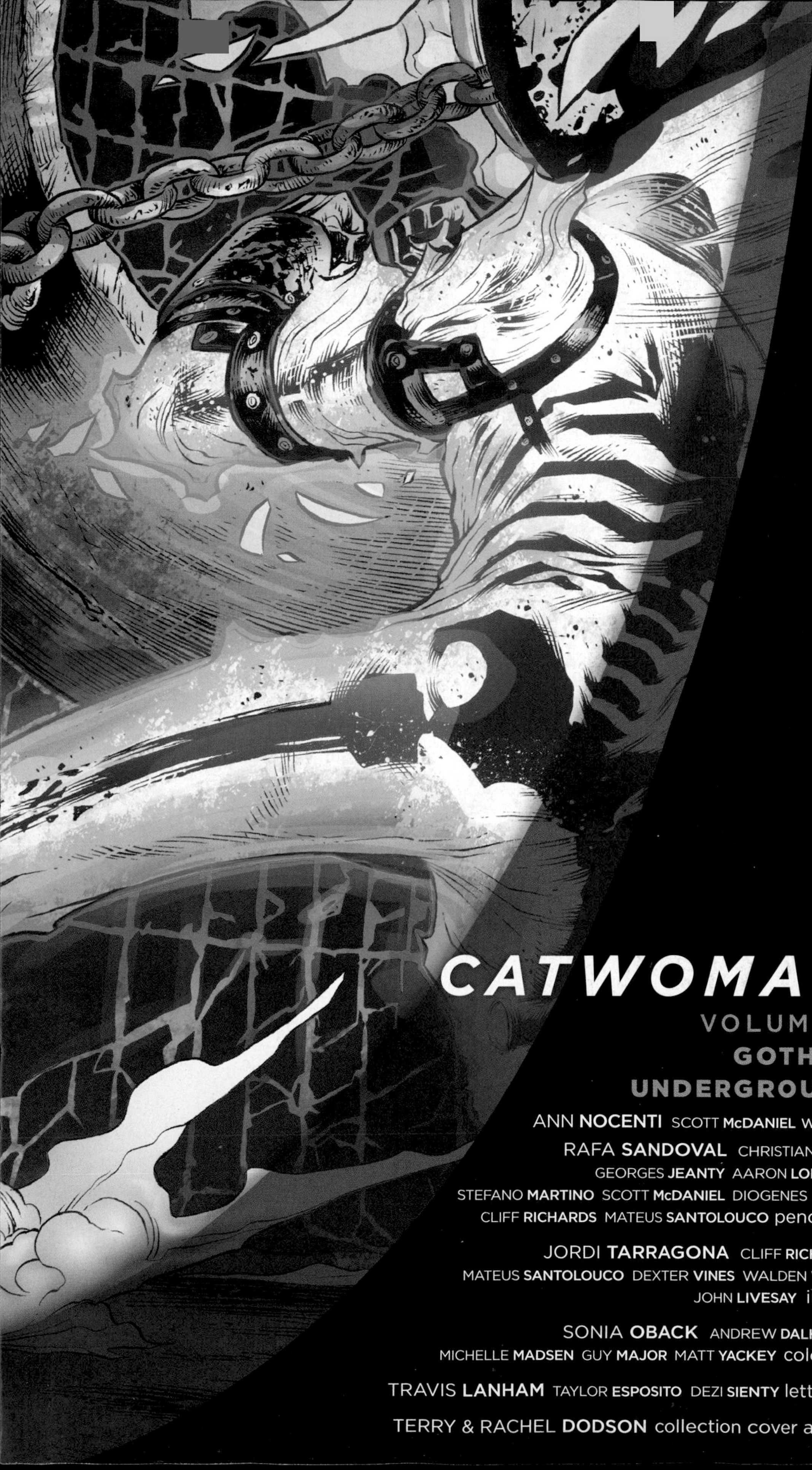

CATWOMAN

VOLUME 4

GOTHAM UNDERGROUND

ANN **NOCENTI** SCOTT **McDANIEL** writers

RAFA **SANDOVAL** CHRISTIAN **DUCE**
GEORGES **JEANTY** AARON **LOPRESTI**
STEFANO **MARTINO** SCOTT **McDANIEL** DIOGENES **NEVES**
CLIFF **RICHARDS** MATEUS **SANTOLOUCO** pencillers

JORDI **TARRAGONA** CLIFF **RICHARDS**
MATEUS **SANTOLOUCO** DEXTER **VINES** WALDEN **WONG**
JOHN **LIVESAY** inkers

SONIA **OBACK** ANDREW **DALHOUSE**
MICHELLE **MADSEN** GUY **MAJOR** MATT **YACKEY** colorists

TRAVIS **LANHAM** TAYLOR **ESPOSITO** DEZI **SIENTY** letterers

TERRY & RACHEL **DODSON** collection cover artists

RACHEL GLUCKSTERN Editor – Original Series DARREN SHAN Assistant Editor– Original Series ROBIN WILDMAN Editor
ROBBIN BROSTERMAN Design Director – Books ROBBIE BIEDERMAN Publication Design

BOB HARRAS Senior VP – Editor-in-Chief, DC Comics

DIANE NELSON President DAN DIDIO and JIM LEE Co-Publishers
GEOFF JOHNS Chief Creative Officer
JOHN ROOD Executive VP – Sales, Marketing and Business Development
AMY GENKINS Senior VP – Business and Legal Affairs NAIRI GARDINER Senior VP – Finance
JEFF BOISON VP – Publishing Planning MARK CHIARELLO VP – Art Direction and Design
JOHN CUNNINGHAM VP – Marketing TERRI CUNNINGHAM VP – Editorial Administration
ALISON GILL Senior VP – Manufacturing and Operations HANK KANALZ Senior VP – Vertigo and Integrated Publishing
JAY KOGAN VP – Business and Legal Affairs, Publishing JACK MAHAN VP – Business Affairs, Talent
NICK NAPOLITANO VP – Manufacturing Administration SUE POHJA VP – Book Sales
COURTNEY SIMMONS Senior VP – Publicity BOB WAYNE Senior VP – Sales

CATWOMAN VOLUME 4: GOTHAM UNDERGROUND

Originally published in single magazine form as CATWOMAN #19-24, #26, CATWOMAN ANNUAL #1, BATMAN: THE DARK KNIGHT #23.4
© 2013, 2014 DC Comics. All Rights Reserved. All characters, their distinctive likenesses and related elements featured
in this publication are trademarks of DC Comics. The stories, characters and incidents featured in
this publication are entirely fictional. DC Comics does not read or accept unsolicited ideas, stories or artwork.

DC Comics, 1700 Broadway, New York, NY 10019
A Warner Bros. Entertainment Company.
Printed by RR Donnelley, Salem, VA, USA. 4/25/14. First Printing.
ISBN: 978-1-4012-4627-3

Library of Congress Cataloging-in-Publication Data

Nocenti, Ann, author.
Catwoman. Vol. 4, Gotham Underground / Ann Nocenti ; illustrated by Rafa Sandoval ; illustrated by Jordi Tarrogana.
pages cm. — (The New 52!)
ISBN 978-1-4012-4627-3 (paperback)
1. Graphic novels. I. Sandoval, Rafa, illustrator. II. Tarrogana, Jordi, illustrator. III. Title. IV. Title: Gotham Underground.
PN6728.C39N64 2014
741.5'973—dc23
2014008596

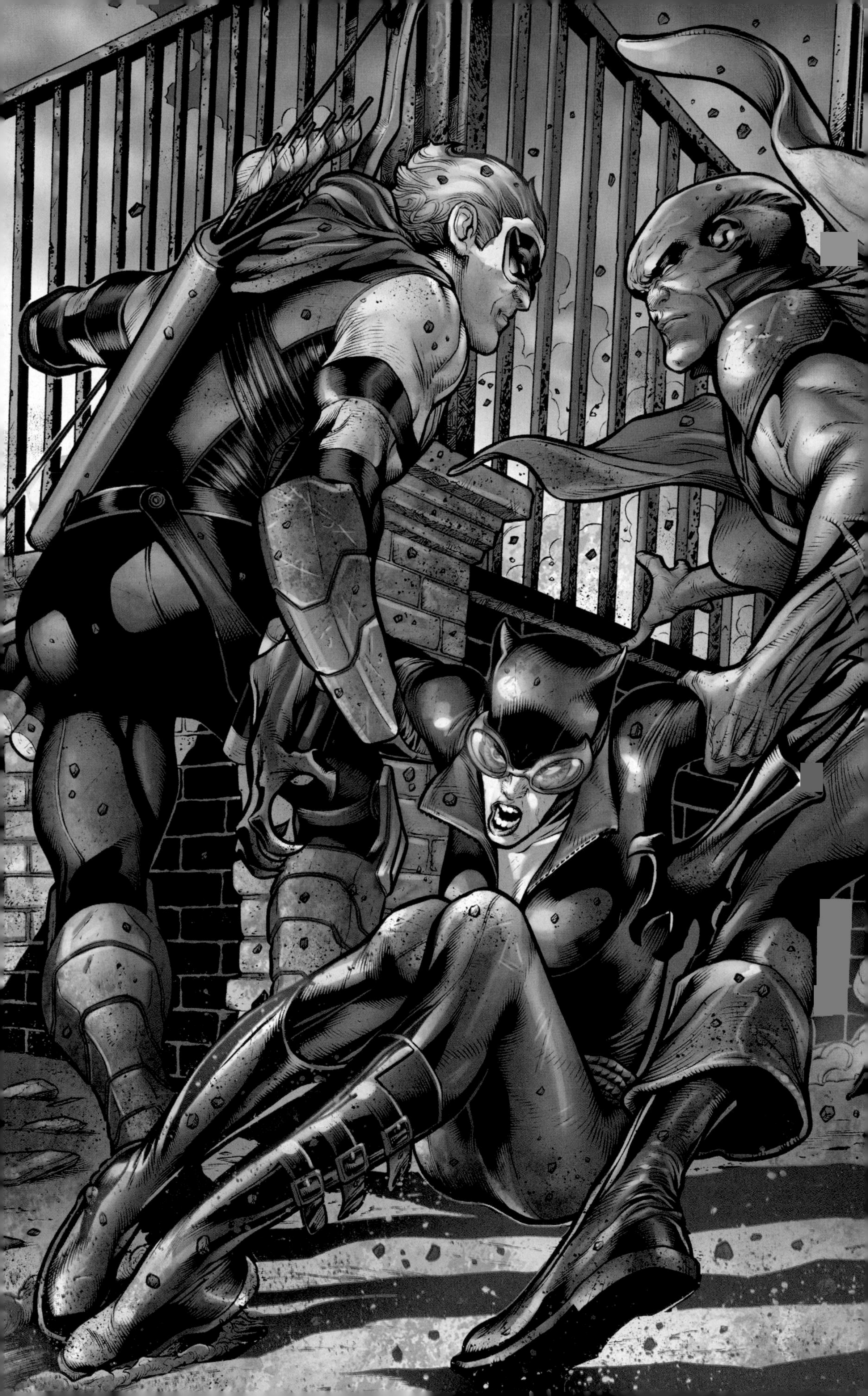

ANN NOCENTI
writer

RAFA SANDOVAL, CLIFF RICHARDS & STEFANO MARTINO
pencillers

JORDI TARRAGONA, CLIFF RICHARDS & WALDEN WONG
inkers

SONIA OBACK
colorist

RAFA SANDOVAL & JORDI TARRAGONA with SONIA OBACK
cover artists

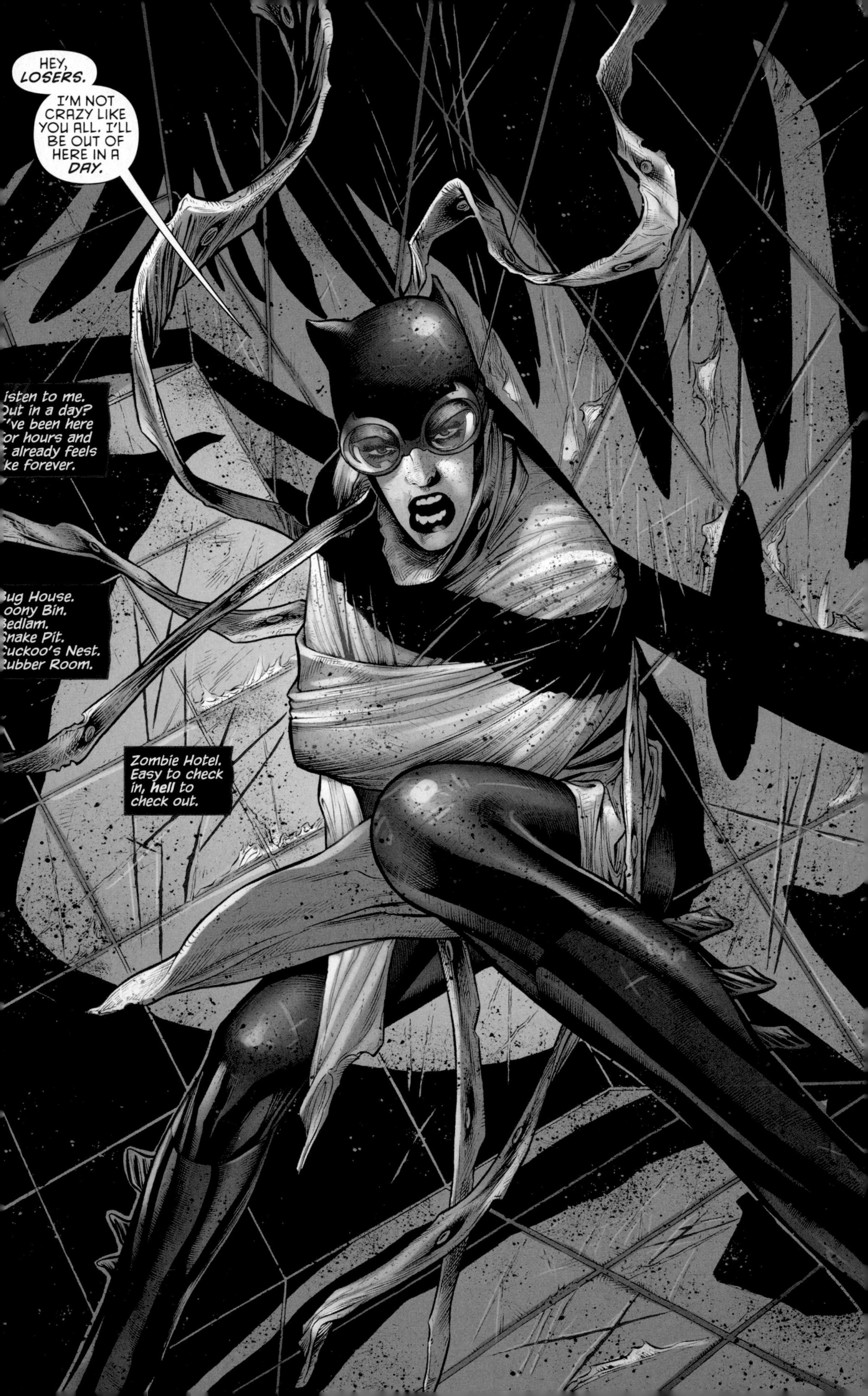
HEY, LOSERS.
I'M NOT CRAZY LIKE YOU ALL. I'LL BE OUT OF HERE IN A DAY.
isten to me.)ut in a day? 've been here or hours and t already feels ke forever.
Bug House. oony Bin. Bedlam. Snake Pit. Cuckoo's Nest. Rubber Room.
Zombie Hotel. Easy to check in, hell to check out.

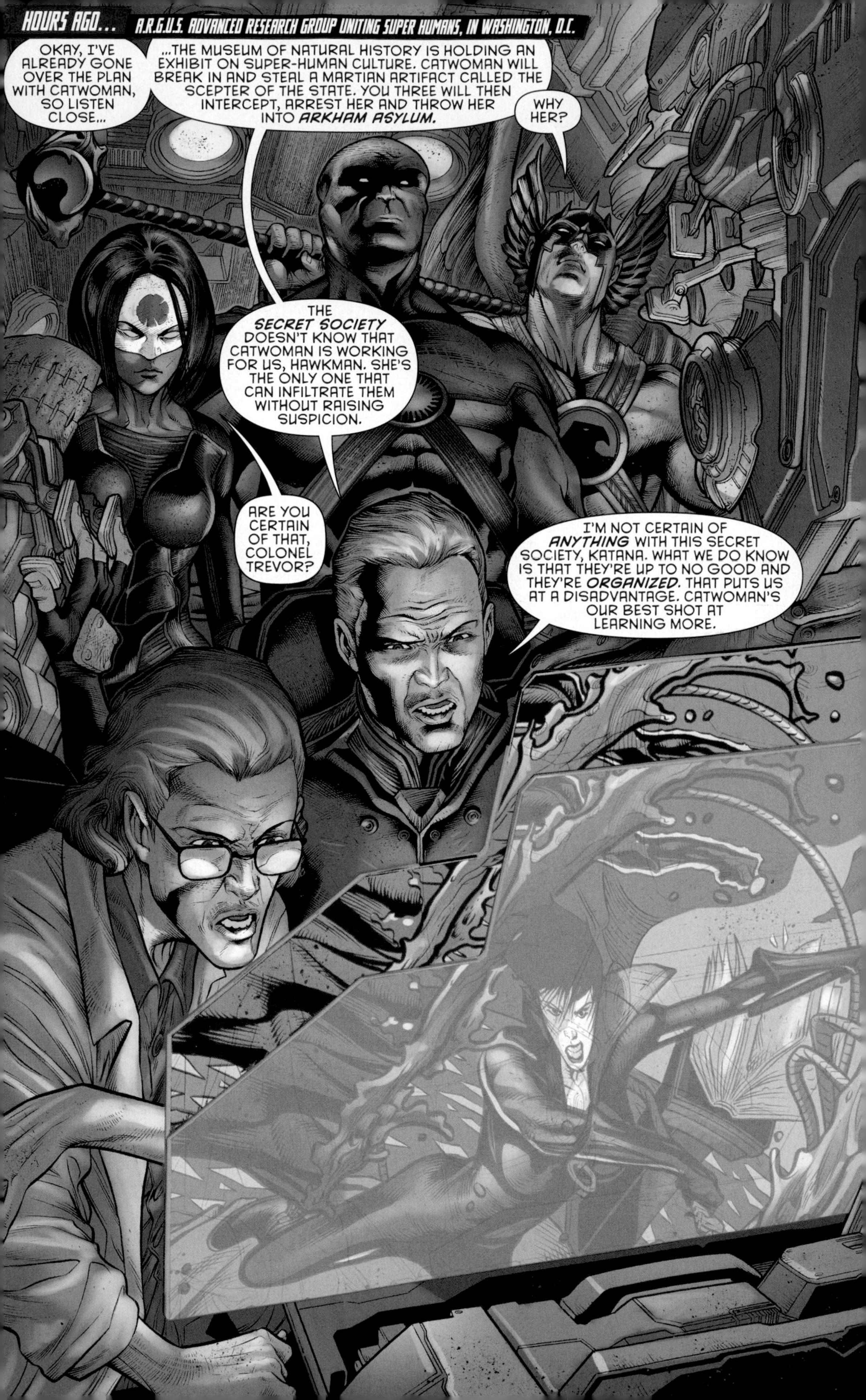
HOURS AGO... A.R.G.U.S. ADVANCED RESEARCH GROUP UNITING SUPER HUMANS, IN WASHINGTON, D.C.
OKAY, I'VE ALREADY GONE OVER THE PLAN WITH CATWOMAN, SO LISTEN CLOSE...
...THE MUSEUM OF NATURAL HISTORY IS HOLDING AN EXHIBIT ON SUPER-HUMAN CULTURE. CATWOMAN WILL BREAK IN AND STEAL A MARTIAN ARTIFACT CALLED THE SCEPTER OF THE STATE. YOU THREE WILL THEN INTERCEPT, ARREST HER AND THROW HER INTO ARKHAM ASYLUM.
WHY HER?
THE SECRET SOCIETY DOESN'T KNOW THAT CATWOMAN IS WORKING FOR US, HAWKMAN. SHE'S THE ONLY ONE THAT CAN INFILTRATE THEM WITHOUT RAISING SUSPICION.
ARE YOU CERTAIN OF THAT, COLONEL TREVOR?
I'M NOT CERTAIN OF ANYTHING WITH THIS SECRET SOCIETY, KATANA. WHAT WE DO KNOW IS THAT THEY'RE UP TO NO GOOD AND THEY'RE ORGANIZED. THAT PUTS US AT A DISADVANTAGE. CATWOMAN'S OUR BEST SHOT AT LEARNING MORE.

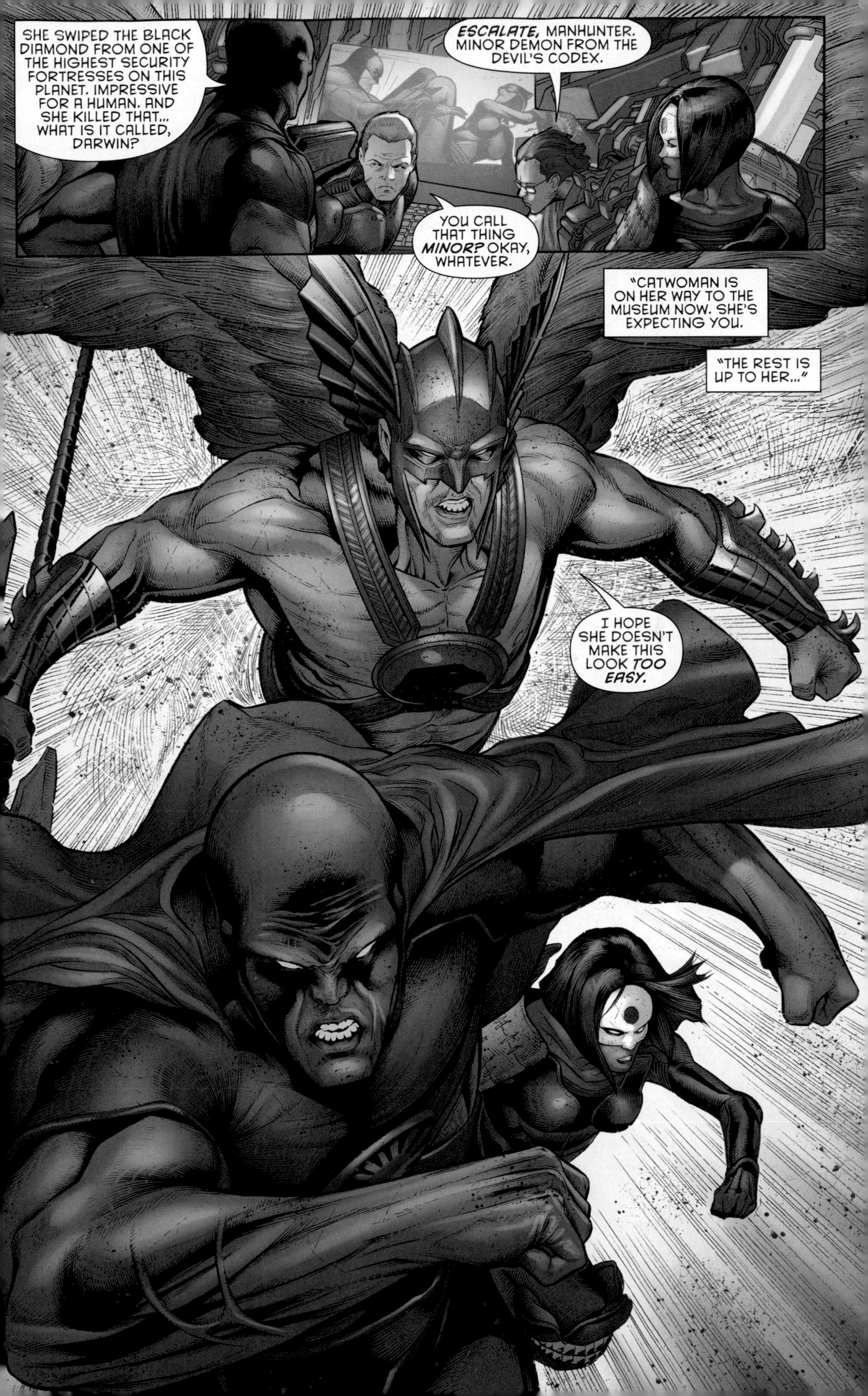

SHE SWIPED THE BLACK DIAMOND FROM ONE OF THE HIGHEST SECURITY FORTRESSES ON THIS PLANET. IMPRESSIVE FOR A HUMAN. AND SHE KILLED THAT... WHAT IS IT CALLED, DARWIN?
ESCALATE, MANHUNTER. MINOR DEMON FROM THE DEVIL'S CODEX.
YOU CALL THAT THING MINOR? OKAY, WHATEVER.
"CATWOMAN IS ON HER WAY TO THE MUSEUM NOW. SHE'S EXPECTING YOU.
"THE REST IS UP TO HER..."
I HOPE SHE DOESN'T MAKE THIS LOOK TOO EASY.

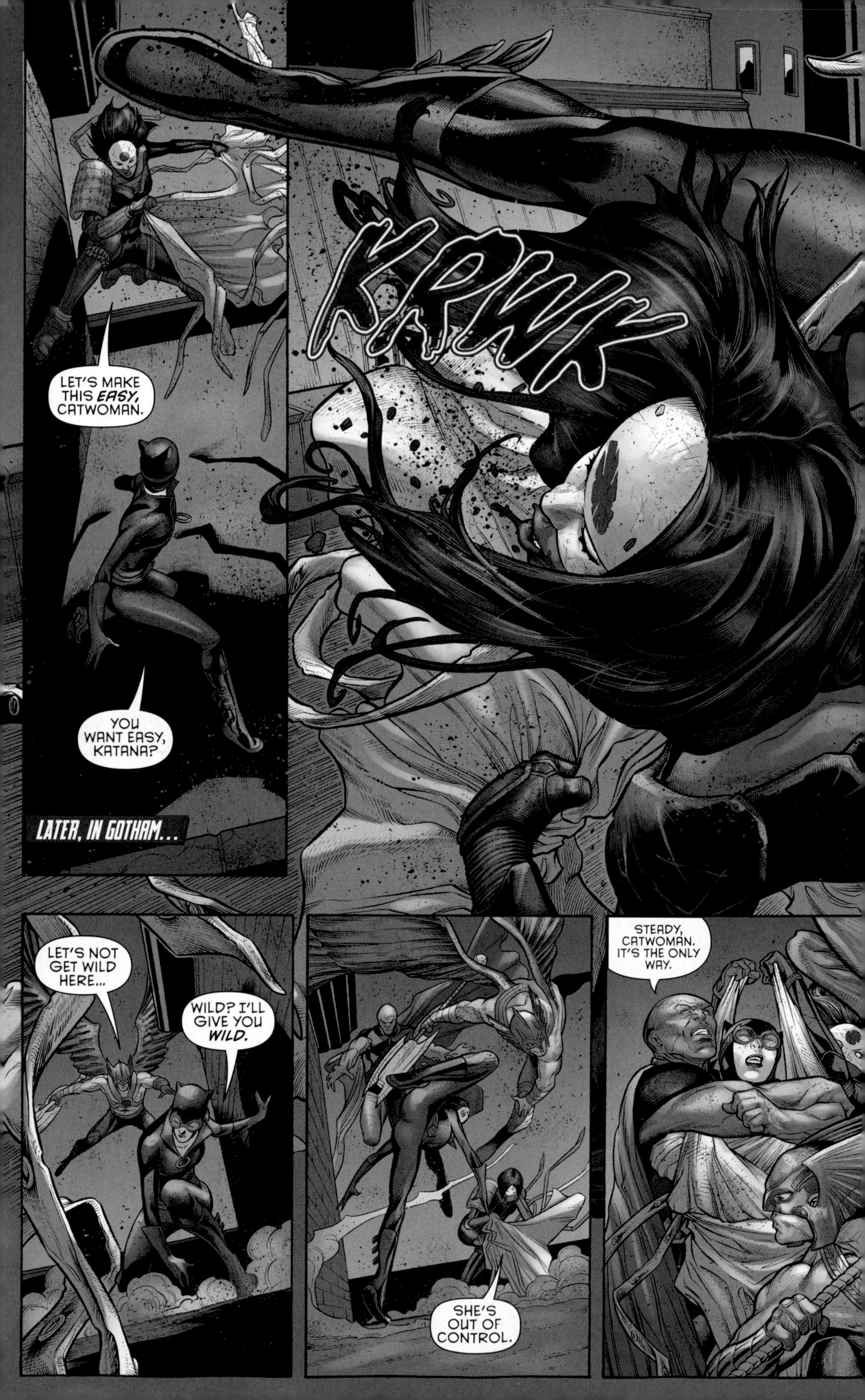

LET'S MAKE THIS *EASY,* CATWOMAN.
YOU WANT EASY, KATANA?
KRUNK
LATER, IN GOTHAM...
LET'S NOT GET WILD HERE...
WILD? I'LL GIVE YOU *WILD.*
SHE'S OUT OF CONTROL.
STEADY, CATWOMAN. IT'S THE ONLY WAY.

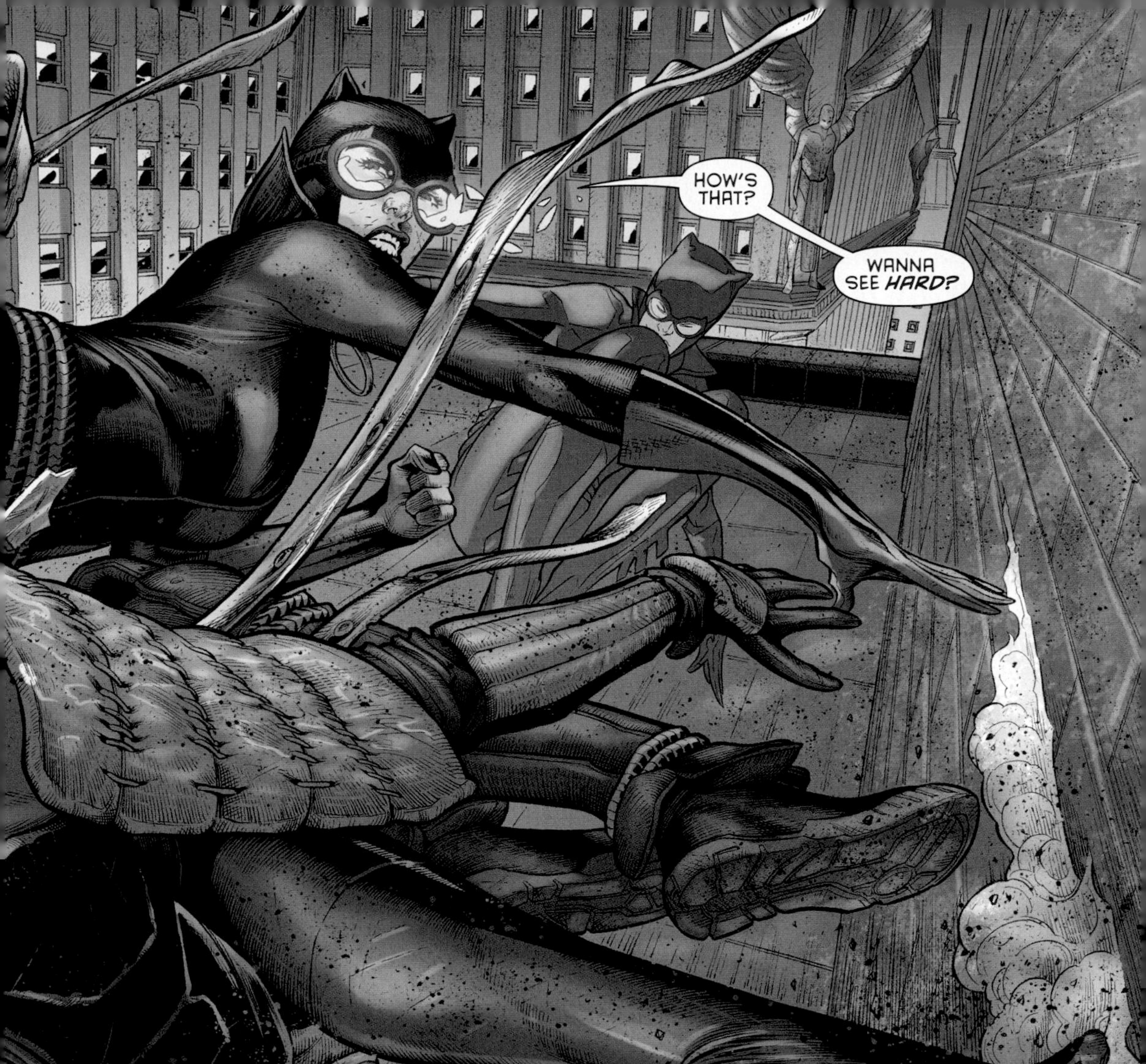
HOW'S THAT?
WANNA SEE HARD?

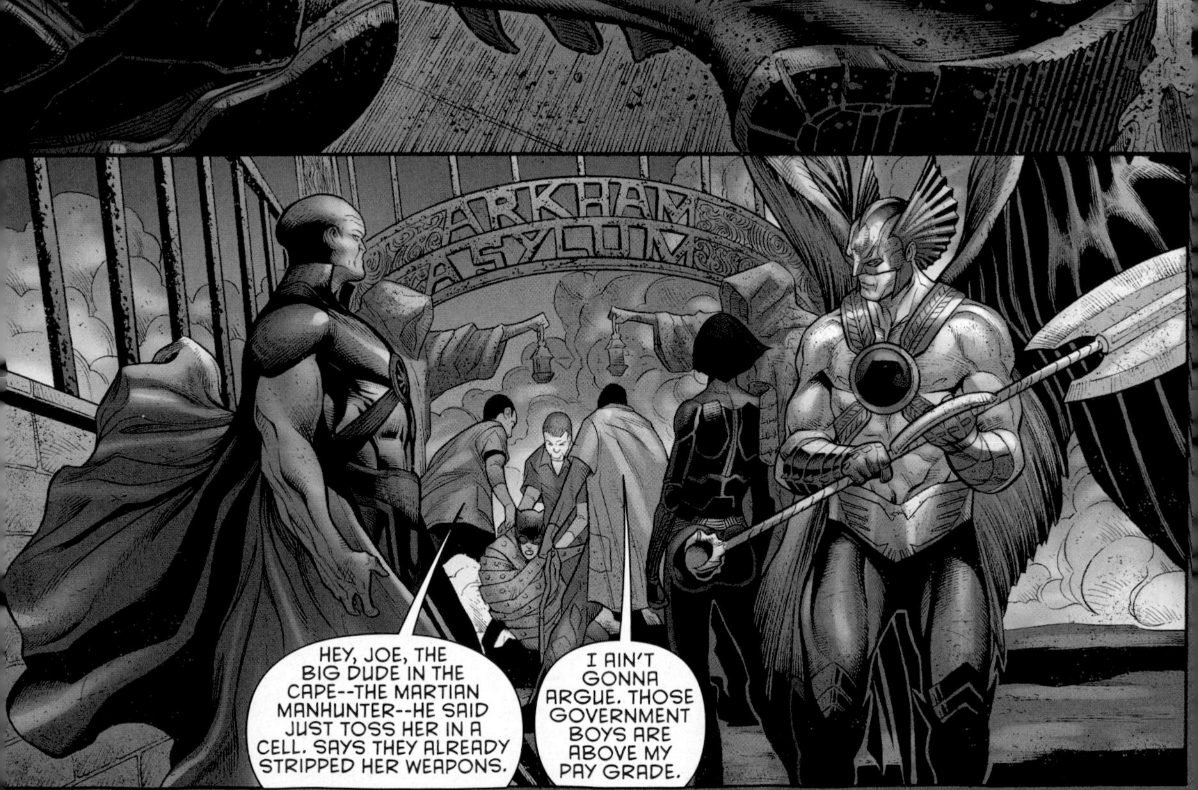
HEY, JOE, THE BIG DUDE IN THE CAPE--THE MARTIAN MANHUNTER--HE SAID JUST TOSS HER IN A CELL. SAYS THEY ALREADY STRIPPED HER WEAPONS.
I AIN'T GONNA ARGUE. THOSE GOVERNMENT BOYS ARE ABOVE MY PAY GRADE.

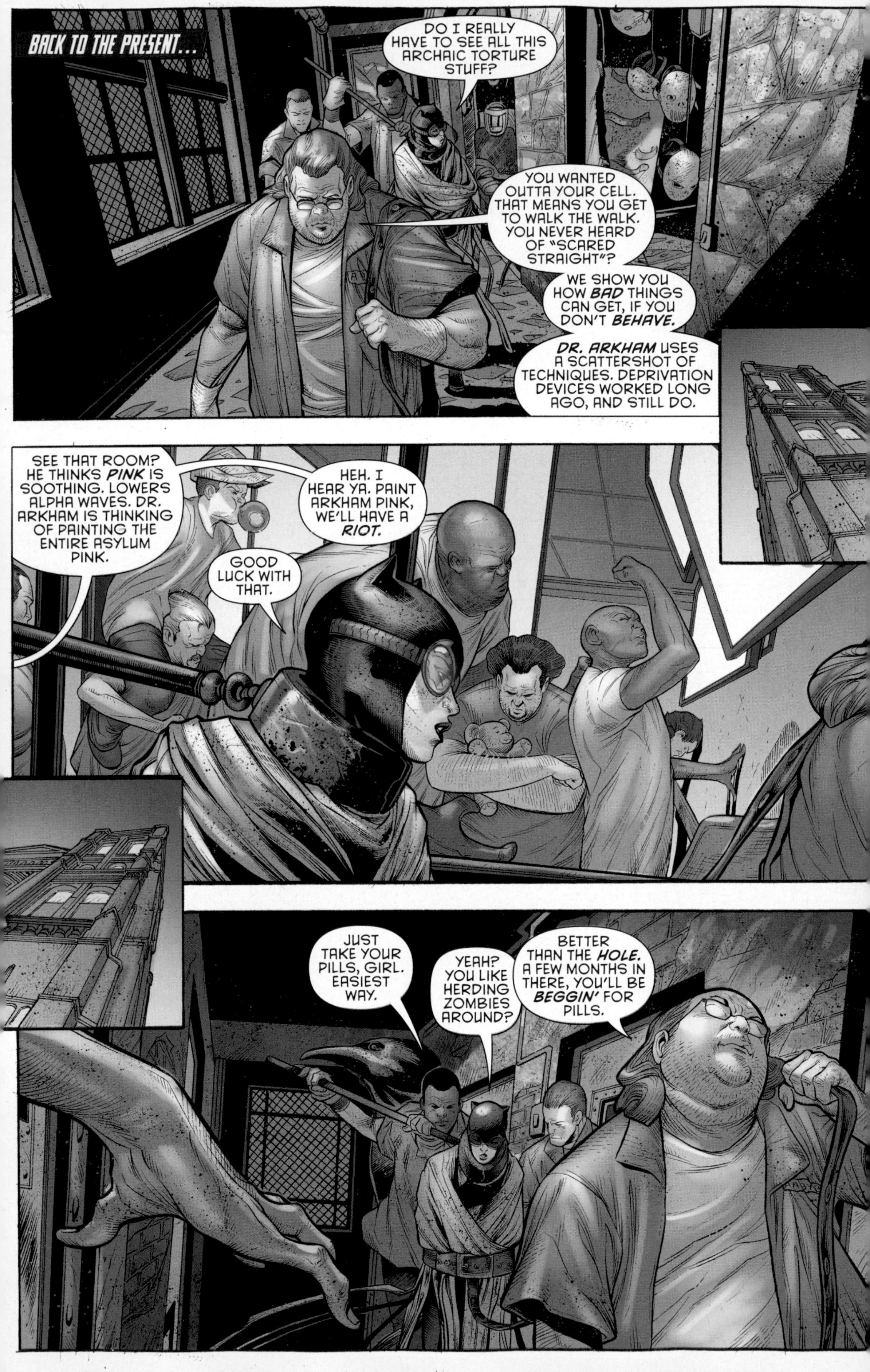
BACK TO THE PRESENT...
DO I REALLY HAVE TO SEE ALL THIS ARCHAIC TORTURE STUFF?
YOU WANTED OUTTA YOUR CELL. THAT MEANS YOU GET TO WALK THE WALK. YOU NEVER HEARD OF "SCARED STRAIGHT"?
WE SHOW YOU HOW BAD THINGS CAN GET, IF YOU DON'T BEHAVE.
DR. ARKHAM USES A SCATTERSHOT OF TECHNIQUES. DEPRIVATION DEVICES WORKED LONG AGO, AND STILL DO.
SEE THAT ROOM? HE THINKS PINK IS SOOTHING. LOWERS ALPHA WAVES. DR. ARKHAM IS THINKING OF PAINTING THE ENTIRE ASYLUM PINK.
HEH. I HEAR YA. PAINT ARKHAM PINK, WE'LL HAVE A RIOT.
GOOD LUCK WITH THAT.
JUST TAKE YOUR PILLS, GIRL. EASIEST WAY.
YEAH? YOU LIKE HERDING ZOMBIES AROUND?
BETTER THAN THE HOLE. A FEW MONTHS IN THERE, YOU'LL BE BEGGIN' FOR PILLS.

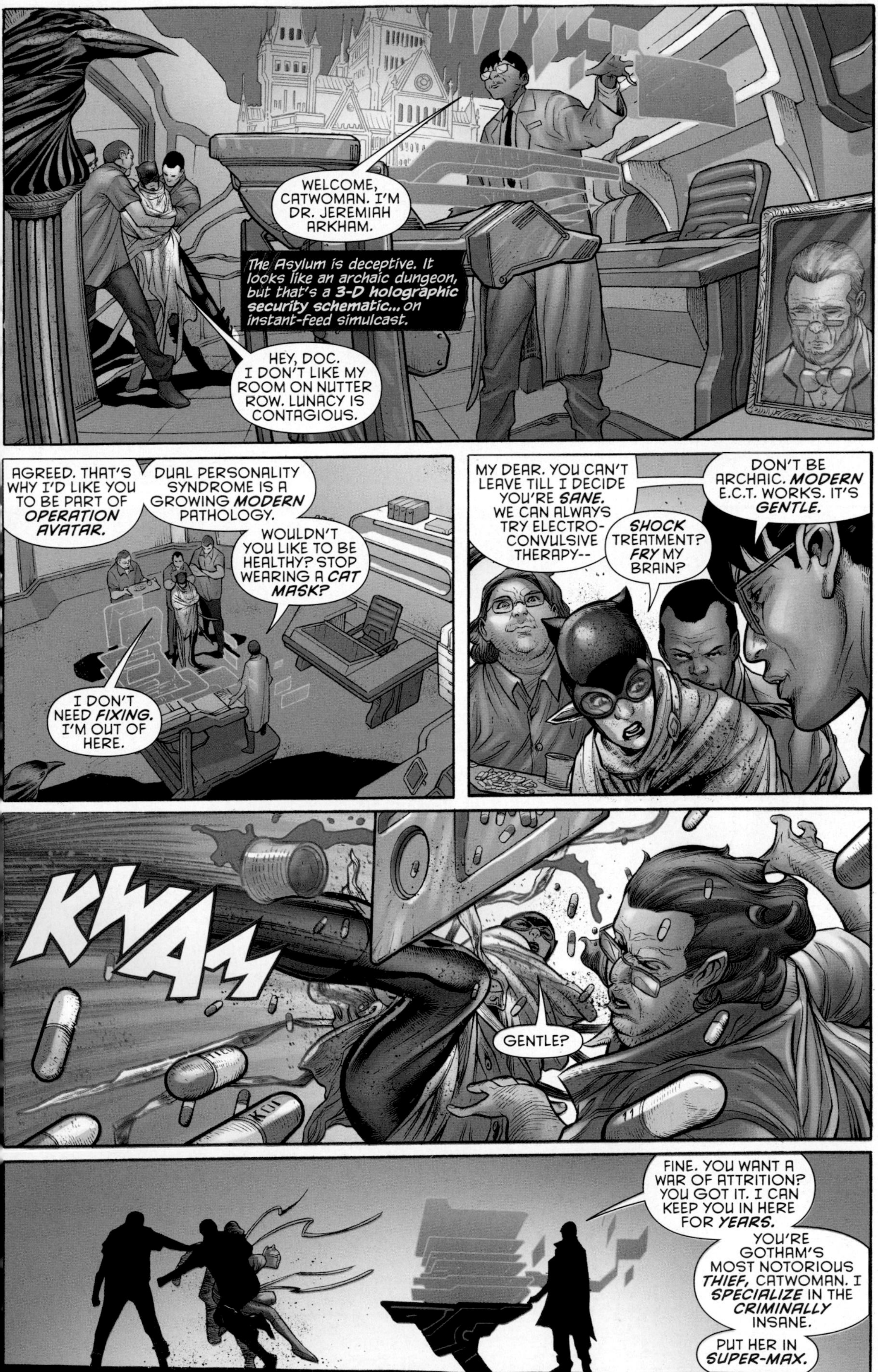

WELCOME, CATWOMAN. I'M DR. JEREMIAH ARKHAM.
The Asylum is deceptive. It looks like an archaic dungeon, but that's a 3-D holographic security schematic... on instant-feed simulcast.
HEY, DOC. I DON'T LIKE MY ROOM ON NUTTER ROW. LUNACY IS CONTAGIOUS.
AGREED. THAT'S WHY I'D LIKE YOU TO BE PART OF OPERATION AVATAR.
DUAL PERSONALITY SYNDROME IS A GROWING MODERN PATHOLOGY.
WOULDN'T YOU LIKE TO BE HEALTHY? STOP WEARING A CAT MASK?
I DON'T NEED FIXING. I'M OUT OF HERE.
MY DEAR. YOU CAN'T LEAVE TILL I DECIDE YOU'RE SANE. WE CAN ALWAYS TRY ELECTRO-CONVULSIVE THERAPY--
SHOCK TREATMENT? FRY MY BRAIN?
DON'T BE ARCHAIC. MODERN E.C.T. WORKS. IT'S GENTLE.
KWAM
GENTLE?
FINE. YOU WANT A WAR OF ATTRITION? YOU GOT IT. I CAN KEEP YOU IN HERE FOR YEARS.
YOU'RE GOTHAM'S MOST NOTORIOUS THIEF, CATWOMAN. I SPECIALIZE IN THE CRIMINALLY INSANE.
PUT HER IN SUPER-MAX.

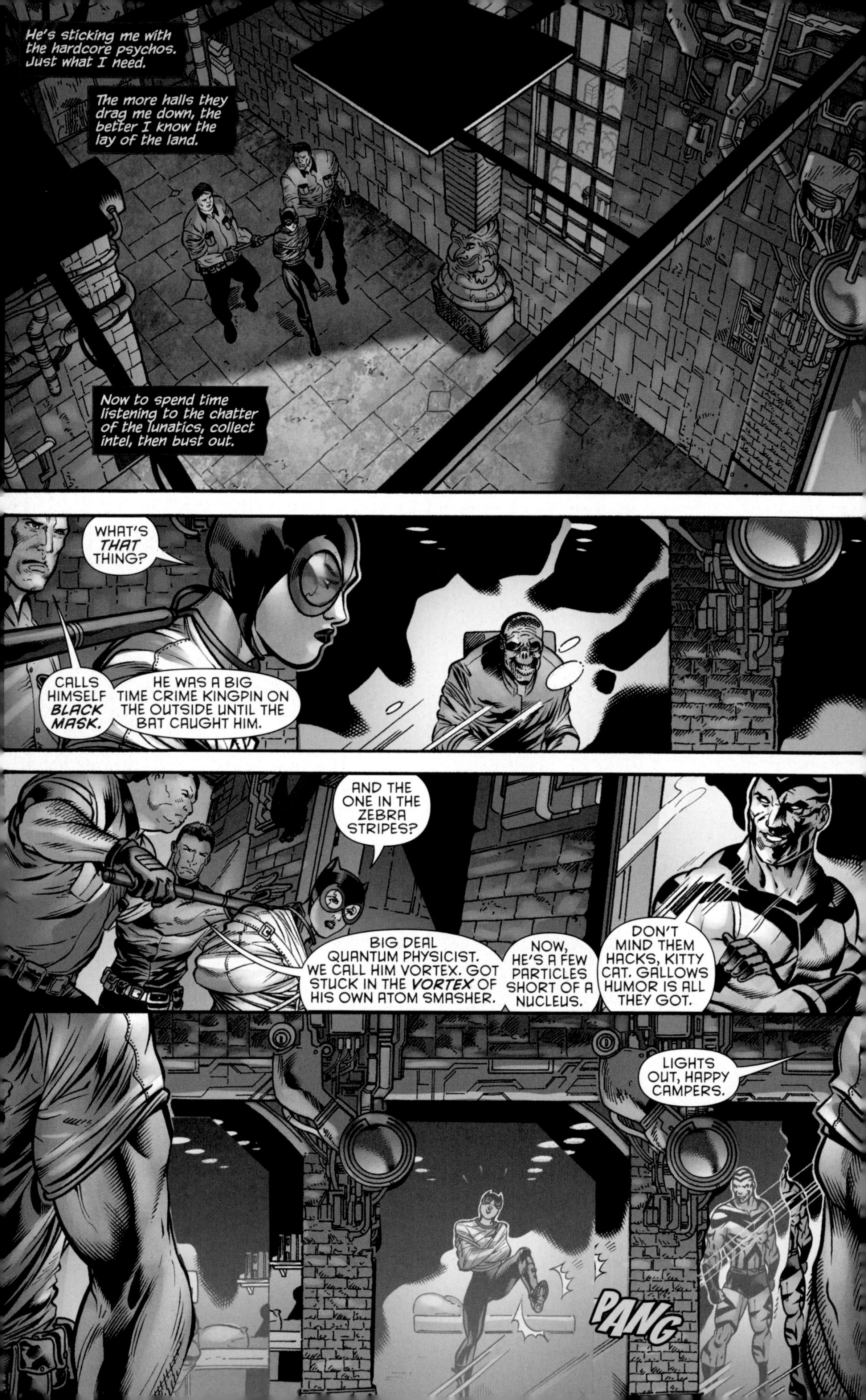
He's sticking me with the hardcore psychos. Just what I need.
The more halls they drag me down, the better I know the lay of the land.
Now to spend time listening to the chatter of the lunatics, collect intel, then bust out.
WHAT'S THAT THING?
CALLS HIMSELF BLACK MASK.
HE WAS A BIG TIME CRIME KINGPIN ON THE OUTSIDE UNTIL THE BAT CAUGHT HIM.
AND THE ONE IN THE ZEBRA STRIPES?
BIG DEAL QUANTUM PHYSICIST. WE CALL HIM VORTEX. GOT STUCK IN THE VORTEX OF HIS OWN ATOM SMASHER.
NOW, HE'S A FEW PARTICLES SHORT OF A NUCLEUS.
DON'T MIND THEM HACKS, KITTY CAT. GALLOWS HUMOR IS ALL THEY GOT.
LIGHTS OUT, HAPPY CAMPERS.
PANG

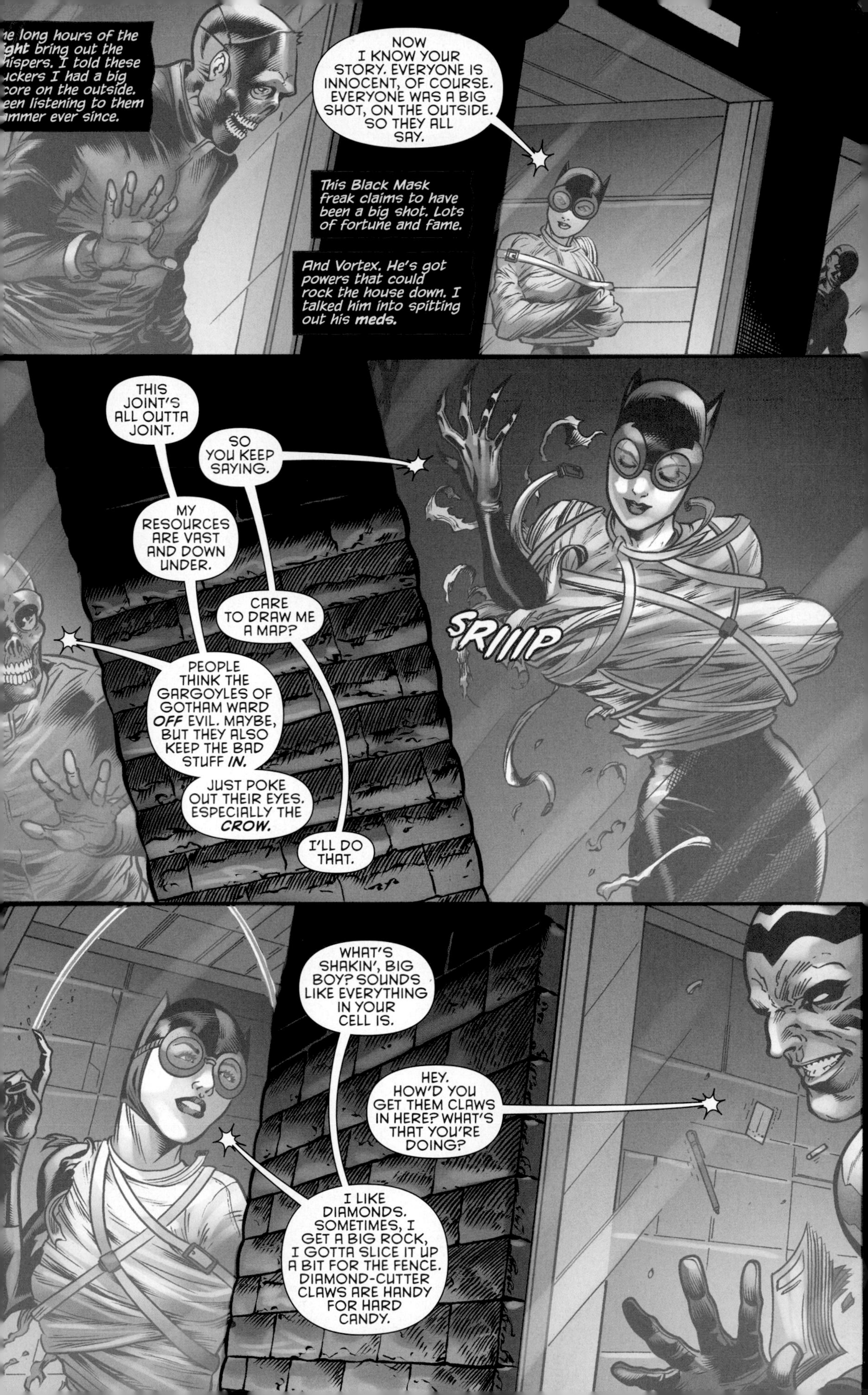

...e long hours of the ...ight bring out the ...hispers. I told these ...uckers I had a big ...core on the outside. ...een listening to them ...ammer ever since.
NOW I KNOW YOUR STORY. EVERYONE IS INNOCENT, OF COURSE. EVERYONE WAS A BIG SHOT, ON THE OUTSIDE. SO THEY ALL SAY.
This Black Mask freak claims to have been a big shot. Lots of fortune and fame.
And Vortex. He's got powers that could rock the house down. I talked him into spitting out his meds.
THIS JOINT'S ALL OUTTA JOINT.
SO YOU KEEP SAYING.
MY RESOURCES ARE VAST AND DOWN UNDER.
CARE TO DRAW ME A MAP?
PEOPLE THINK THE GARGOYLES OF GOTHAM WARD OFF EVIL. MAYBE, BUT THEY ALSO KEEP THE BAD STUFF IN.
JUST POKE OUT THEIR EYES. ESPECIALLY THE CROW.
I'LL DO THAT.
SRIIIP
WHAT'S SHAKIN', BIG BOY? SOUNDS LIKE EVERYTHING IN YOUR CELL IS.
HEY. HOW'D YOU GET THEM CLAWS IN HERE? WHAT'S THAT YOU'RE DOING?
I LIKE DIAMONDS. SOMETIMES, I GET A BIG ROCK, I GOTTA SLICE IT UP A BIT FOR THE FENCE. DIAMOND-CUTTER CLAWS ARE HANDY FOR HARD CANDY.

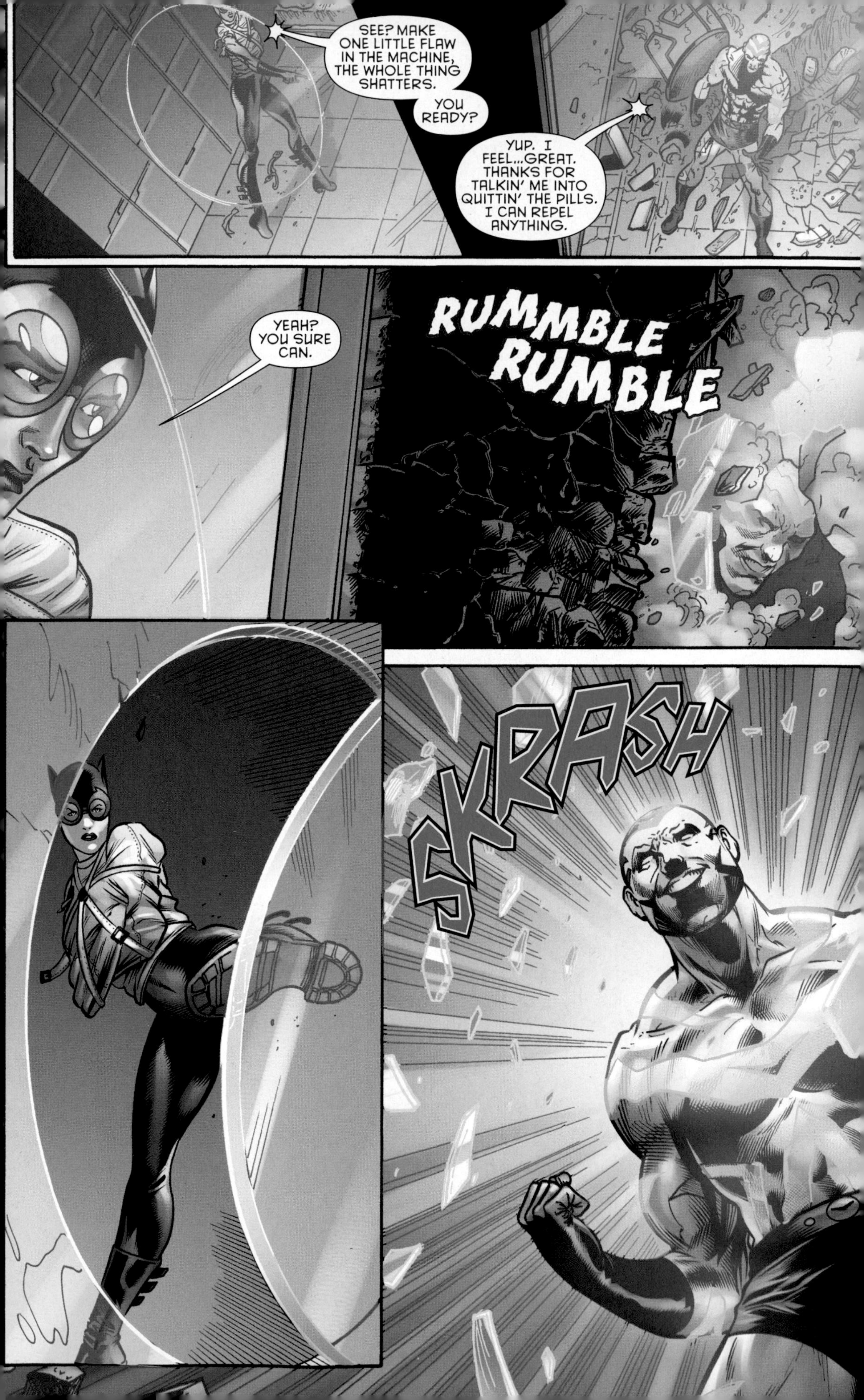
SEE? MAKE ONE LITTLE FLAW IN THE MACHINE, THE WHOLE THING SHATTERS.
YOU READY?
YUP. I FEEL...GREAT. THANKS FOR TALKIN' ME INTO QUITTIN' THE PILLS. I CAN REPEL ANYTHING.
YEAH? YOU SURE CAN.
RUMMBLE RUMBLE
SKRASH

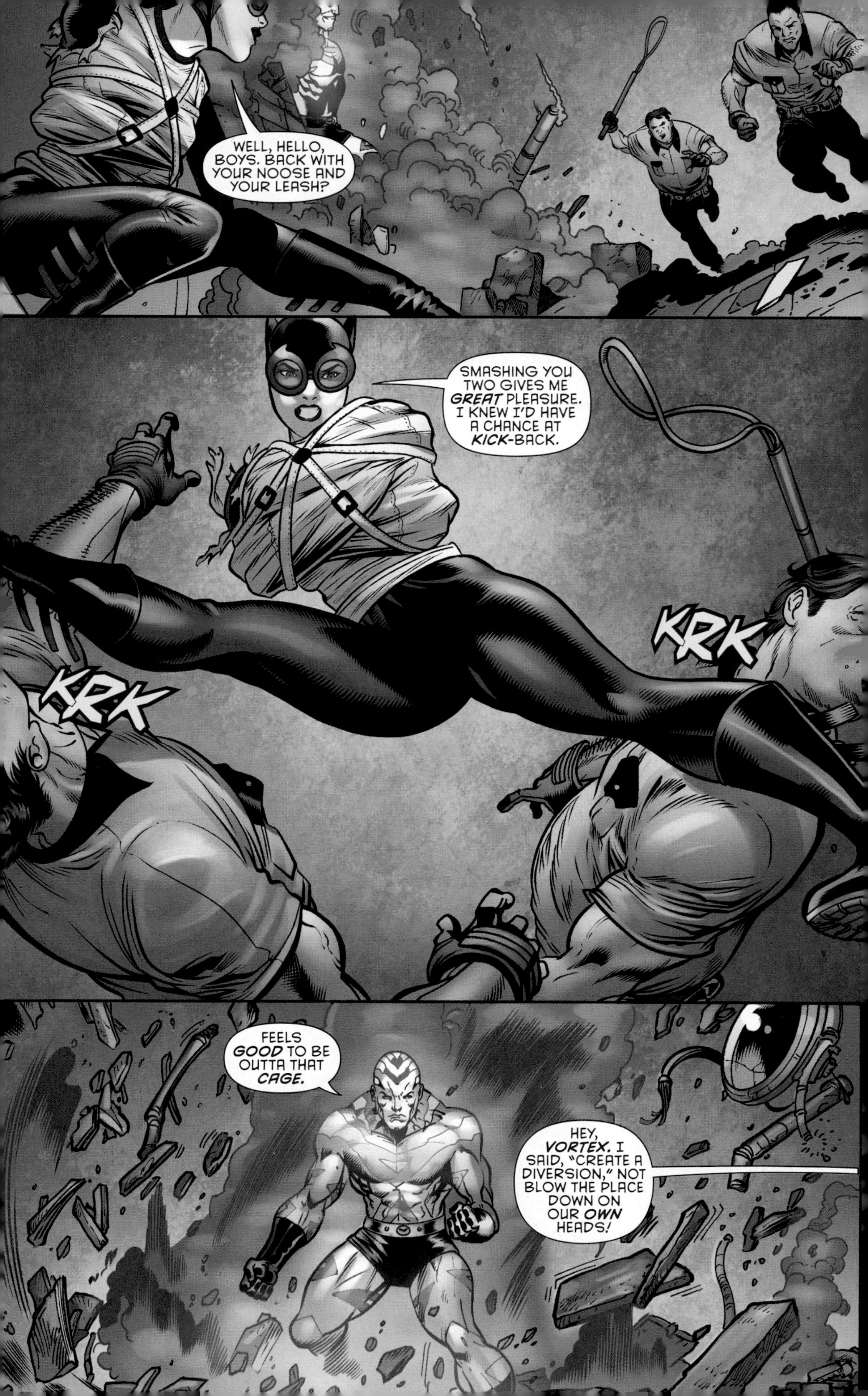
WELL, HELLO, BOYS. BACK WITH YOUR NOOSE AND YOUR LEASH?
SMASHING YOU TWO GIVES ME GREAT PLEASURE. I KNEW I'D HAVE A CHANCE AT KICK-BACK.
KRK
KRK
FEELS GOOD TO BE OUTTA THAT CAGE.
HEY, VORTEX. I SAID, "CREATE A DIVERSION," NOT BLOW THE PLACE DOWN ON OUR OWN HEADS!

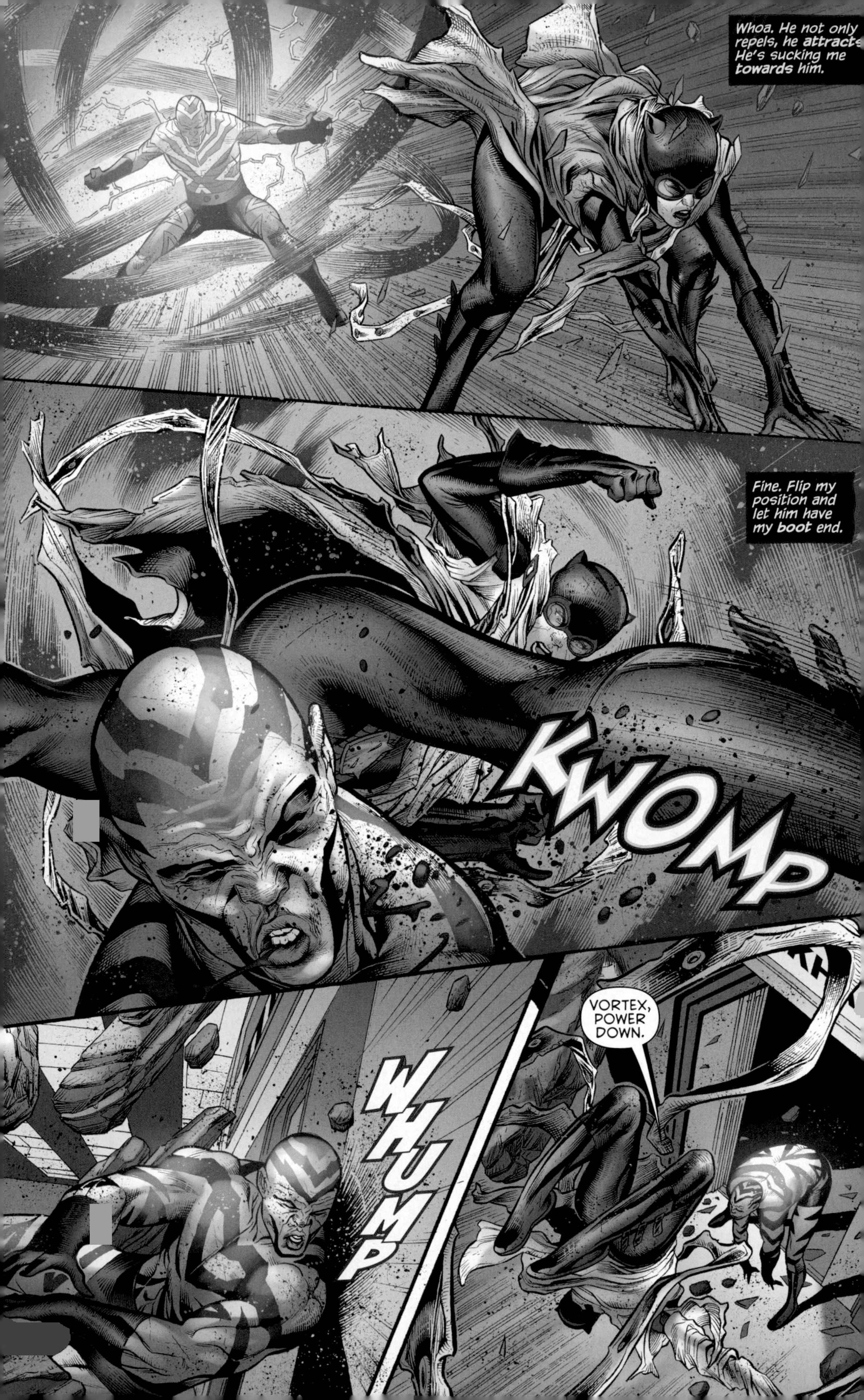

Whoa. He not only repels, he attracts. He's sucking me towards him.
Fine. Flip my position and let him have my boot end.
KWOMP
WHUMP
VORTEX, POWER DOWN.

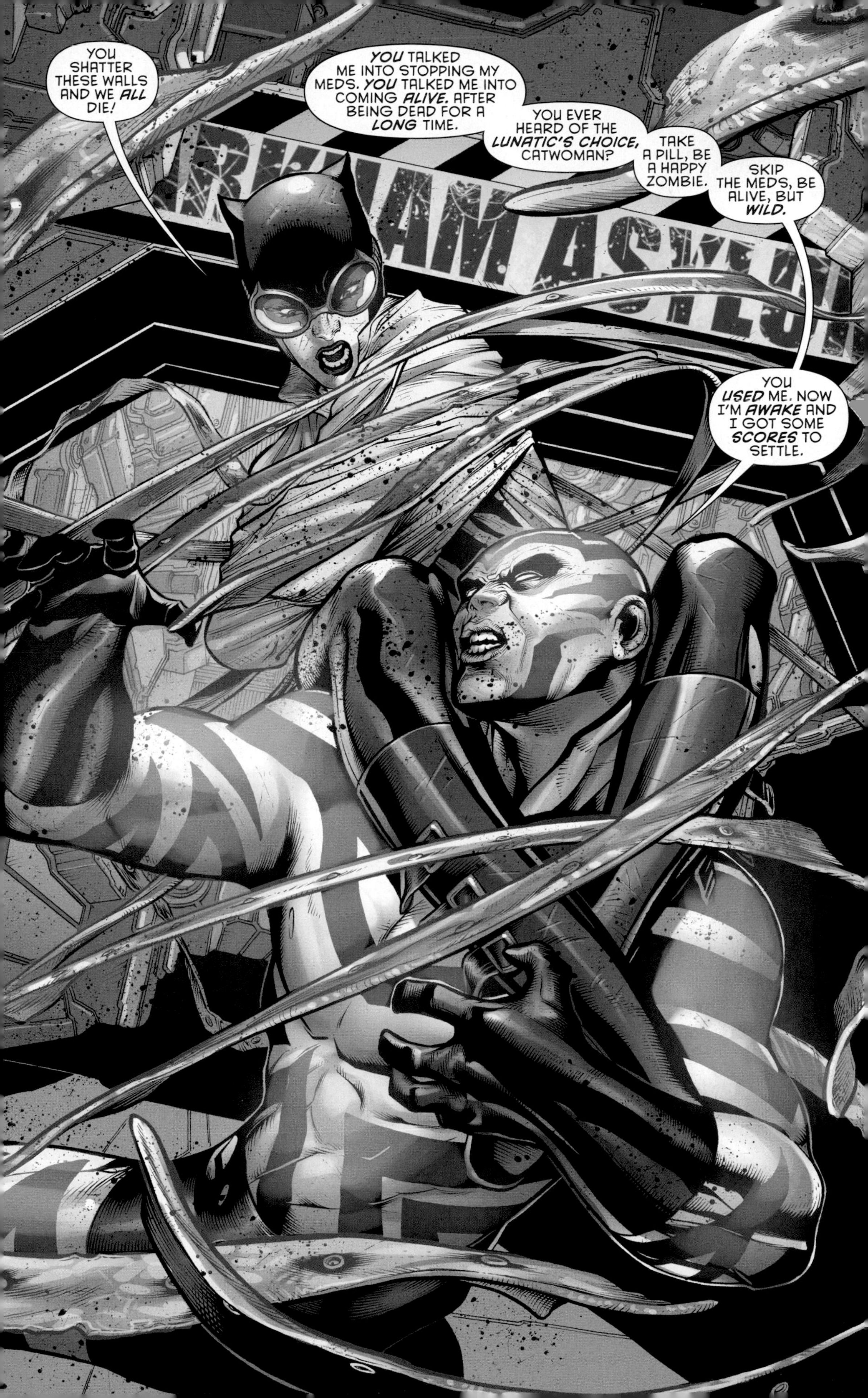
YOU SHATTER THESE WALLS AND WE ALL DIE!
YOU TALKED ME INTO STOPPING MY MEDS. YOU TALKED ME INTO COMING ALIVE. AFTER BEING DEAD FOR A LONG TIME.
YOU EVER HEARD OF THE LUNATIC'S CHOICE, CATWOMAN?
TAKE A PILL, BE A HAPPY ZOMBIE.
SKIP THE MEDS, BE ALIVE, BUT WILD.
YOU USED ME. NOW I'M AWAKE AND I GOT SOME SCORES TO SETTLE.

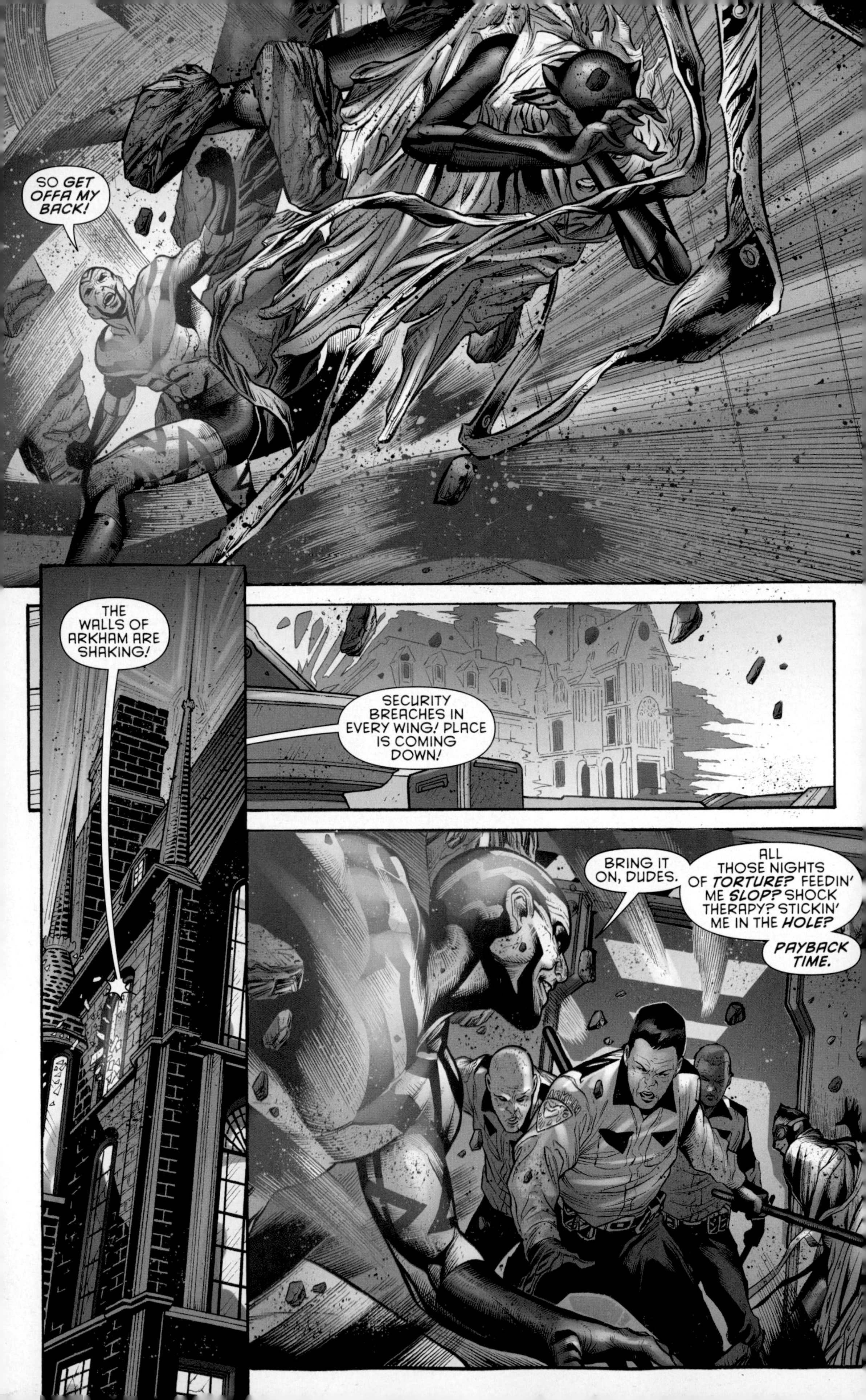
SO GET OFFA MY BACK!
THE WALLS OF ARKHAM ARE SHAKING!
SECURITY BREACHES IN EVERY WING! PLACE IS COMING DOWN!
BRING IT ON, DUDES.
ALL THOSE NIGHTS OF TORTURE? FEEDIN' ME SLOP? SHOCK THERAPY? STICKIN' ME IN THE HOLE?
PAYBACK TIME.

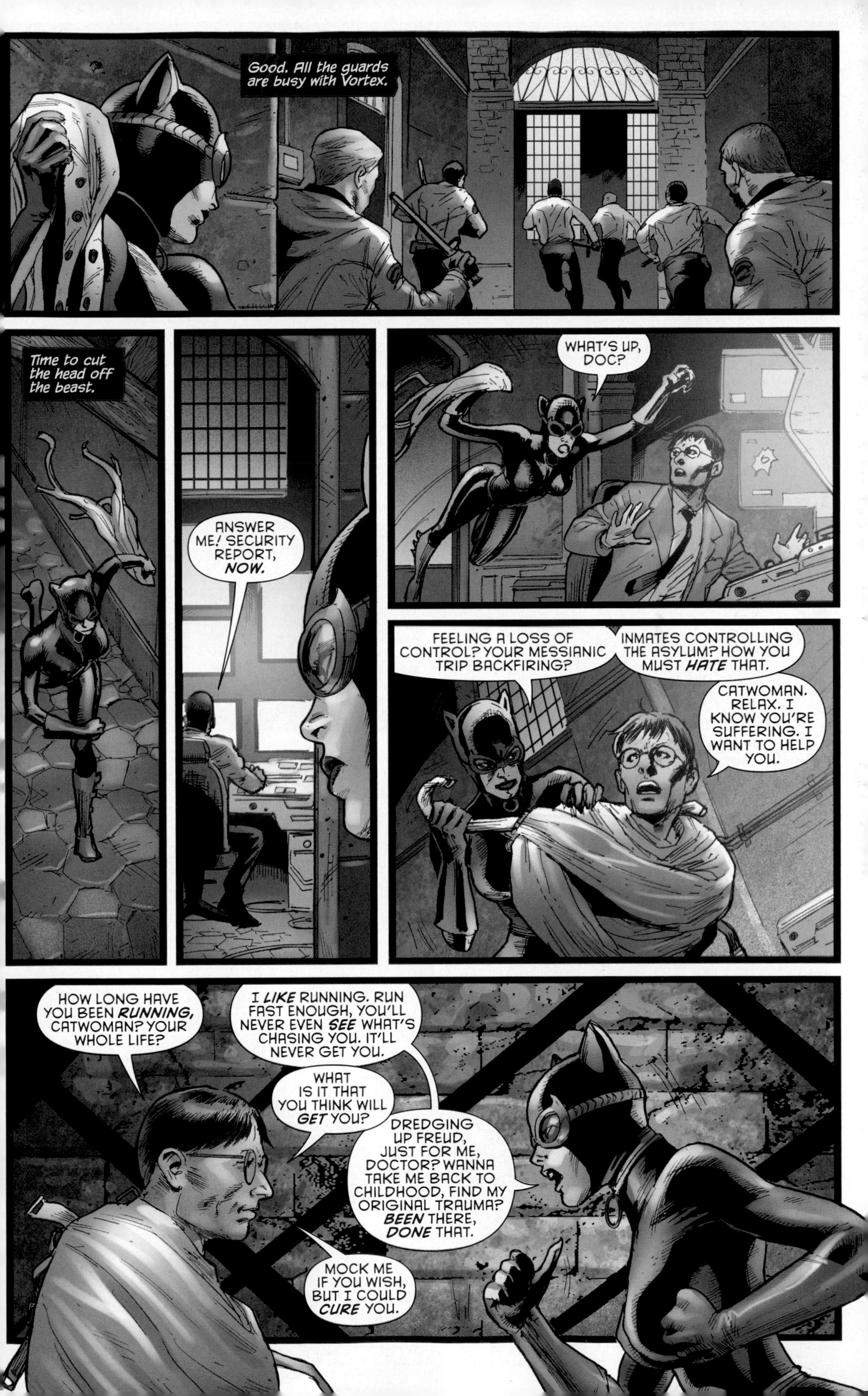
Good. All the guards are busy with Vortex.
Time to cut the head off the beast.
ANSWER ME! SECURITY REPORT, NOW.
WHAT'S UP, DOC?
FEELING A LOSS OF CONTROL? YOUR MESSIANIC TRIP BACKFIRING?
INMATES CONTROLLING THE ASYLUM? HOW YOU MUST HATE THAT.
CATWOMAN. RELAX. I KNOW YOU'RE SUFFERING. I WANT TO HELP YOU.
HOW LONG HAVE YOU BEEN RUNNING, CATWOMAN? YOUR WHOLE LIFE?
I LIKE RUNNING. RUN FAST ENOUGH, YOU'LL NEVER EVEN SEE WHAT'S CHASING YOU. IT'LL NEVER GET YOU.
WHAT IS IT THAT YOU THINK WILL GET YOU?
DREDGING UP FREUD, JUST FOR ME, DOCTOR? WANNA TAKE ME BACK TO CHILDHOOD, FIND MY ORIGINAL TRAUMA? BEEN THERE, DONE THAT.
MOCK ME IF YOU WISH, BUT I COULD CURE YOU.

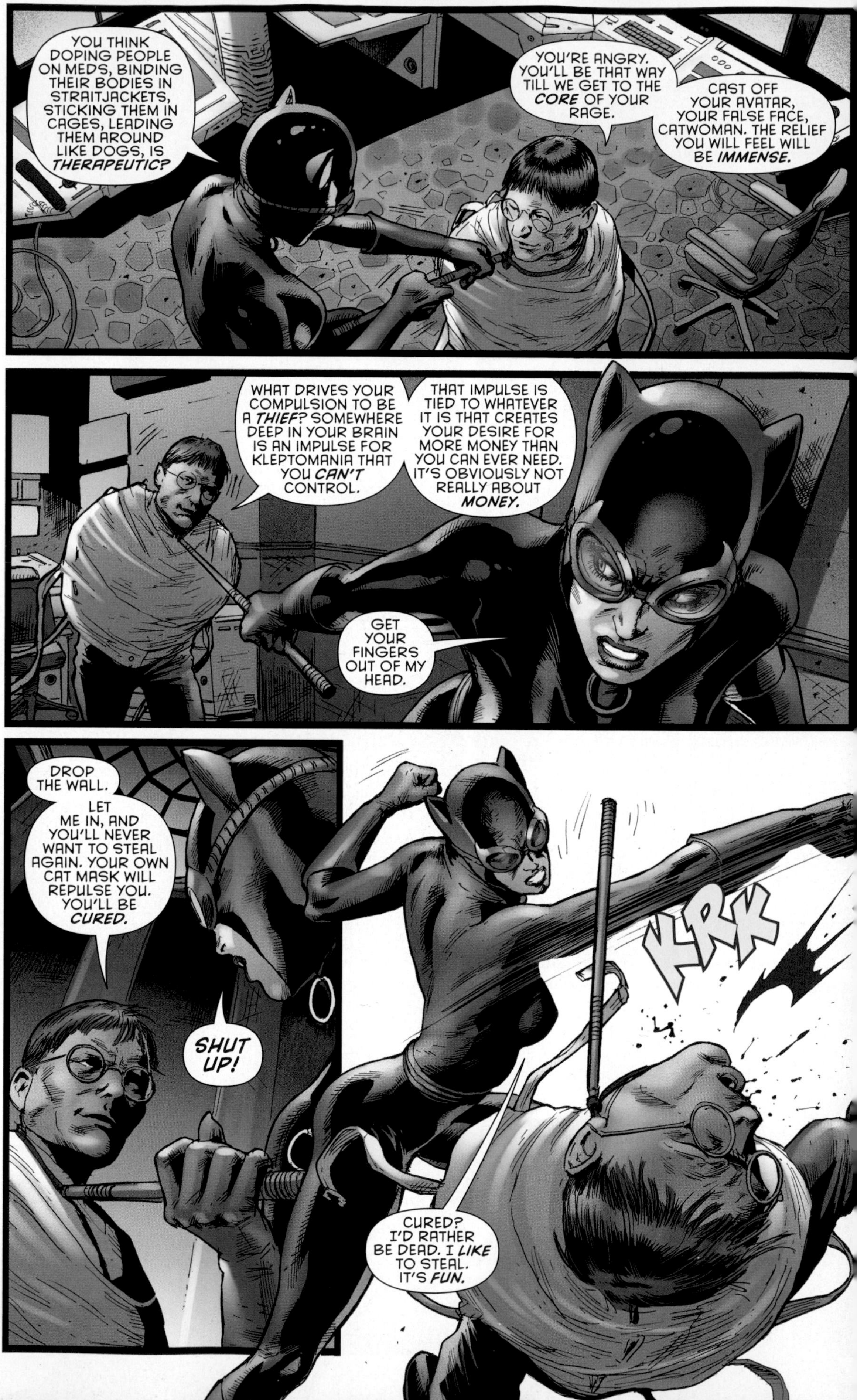
YOU THINK DOPING PEOPLE ON MEDS, BINDING THEIR BODIES IN STRAITJACKETS, STICKING THEM IN CAGES, LEADING THEM AROUND LIKE DOGS, IS *THERAPEUTIC?*
YOU'RE ANGRY. YOU'LL BE THAT WAY TILL WE GET TO THE *CORE* OF YOUR RAGE.
CAST OFF YOUR AVATAR, YOUR FALSE FACE, CATWOMAN. THE RELIEF YOU WILL FEEL WILL BE *IMMENSE.*
WHAT DRIVES YOUR COMPULSION TO BE A *THIEF?* SOMEWHERE DEEP IN YOUR BRAIN IS AN IMPULSE FOR KLEPTOMANIA THAT YOU *CAN'T* CONTROL.
THAT IMPULSE IS TIED TO WHATEVER IT IS THAT CREATES YOUR DESIRE FOR MORE MONEY THAN YOU CAN EVER NEED. IT'S OBVIOUSLY NOT REALLY ABOUT *MONEY.*
GET YOUR FINGERS OUT OF MY HEAD.
DROP THE WALL.
LET ME IN, AND YOU'LL NEVER WANT TO STEAL AGAIN. YOUR OWN CAT MASK WILL REPULSE YOU. YOU'LL BE *CURED.*
SHUT UP!
KRK
CURED? I'D RATHER BE DEAD. I *LIKE* TO STEAL. IT'S *FUN.*

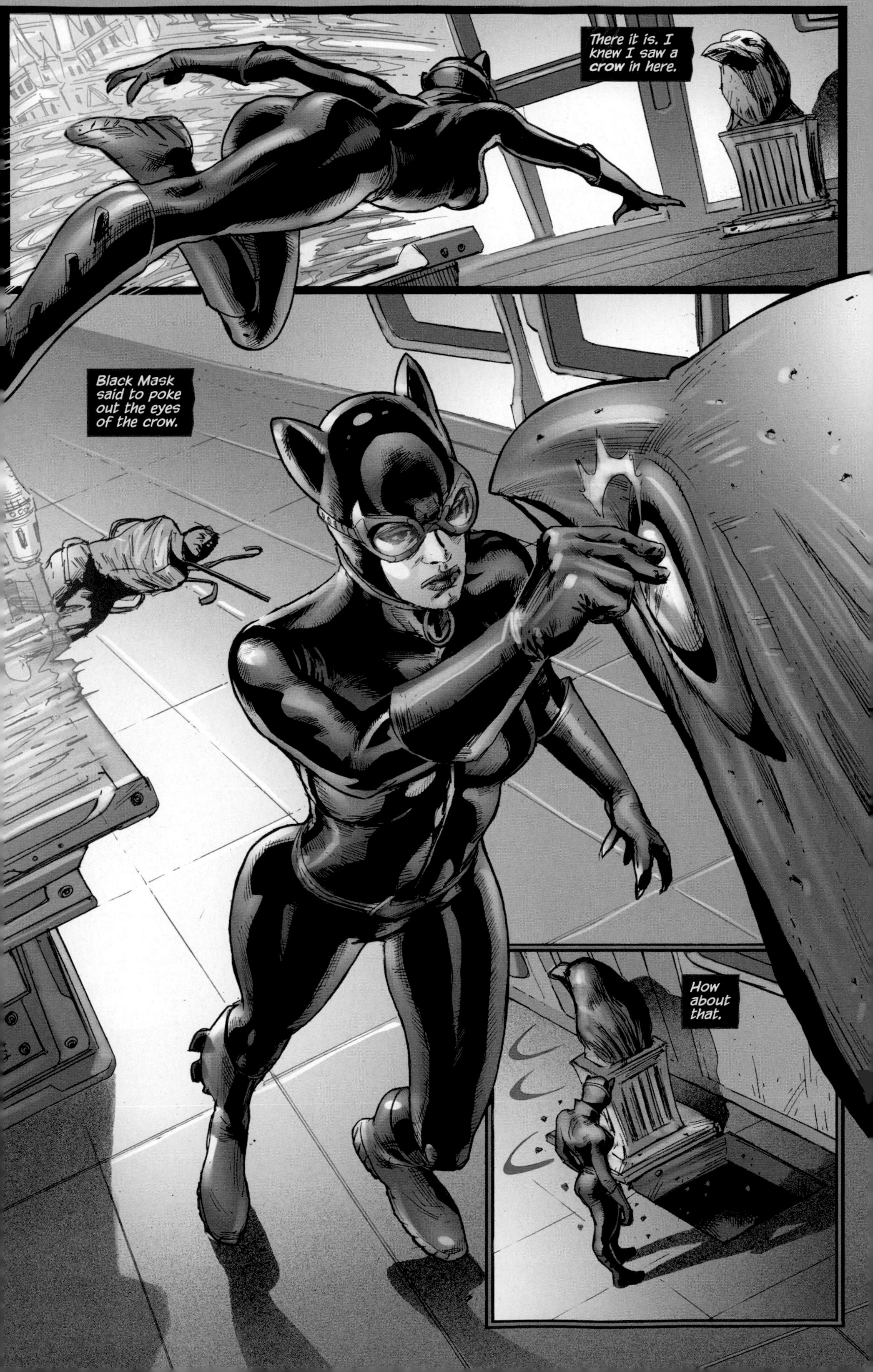
There it is. I knew I saw a crow in here.
Black Mask said to poke out the eyes of the crow.
How about that.

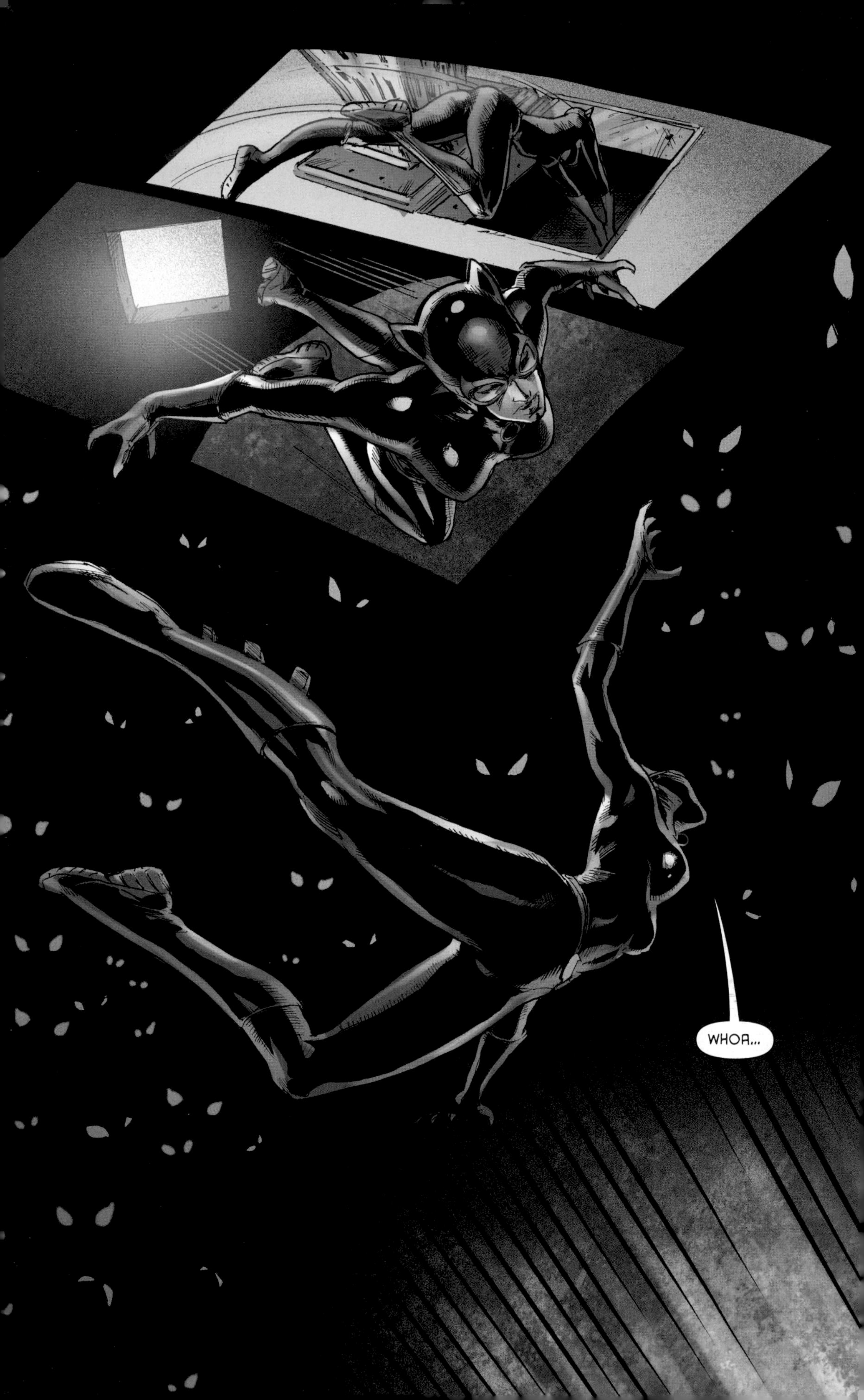
WHOA...

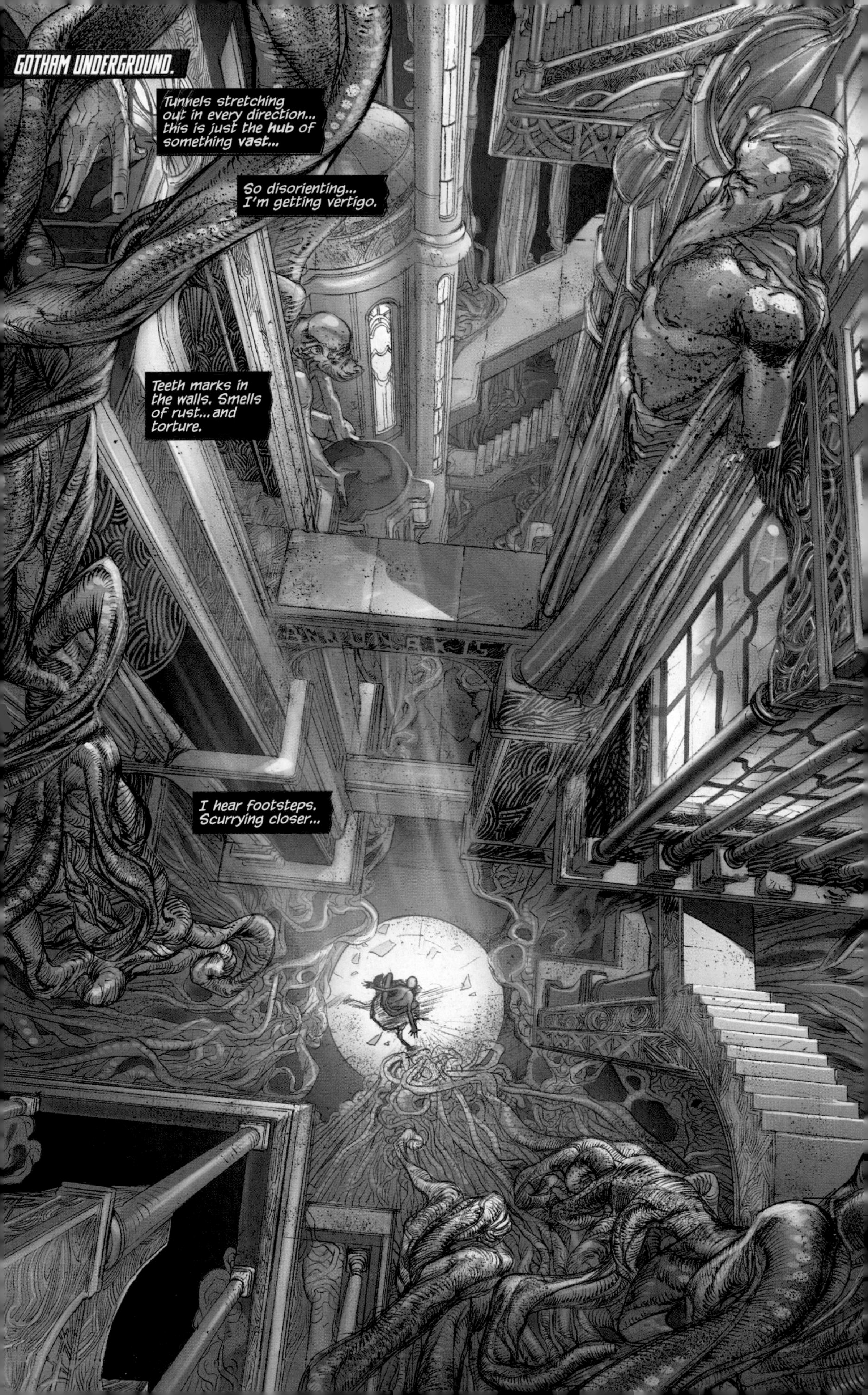
GOTHAM UNDERGROUND.
Tunnels stretching out in every direction... this is just the **hub** of something **vast**...
So disorienting... I'm getting vertigo.
Teeth marks in the walls. Smells of rust... and torture.
I hear footsteps. Scurrying closer...

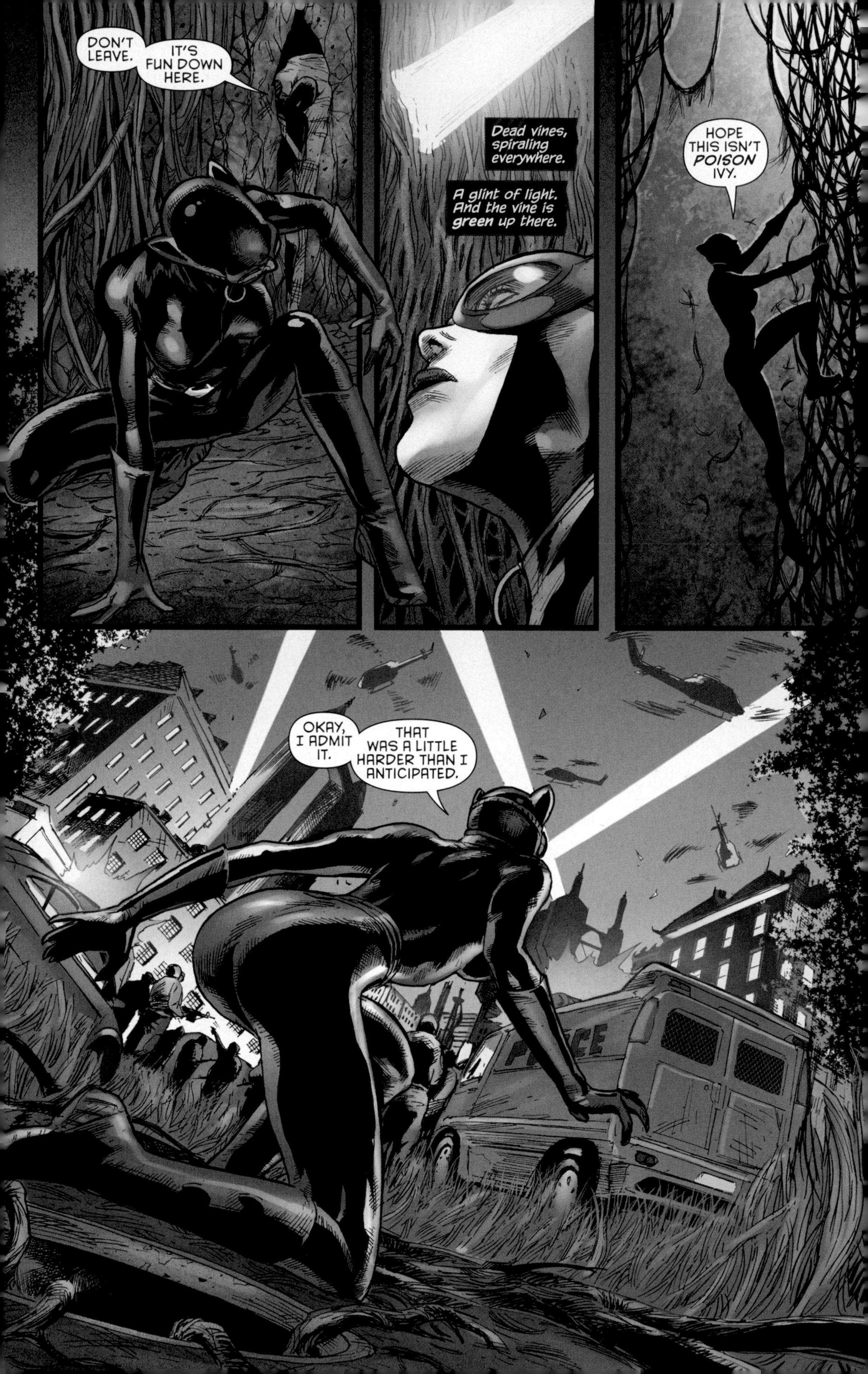
DON'T LEAVE.
IT'S FUN DOWN HERE.
Dead vines, spiraling everywhere.
A glint of light. And the vine is green up there.
HOPE THIS ISN'T POISON IVY.
OKAY, I ADMIT IT.
THAT WAS A LITTLE HARDER THAN I ANTICIPATED.
POLICE

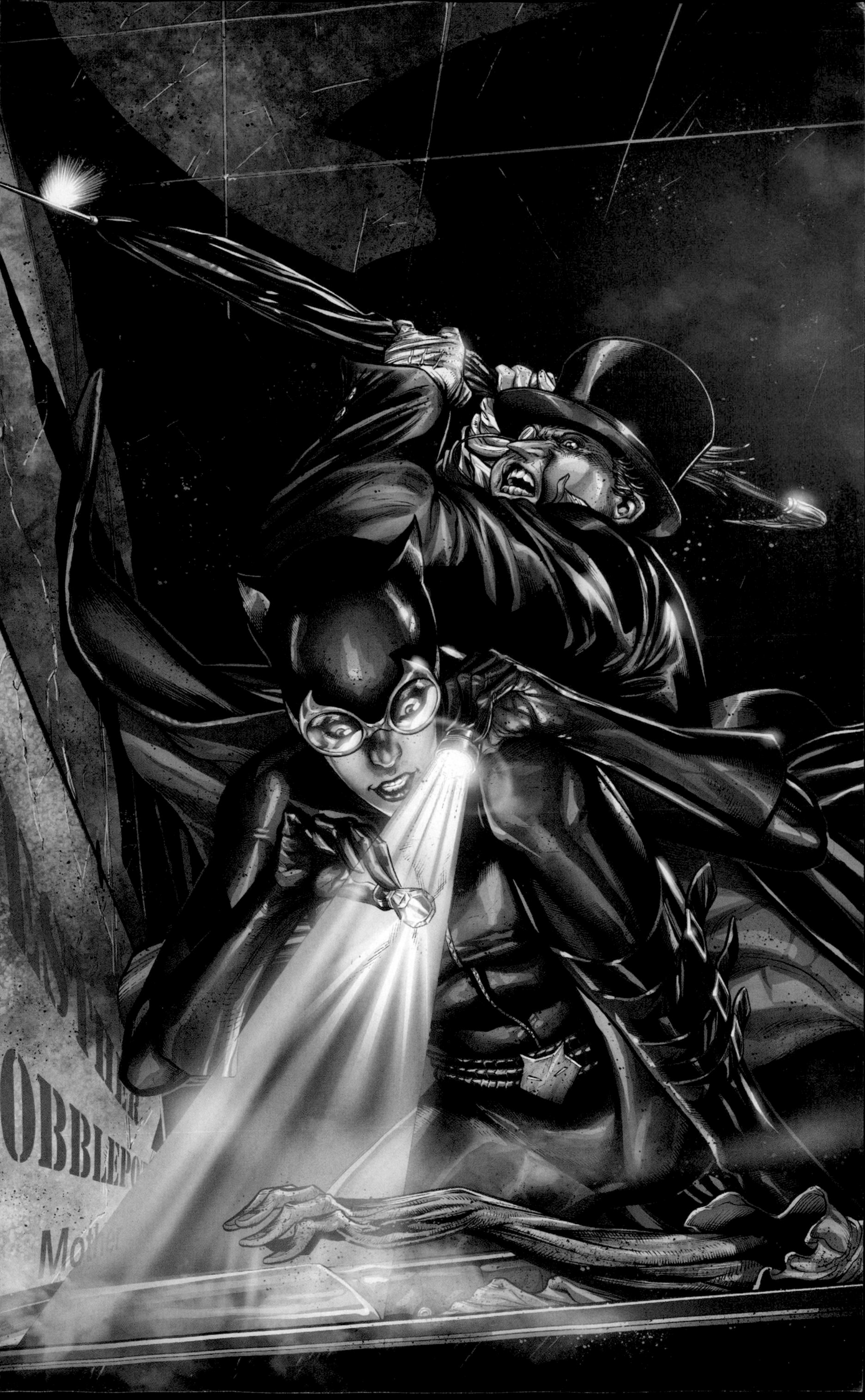

ANN NOCENTI
writer

RAFA SANDOVAL, DIOGENES NEVES & MATEUS SANTOLOUCO
pencillers

JORDI TARRAGONA & MATEUS SANTOLOUCO
inkers

SONIA OBACK & GUY MAJOR
colorists

RAFA SANDOVAL & JORDI TARRAGONA with ULISES ARREOLA
cover artists

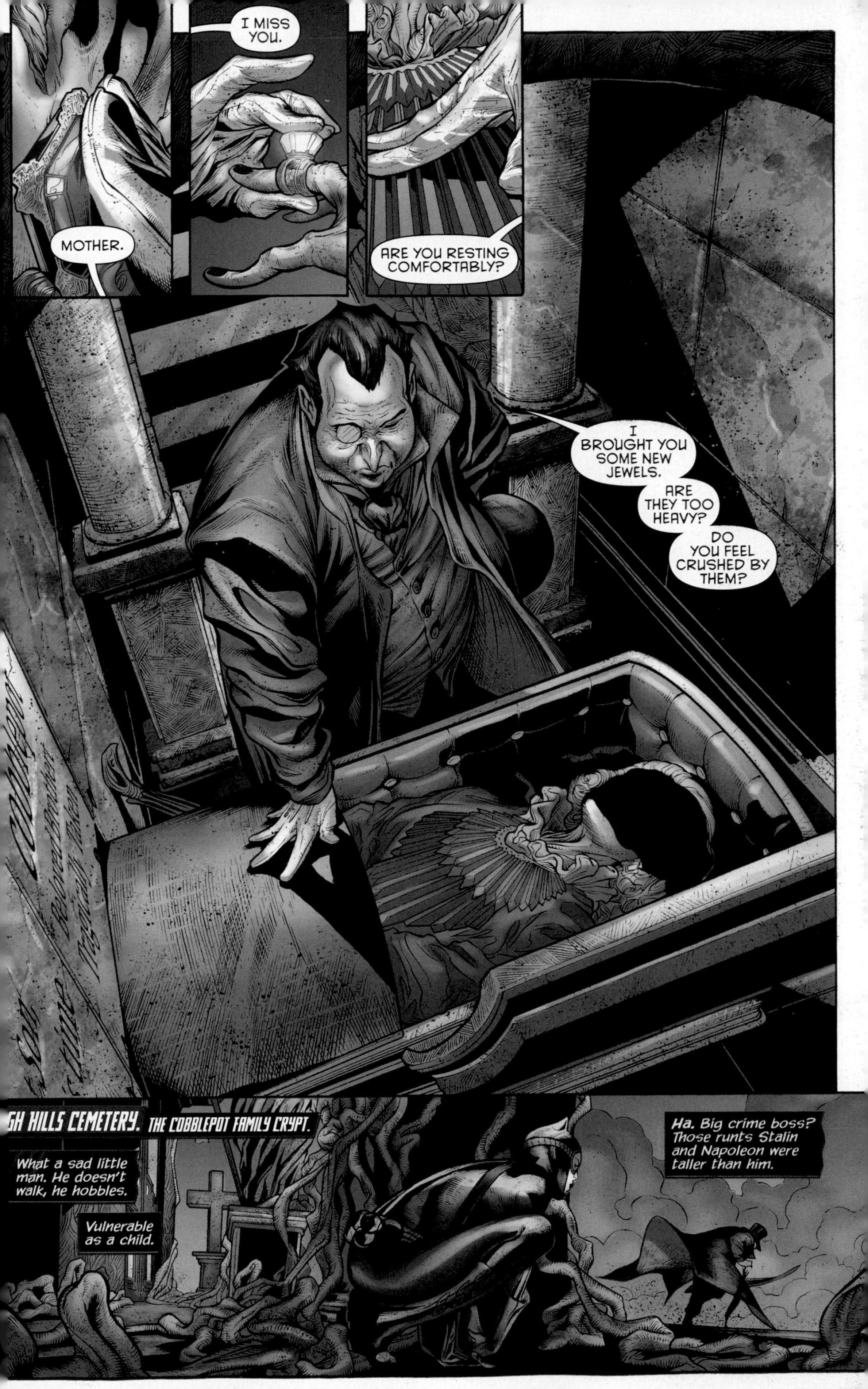

MOTHER.
I MISS YOU.
ARE YOU RESTING COMFORTABLY?
I BROUGHT YOU SOME NEW JEWELS.
ARE THEY TOO HEAVY?
DO YOU FEEL CRUSHED BY THEM?
GH HILLS CEMETERY.
THE COBBLEPOT FAMILY CRYPT.
What a sad little man. He doesn't walk, he hobbles.
Vulnerable as a child.
Ha. Big crime boss? Those runts Stalin and Napoleon were taller than him.

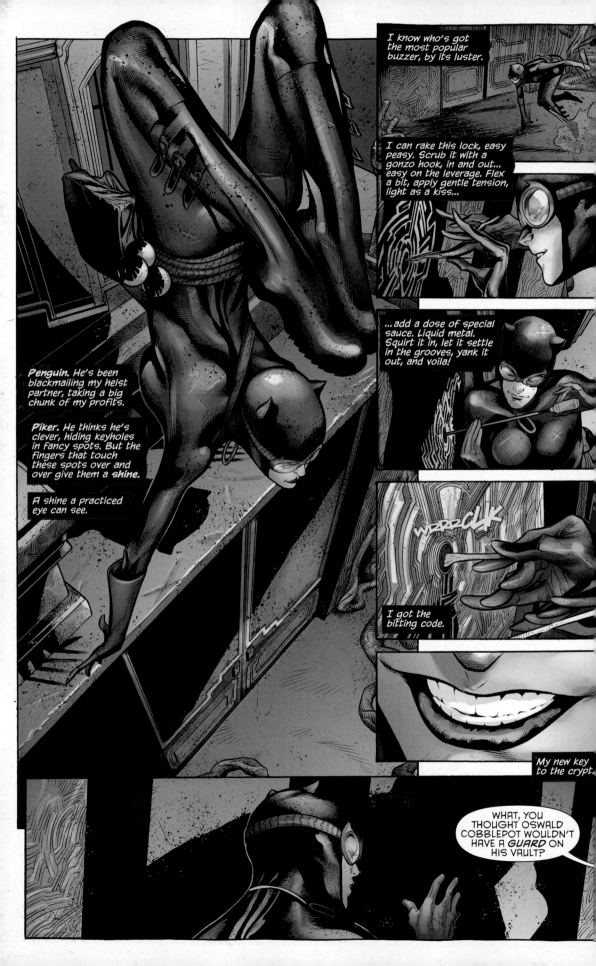

I know who's got the most popular buzzer, by its luster.

I can rake this lock, easy peasy. Scrub it with a gonzo hook, in and out... easy on the leverage. Flex a bit, apply gentle tension, light as a kiss...

...add a dose of special sauce. Liquid metal. Squirt it in, let it settle in the grooves, yank it out, and voila!

Penguin. He's been blackmailing my heist partner, taking a big chunk of my profits.

Piker. He thinks he's clever, hiding keyholes in fancy spots. But the fingers that touch these spots over and over give them a shine.

A shine a practiced eye can see.

WRRRCLK

I got the bitting code.

My new key to the crypt.

WHAT, YOU THOUGHT OSWALD COBBLEPOT WOULDN'T HAVE A *GUARD* ON HIS VAULT?

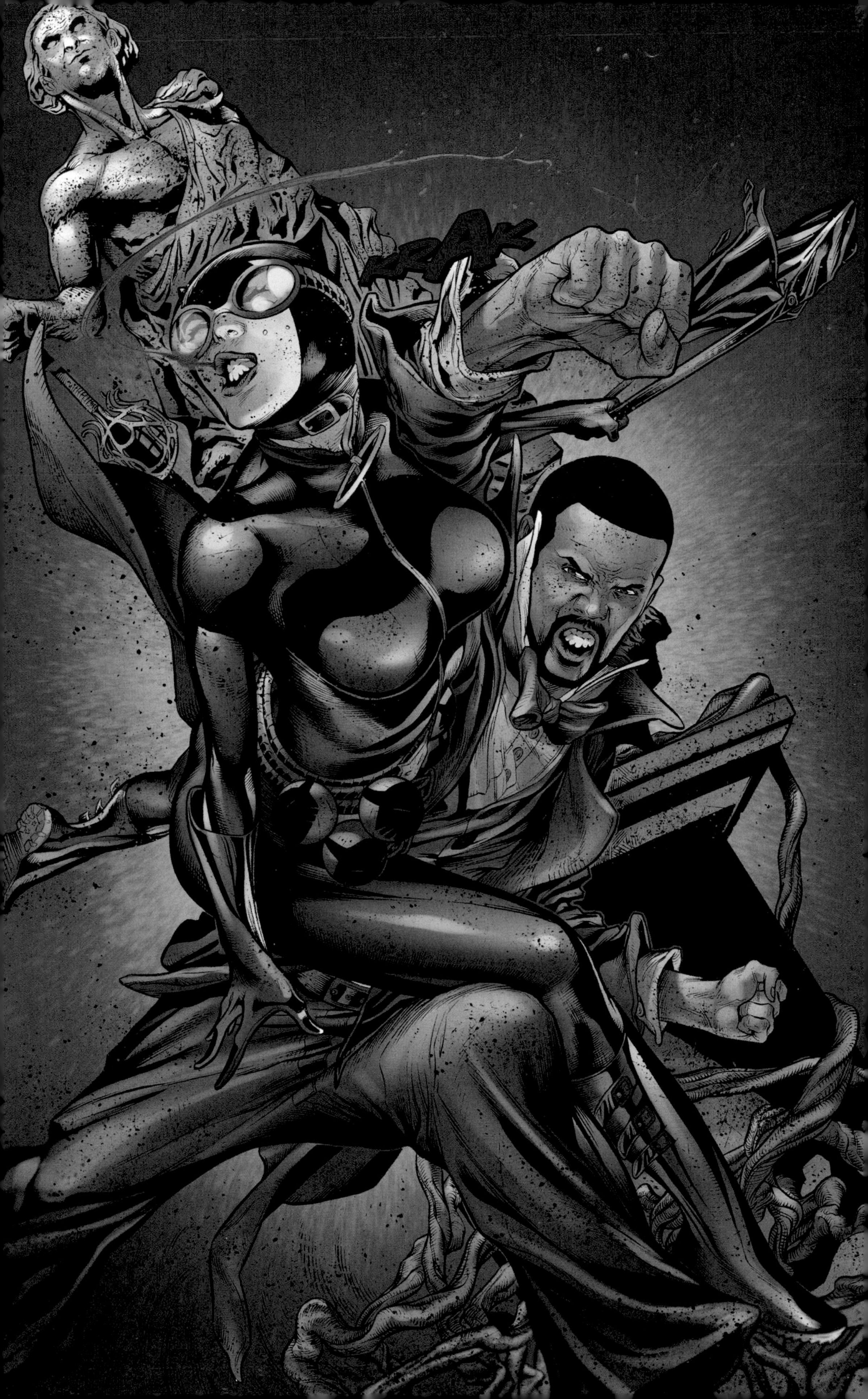

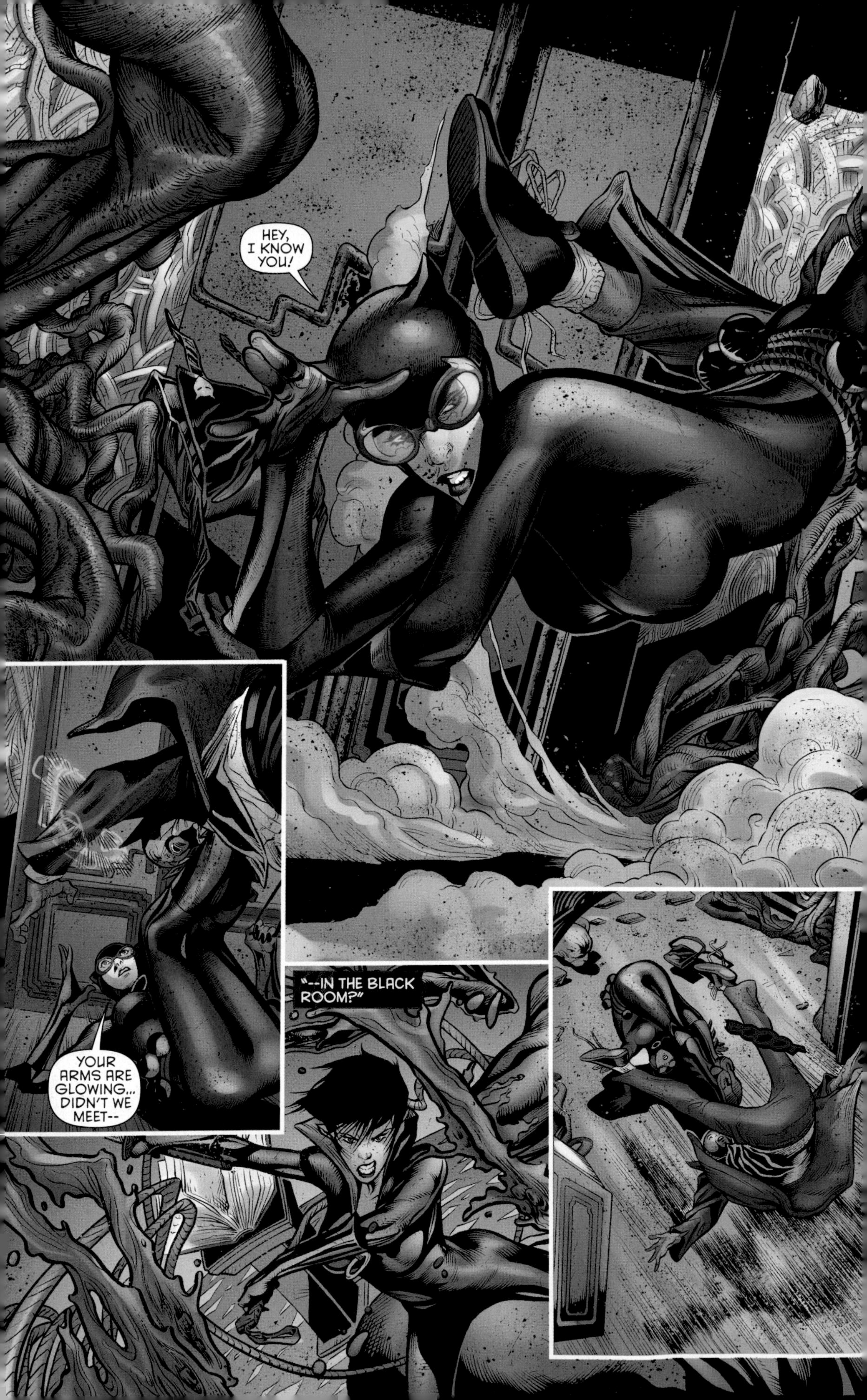
HEY, I KNOW YOU!
YOUR ARMS ARE GLOWING... DIDN'T WE MEET--
"--IN THE BLACK ROOM?"

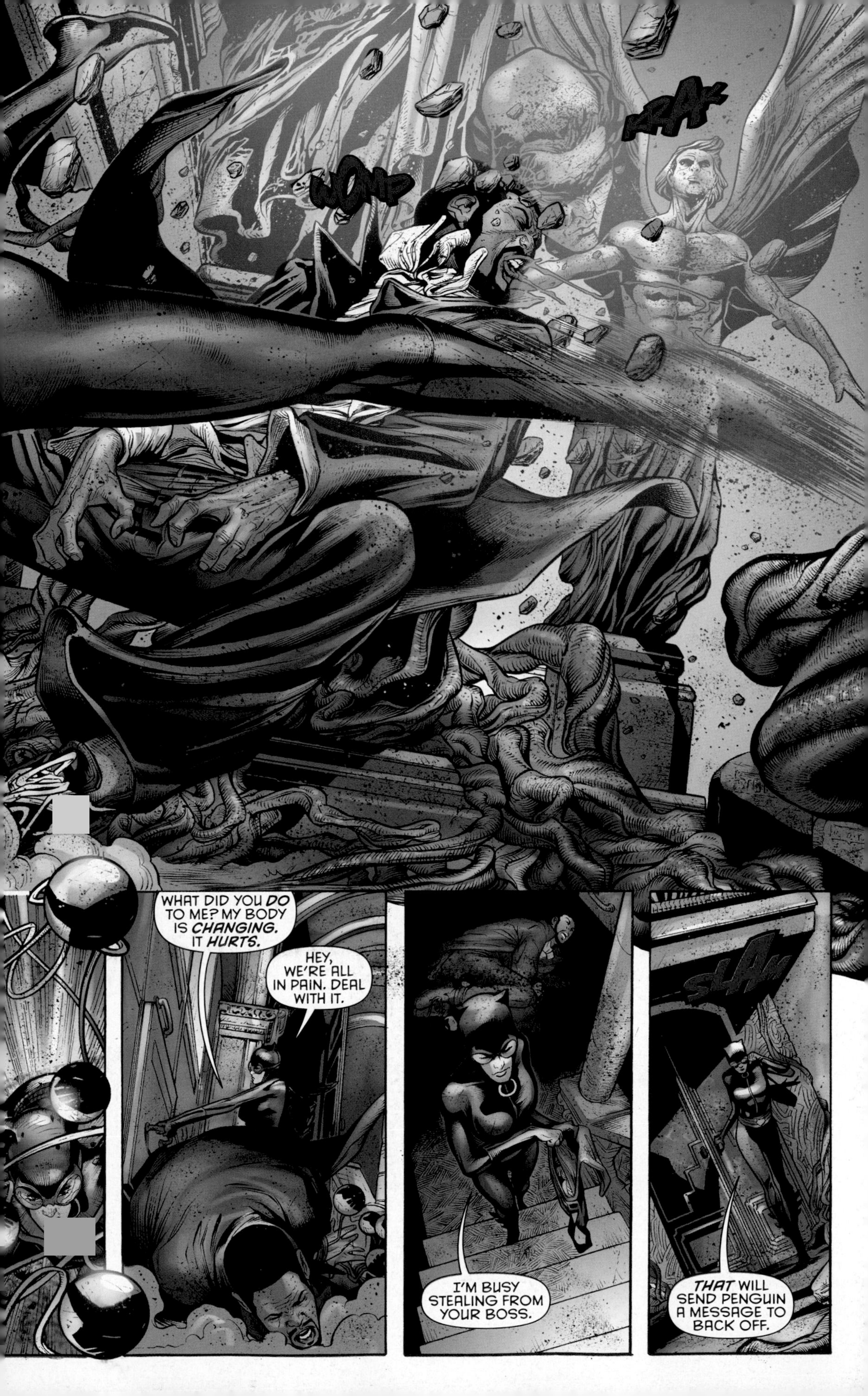
WOMP
KRAK
WHAT DID YOU DO TO ME? MY BODY IS CHANGING. IT HURTS.
HEY, WE'RE ALL IN PAIN. DEAL WITH IT.
I'M BUSY STEALING FROM YOUR BOSS.
SLAM
THAT WILL SEND PENGUIN A MESSAGE TO BACK OFF.

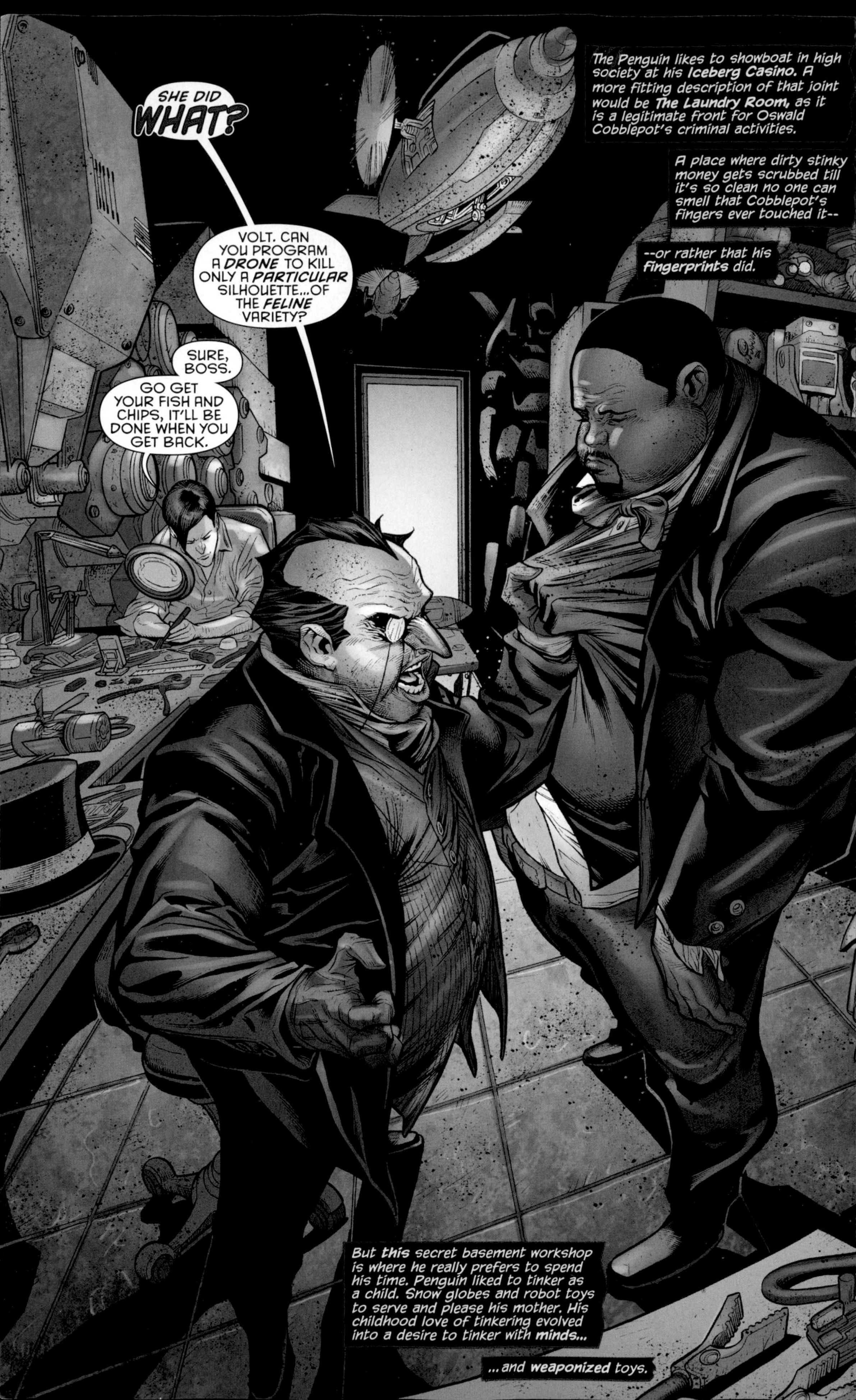
The Penguin likes to showboat in high society at his Iceberg Casino. A more fitting description of that joint would be The Laundry Room, as it is a legitimate front for Oswald Cobblepot's criminal activities.
A place where dirty stinky money gets scrubbed till it's so clean no one can smell that Cobblepot's fingers ever touched it--
--or rather that his fingerprints did.
SHE DID WHAT?
VOLT. CAN YOU PROGRAM A DRONE TO KILL ONLY A PARTICULAR SILHOUETTE...OF THE FELINE VARIETY?
SURE, BOSS.
GO GET YOUR FISH AND CHIPS, IT'LL BE DONE WHEN YOU GET BACK.
But this secret basement workshop is where he really prefers to spend his time. Penguin liked to tinker as a child. Snow globes and robot toys to serve and please his mother. His childhood love of tinkering evolved into a desire to tinker with minds...
...and weaponized toys.

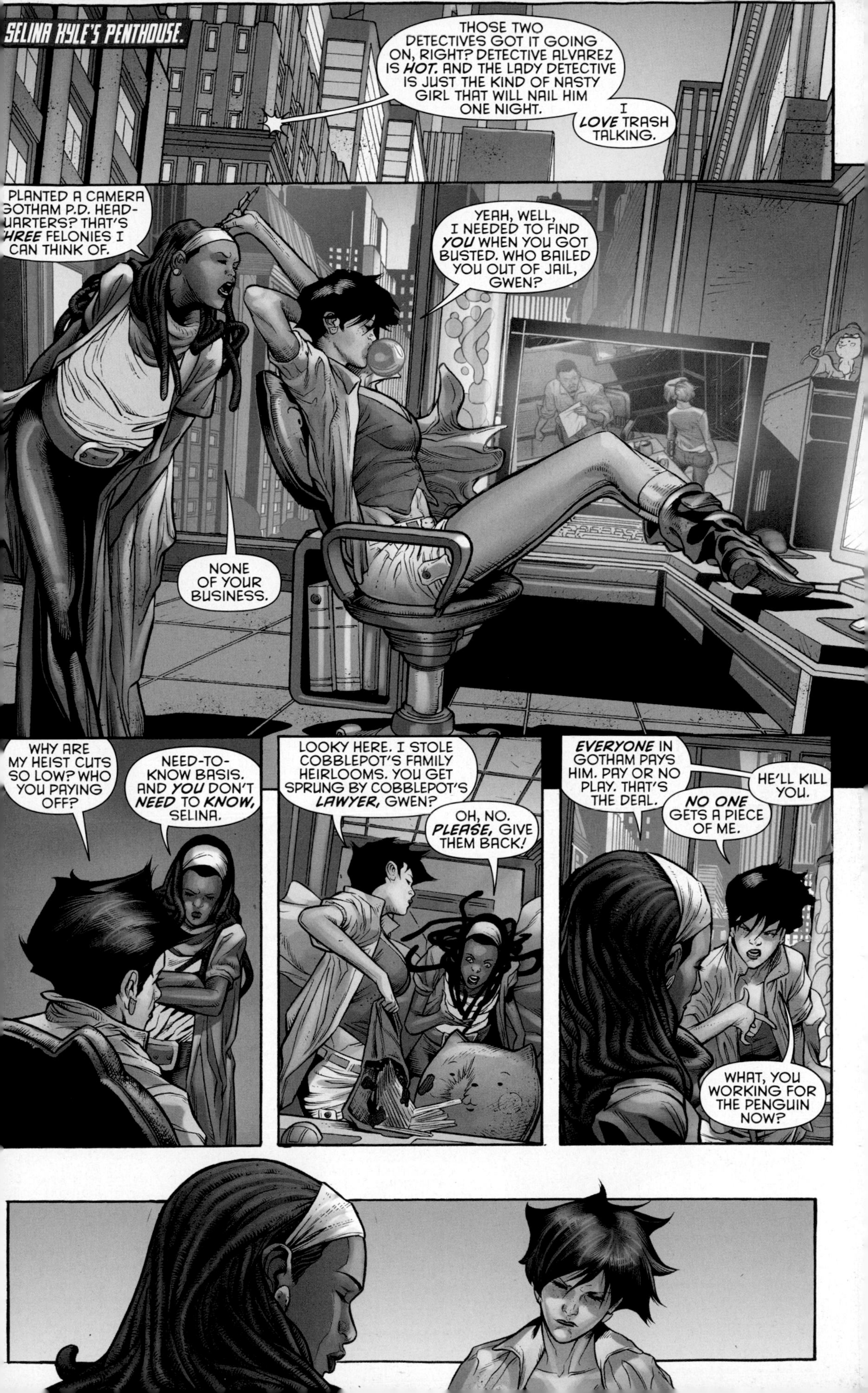

SELINA KYLE'S PENTHOUSE.
THOSE TWO DETECTIVES GOT IT GOING ON, RIGHT? DETECTIVE ALVAREZ IS HOT. AND THE LADY DETECTIVE IS JUST THE KIND OF NASTY GIRL THAT WILL NAIL HIM ONE NIGHT.
I LOVE TRASH TALKING.
PLANTED A CAMERA GOTHAM P.D. HEAD- UARTERS? THAT'S HREE FELONIES I CAN THINK OF.
YEAH, WELL, I NEEDED TO FIND YOU WHEN YOU GOT BUSTED. WHO BAILED YOU OUT OF JAIL, GWEN?
NONE OF YOUR BUSINESS.
WHY ARE MY HEIST CUTS SO LOW? WHO YOU PAYING OFF?
NEED-TO-KNOW BASIS. AND YOU DON'T NEED TO KNOW, SELINA.
LOOKY HERE. I STOLE COBBLEPOT'S FAMILY HEIRLOOMS. YOU GET SPRUNG BY COBBLEPOT'S LAWYER, GWEN?
OH, NO. PLEASE, GIVE THEM BACK!
EVERYONE IN GOTHAM PAYS HIM. PAY OR NO PLAY. THAT'S THE DEAL.
HE'LL KILL YOU.
NO ONE GETS A PIECE OF ME.
WHAT, YOU WORKING FOR THE PENGUIN NOW?

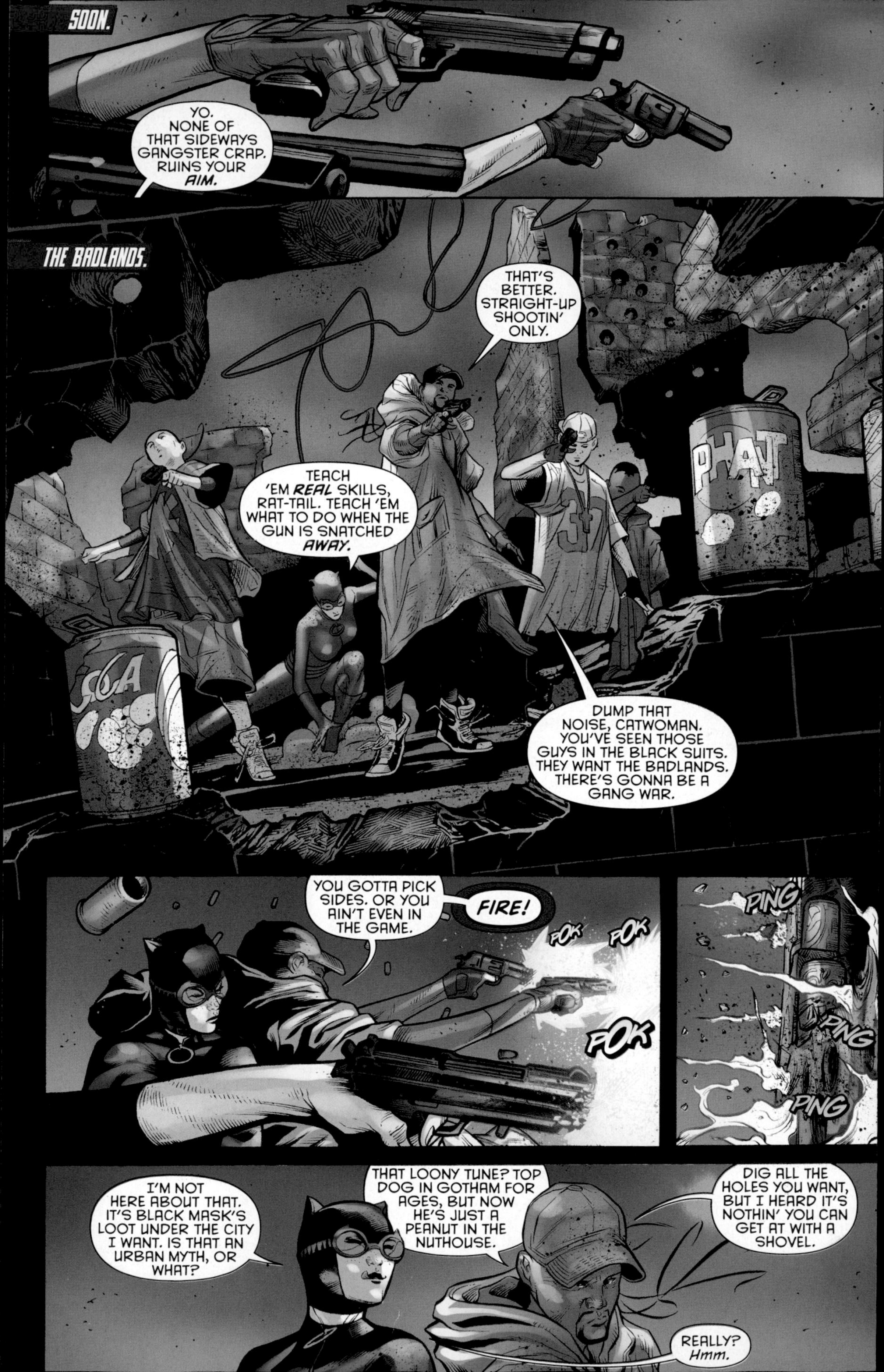
SOON.
YO. NONE OF THAT SIDEWAYS GANGSTER CRAP. RUINS YOUR AIM.
THE BADLANDS.
THAT'S BETTER. STRAIGHT-UP SHOOTIN' ONLY.
TEACH 'EM REAL SKILLS, RAT-TAIL. TEACH 'EM WHAT TO DO WHEN THE GUN IS SNATCHED AWAY.
PHAT
DUMP THAT NOISE, CATWOMAN. YOU'VE SEEN THOSE GUYS IN THE BLACK SUITS. THEY WANT THE BADLANDS. THERE'S GONNA BE A GANG WAR.
YOU GOTTA PICK SIDES. OR YOU AIN'T EVEN IN THE GAME.
FIRE!
FOK
FOK
FOK
PING
PING
PING
I'M NOT HERE ABOUT THAT. IT'S BLACK MASK'S LOOT UNDER THE CITY I WANT. IS THAT AN URBAN MYTH, OR WHAT?
THAT LOONY TUNE? TOP DOG IN GOTHAM FOR AGES, BUT NOW HE'S JUST A PEANUT IN THE NUTHOUSE.
DIG ALL THE HOLES YOU WANT, BUT I HEARD IT'S NOTHIN' YOU CAN GET AT WITH A SHOVEL.
REALLY? Hmm.

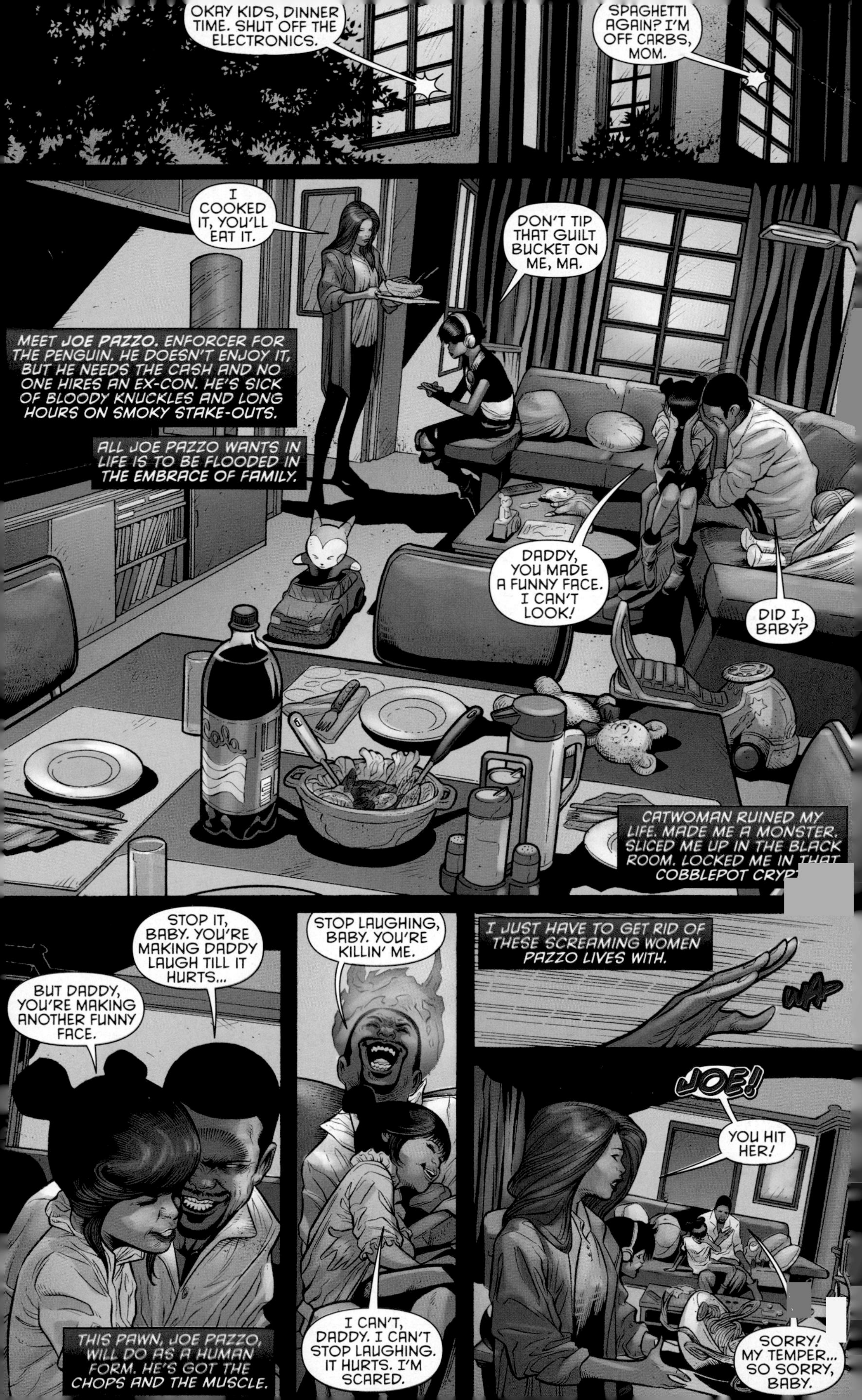

OKAY KIDS, DINNER TIME. SHUT OFF THE ELECTRONICS.
SPAGHETTI AGAIN? I'M OFF CARBS, MOM.
I COOKED IT, YOU'LL EAT IT.
DON'T TIP THAT GUILT BUCKET ON ME, MA.
MEET JOE PAZZO. ENFORCER FOR THE PENGUIN. HE DOESN'T ENJOY IT, BUT HE NEEDS THE CASH AND NO ONE HIRES AN EX-CON. HE'S SICK OF BLOODY KNUCKLES AND LONG HOURS ON SMOKY STAKE-OUTS.
ALL JOE PAZZO WANTS IN LIFE IS TO BE FLOODED IN THE EMBRACE OF FAMILY.
DADDY, YOU MADE A FUNNY FACE. I CAN'T LOOK!
DID I, BABY?
CATWOMAN RUINED MY LIFE. MADE ME A MONSTER. SLICED ME UP IN THE BLACK ROOM. LOCKED ME IN THAT COBBLEPOT CRYPT.
BUT DADDY, YOU'RE MAKING ANOTHER FUNNY FACE.
STOP IT, BABY. YOU'RE MAKING DADDY LAUGH TILL IT HURTS...
THIS PAWN, JOE PAZZO, WILL DO AS A HUMAN FORM. HE'S GOT THE CHOPS AND THE MUSCLE.
STOP LAUGHING, BABY. YOU'RE KILLIN' ME.
I CAN'T, DADDY. I CAN'T STOP LAUGHING. IT HURTS. I'M SCARED.
I JUST HAVE TO GET RID OF THESE SCREAMING WOMEN PAZZO LIVES WITH.
JOE!
YOU HIT HER!
SORRY! MY TEMPER... SO SORRY, BABY.

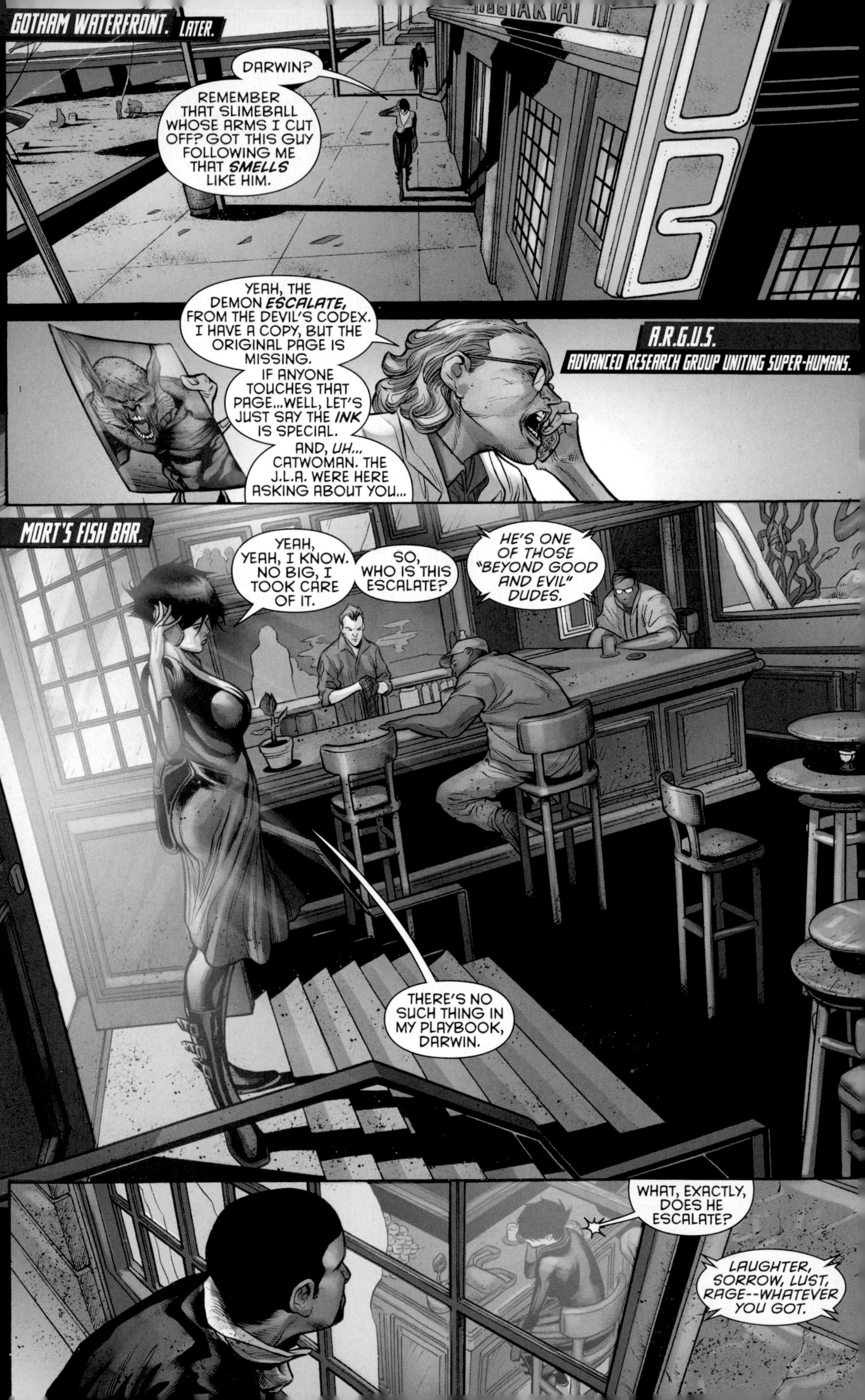
GOTHAM WATERFRONT. LATER.
DARWIN?
REMEMBER THAT SLIMEBALL WHOSE ARMS I CUT OFF? GOT THIS GUY FOLLOWING ME THAT SMELLS LIKE HIM.
YEAH, THE DEMON ESCALATE, FROM THE DEVIL'S CODEX. I HAVE A COPY, BUT THE ORIGINAL PAGE IS MISSING.
IF ANYONE TOUCHES THAT PAGE...WELL, LET'S JUST SAY THE INK IS SPECIAL.
AND, UH... CATWOMAN. THE J.L.A. WERE HERE ASKING ABOUT YOU...
A.R.G.U.S.
ADVANCED RESEARCH GROUP UNITING SUPER-HUMANS.
MORT'S FISH BAR.
YEAH, YEAH, I KNOW. NO BIG, I TOOK CARE OF IT.
SO, WHO IS THIS ESCALATE?
HE'S ONE OF THOSE "BEYOND GOOD AND EVIL" DUDES.
THERE'S NO SUCH THING IN MY PLAYBOOK, DARWIN.
WHAT, EXACTLY, DOES HE ESCALATE?
LAUGHTER, SORROW, LUST, RAGE--WHATEVER YOU GOT.

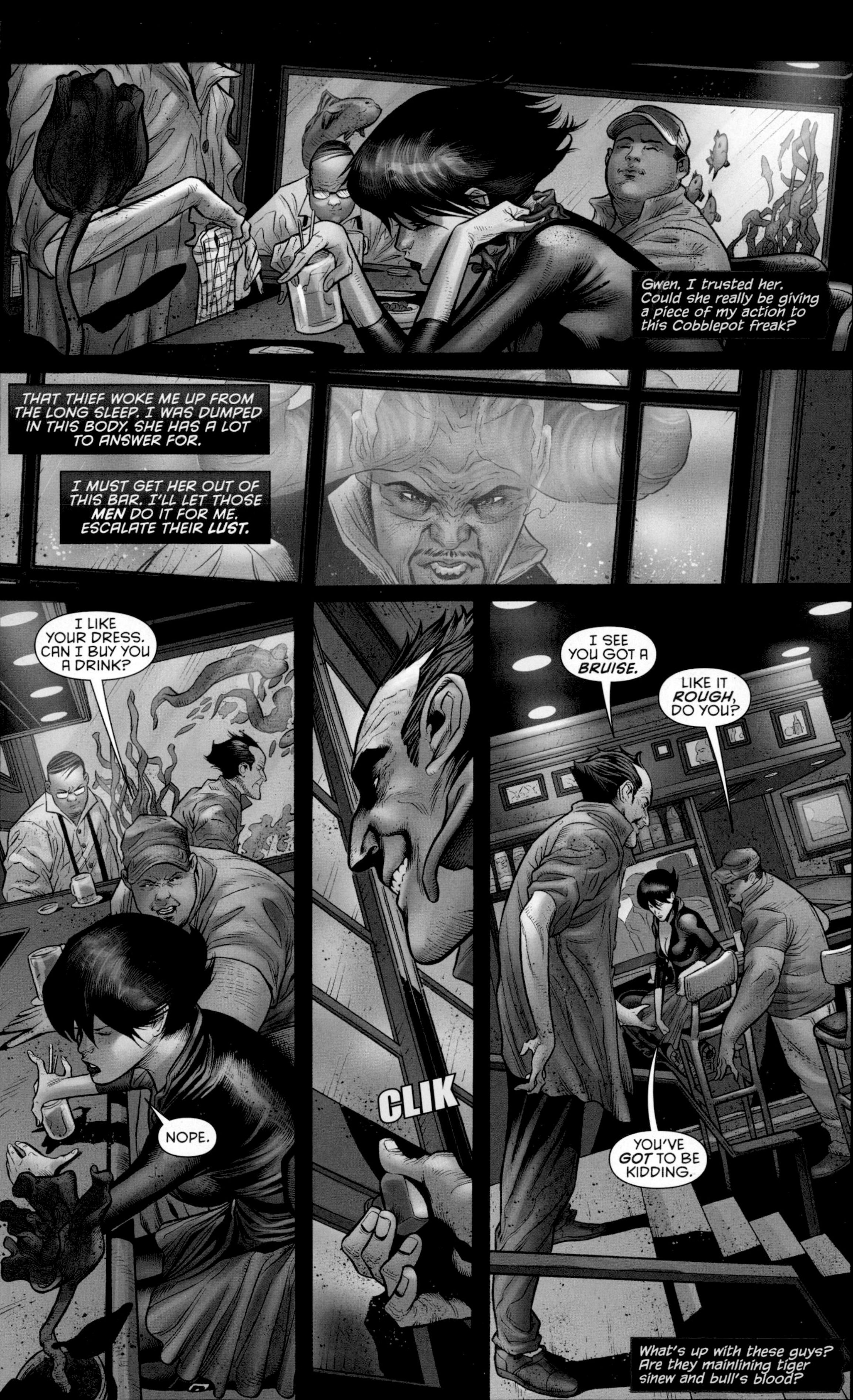

Gwen. I trusted her. Could she really be giving a piece of my action to this Cobblepot freak?
THAT THIEF WOKE ME UP FROM THE LONG SLEEP. I WAS DUMPED IN THIS BODY. SHE HAS A LOT TO ANSWER FOR.
I MUST GET HER OUT OF THIS BAR. I'LL LET THOSE MEN DO IT FOR ME. ESCALATE THEIR LUST.
I LIKE YOUR DRESS. CAN I BUY YOU A DRINK?
NOPE.
CLIK
I SEE YOU GOT A BRUISE.
LIKE IT ROUGH, DO YOU?
YOU'VE GOT TO BE KIDDING.
What's up with these guys? Are they mainlining tiger sinew and bull's blood?

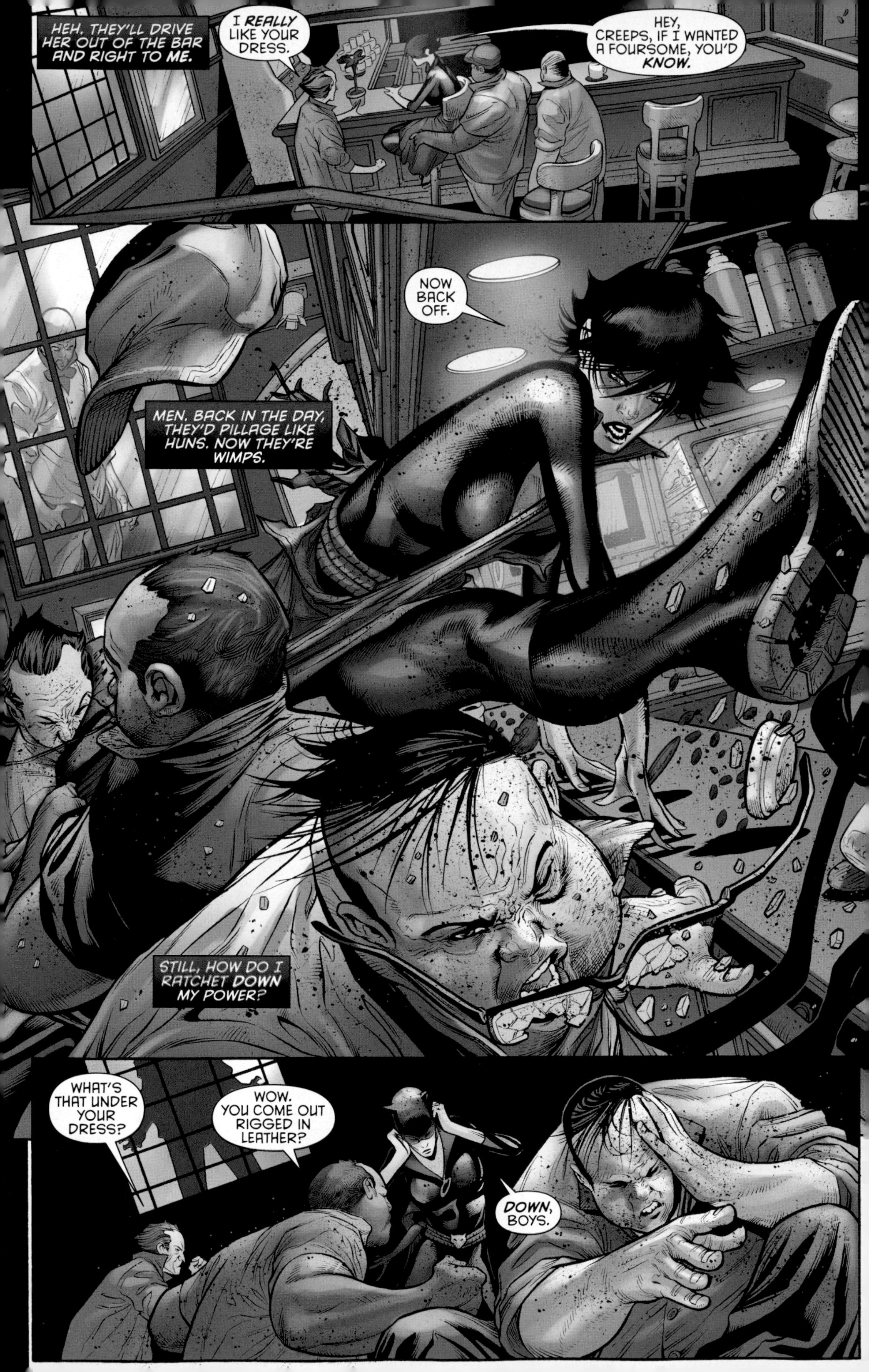
HEH. THEY'LL DRIVE HER OUT OF THE BAR AND RIGHT TO ME.
I REALLY LIKE YOUR DRESS.
HEY, CREEPS, IF I WANTED A FOURSOME, YOU'D KNOW.
NOW BACK OFF.
MEN. BACK IN THE DAY, THEY'D PILLAGE LIKE HUNS. NOW THEY'RE WIMPS.
STILL, HOW DO I RATCHET DOWN MY POWER?
WHAT'S THAT UNDER YOUR DRESS?
WOW. YOU COME OUT RIGGED IN LEATHER?
DOWN, BOYS.

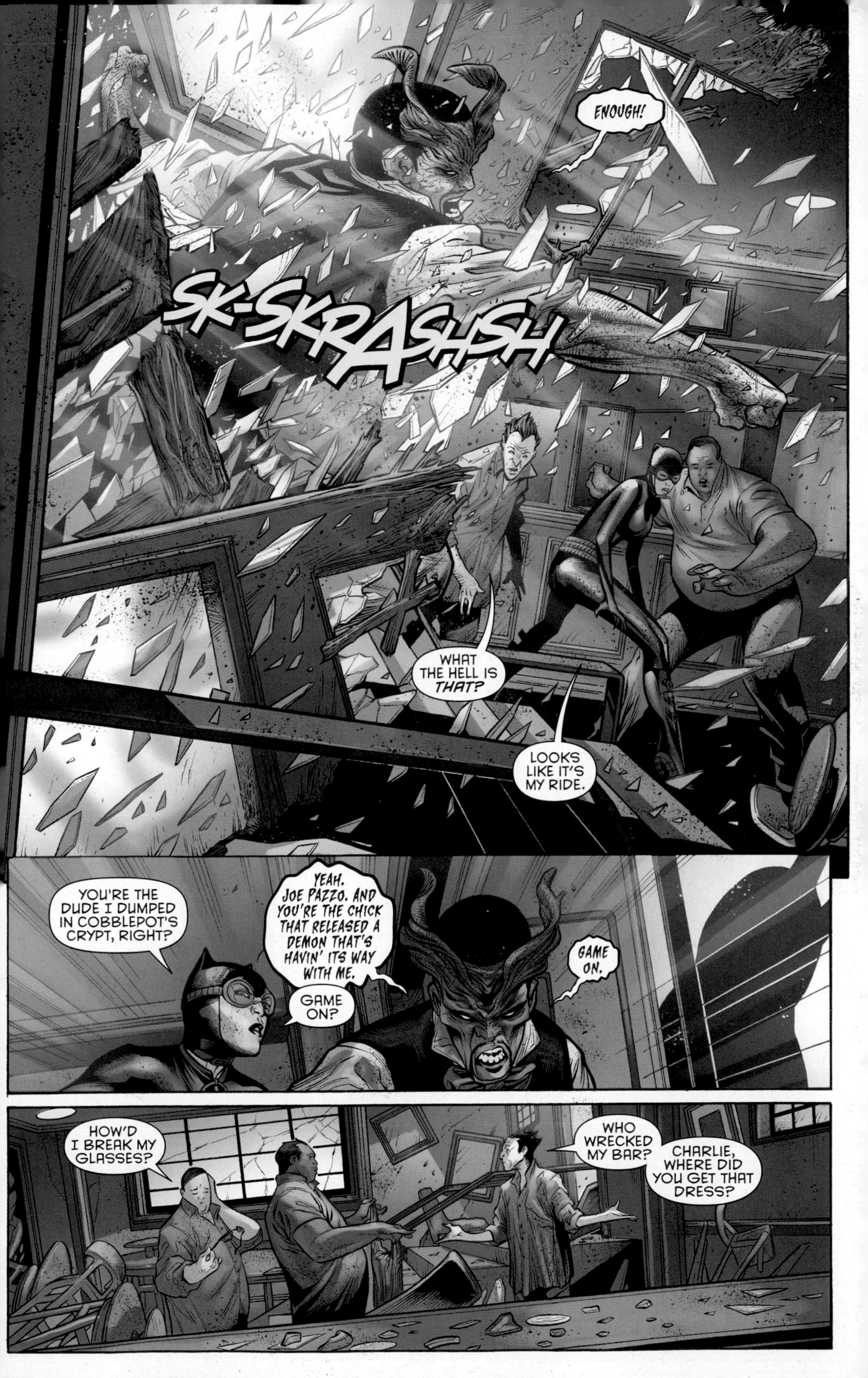
ENOUGH!
SK-SKRASHSH
WHAT THE HELL IS THAT?
LOOKS LIKE IT'S MY RIDE.
YOU'RE THE DUDE I DUMPED IN COBBLEPOT'S CRYPT, RIGHT?
YEAH. JOE PAZZO. AND YOU'RE THE CHICK THAT RELEASED A DEMON THAT'S HAVIN' ITS WAY WITH ME.
GAME ON?
GAME ON.
HOW'D I BREAK MY GLASSES?
WHO WRECKED MY BAR?
CHARLIE, WHERE DID YOU GET THAT DRESS?

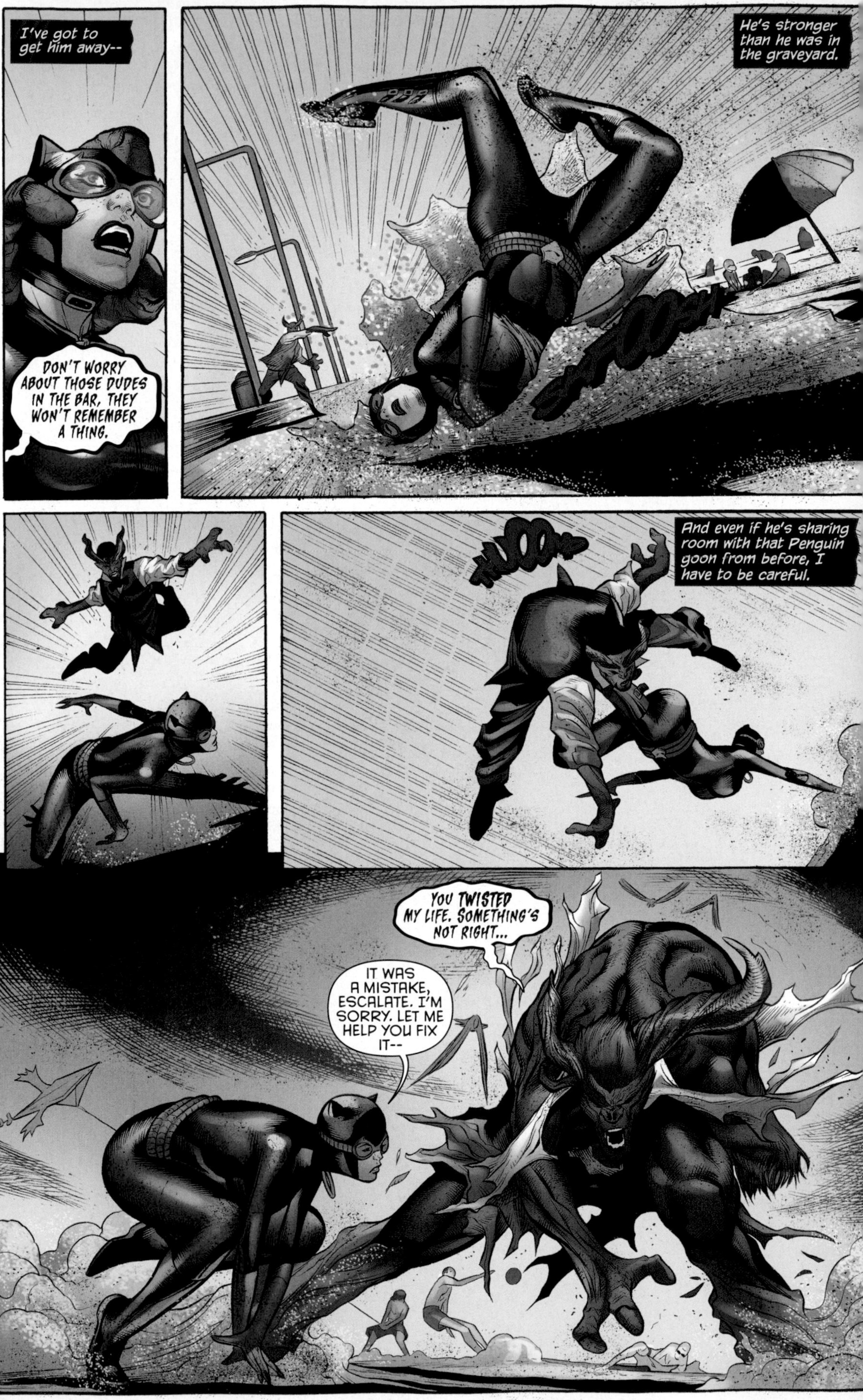
I've got to get him away--
He's stronger than he was in the graveyard.
DON'T WORRY ABOUT THOSE DUDES IN THE BAR, THEY WON'T REMEMBER A THING.
And even if he's sharing room with that Penguin goon from before, I have to be careful.
YOU TWISTED MY LIFE. SOMETHING'S NOT RIGHT...
IT WAS A MISTAKE, ESCALATE. I'M SORRY. LET ME HELP YOU FIX IT--

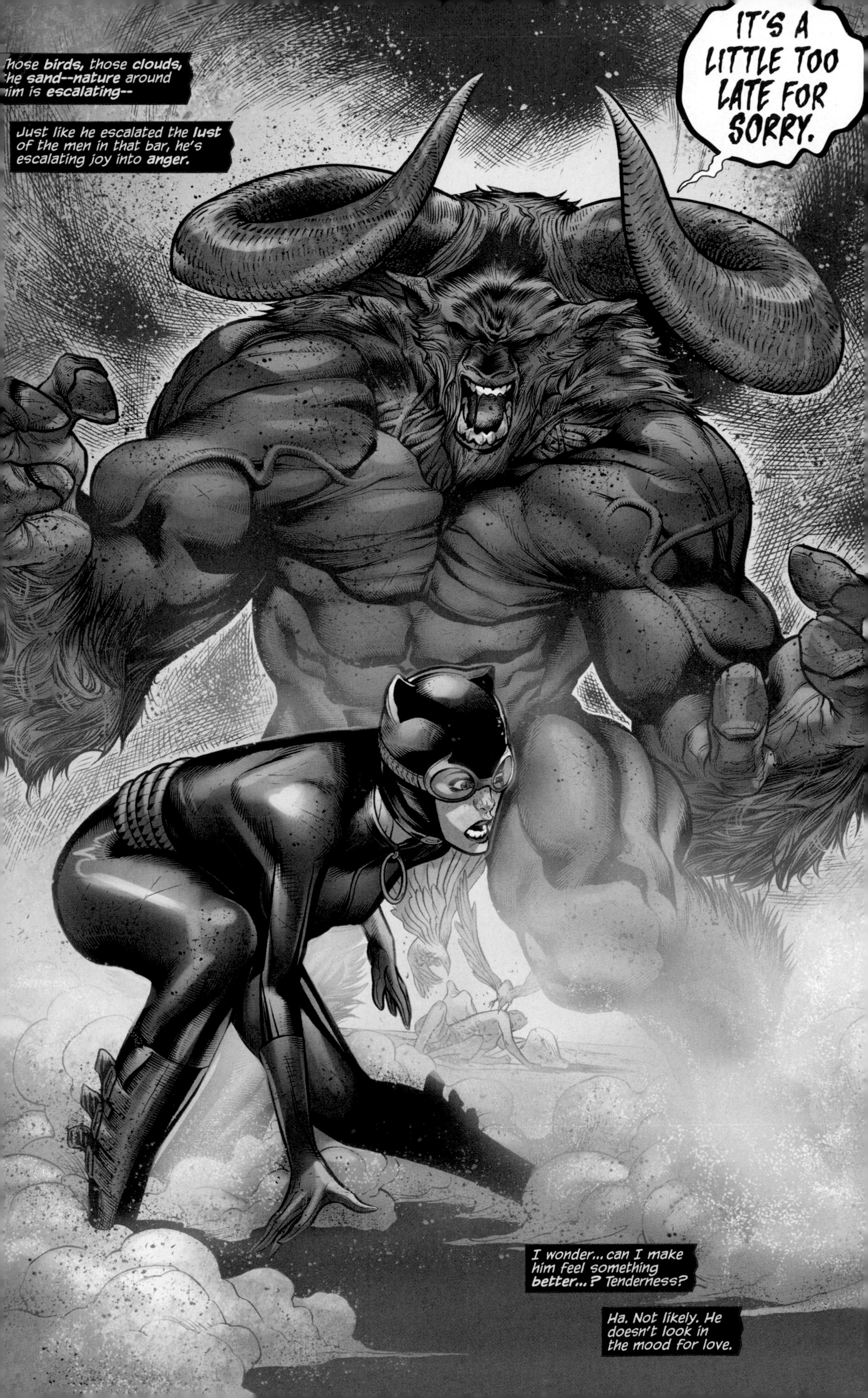

hose birds, those clouds, he sand--nature around im is escalating--
Just like he escalated the lust of the men in that bar, he's escalating joy into anger.
IT'S A LITTLE TOO LATE FOR SORRY.
I wonder... can I make him feel something better...? Tenderness?
Ha. Not likely. He doesn't look in the mood for love.

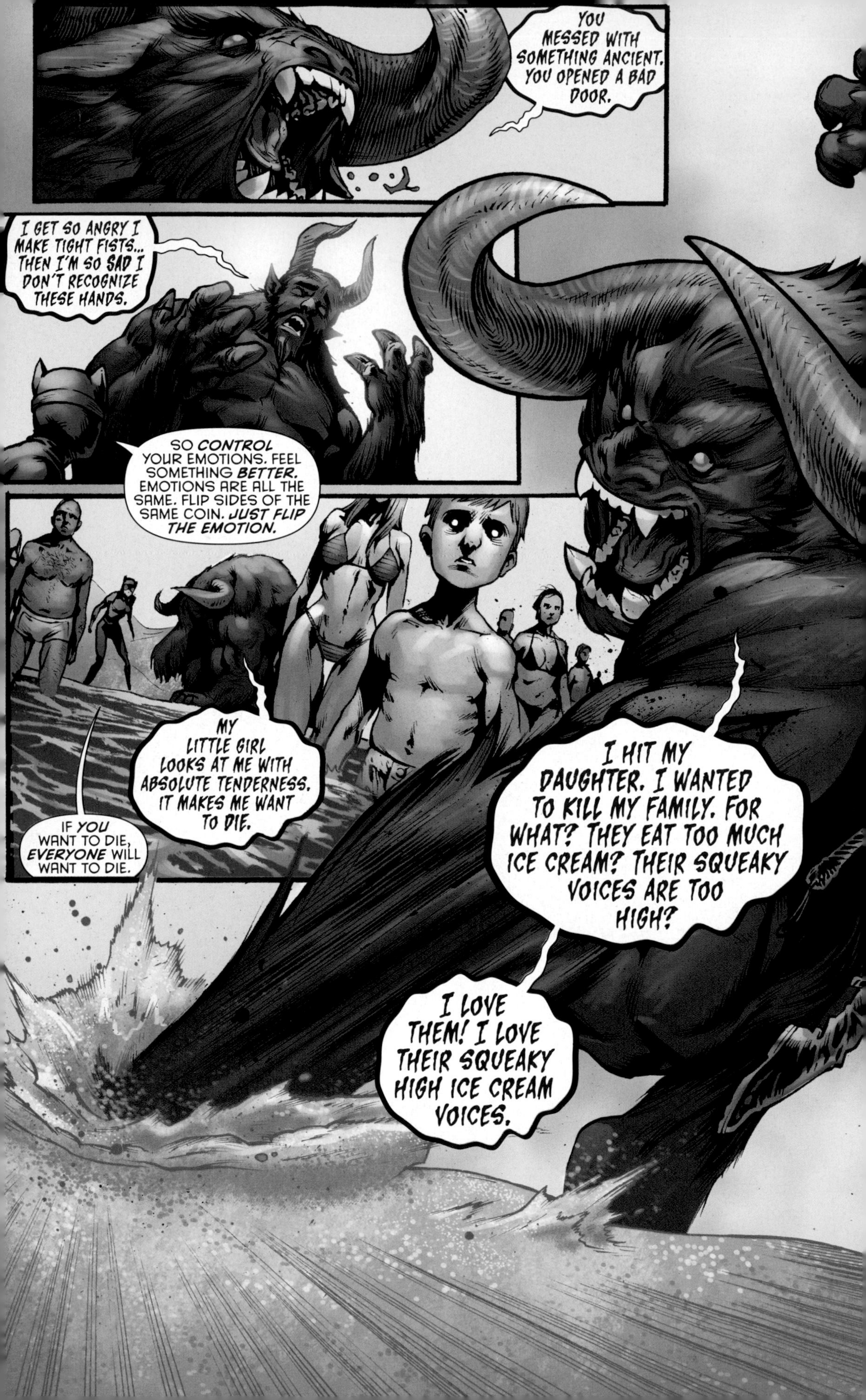

YOU MESSED WITH SOMETHING ANCIENT. YOU OPENED A BAD DOOR.
I GET SO ANGRY I MAKE TIGHT FISTS... THEN I'M SO SAD I DON'T RECOGNIZE THESE HANDS.
SO CONTROL YOUR EMOTIONS. FEEL SOMETHING BETTER. EMOTIONS ARE ALL THE SAME. FLIP SIDES OF THE SAME COIN. JUST FLIP THE EMOTION.
MY LITTLE GIRL LOOKS AT ME WITH ABSOLUTE TENDERNESS. IT MAKES ME WANT TO DIE.
IF YOU WANT TO DIE, EVERYONE WILL WANT TO DIE.
I HIT MY DAUGHTER. I WANTED TO KILL MY FAMILY. FOR WHAT? THEY EAT TOO MUCH ICE CREAM? THEIR SQUEAKY VOICES ARE TOO HIGH?
I LOVE THEM! I LOVE THEIR SQUEAKY HIGH ICE CREAM VOICES.

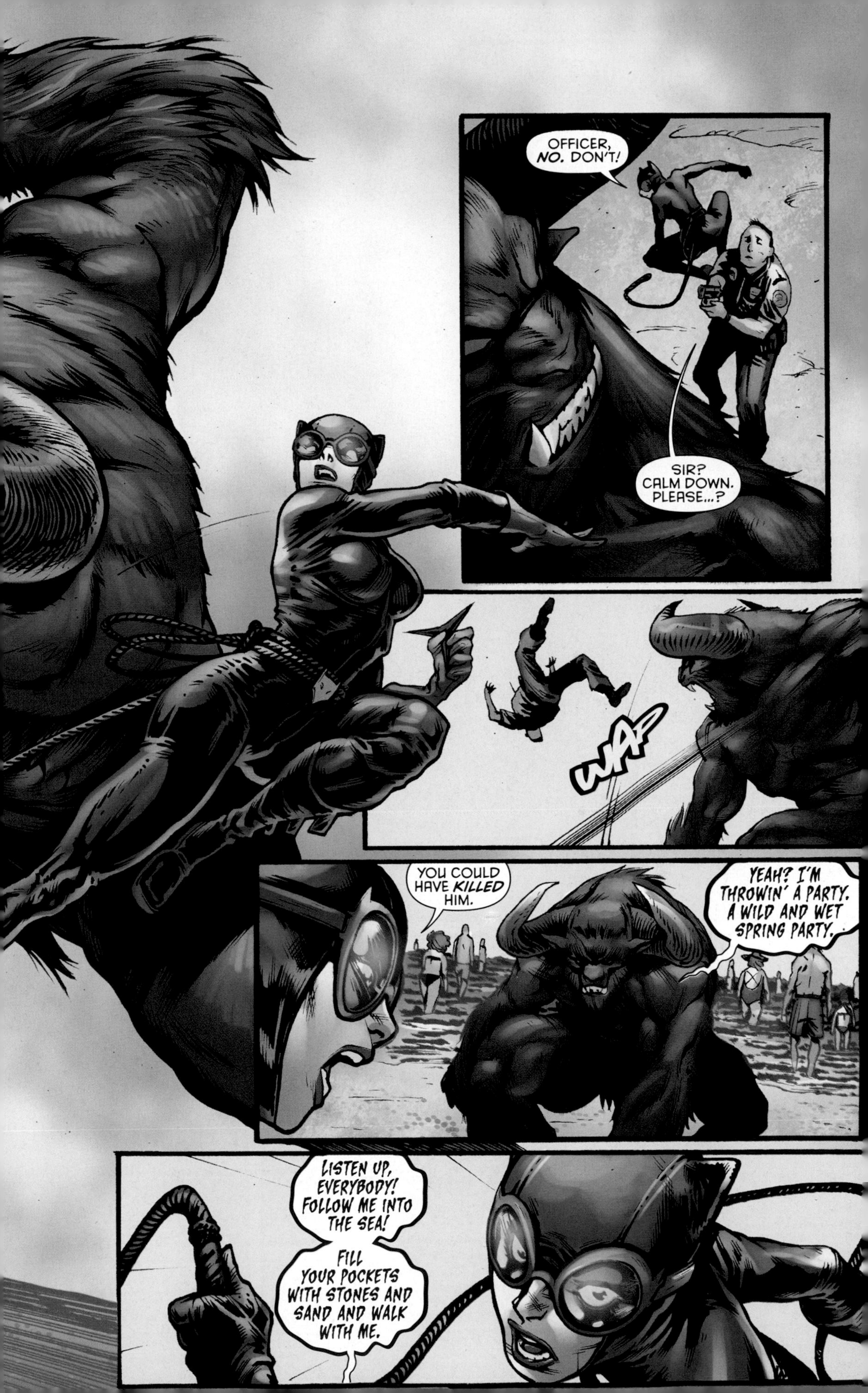
OFFICER, NO. DON'T!
SIR? CALM DOWN. PLEASE...?
WAP
YOU COULD HAVE KILLED HIM.
YEAH? I'M THROWIN' A PARTY. A WILD AND WET SPRING PARTY.
LISTEN UP, EVERYBODY! FOLLOW ME INTO THE SEA!
FILL YOUR POCKETS WITH STONES AND SAND AND WALK WITH ME.

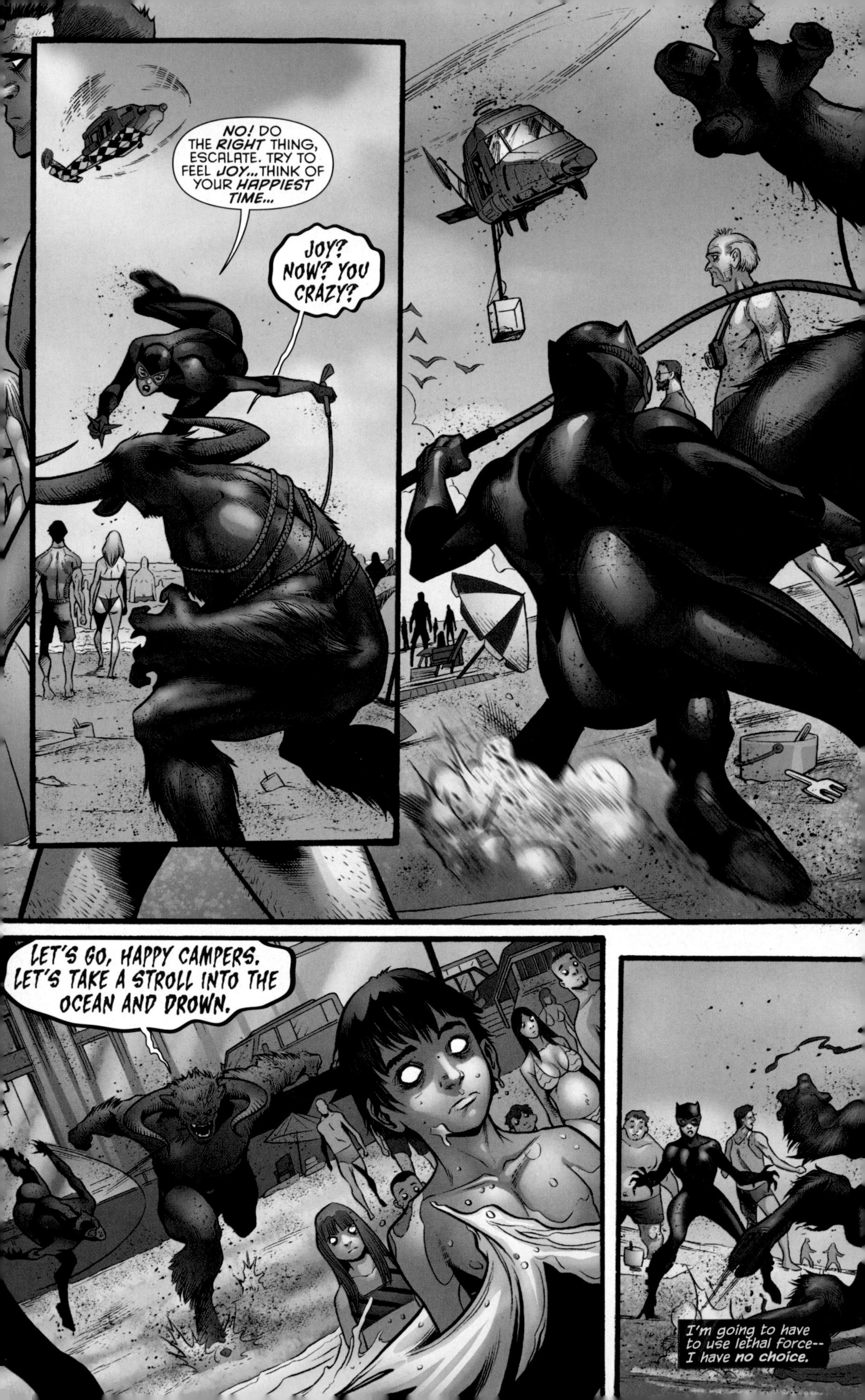
NO! DO THE RIGHT THING, ESCALATE. TRY TO FEEL JOY...THINK OF YOUR HAPPIEST TIME...
JOY? NOW? YOU CRAZY?
LET'S GO, HAPPY CAMPERS. LET'S TAKE A STROLL INTO THE OCEAN AND DROWN.
I'm going to have to use lethal force-- I have no choice.

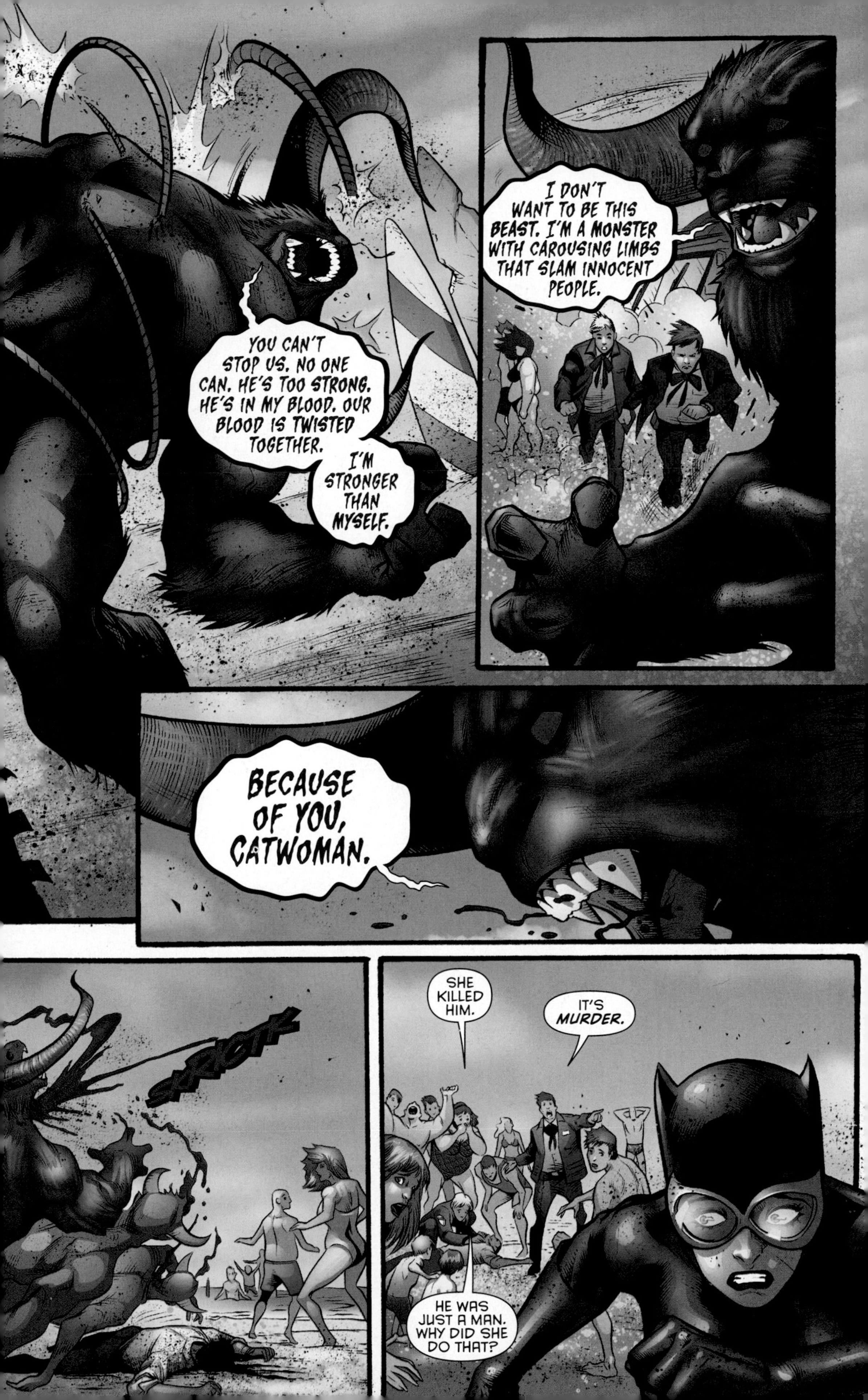
I DON'T WANT TO BE THIS BEAST. I'M A MONSTER WITH CAROUSING LIMBS THAT SLAM INNOCENT PEOPLE.
YOU CAN'T STOP US. NO ONE CAN. HE'S TOO STRONG. HE'S IN MY BLOOD. OUR BLOOD IS TWISTED TOGETHER.
I'M STRONGER THAN MYSELF.
BECAUSE OF YOU, CATWOMAN.
SHE KILLED HIM.
IT'S MURDER.
HE WAS JUST A MAN. WHY DID SHE DO THAT?

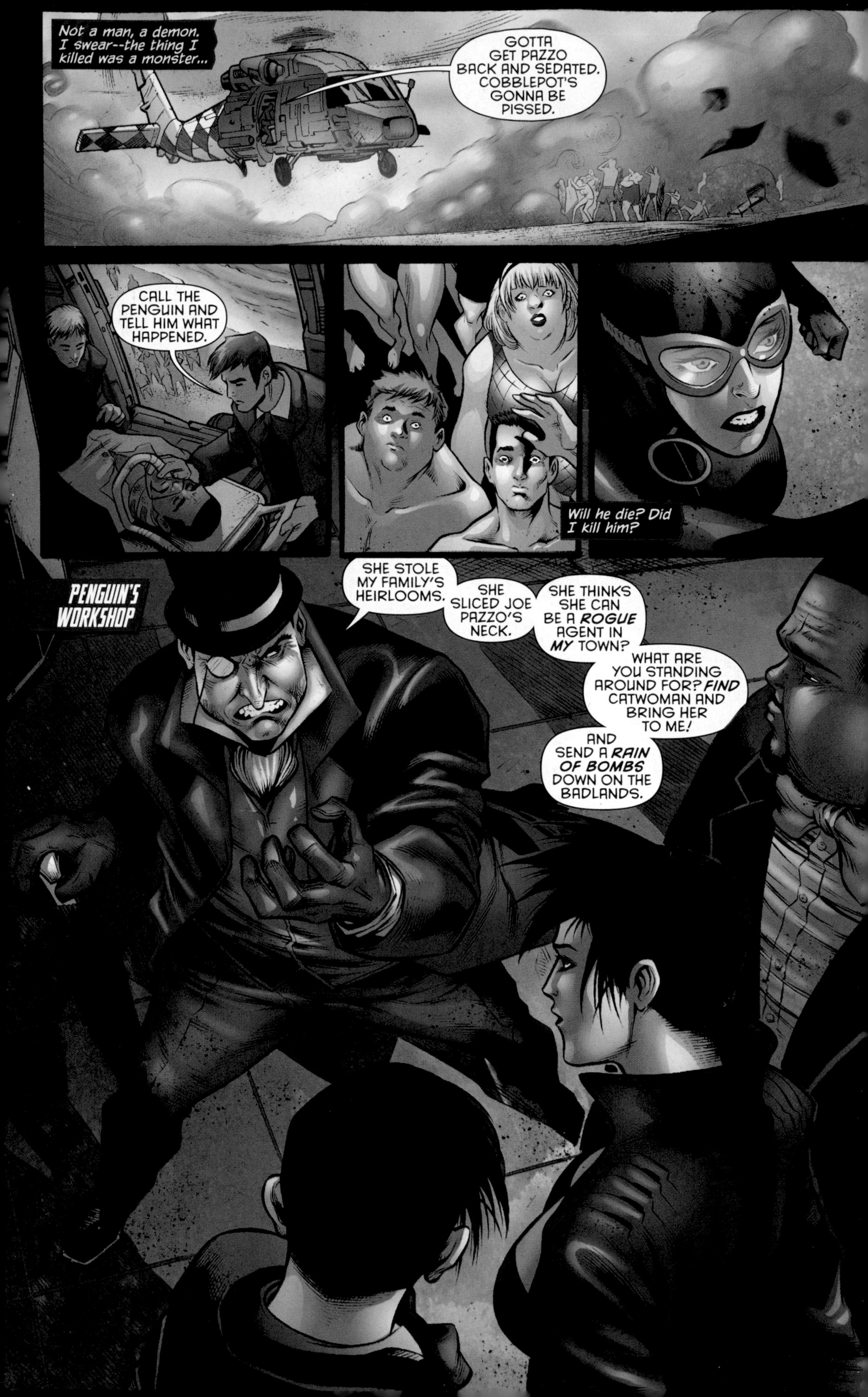
Not a man, a demon. I swear--the thing I killed was a monster...
GOTTA GET PAZZO BACK AND SEDATED. COBBLEPOT'S GONNA BE PISSED.
CALL THE PENGUIN AND TELL HIM WHAT HAPPENED.
Will he die? Did I kill him?
PENGUIN'S WORKSHOP
SHE STOLE MY FAMILY'S HEIRLOOMS.
SHE SLICED JOE PAZZO'S NECK.
SHE THINKS SHE CAN BE A ROGUE AGENT IN MY TOWN?
WHAT ARE YOU STANDING AROUND FOR? FIND CATWOMAN AND BRING HER TO ME!
AND SEND A RAIN OF BOMBS DOWN ON THE BADLANDS.

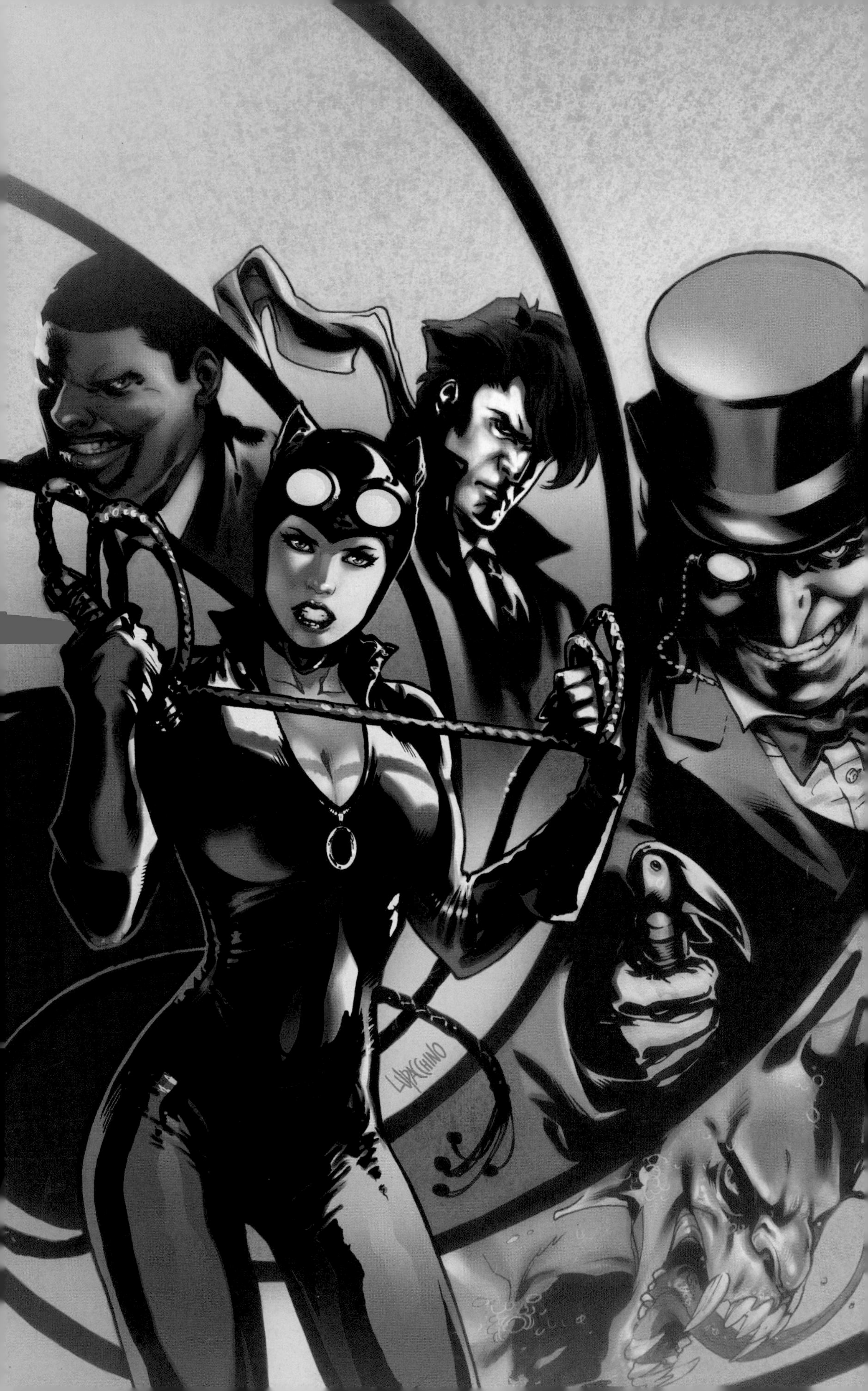
LUPACCHINO

ANN NOCENTI
writer

CHRISTIAN DUCE with AARON LOPRESTI & JOHN LIVESAY
artists

ANDREW DALHOUSE with MATT YACKEY
colorists

EMANUELA LUPACCHINO
cover artist

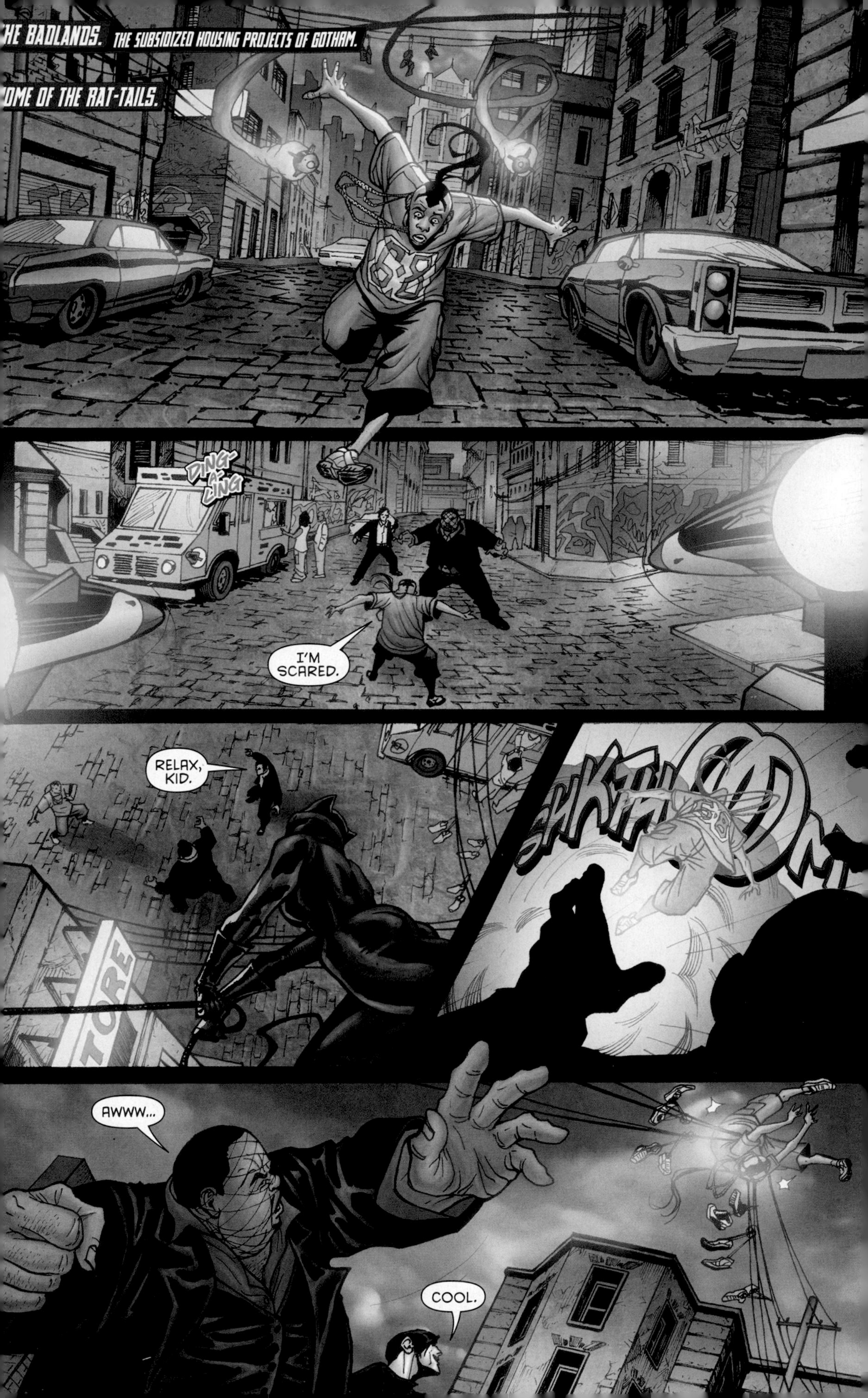
HE BADLANDS. THE SUBSIDIZED HOUSING PROJECTS OF GOTHAM.
OME OF THE RAT-TAILS.
DING-A-LING
I'M SCARED.
RELAX, KID.
AWWW...
COOL.

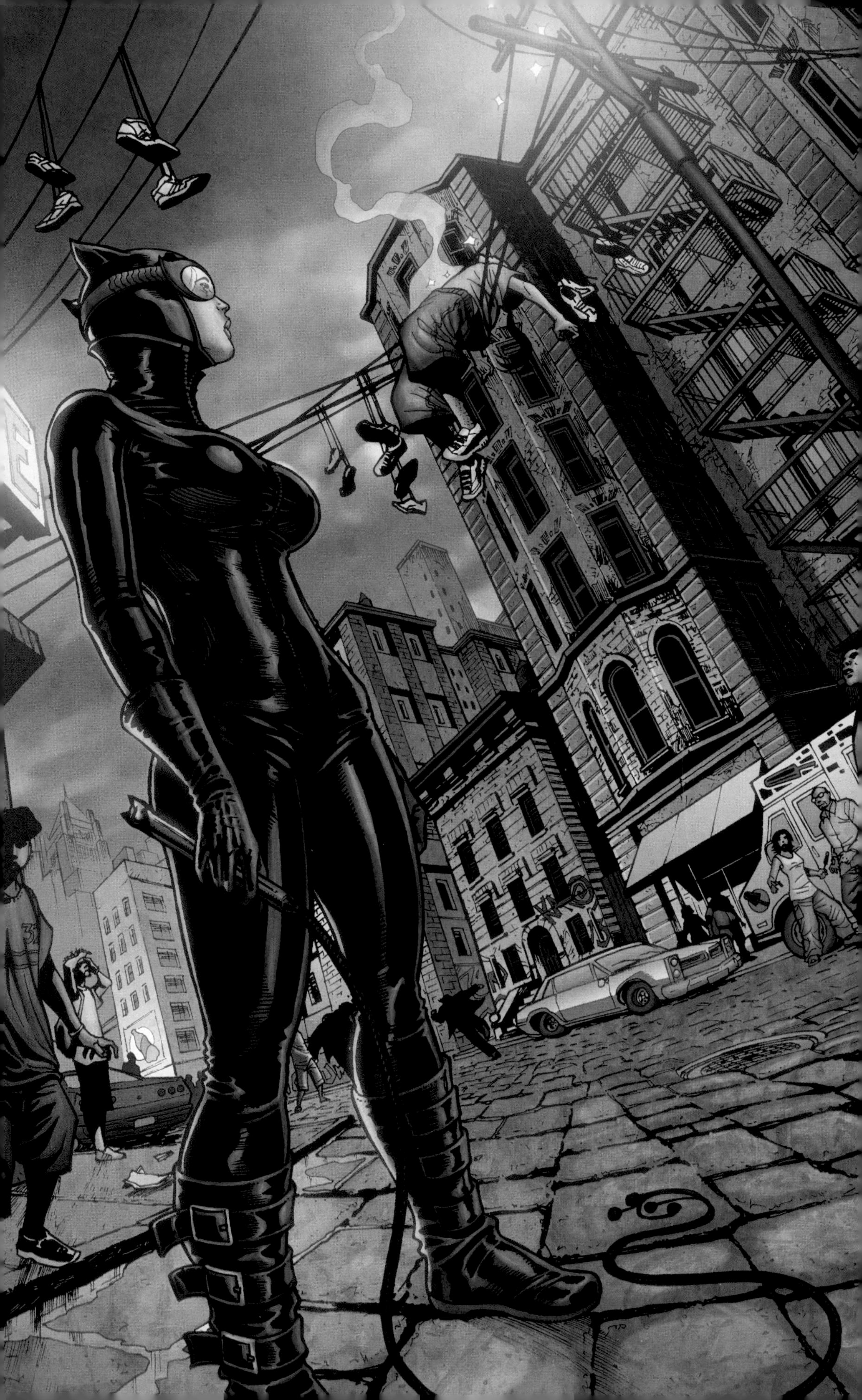

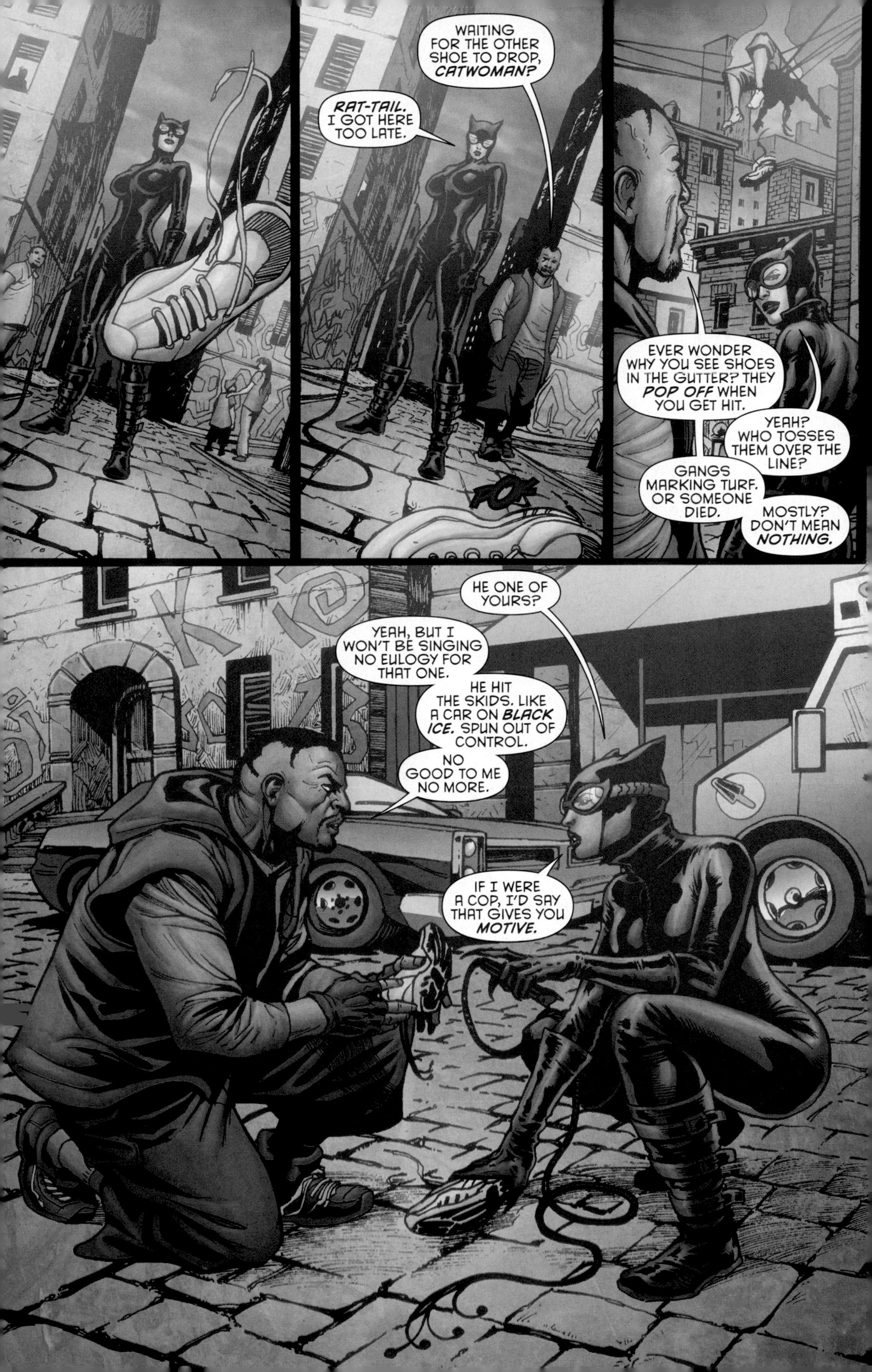
WAITING FOR THE OTHER SHOE TO DROP, CATWOMAN?
RAT-TAIL. I GOT HERE TOO LATE.
POK
EVER WONDER WHY YOU SEE SHOES IN THE GUTTER? THEY POP OFF WHEN YOU GET HIT.
YEAH? WHO TOSSES THEM OVER THE LINE?
GANGS MARKING TURF. OR SOMEONE DIED.
MOSTLY? DON'T MEAN NOTHING.
HE ONE OF YOURS?
YEAH, BUT I WON'T BE SINGING NO EULOGY FOR THAT ONE.
HE HIT THE SKIDS. LIKE A CAR ON BLACK ICE. SPUN OUT OF CONTROL.
NO GOOD TO ME NO MORE.
IF I WERE A COP, I'D SAY THAT GIVES YOU MOTIVE.

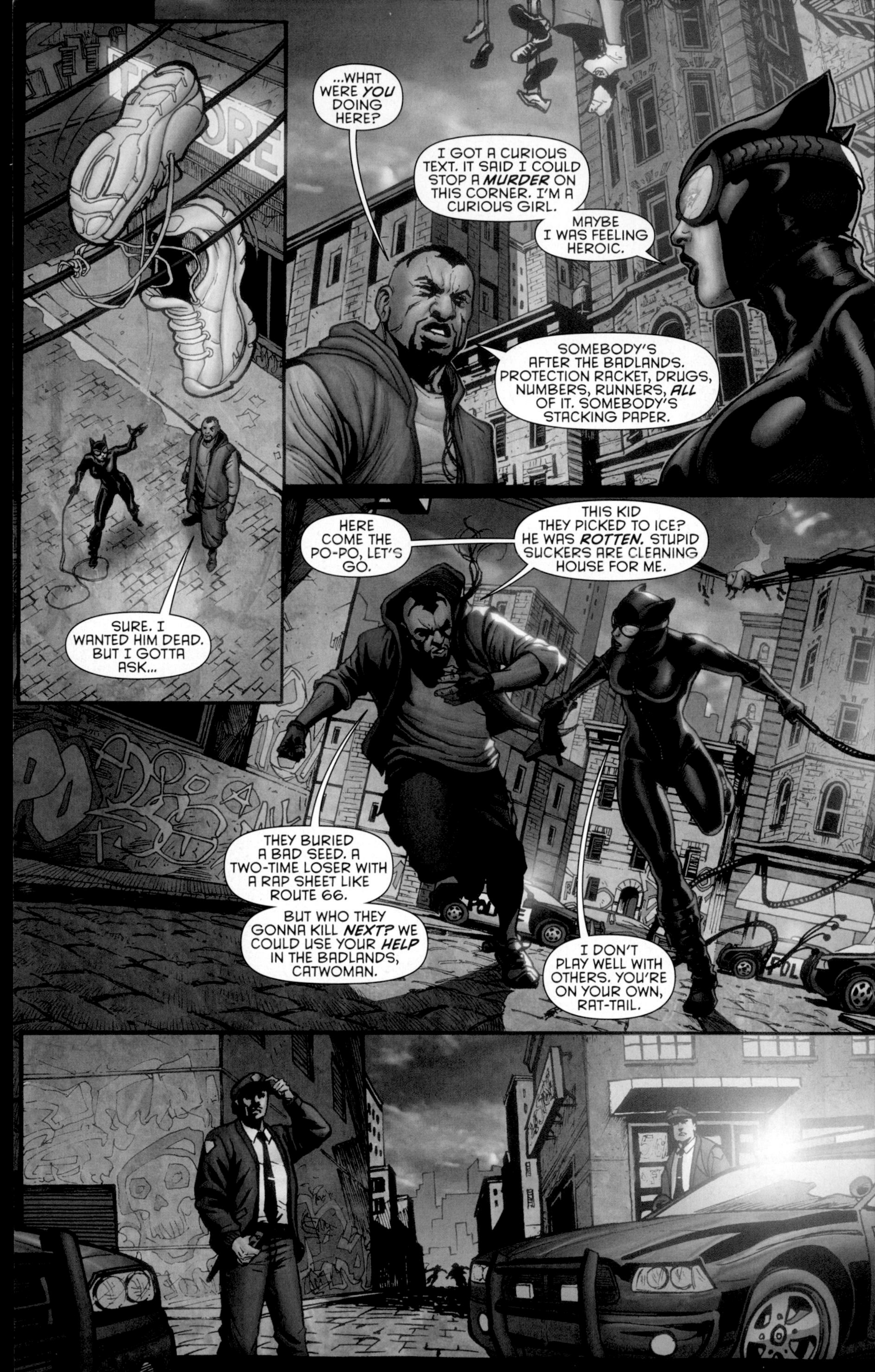
...WHAT WERE YOU DOING HERE?
I GOT A CURIOUS TEXT. IT SAID I COULD STOP A MURDER ON THIS CORNER. I'M A CURIOUS GIRL.
MAYBE I WAS FEELING HEROIC.
SOMEBODY'S AFTER THE BADLANDS. PROTECTION RACKET, DRUGS, NUMBERS, RUNNERS, ALL OF IT. SOMEBODY'S STACKING PAPER.
SURE. I WANTED HIM DEAD. BUT I GOTTA ASK...
HERE COME THE PO-PO, LET'S GO.
THIS KID THEY PICKED TO ICE? HE WAS ROTTEN. STUPID SUCKERS ARE CLEANING HOUSE FOR ME.
THEY BURIED A BAD SEED. A TWO-TIME LOSER WITH A RAP SHEET LIKE ROUTE 66.
BUT WHO THEY GONNA KILL NEXT? WE COULD USE YOUR HELP IN THE BADLANDS, CATWOMAN.
I DON'T PLAY WELL WITH OTHERS. YOU'RE ON YOUR OWN, RAT-TAIL.

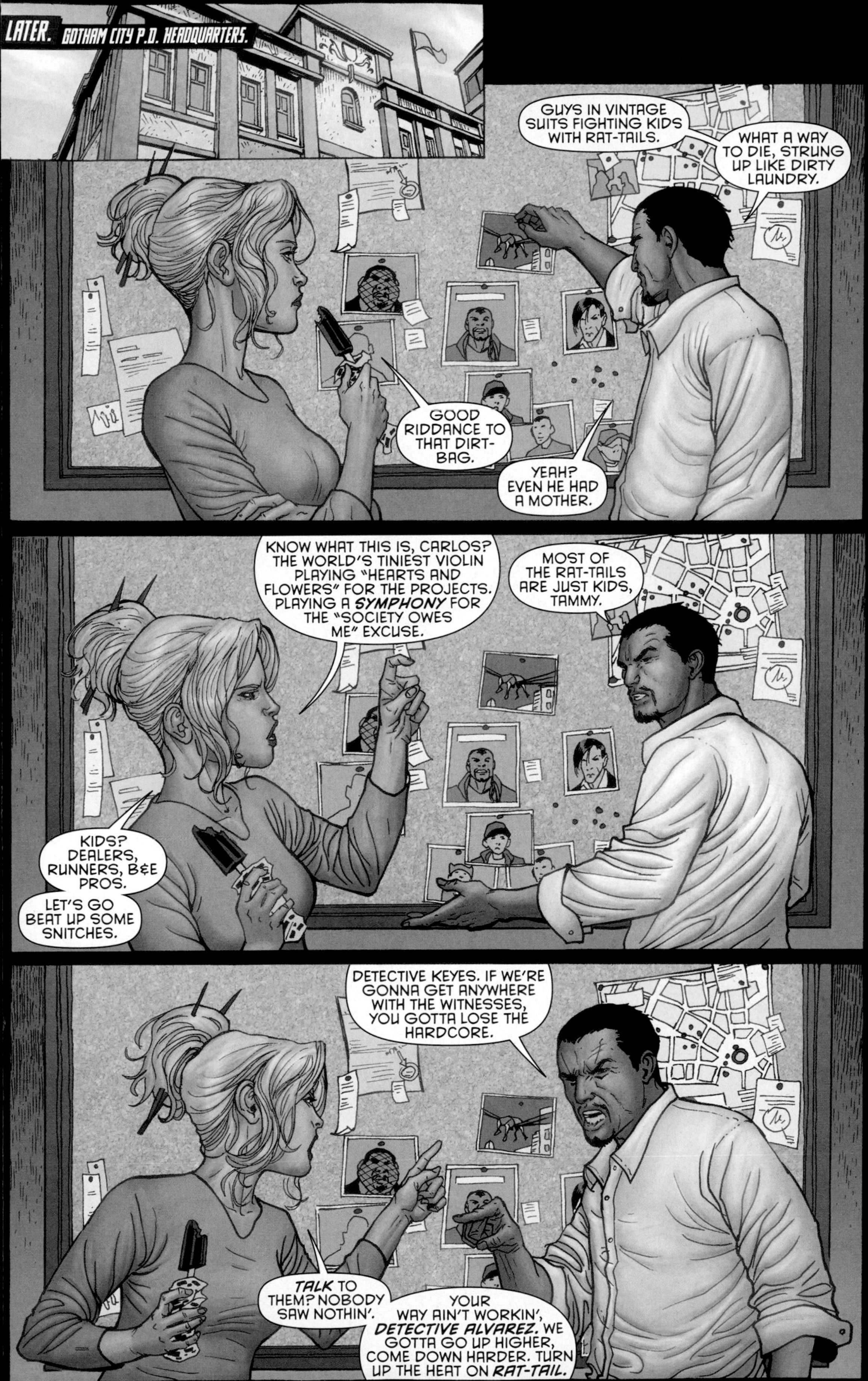
LATER. GOTHAM CITY P.D. HEADQUARTERS.
GUYS IN VINTAGE SUITS FIGHTING KIDS WITH RAT-TAILS.
WHAT A WAY TO DIE, STRUNG UP LIKE DIRTY LAUNDRY.
GOOD RIDDANCE TO THAT DIRT-BAG.
YEAH? EVEN HE HAD A MOTHER.
KNOW WHAT THIS IS, CARLOS? THE WORLD'S TINIEST VIOLIN PLAYING "HEARTS AND FLOWERS" FOR THE PROJECTS. PLAYING A *SYMPHONY* FOR THE "SOCIETY OWES ME" EXCUSE.
MOST OF THE RAT-TAILS ARE JUST KIDS, TAMMY.
KIDS? DEALERS, RUNNERS, B&E PROS.
LET'S GO BEAT UP SOME SNITCHES.
DETECTIVE KEYES. IF WE'RE GONNA GET ANYWHERE WITH THE WITNESSES, YOU GOTTA LOSE THE HARDCORE.
TALK TO THEM? NOBODY SAW NOTHIN'.
YOUR WAY AIN'T WORKIN', ***DETECTIVE ALVAREZ.*** WE GOTTA GO UP HIGHER, COME DOWN HARDER. TURN UP THE HEAT ON *RAT-TAIL.*

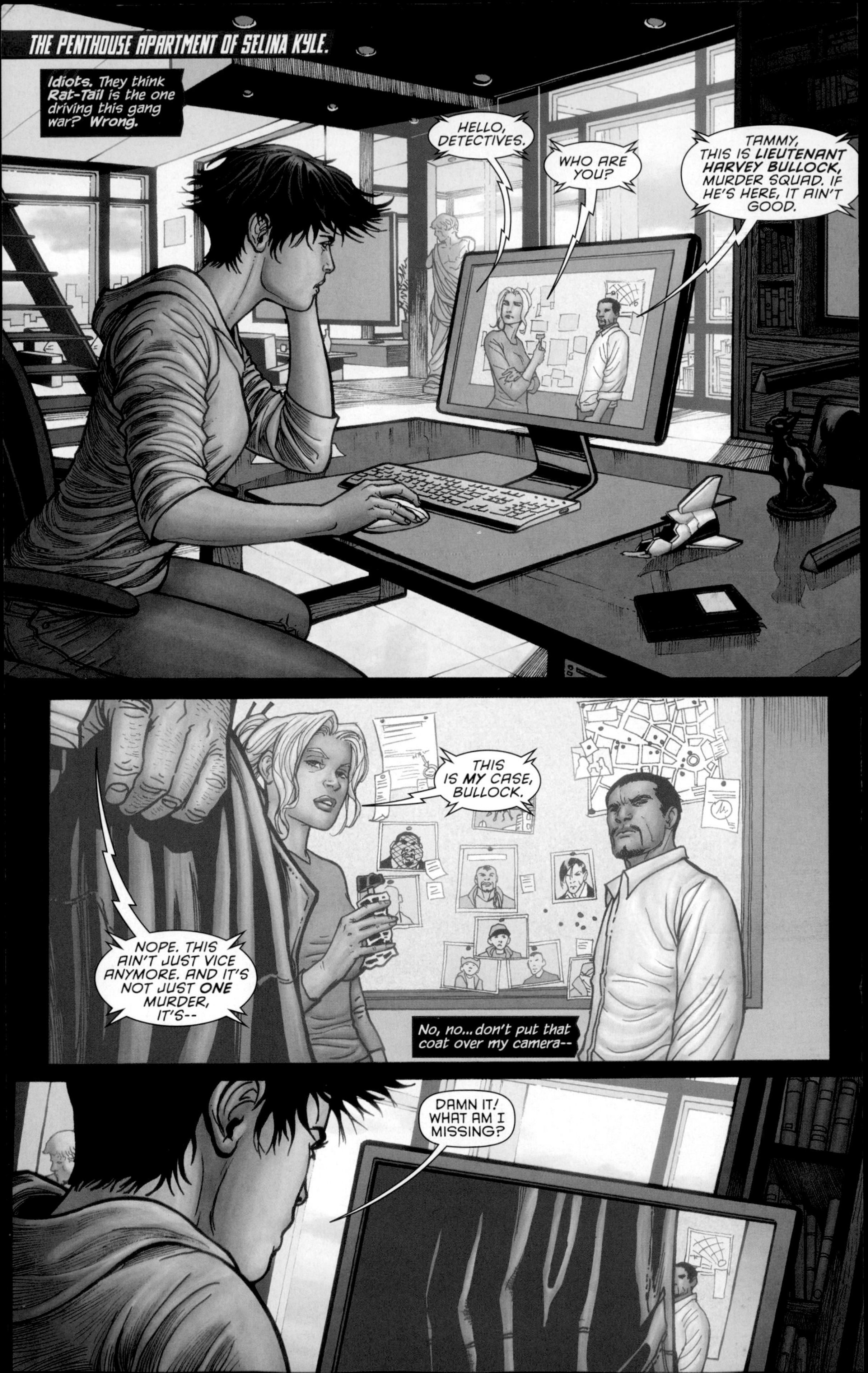
THE PENTHOUSE APARTMENT OF SELINA KYLE.
Idiots. They think Rat-Tail is the one driving this gang war? Wrong.
HELLO, DETECTIVES.
WHO ARE YOU?
TAMMY, THIS IS LIEUTENANT HARVEY BULLOCK, MURDER SQUAD. IF HE'S HERE, IT AIN'T GOOD.
THIS IS MY CASE, BULLOCK.
NOPE. THIS AIN'T JUST VICE ANYMORE. AND IT'S NOT JUST ONE MURDER, IT'S--
No, no...don't put that coat over my camera--
DAMN IT! WHAT AM I MISSING?

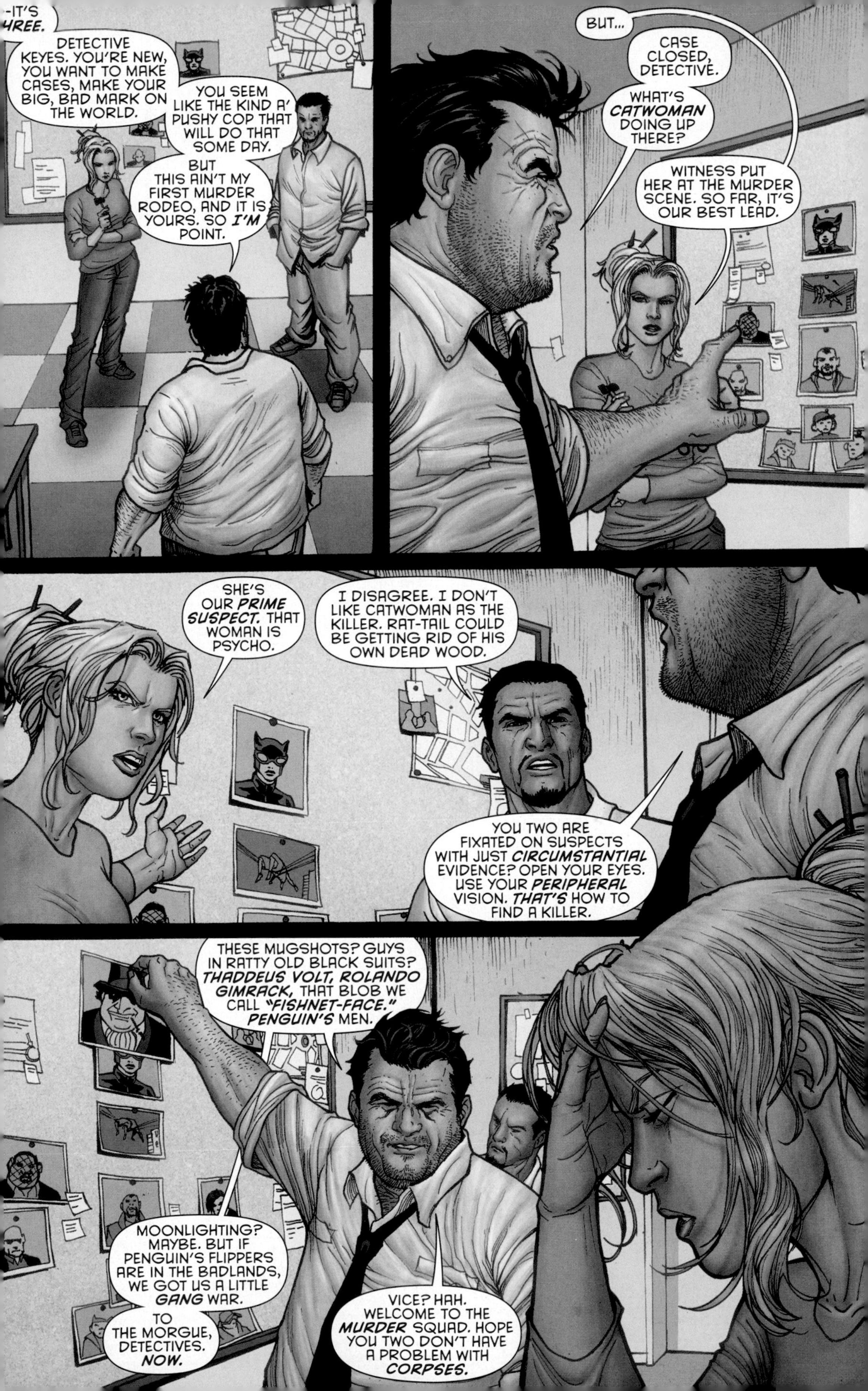
-IT'S
HREE.
DETECTIVE KEYES. YOU'RE NEW, YOU WANT TO MAKE CASES, MAKE YOUR BIG, BAD MARK ON THE WORLD.
YOU SEEM LIKE THE KIND A' PUSHY COP THAT WILL DO THAT SOME DAY.
BUT THIS AIN'T MY FIRST MURDER RODEO, AND IT IS YOURS. SO I'M POINT.
BUT...
CASE CLOSED, DETECTIVE.
WHAT'S CATWOMAN DOING UP THERE?
WITNESS PUT HER AT THE MURDER SCENE. SO FAR, IT'S OUR BEST LEAD.
SHE'S OUR PRIME SUSPECT. THAT WOMAN IS PSYCHO.
I DISAGREE. I DON'T LIKE CATWOMAN AS THE KILLER. RAT-TAIL COULD BE GETTING RID OF HIS OWN DEAD WOOD.
YOU TWO ARE FIXATED ON SUSPECTS WITH JUST CIRCUMSTANTIAL EVIDENCE? OPEN YOUR EYES. USE YOUR PERIPHERAL VISION. THAT'S HOW TO FIND A KILLER.
THESE MUGSHOTS? GUYS IN RATTY OLD BLACK SUITS? THADDEUS VOLT, ROLANDO GIMRACK, THAT BLOB WE CALL "FISHNET-FACE." PENGUIN'S MEN.
MOONLIGHTING? MAYBE. BUT IF PENGUIN'S FLIPPERS ARE IN THE BADLANDS, WE GOT US A LITTLE GANG WAR.
TO THE MORGUE, DETECTIVES. NOW.
VICE? HAH. WELCOME TO THE MURDER SQUAD. HOPE YOU TWO DON'T HAVE A PROBLEM WITH CORPSES.

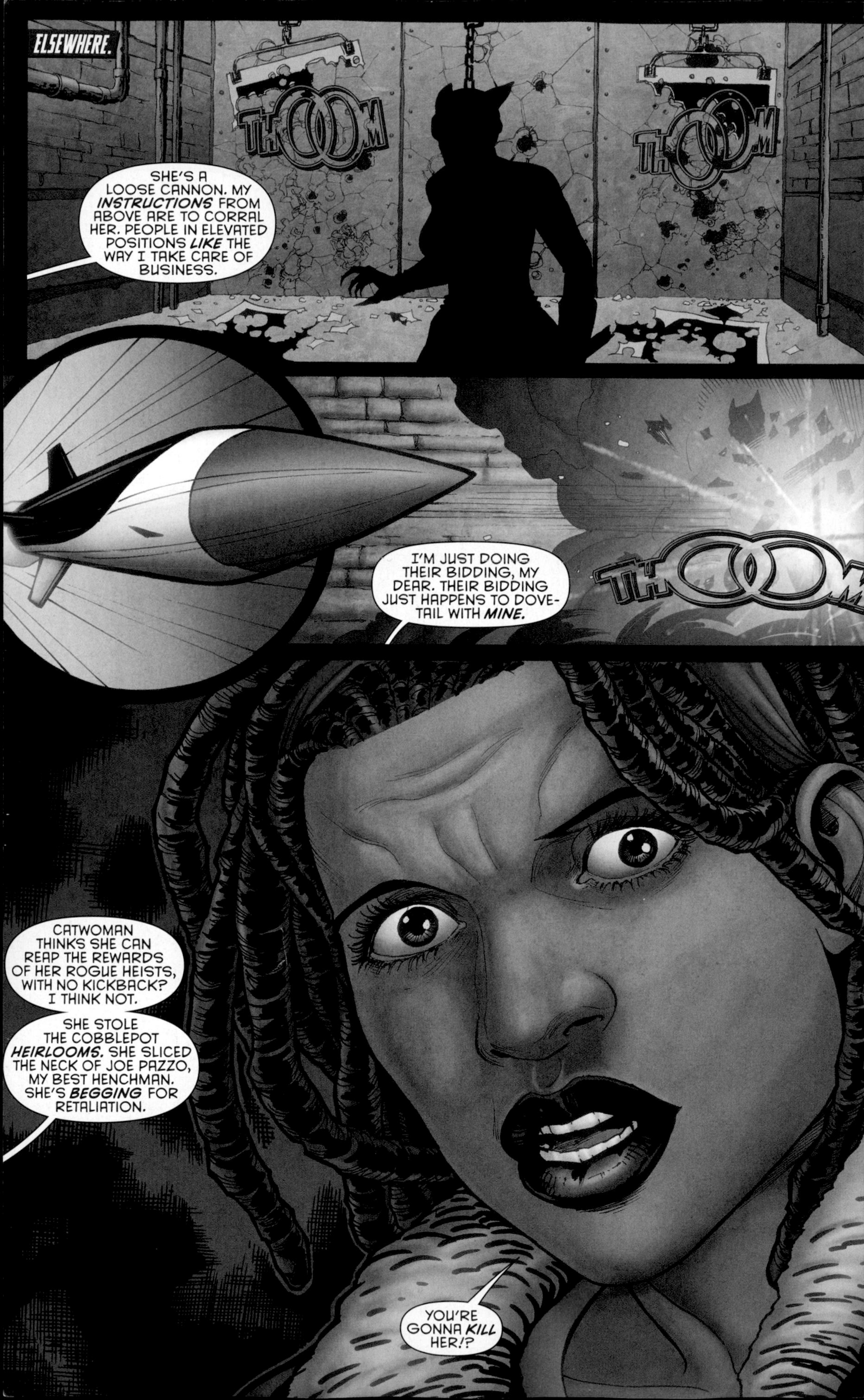
ELSEWHERE.
THOOM
THOOM
SHE'S A LOOSE CANNON. MY INSTRUCTIONS FROM ABOVE ARE TO CORRAL HER. PEOPLE IN ELEVATED POSITIONS LIKE THE WAY I TAKE CARE OF BUSINESS.
I'M JUST DOING THEIR BIDDING, MY DEAR. THEIR BIDDING JUST HAPPENS TO DOVE-TAIL WITH MINE.
CATWOMAN THINKS SHE CAN REAP THE REWARDS OF HER ROGUE HEISTS, WITH NO KICKBACK? I THINK NOT.
SHE STOLE THE COBBLEPOT HEIRLOOMS. SHE SLICED THE NECK OF JOE PAZZO, MY BEST HENCHMAN. SHE'S BEGGING FOR RETALIATION.
YOU'RE GONNA KILL HER!?

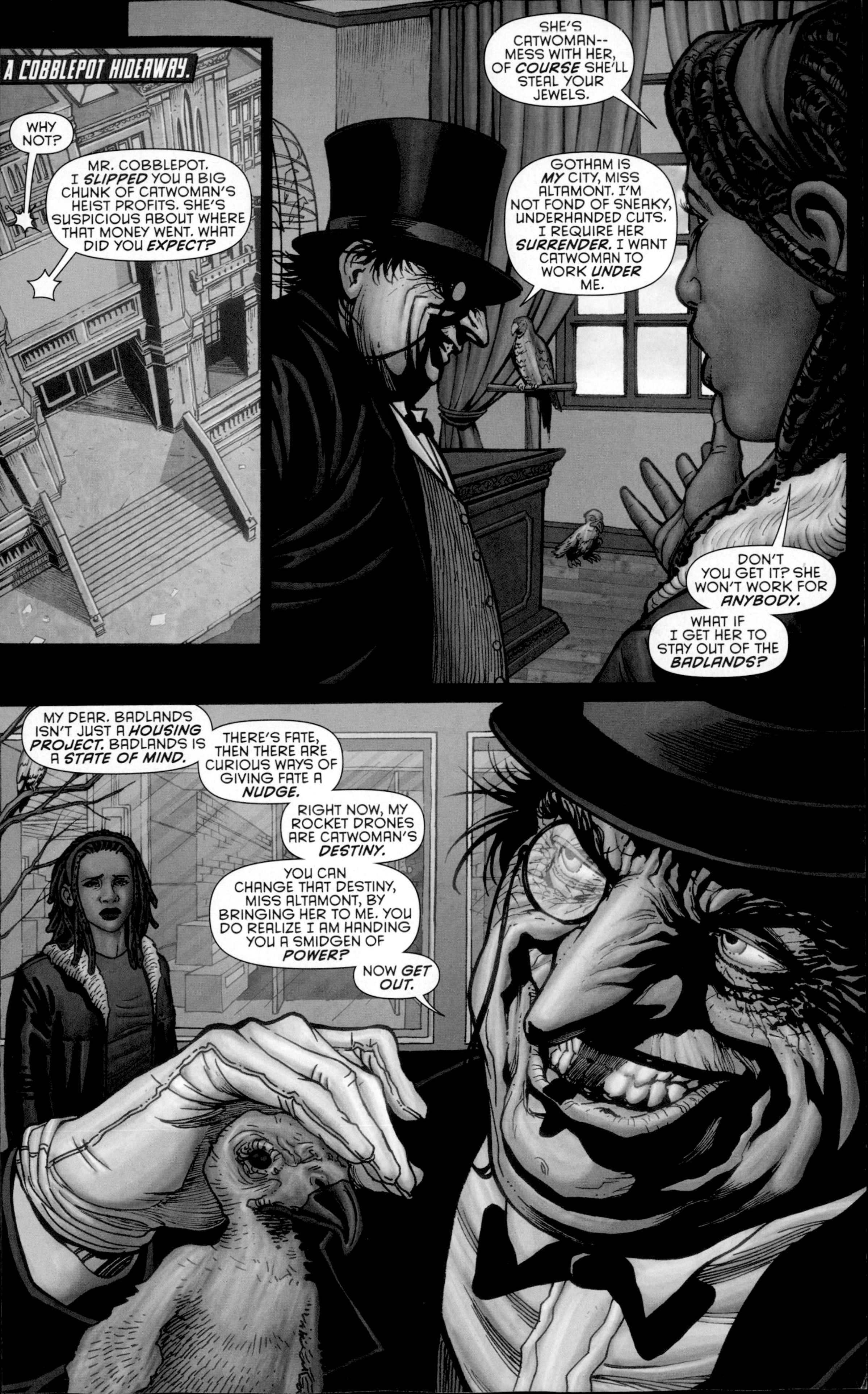
A COBBLEPOT HIDEAWAY.
SHE'S CATWOMAN-- MESS WITH HER, OF COURSE SHE'LL STEAL YOUR JEWELS.
WHY NOT?
MR. COBBLEPOT. I SLIPPED YOU A BIG CHUNK OF CATWOMAN'S HEIST PROFITS. SHE'S SUSPICIOUS ABOUT WHERE THAT MONEY WENT. WHAT DID YOU EXPECT?
GOTHAM IS MY CITY, MISS ALTAMONT. I'M NOT FOND OF SNEAKY, UNDERHANDED CUTS. I REQUIRE HER SURRENDER. I WANT CATWOMAN TO WORK UNDER ME.
DON'T YOU GET IT? SHE WON'T WORK FOR ANYBODY.
WHAT IF I GET HER TO STAY OUT OF THE BADLANDS?
MY DEAR. BADLANDS ISN'T JUST A HOUSING PROJECT. BADLANDS IS A STATE OF MIND.
THERE'S FATE, THEN THERE ARE CURIOUS WAYS OF GIVING FATE A NUDGE.
RIGHT NOW, MY ROCKET DRONES ARE CATWOMAN'S DESTINY.
YOU CAN CHANGE THAT DESTINY, MISS ALTAMONT, BY BRINGING HER TO ME. YOU DO REALIZE I AM HANDING YOU A SMIDGEN OF POWER?
NOW GET OUT.

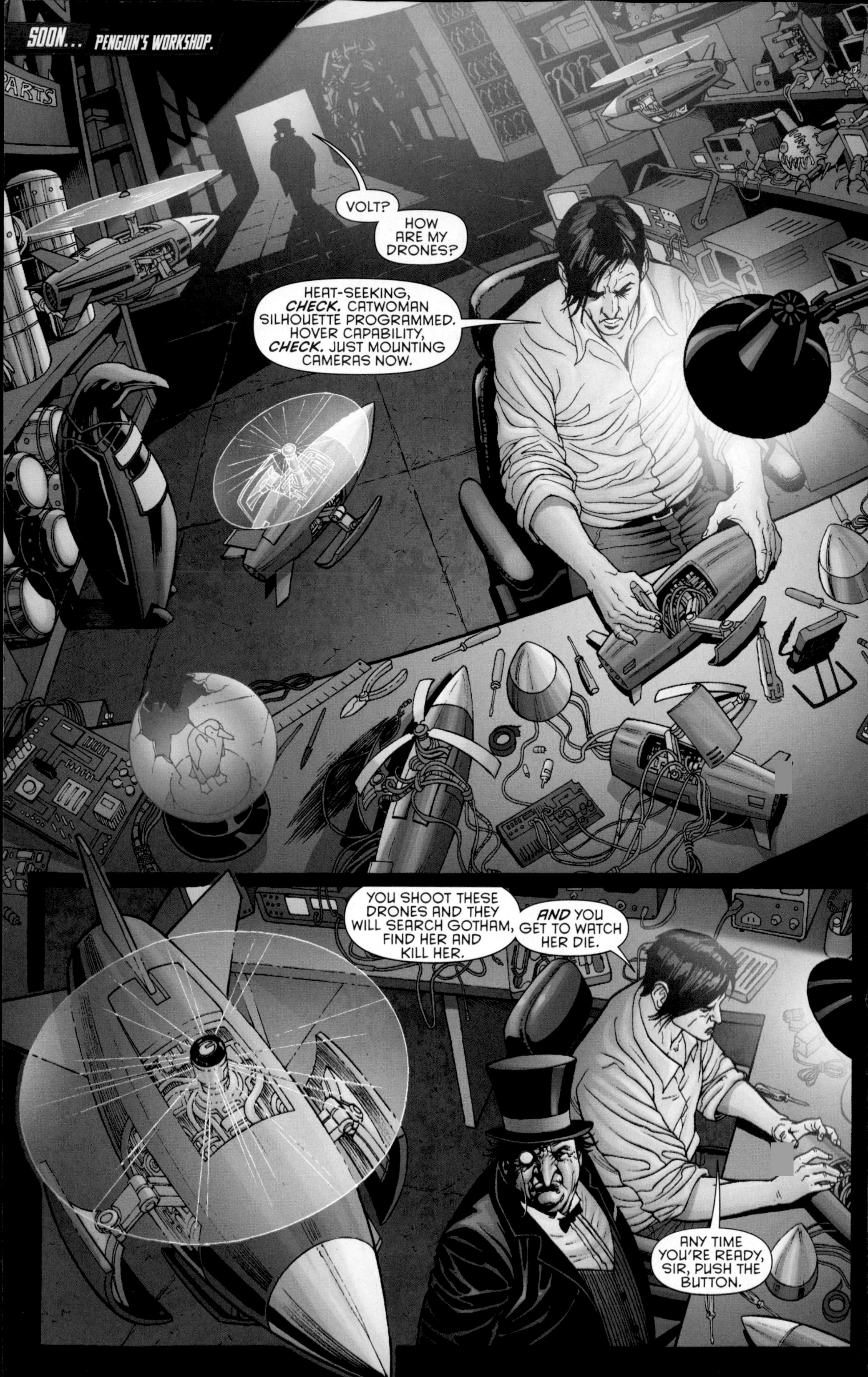
SOON... PENGUIN'S WORKSHOP.
PARTS
VOLT?
HOW ARE MY DRONES?
HEAT-SEEKING, CHECK. CATWOMAN SILHOUETTE PROGRAMMED. HOVER CAPABILITY, CHECK. JUST MOUNTING CAMERAS NOW.
YOU SHOOT THESE DRONES AND THEY WILL SEARCH GOTHAM, FIND HER AND KILL HER.
AND YOU GET TO WATCH HER DIE.
ANY TIME YOU'RE READY, SIR, PUSH THE BUTTON.

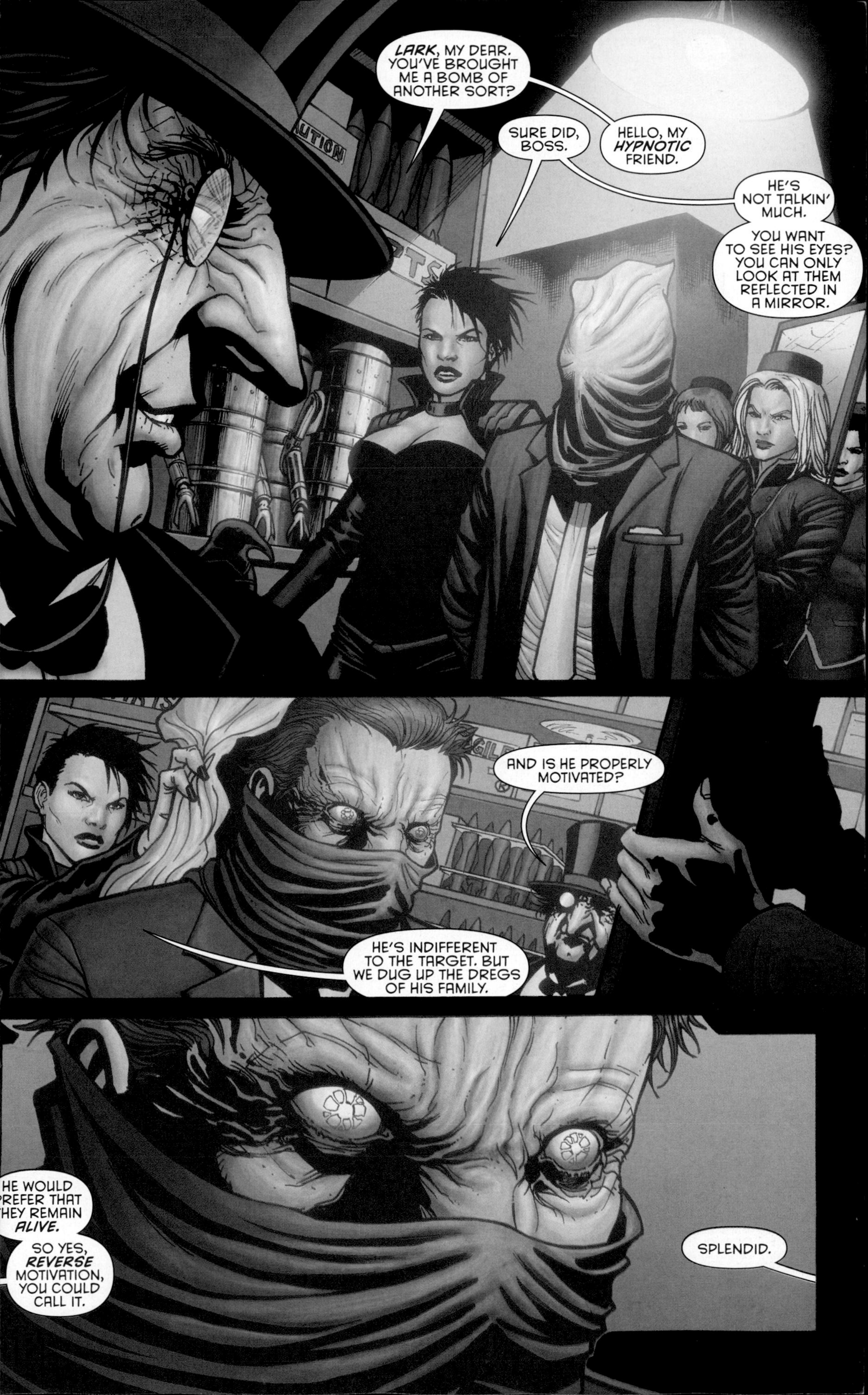
LARK, MY DEAR. YOU'VE BROUGHT ME A BOMB OF ANOTHER SORT?
SURE DID, BOSS.
HELLO, MY HYPNOTIC FRIEND.
HE'S NOT TALKIN' MUCH.
YOU WANT TO SEE HIS EYES? YOU CAN ONLY LOOK AT THEM REFLECTED IN A MIRROR.
AND IS HE PROPERLY MOTIVATED?
HE'S INDIFFERENT TO THE TARGET. BUT WE DUG UP THE DREGS OF HIS FAMILY.
HE WOULD PREFER THAT THEY REMAIN ALIVE.
SO YES, REVERSE MOTIVATION, YOU COULD CALL IT.
SPLENDID.

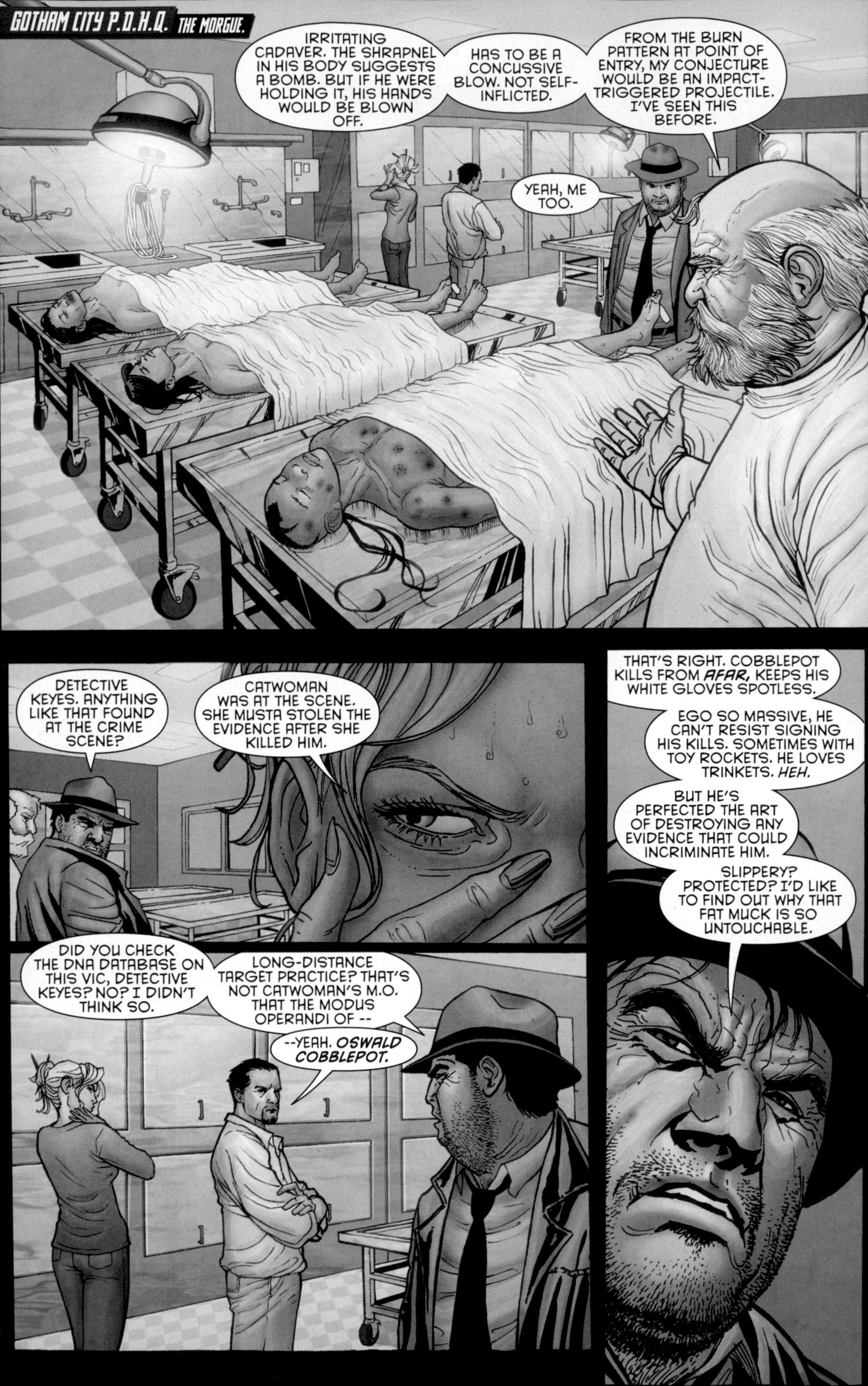
GOTHAM CITY P.D.H.Q. THE MORGUE.
IRRITATING CADAVER. THE SHRAPNEL IN HIS BODY SUGGESTS A BOMB. BUT IF HE WERE HOLDING IT, HIS HANDS WOULD BE BLOWN OFF.
HAS TO BE A CONCUSSIVE BLOW. NOT SELF-INFLICTED.
FROM THE BURN PATTERN AT POINT OF ENTRY, MY CONJECTURE WOULD BE AN IMPACT-TRIGGERED PROJECTILE. I'VE SEEN THIS BEFORE.
YEAH, ME TOO.
DETECTIVE KEYES. ANYTHING LIKE THAT FOUND AT THE CRIME SCENE?
CATWOMAN WAS AT THE SCENE. SHE MUSTA STOLEN THE EVIDENCE AFTER SHE KILLED HIM.
DID YOU CHECK THE DNA DATABASE ON THIS VIC, DETECTIVE KEYES? NO? I DIDN'T THINK SO.
LONG-DISTANCE TARGET PRACTICE? THAT'S NOT CATWOMAN'S M.O. THAT THE MODUS OPERANDI OF --
--YEAH. OSWALD COBBLEPOT.
THAT'S RIGHT. COBBLEPOT KILLS FROM AFAR, KEEPS HIS WHITE GLOVES SPOTLESS.
EGO SO MASSIVE, HE CAN'T RESIST SIGNING HIS KILLS. SOMETIMES WITH TOY ROCKETS. HE LOVES TRINKETS. HEH.
BUT HE'S PERFECTED THE ART OF DESTROYING ANY EVIDENCE THAT COULD INCRIMINATE HIM.
SLIPPERY? PROTECTED? I'D LIKE TO FIND OUT WHY THAT FAT MUCK IS SO UNTOUCHABLE.

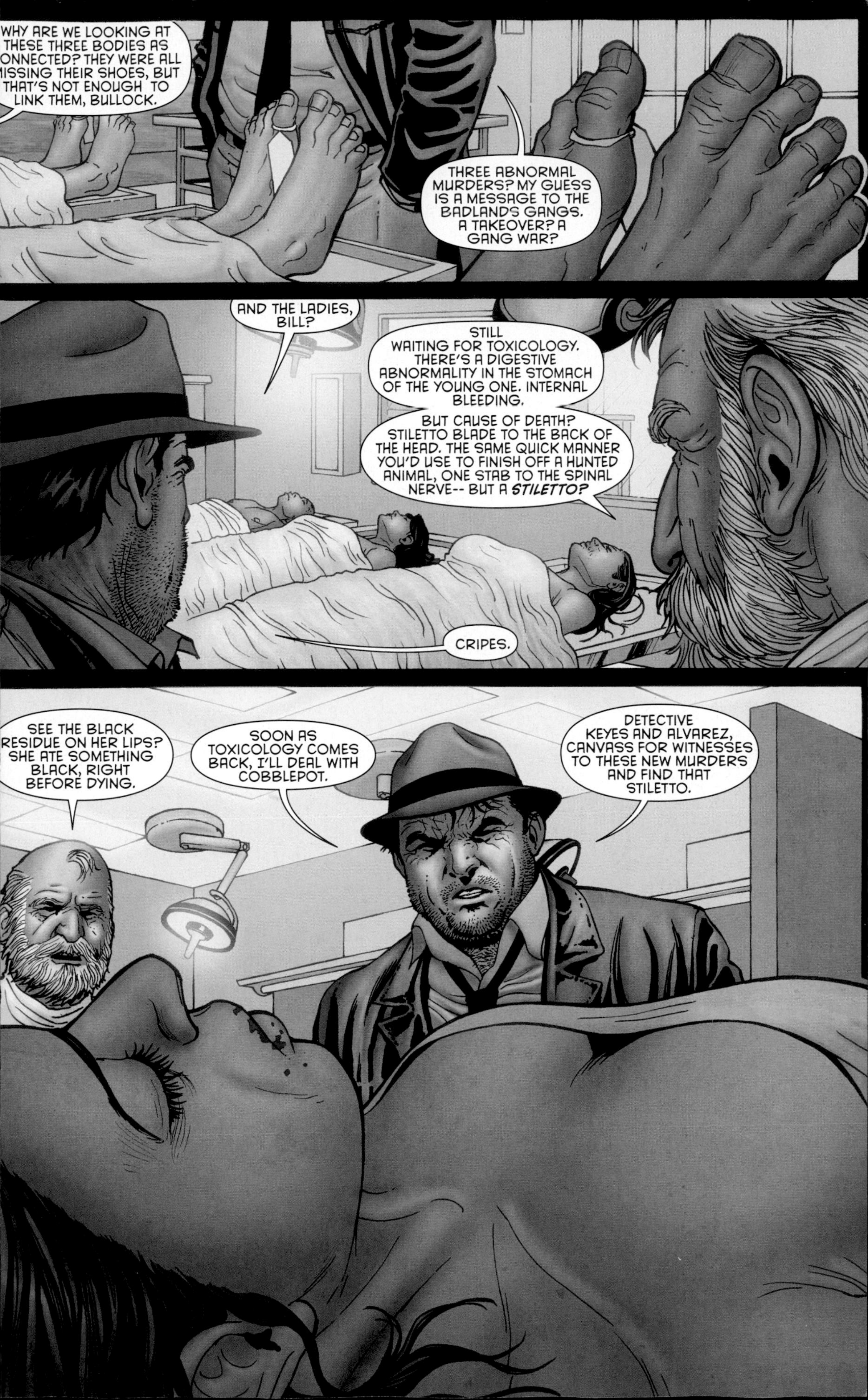
WHY ARE WE LOOKING AT THESE THREE BODIES AS CONNECTED? THEY WERE ALL MISSING THEIR SHOES, BUT THAT'S NOT ENOUGH TO LINK THEM, BULLOCK.
THREE ABNORMAL MURDERS? MY GUESS IS A MESSAGE TO THE BADLAND'S GANGS. A TAKEOVER? A GANG WAR?
AND THE LADIES, BILL?
STILL WAITING FOR TOXICOLOGY. THERE'S A DIGESTIVE ABNORMALITY IN THE STOMACH OF THE YOUNG ONE. INTERNAL BLEEDING.
BUT CAUSE OF DEATH? STILETTO BLADE TO THE BACK OF THE HEAD. THE SAME QUICK MANNER YOU'D USE TO FINISH OFF A HUNTED ANIMAL, ONE STAB TO THE SPINAL NERVE-- BUT A *STILETTO?*
CRIPES.
SEE THE BLACK RESIDUE ON HER LIPS? SHE ATE SOMETHING BLACK, RIGHT BEFORE DYING.
SOON AS TOXICOLOGY COMES BACK, I'LL DEAL WITH COBBLEPOT.
DETECTIVE KEYES AND ALVAREZ, CANVASS FOR WITNESSES TO THESE NEW MURDERS AND FIND THAT STILETTO.

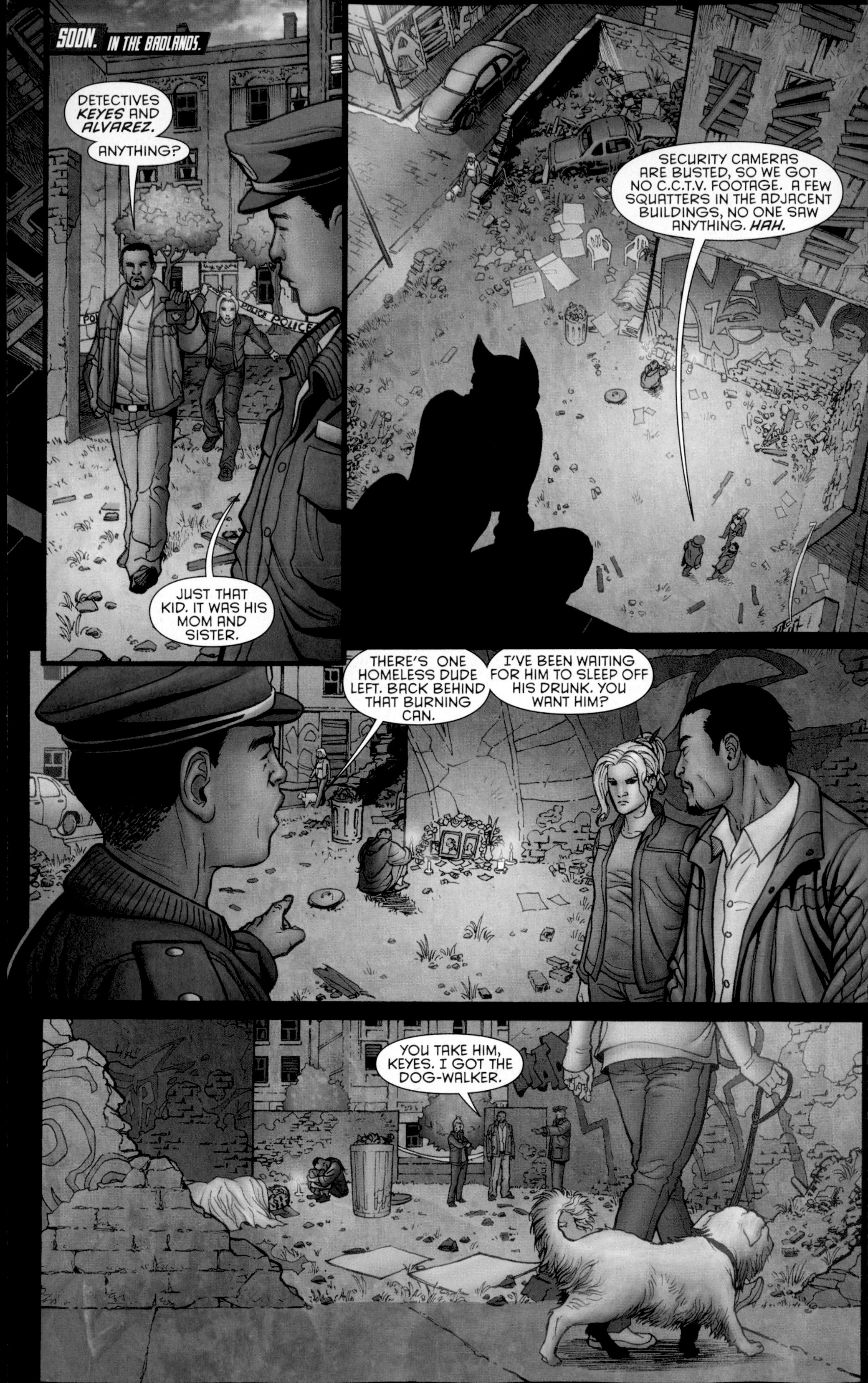
SOON. IN THE BADLANDS.
DETECTIVES KEYES AND ALVAREZ.
ANYTHING?
JUST THAT KID. IT WAS HIS MOM AND SISTER.
SECURITY CAMERAS ARE BUSTED, SO WE GOT NO C.C.T.V. FOOTAGE. A FEW SQUATTERS IN THE ADJACENT BUILDINGS, NO ONE SAW ANYTHING. HAH.
THERE'S ONE HOMELESS DUDE LEFT. BACK BEHIND THAT BURNING CAN.
I'VE BEEN WAITING FOR HIM TO SLEEP OFF HIS DRUNK. YOU WANT HIM?
YOU TAKE HIM, KEYES. I GOT THE DOG-WALKER.

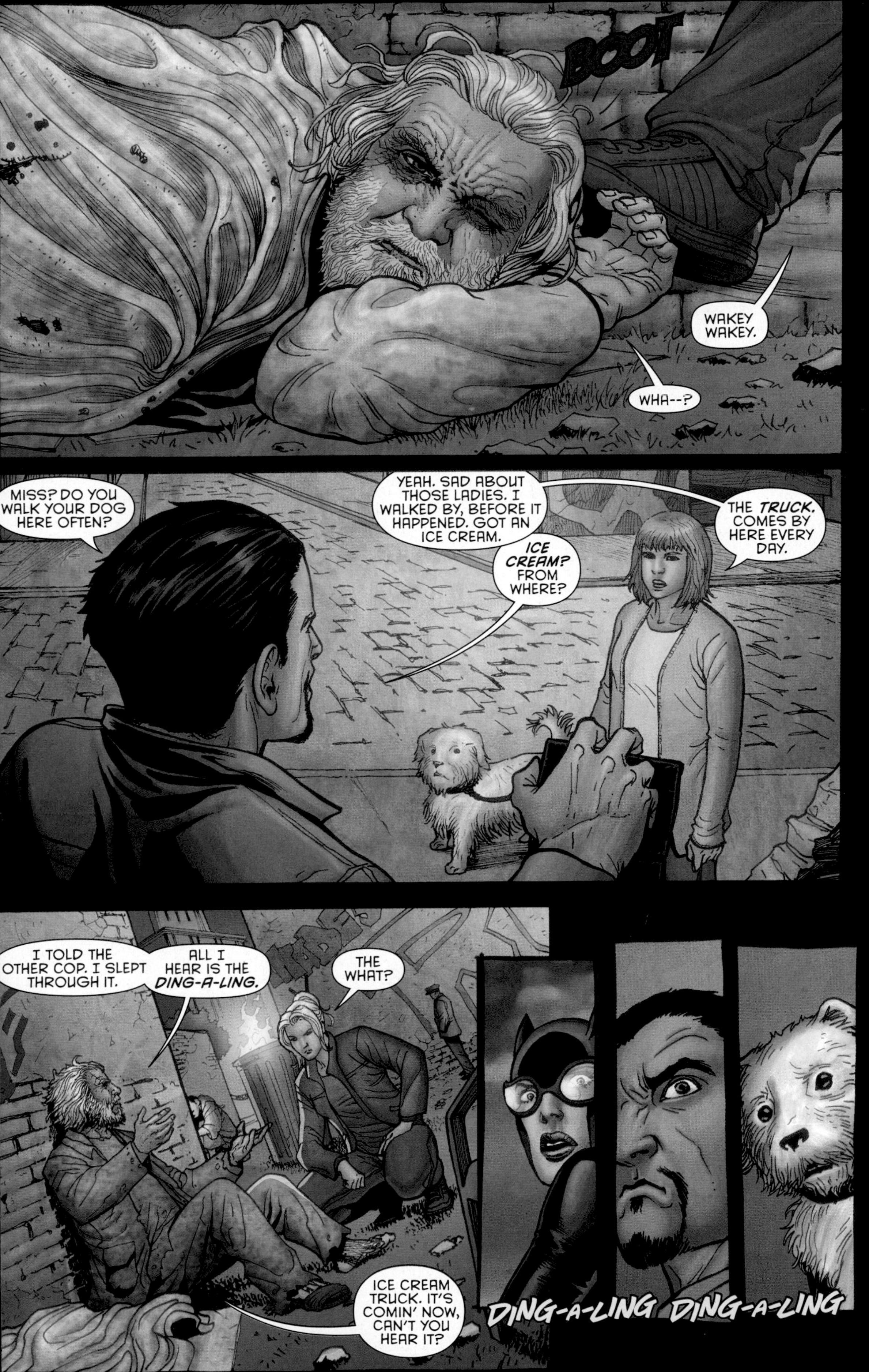
BOOT
WAKEY WAKEY.
WHA--?
MISS? DO YOU WALK YOUR DOG HERE OFTEN?
YEAH. SAD ABOUT THOSE LADIES. I WALKED BY, BEFORE IT HAPPENED. GOT AN ICE CREAM.
ICE CREAM? FROM WHERE?
THE TRUCK. COMES BY HERE EVERY DAY.
I TOLD THE OTHER COP. I SLEPT THROUGH IT.
ALL I HEAR IS THE DING-A-LING.
THE WHAT?
ICE CREAM TRUCK. IT'S COMIN' NOW, CAN'T YOU HEAR IT?
DING-A-LING DING-A-LING

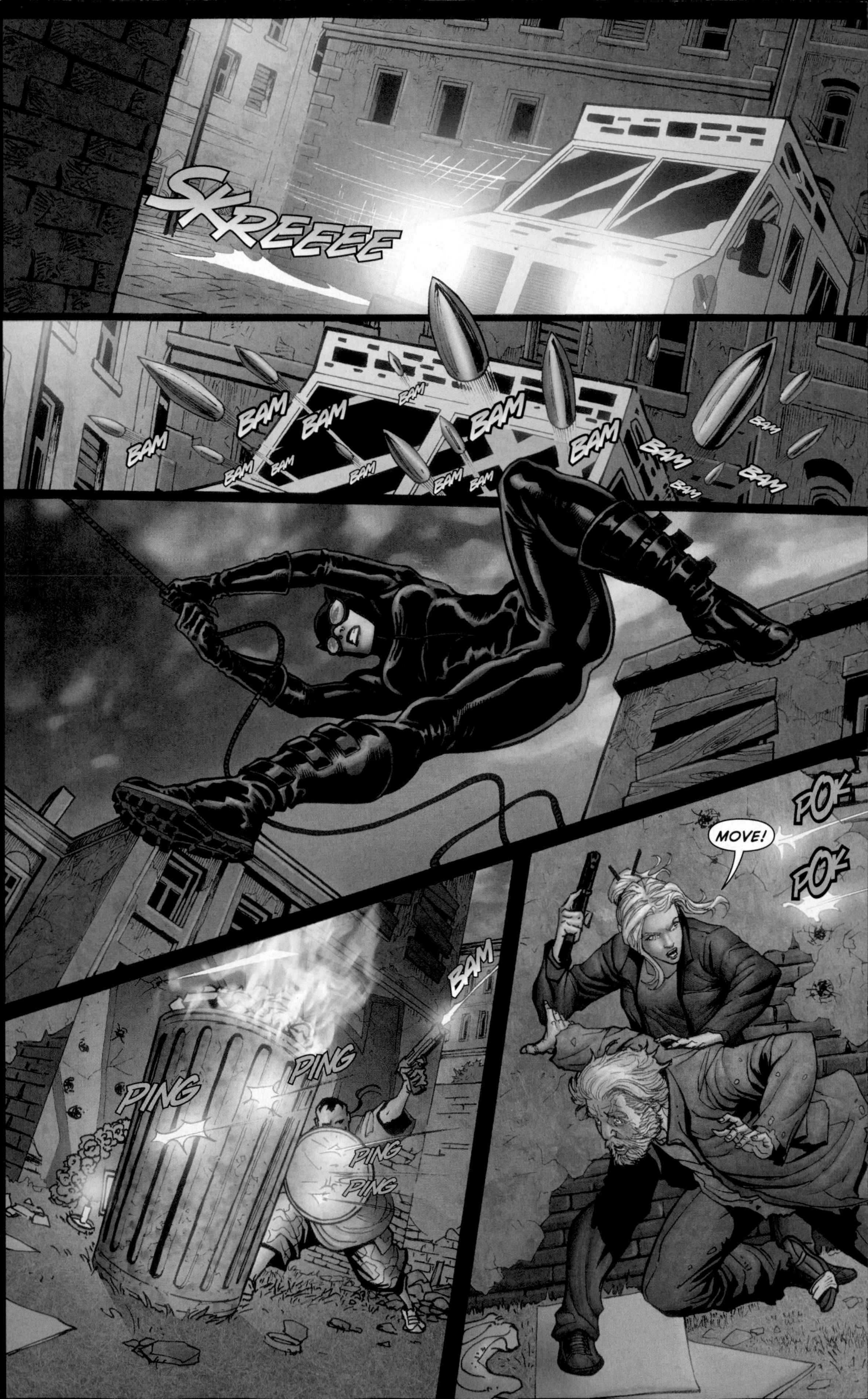
SKREEEEE
BAM
BAM
BAM
BAM
BAM
BAM
BAM
BAM
BAM
BAM
BAM
BAM
BAM
BAM
BAM
POK
MOVE!
POK
BAM
PING
PING
PING
PING

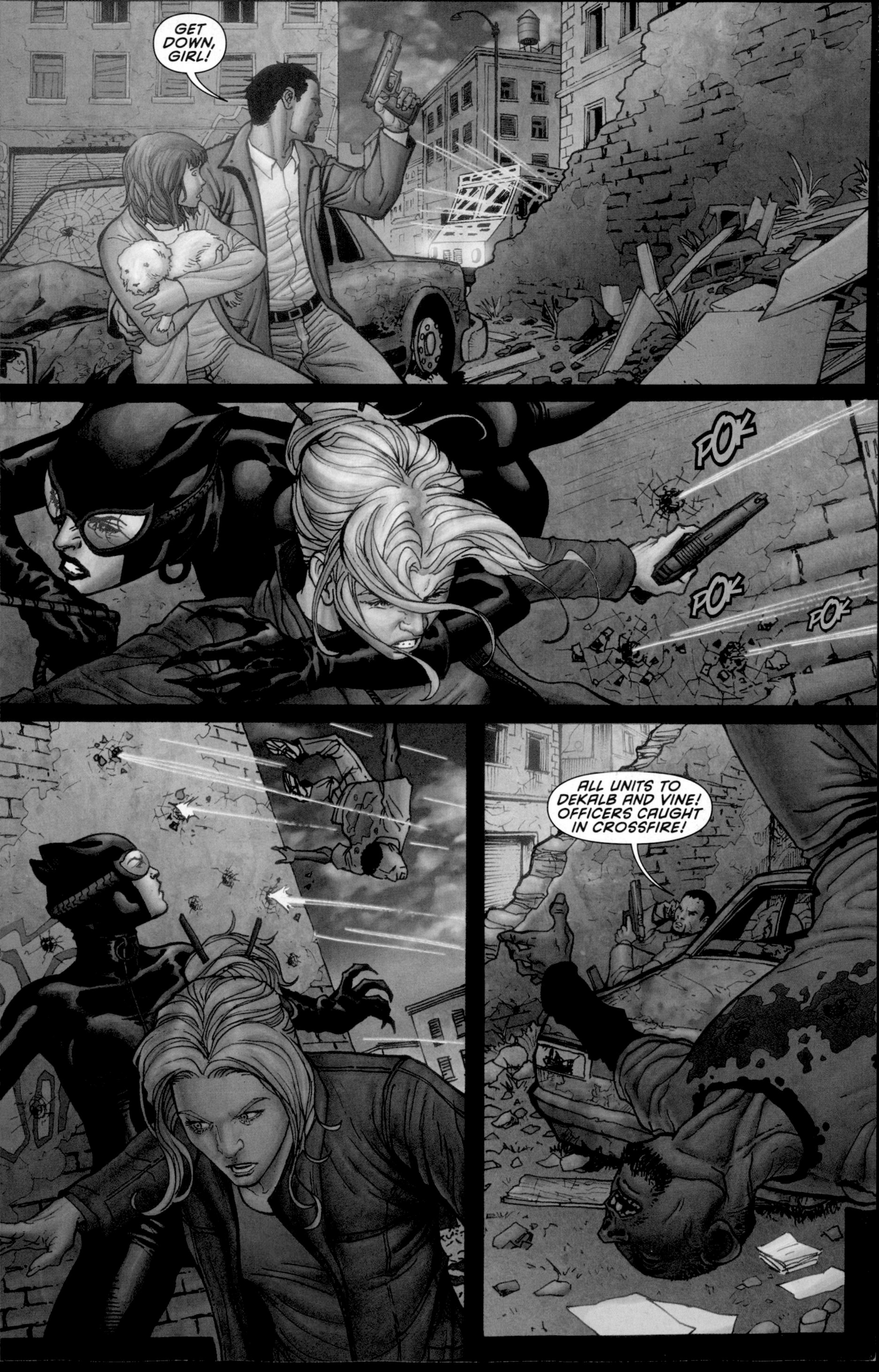
GET DOWN, GIRL!
POK
POK
POK
ALL UNITS TO DEKALB AND VINE! OFFICERS CAUGHT IN CROSSFIRE!

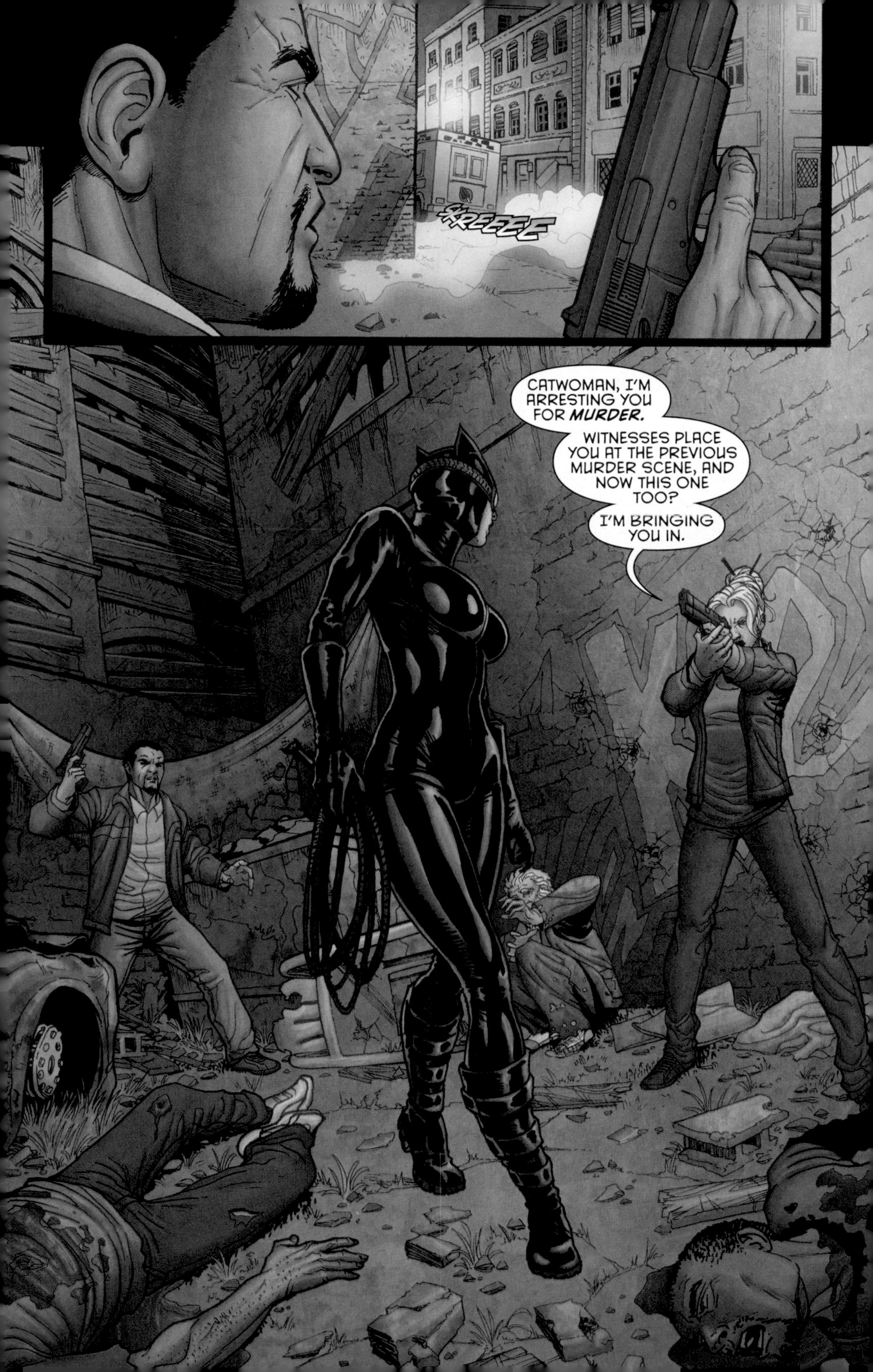
SKREEEE
CATWOMAN, I'M ARRESTING YOU FOR MURDER.
WITNESSES PLACE YOU AT THE PREVIOUS MURDER SCENE, AND NOW THIS ONE TOO?
I'M BRINGING YOU IN.

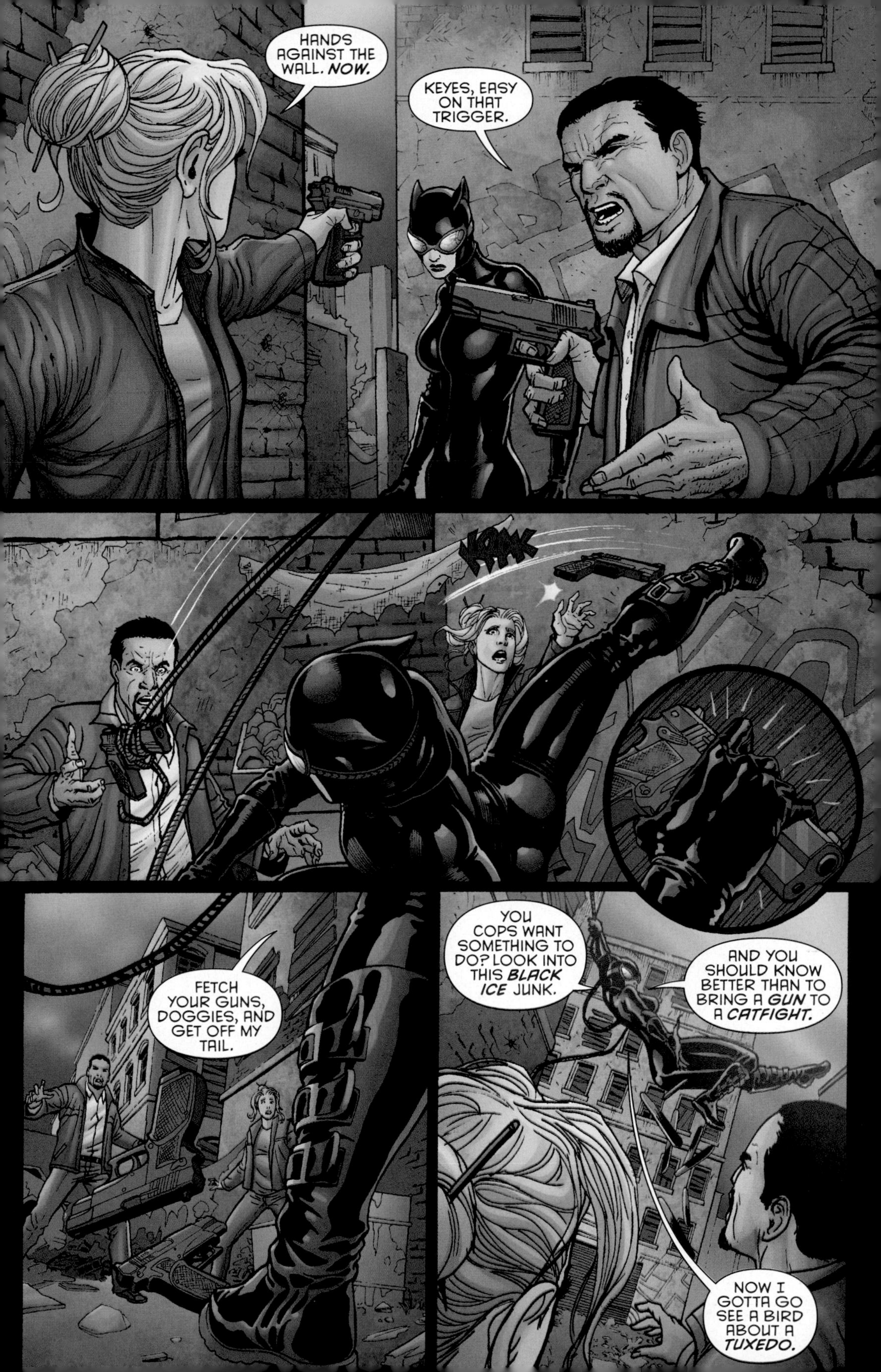
HANDS AGAINST THE WALL. NOW.
KEYES, EASY ON THAT TRIGGER.
FETCH YOUR GUNS, DOGGIES, AND GET OFF MY TAIL.
YOU COPS WANT SOMETHING TO DO? LOOK INTO THIS BLACK ICE JUNK.
AND YOU SHOULD KNOW BETTER THAN TO BRING A GUN TO A CATFIGHT.
NOW I GOTTA GO SEE A BIRD ABOUT A TUXEDO.

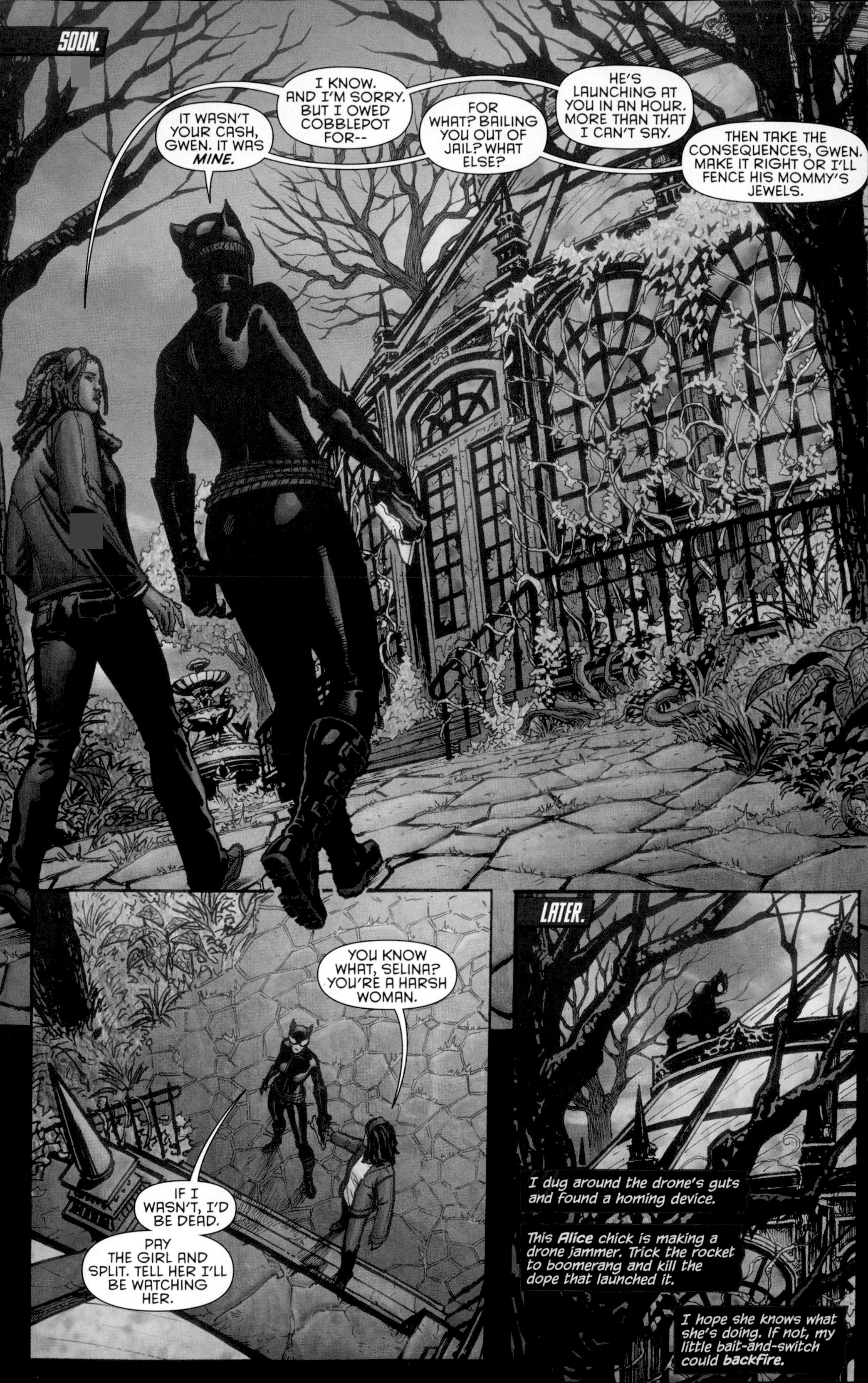
SOON.
IT WASN'T YOUR CASH, GWEN. IT WAS *MINE.*
I KNOW. AND I'M SORRY. BUT I OWED COBBLEPOT FOR--
FOR WHAT? BAILING YOU OUT OF JAIL? WHAT ELSE?
HE'S LAUNCHING AT YOU IN AN HOUR. MORE THAN THAT I CAN'T SAY.
THEN TAKE THE CONSEQUENCES, GWEN. MAKE IT RIGHT OR I'LL FENCE HIS MOMMY'S JEWELS.
YOU KNOW WHAT, SELINA? YOU'RE A HARSH WOMAN.
IF I WASN'T, I'D BE DEAD.
PAY THE GIRL AND SPLIT. TELL HER I'LL BE WATCHING HER.
LATER.
I dug around the drone's guts and found a homing device.
This **Alice** chick is making a drone jammer. Trick the rocket to boomerang and kill the dope that launched it.
I hope she knows what she's doing. If not, my little bait-and-switch could **backfire.**

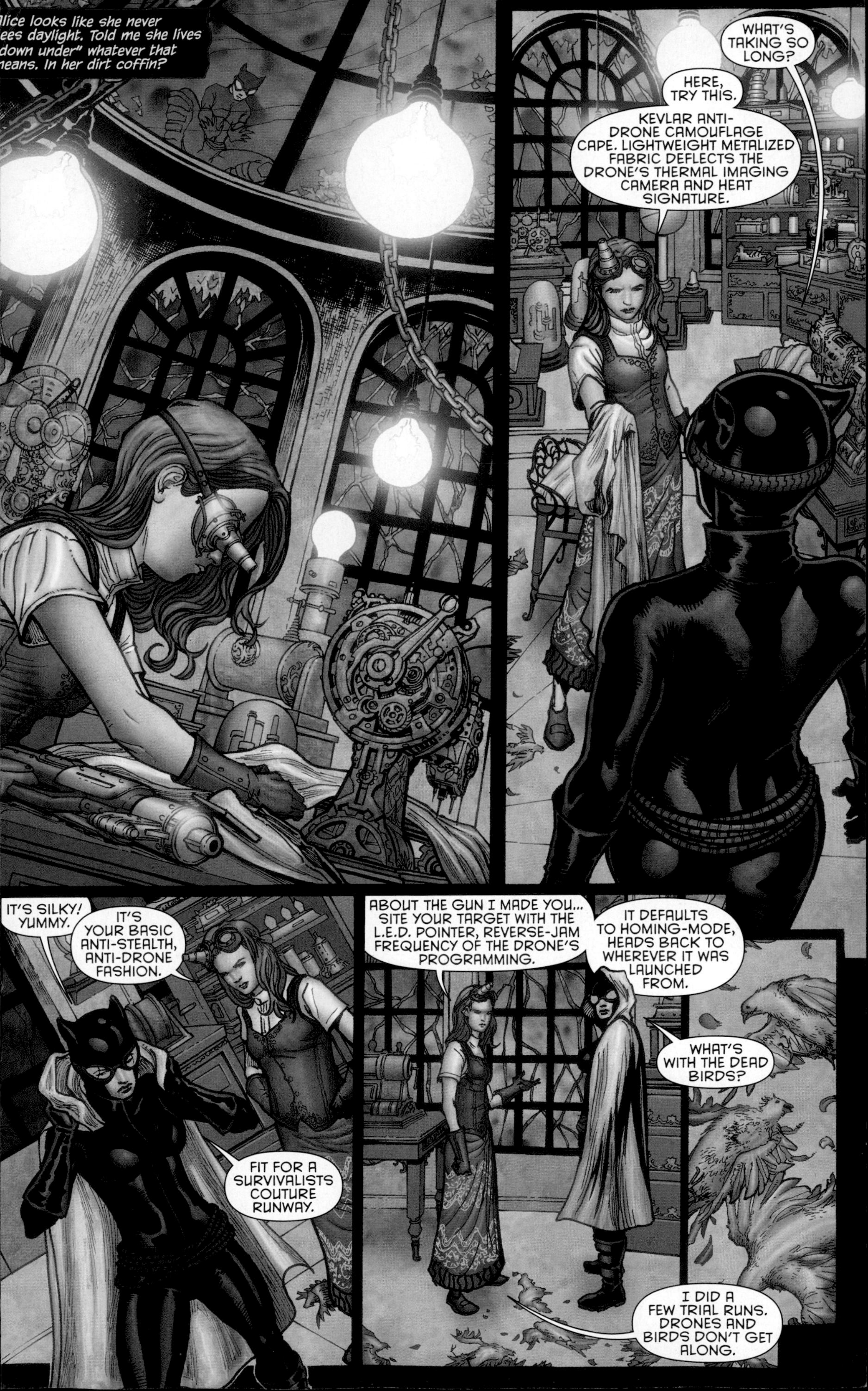

Alice looks like she never sees daylight. Told me she lives "down under" whatever that means. In her dirt coffin?
WHAT'S TAKING SO LONG?
HERE, TRY THIS.
KEVLAR ANTI-DRONE CAMOUFLAGE CAPE. LIGHTWEIGHT METALIZED FABRIC DEFLECTS THE DRONE'S THERMAL IMAGING CAMERA AND HEAT SIGNATURE.
IT'S SILKY! YUMMY.
IT'S YOUR BASIC ANTI-STEALTH, ANTI-DRONE FASHION.
FIT FOR A SURVIVALISTS COUTURE RUNWAY.
ABOUT THE GUN I MADE YOU... SITE YOUR TARGET WITH THE L.E.D. POINTER, REVERSE-JAM FREQUENCY OF THE DRONE'S PROGRAMMING.
IT DEFAULTS TO HOMING-MODE, HEADS BACK TO WHEREVER IT WAS LAUNCHED FROM.
WHAT'S WITH THE DEAD BIRDS?
I DID A FEW TRIAL RUNS. DRONES AND BIRDS DON'T GET ALONG.

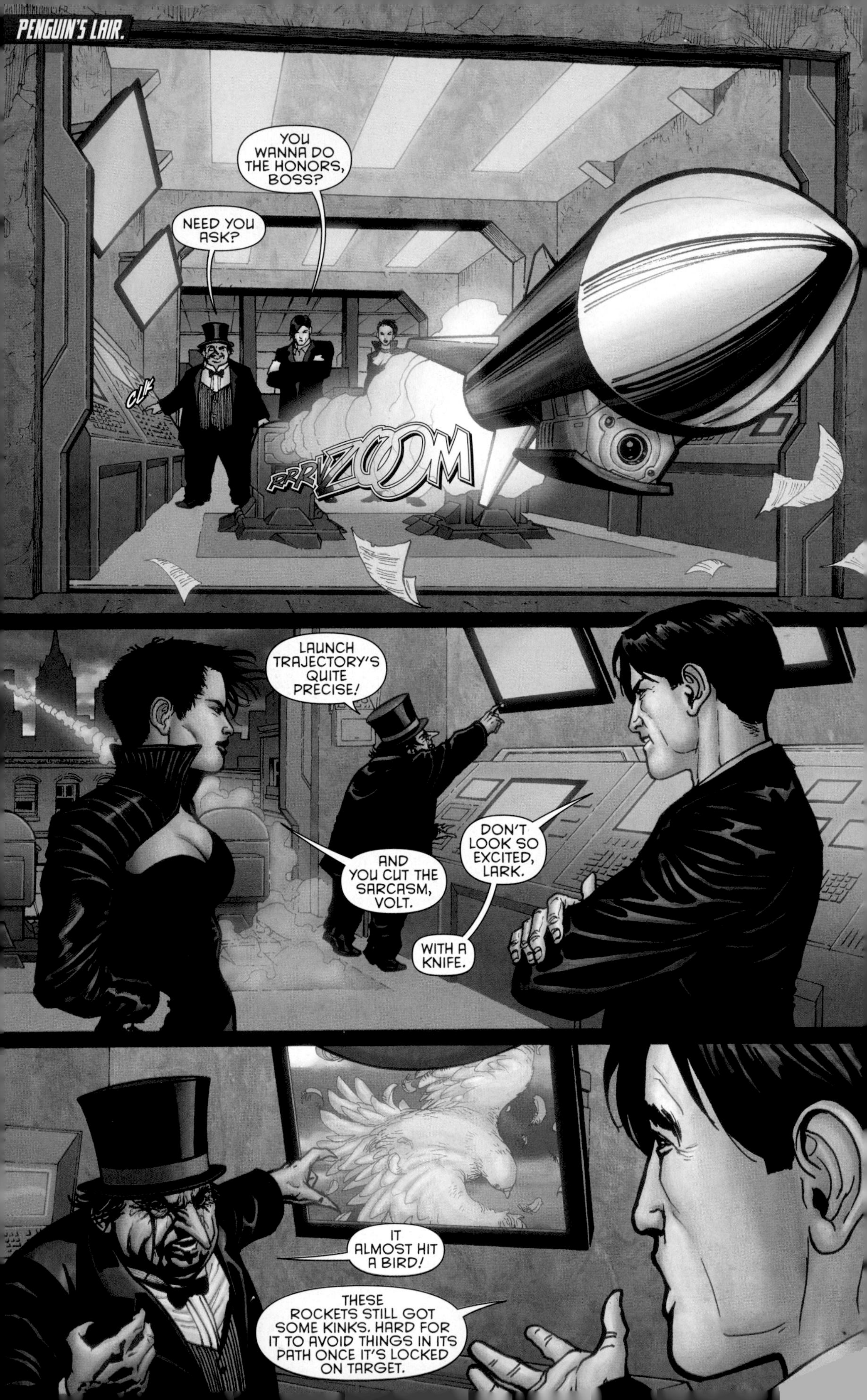
PENGUIN'S LAIR.
YOU WANNA DO THE HONORS, BOSS?
NEED YOU ASK?
CLIK
RRRVZOOOM
LAUNCH TRAJECTORY'S QUITE PRECISE!
DON'T LOOK SO EXCITED, LARK.
AND YOU CUT THE SARCASM, VOLT.
WITH A KNIFE.
IT ALMOST HIT A BIRD!
THESE ROCKETS STILL GOT SOME KINKS. HARD FOR IT TO AVOID THINGS IN ITS PATH ONCE IT'S LOCKED ON TARGET.

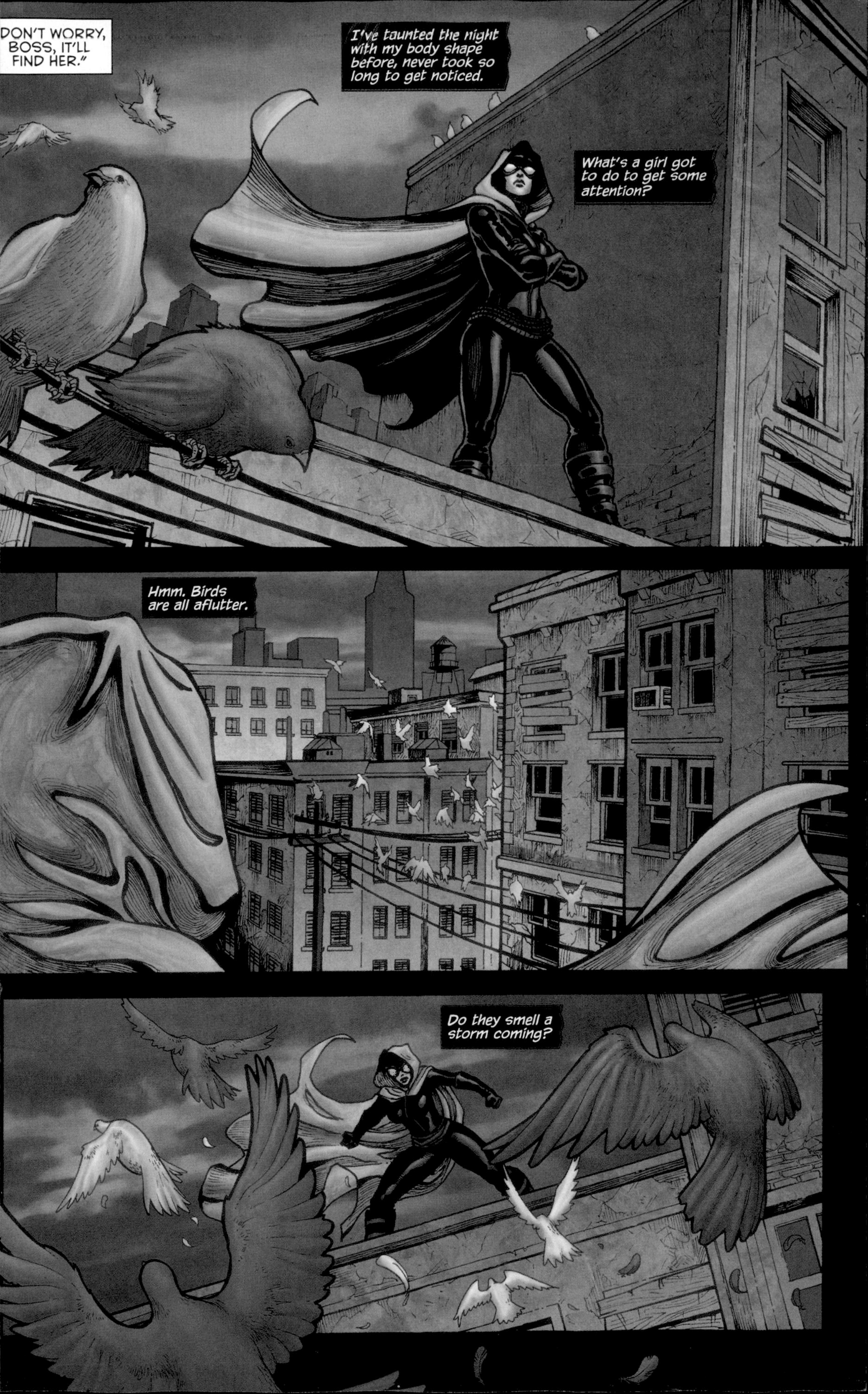
"DON'T WORRY, BOSS, IT'LL FIND HER."
I've taunted the night with my body shape before, never took so long to get noticed.
What's a girl got to do to get some attention?
Hmm. Birds are all aflutter.
Do they smell a storm coming?

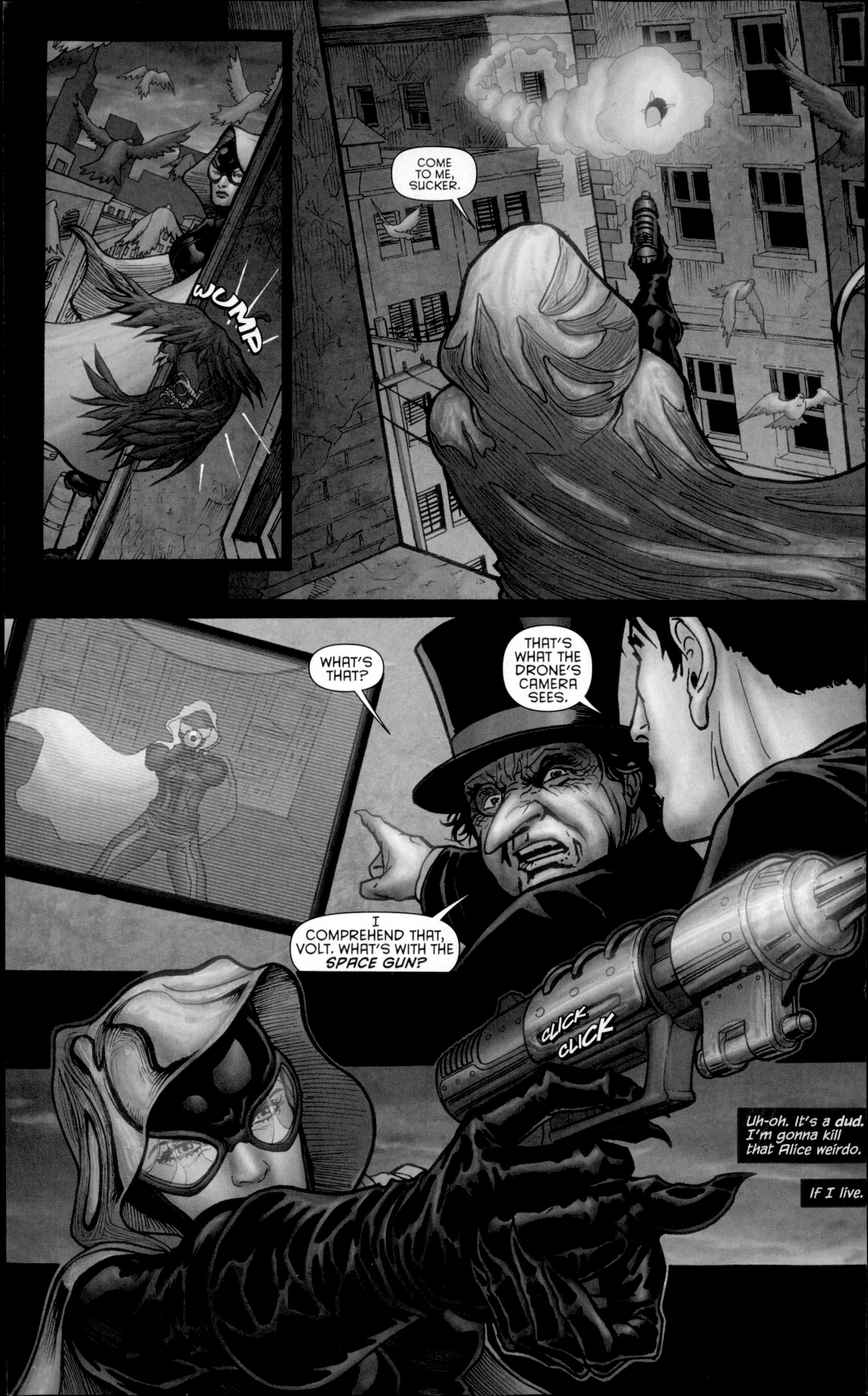
WUMP
COME TO ME, SUCKER.
WHAT'S THAT?
THAT'S WHAT THE DRONE'S CAMERA SEES.
I COMPREHEND THAT, VOLT. WHAT'S WITH THE *SPACE GUN?*
CLICK CLICK
Uh-oh. It's a **dud.** I'm gonna kill that Alice weirdo.
If I live.

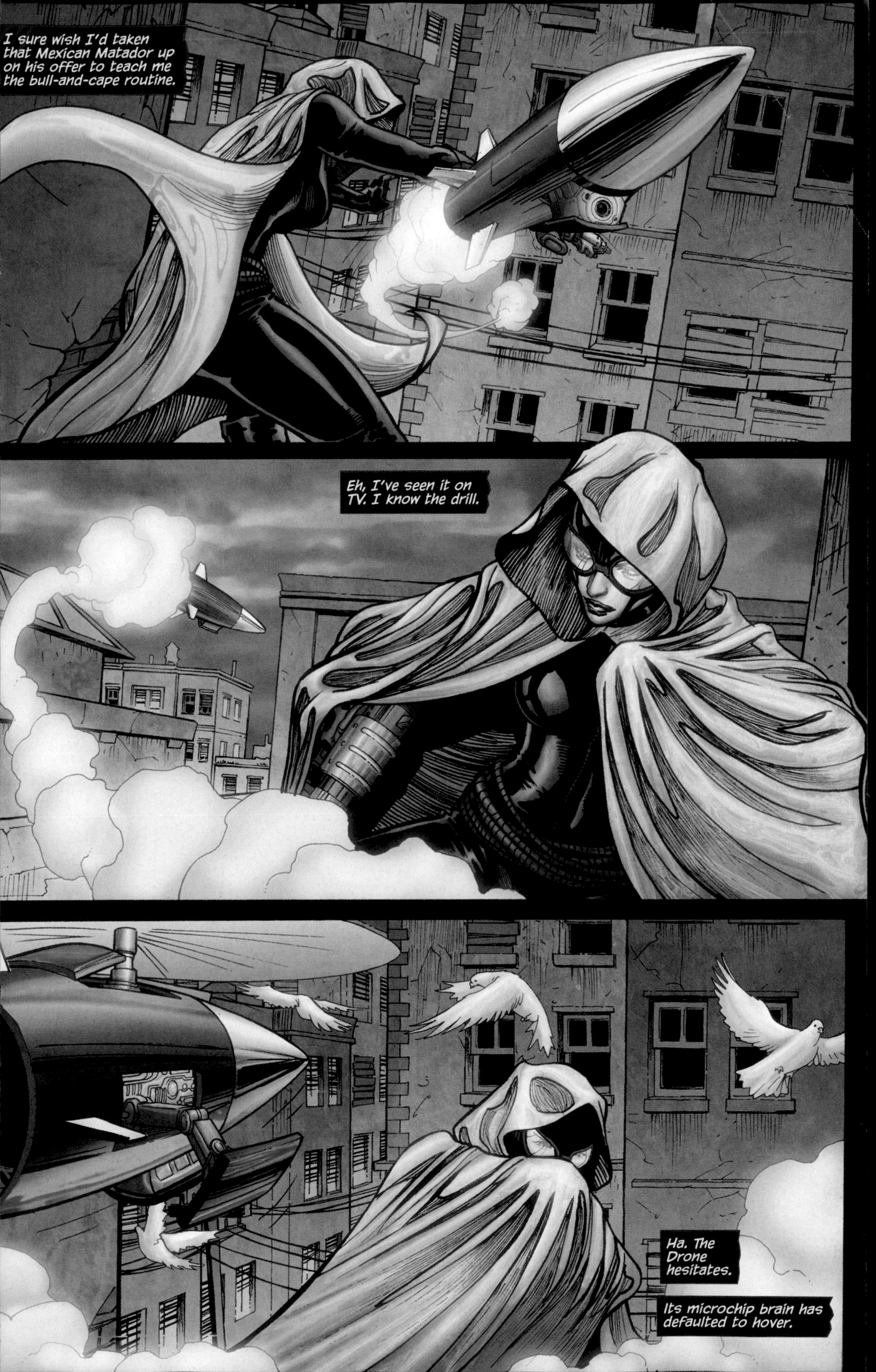
I sure wish I'd taken that Mexican Matador up on his offer to teach me the bull-and-cape routine.
Eh, I've seen it on TV. I know the drill.
Ha. The Drone hesitates.
Its microchip brain has defaulted to hover.

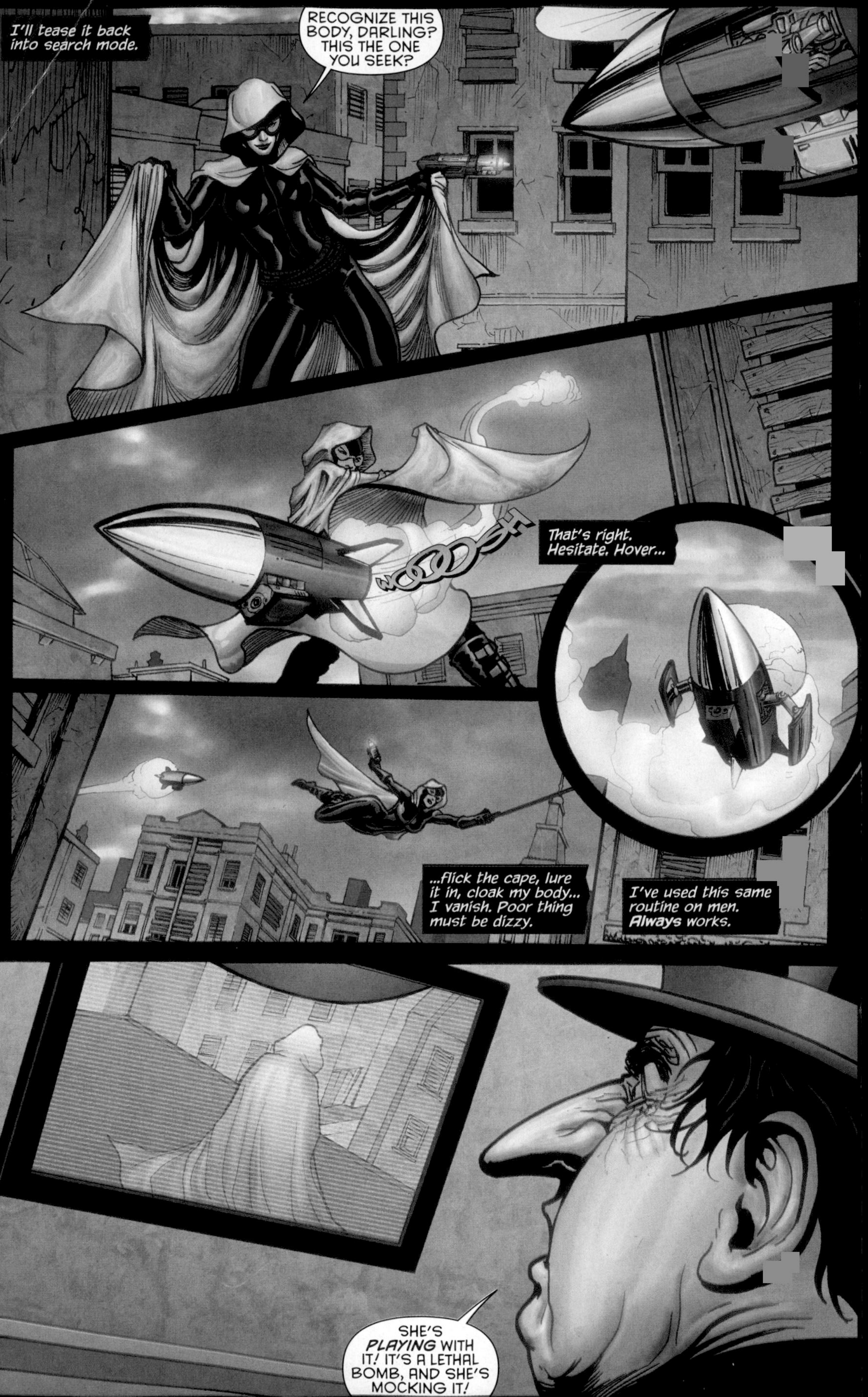
I'll tease it back into search mode.
RECOGNIZE THIS BODY, DARLING? THIS THE ONE YOU SEEK?
WOOOSH
That's right. Hesitate. Hover...
...flick the cape, lure it in, cloak my body... I vanish. Poor thing must be dizzy.
I've used this same routine on men. **Always** works.
SHE'S ***PLAYING*** WITH IT! IT'S A LETHAL BOMB, AND SHE'S MOCKING IT!

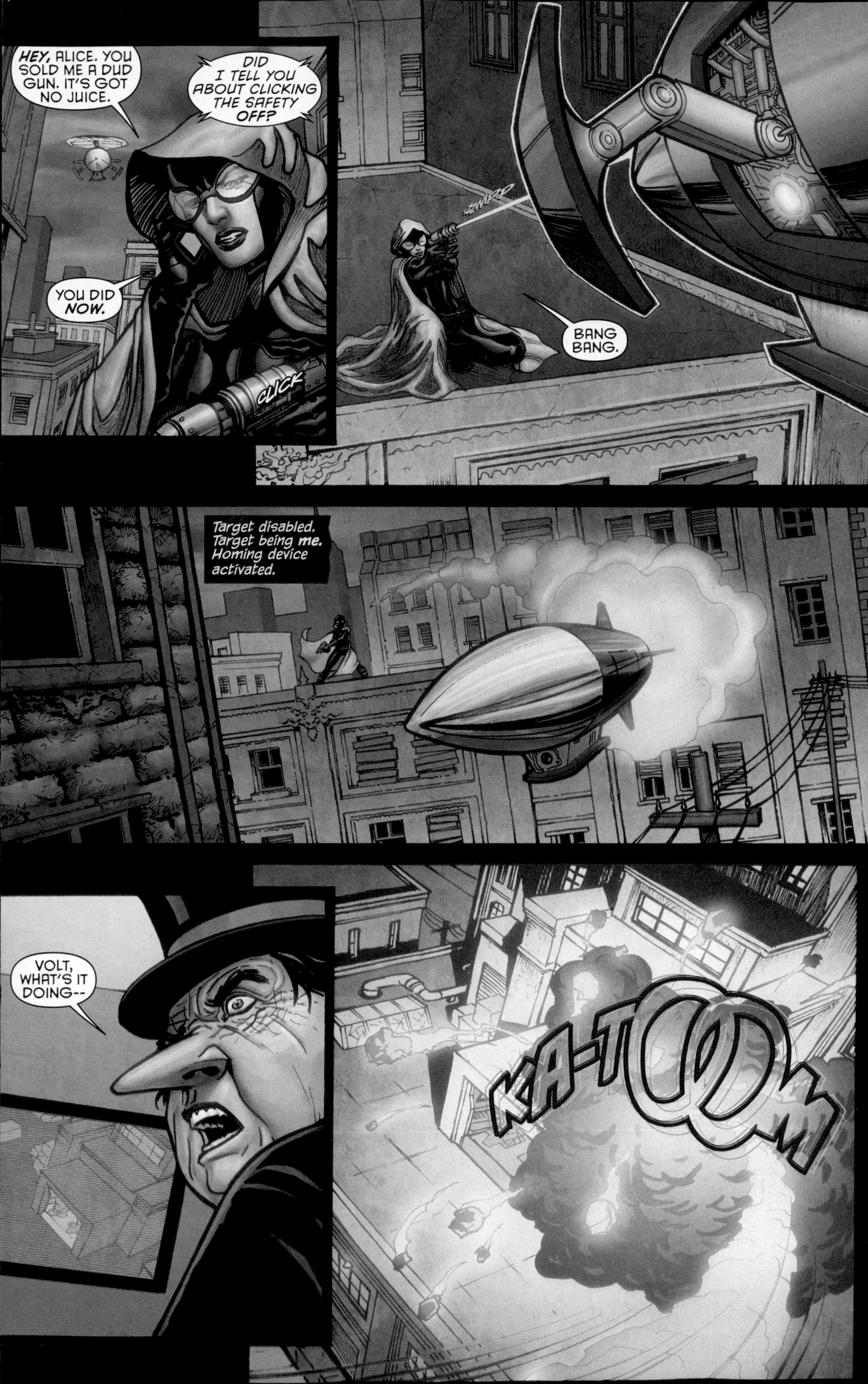
HEY, ALICE. YOU SOLD ME A DUD GUN. IT'S GOT NO JUICE.
DID I TELL YOU ABOUT CLICKING THE SAFETY OFF?
YOU DID NOW.
CLICK
BANG BANG.
Target disabled. Target being me. Homing device activated.
VOLT, WHAT'S IT DOING--
KA-TOOOM

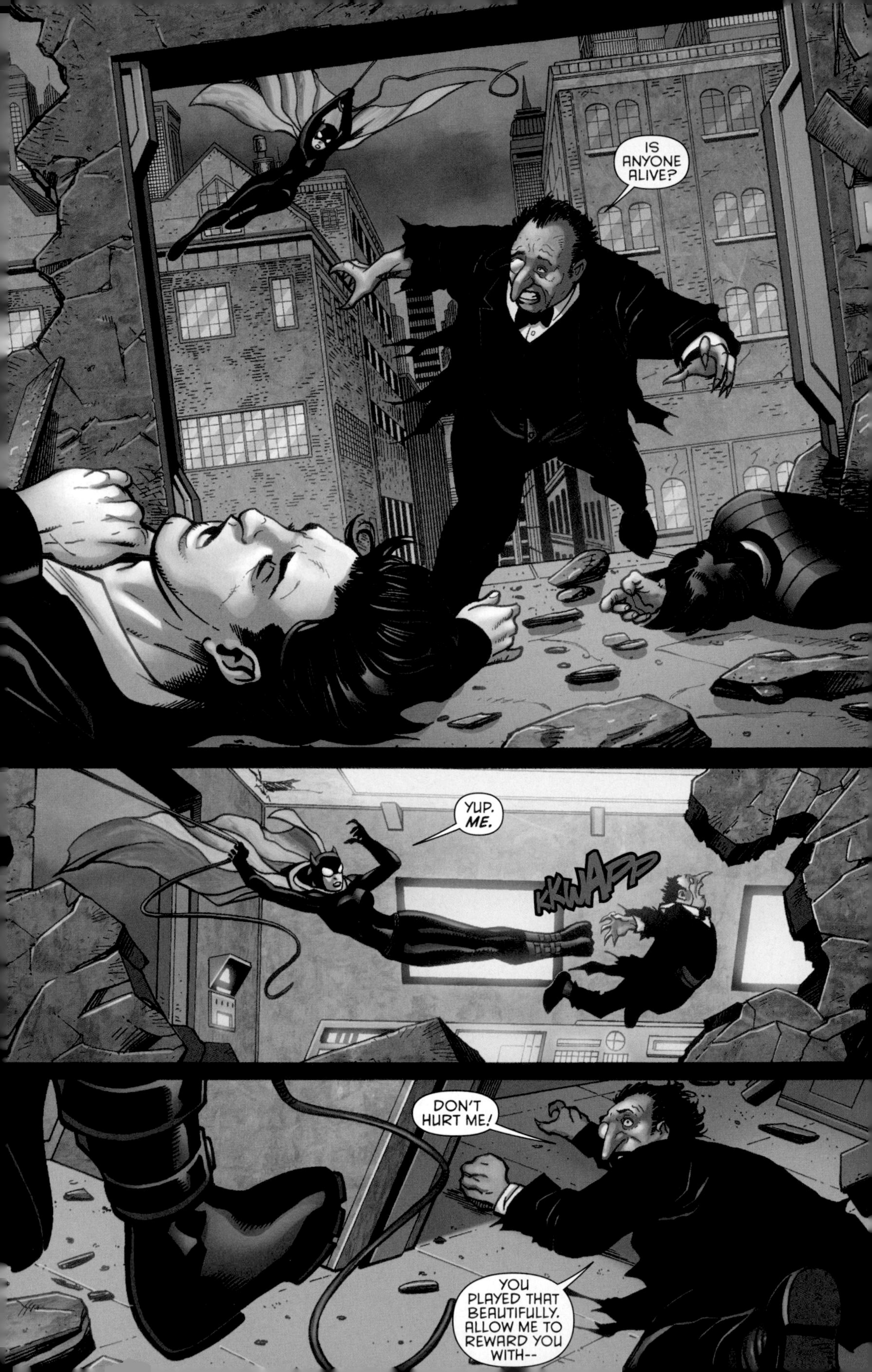
IS ANYONE ALIVE?
YUP. ME.
KKWAPP
DON'T HURT ME!
YOU PLAYED THAT BEAUTIFULLY. ALLOW ME TO REWARD YOU WITH--

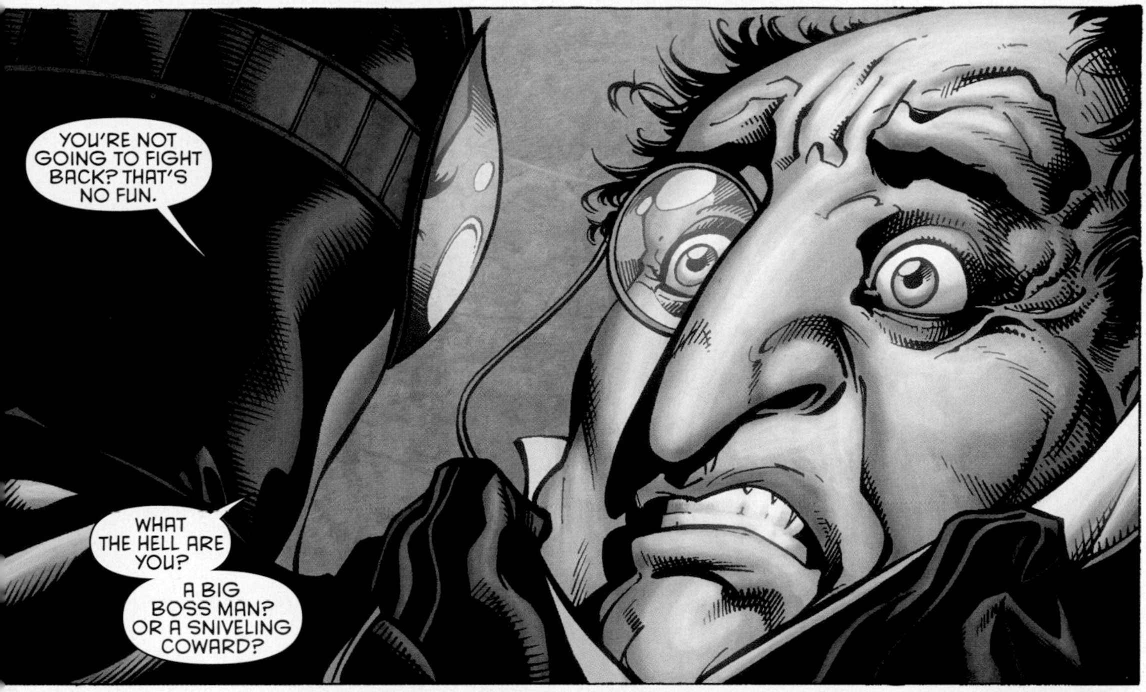
YOU'RE NOT GOING TO FIGHT BACK? THAT'S NO FUN.
WHAT THE HELL ARE YOU?
A BIG BOSS MAN? OR A SNIVELING COWARD?

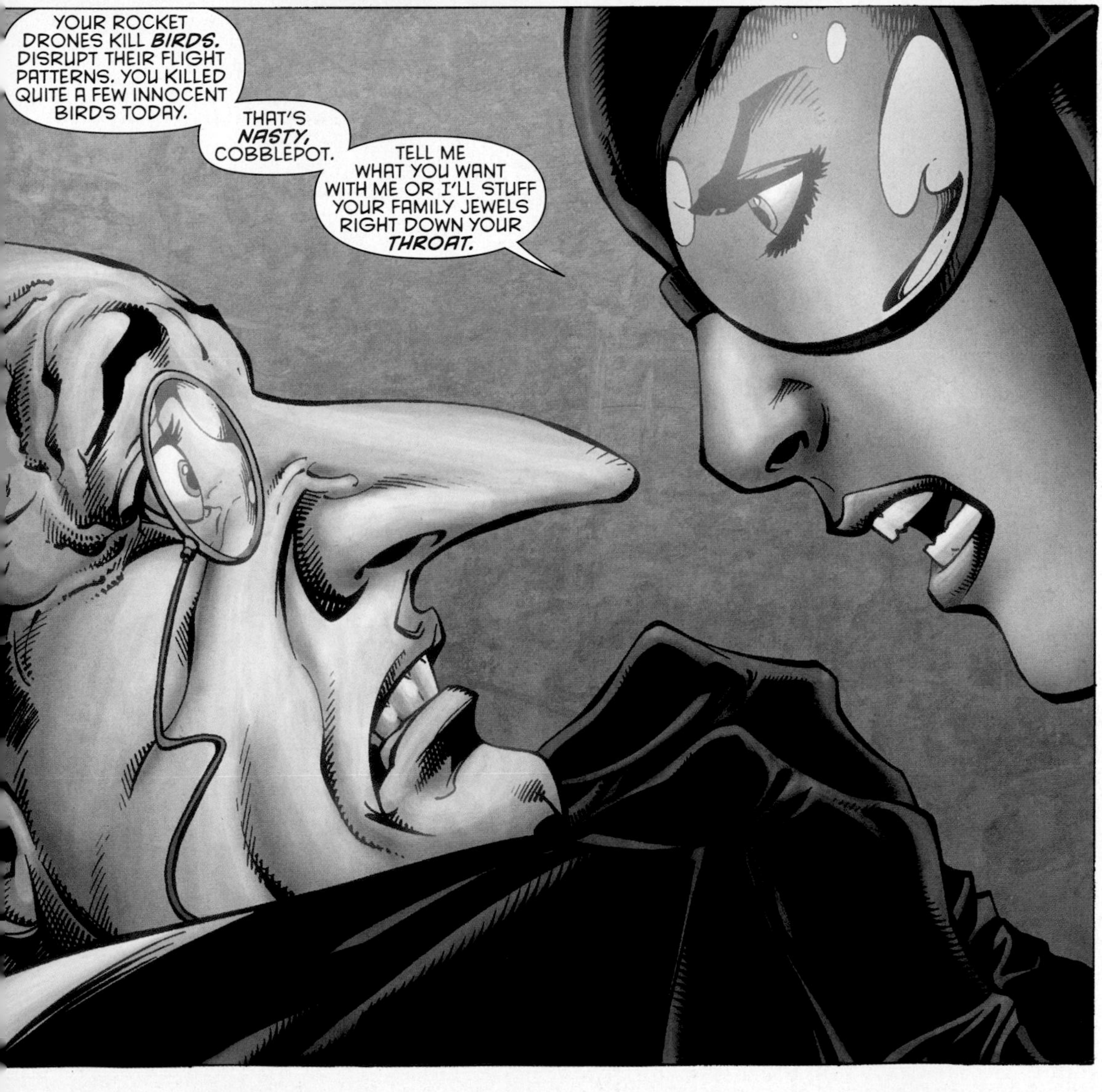
YOUR ROCKET DRONES KILL BIRDS. DISRUPT THEIR FLIGHT PATTERNS. YOU KILLED QUITE A FEW INNOCENT BIRDS TODAY.
THAT'S NASTY, COBBLEPOT.
TELL ME WHAT YOU WANT WITH ME OR I'LL STUFF YOUR FAMILY JEWELS RIGHT DOWN YOUR THROAT.

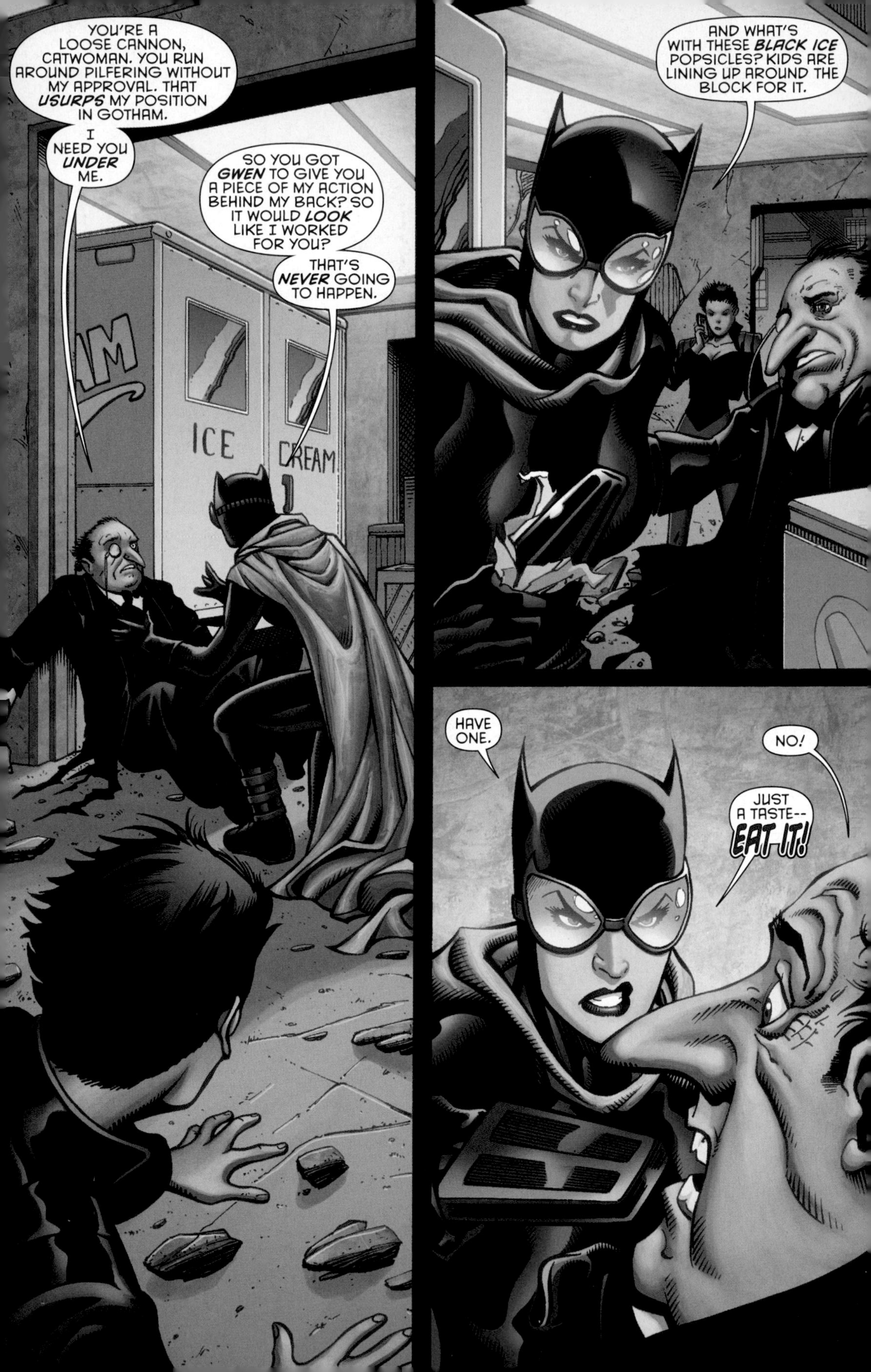
YOU'RE A LOOSE CANNON, CATWOMAN. YOU RUN AROUND PILFERING WITHOUT MY APPROVAL. THAT USURPS MY POSITION IN GOTHAM.
I NEED YOU UNDER ME.
SO YOU GOT GWEN TO GIVE YOU A PIECE OF MY ACTION BEHIND MY BACK? SO IT WOULD LOOK LIKE I WORKED FOR YOU?
THAT'S NEVER GOING TO HAPPEN.
ICE CREAM
AND WHAT'S WITH THESE BLACK ICE POPSICLES? KIDS ARE LINING UP AROUND THE BLOCK FOR IT.
HAVE ONE.
NO!
JUST A TASTE-- EAT IT!

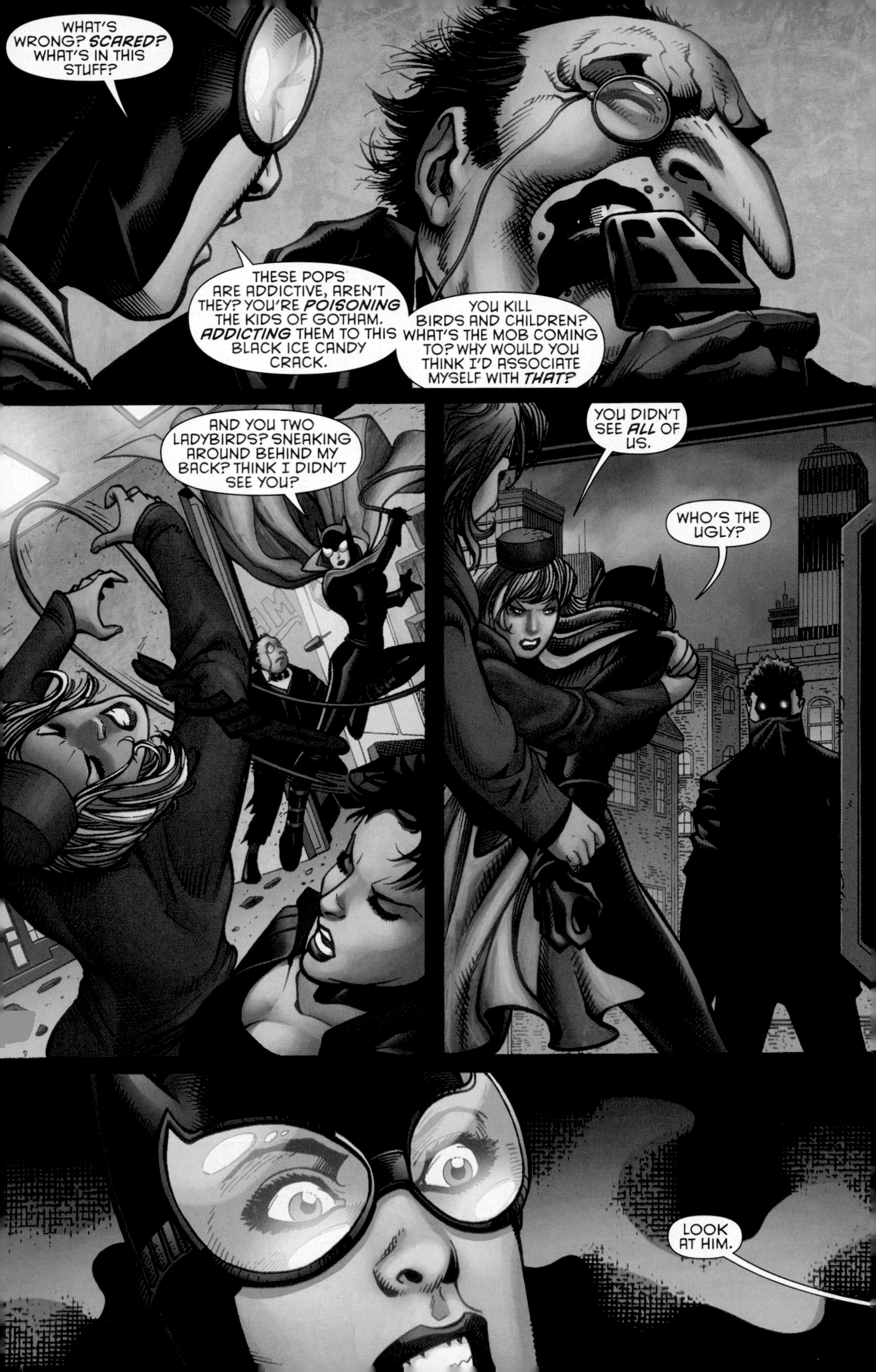
WHAT'S WRONG? SCARED? WHAT'S IN THIS STUFF?
THESE POPS ARE ADDICTIVE, AREN'T THEY? YOU'RE POISONING THE KIDS OF GOTHAM. ADDICTING THEM TO THIS BLACK ICE CANDY CRACK.
YOU KILL BIRDS AND CHILDREN? WHAT'S THE MOB COMING TO? WHY WOULD YOU THINK I'D ASSOCIATE MYSELF WITH THAT?
AND YOU TWO LADYBIRDS? SNEAKING AROUND BEHIND MY BACK? THINK I DIDN'T SEE YOU?
YOU DIDN'T SEE ALL OF US.
WHO'S THE UGLY?
LOOK AT HIM.

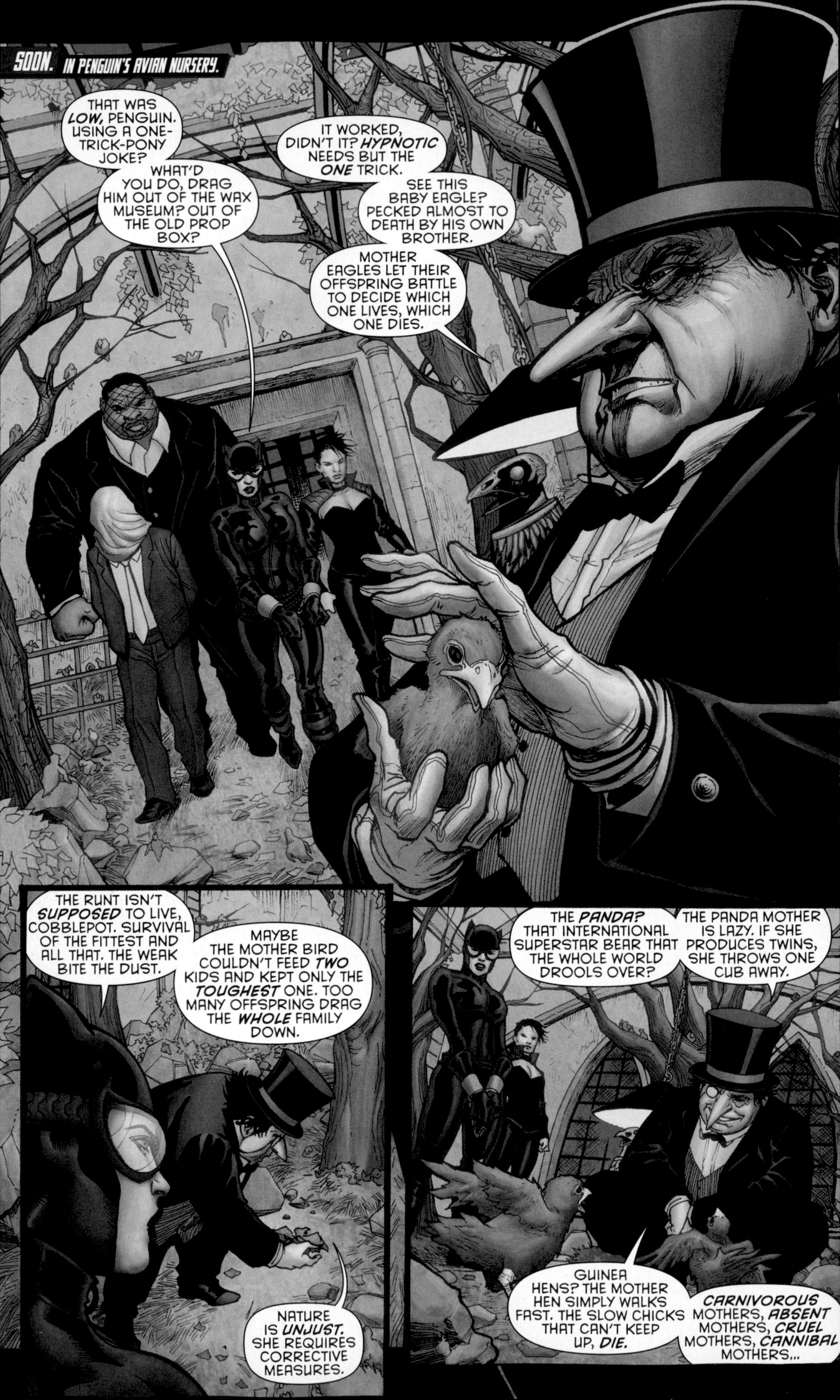
SOON. IN PENGUIN'S AVIAN NURSERY.
THAT WAS LOW, PENGUIN. USING A ONE-TRICK-PONY JOKE?
WHAT'D YOU DO, DRAG HIM OUT OF THE WAX MUSEUM? OUT OF THE OLD PROP BOX?
IT WORKED, DIDN'T IT? HYPNOTIC NEEDS BUT THE ONE TRICK.
SEE THIS BABY EAGLE? PECKED ALMOST TO DEATH BY HIS OWN BROTHER.
MOTHER EAGLES LET THEIR OFFSPRING BATTLE TO DECIDE WHICH ONE LIVES, WHICH ONE DIES.
THE RUNT ISN'T SUPPOSED TO LIVE, COBBLEPOT. SURVIVAL OF THE FITTEST AND ALL THAT. THE WEAK BITE THE DUST.
MAYBE THE MOTHER BIRD COULDN'T FEED TWO KIDS AND KEPT ONLY THE TOUGHEST ONE. TOO MANY OFFSPRING DRAG THE WHOLE FAMILY DOWN.
NATURE IS UNJUST. SHE REQUIRES CORRECTIVE MEASURES.
THE PANDA? THAT INTERNATIONAL SUPERSTAR BEAR THAT THE WHOLE WORLD DROOLS OVER?
THE PANDA MOTHER IS LAZY. IF SHE PRODUCES TWINS, SHE THROWS ONE CUB AWAY.
GUINEA HENS? THE MOTHER HEN SIMPLY WALKS FAST. THE SLOW CHICKS THAT CAN'T KEEP UP, DIE.
CARNIVOROUS MOTHERS, ABSENT MOTHERS, CRUEL MOTHERS, CANNIBAL MOTHERS...

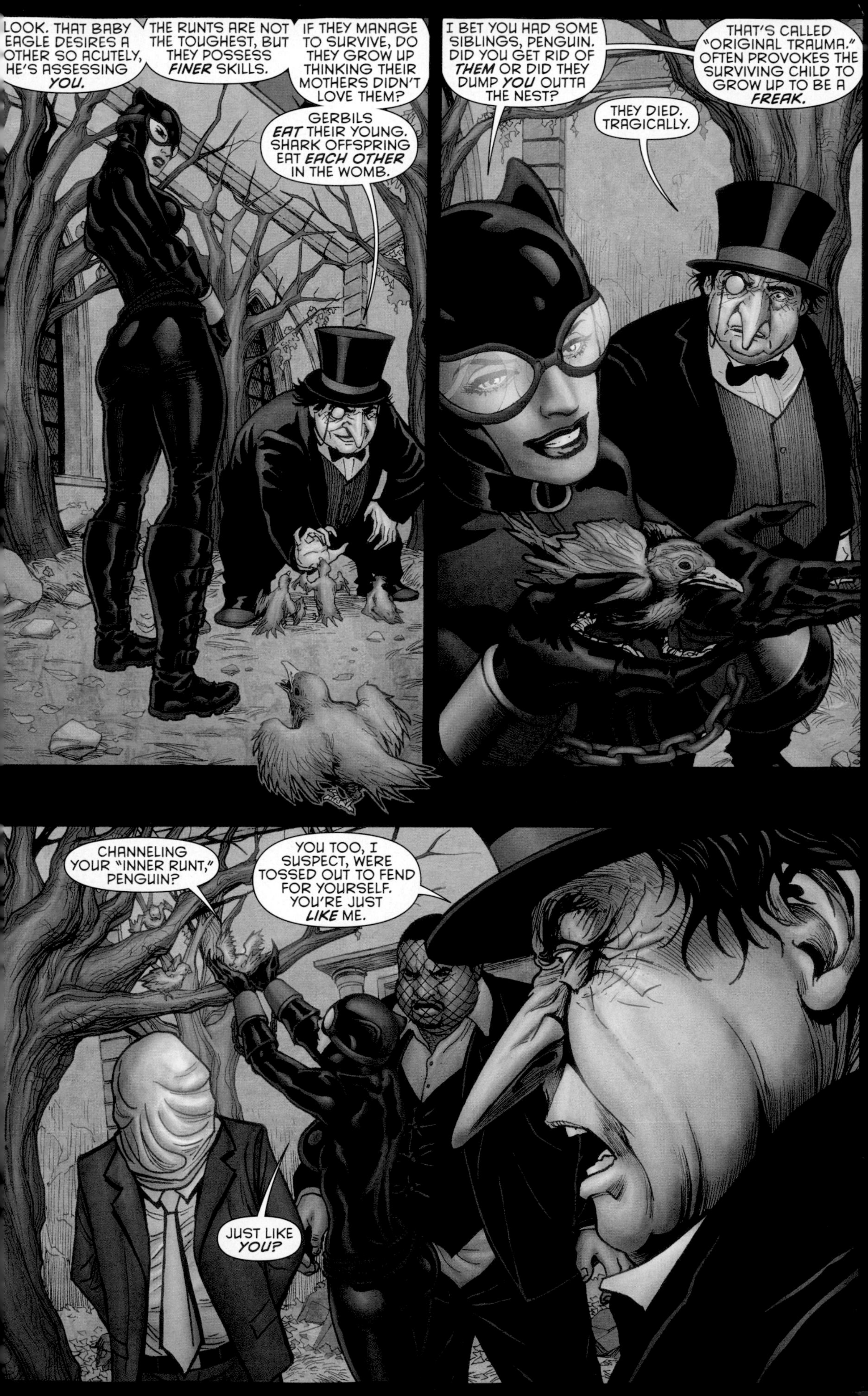
LOOK. THAT BABY EAGLE DESIRES A OTHER SO ACUTELY, HE'S ASSESSING *YOU.*
THE RUNTS ARE NOT THE TOUGHEST, BUT THEY POSSESS *FINER* SKILLS.
IF THEY MANAGE TO SURVIVE, DO THEY GROW UP THINKING THEIR MOTHERS DIDN'T LOVE THEM?
GERBILS *EAT* THEIR YOUNG. SHARK OFFSPRING EAT *EACH OTHER* IN THE WOMB.
I BET YOU HAD SOME SIBLINGS, PENGUIN. DID YOU GET RID OF *THEM* OR DID THEY DUMP *YOU* OUTTA THE NEST?
THAT'S CALLED "ORIGINAL TRAUMA." OFTEN PROVOKES THE SURVIVING CHILD TO GROW UP TO BE A *FREAK.*
THEY DIED. TRAGICALLY.
CHANNELING YOUR "INNER RUNT," PENGUIN?
YOU TOO, I SUSPECT, WERE TOSSED OUT TO FEND FOR YOURSELF. YOU'RE JUST *LIKE* ME.
JUST LIKE *YOU?*

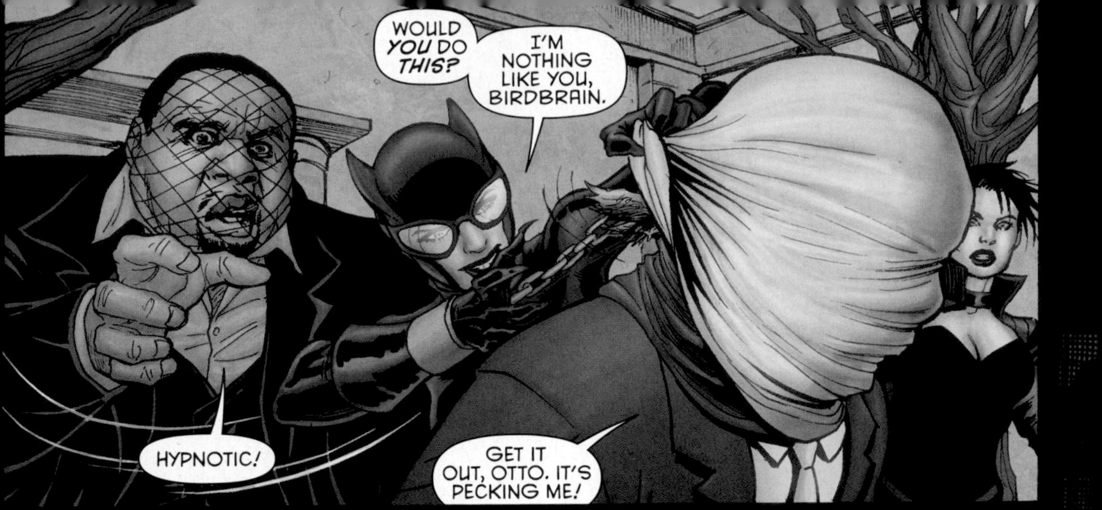

WOULD YOU DO THIS?
I'M NOTHING LIKE YOU, BIRDBRAIN.
HYPNOTIC!
GET IT OUT, OTTO. IT'S PECKING ME!

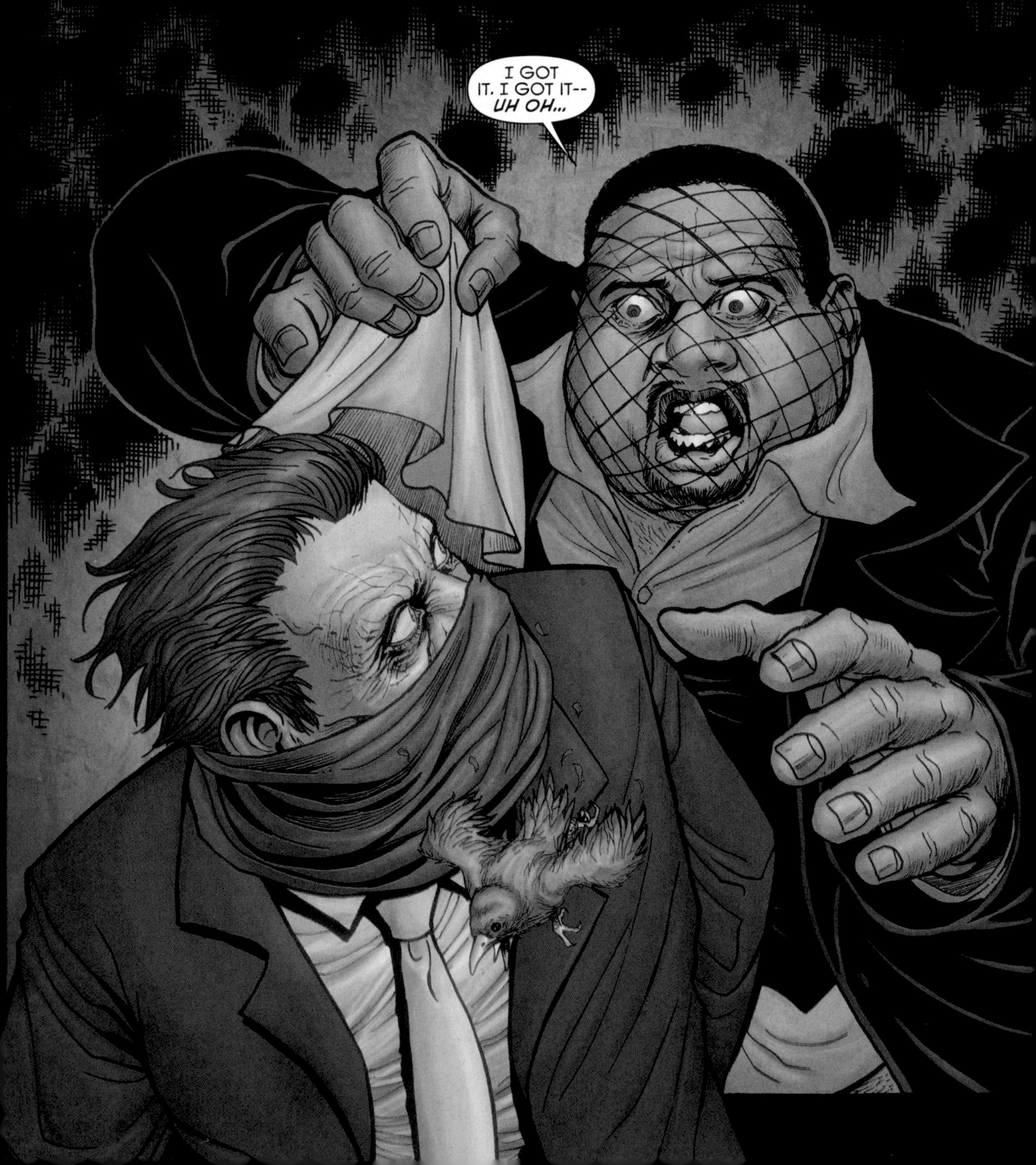

I GOT IT. I GOT IT-- UH OH...

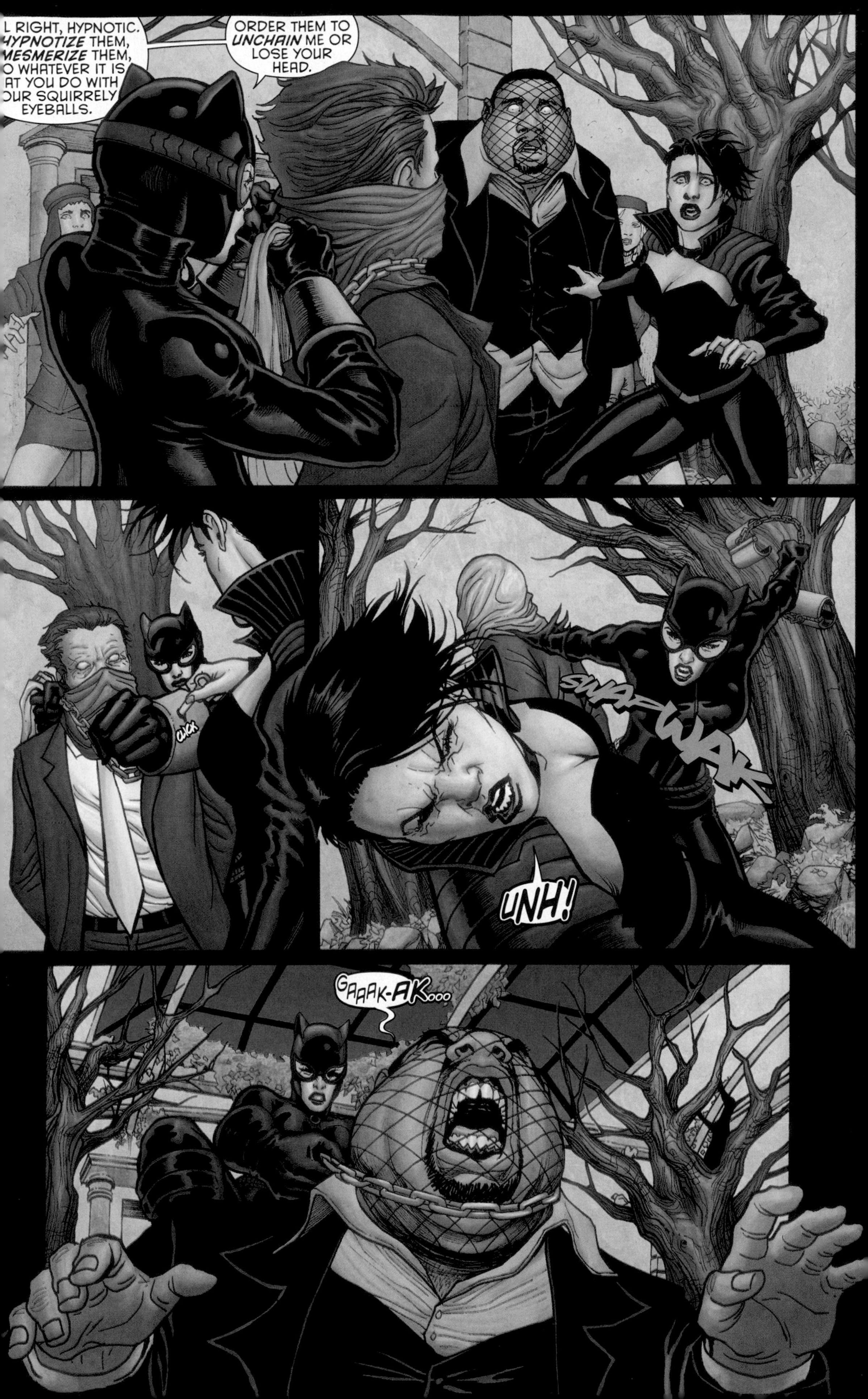
L RIGHT, HYPNOTIC. HYPNOTIZE THEM, MESMERIZE THEM, O WHATEVER IT IS AT YOU DO WITH OUR SQUIRRELY EYEBALLS.
ORDER THEM TO UNCHAIN ME OR LOSE YOUR HEAD.
CLICK
SWAPWAK
UNH!
GAAAK-AK...

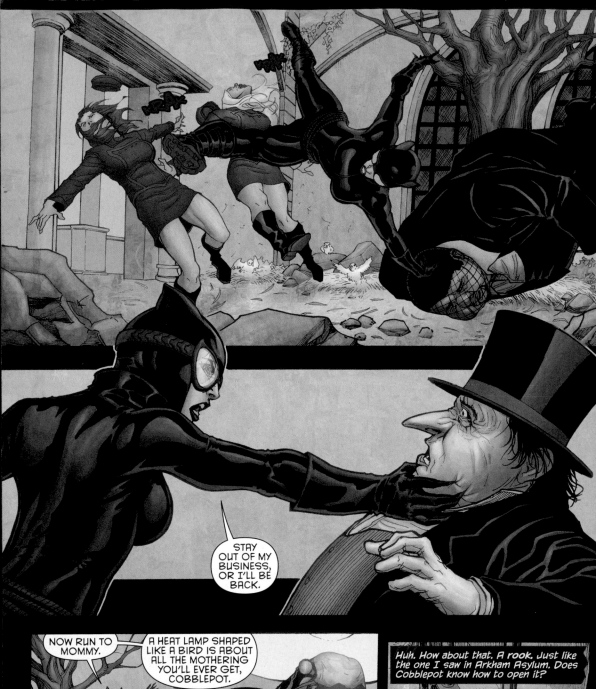

STAY OUT OF MY BUSINESS, OR I'LL BE BACK.

NOW RUN TO MOMMY.

A HEAT LAMP SHAPED LIKE A BIRD IS ABOUT ALL THE MOTHERING YOU'LL EVER GET, COBBLEPOT.

Huh. How about that. A *rook*. Just like the one I saw in Arkham Asylum. Does Cobblepot know how to open it?

Does it lead to what I saw under Gotham?

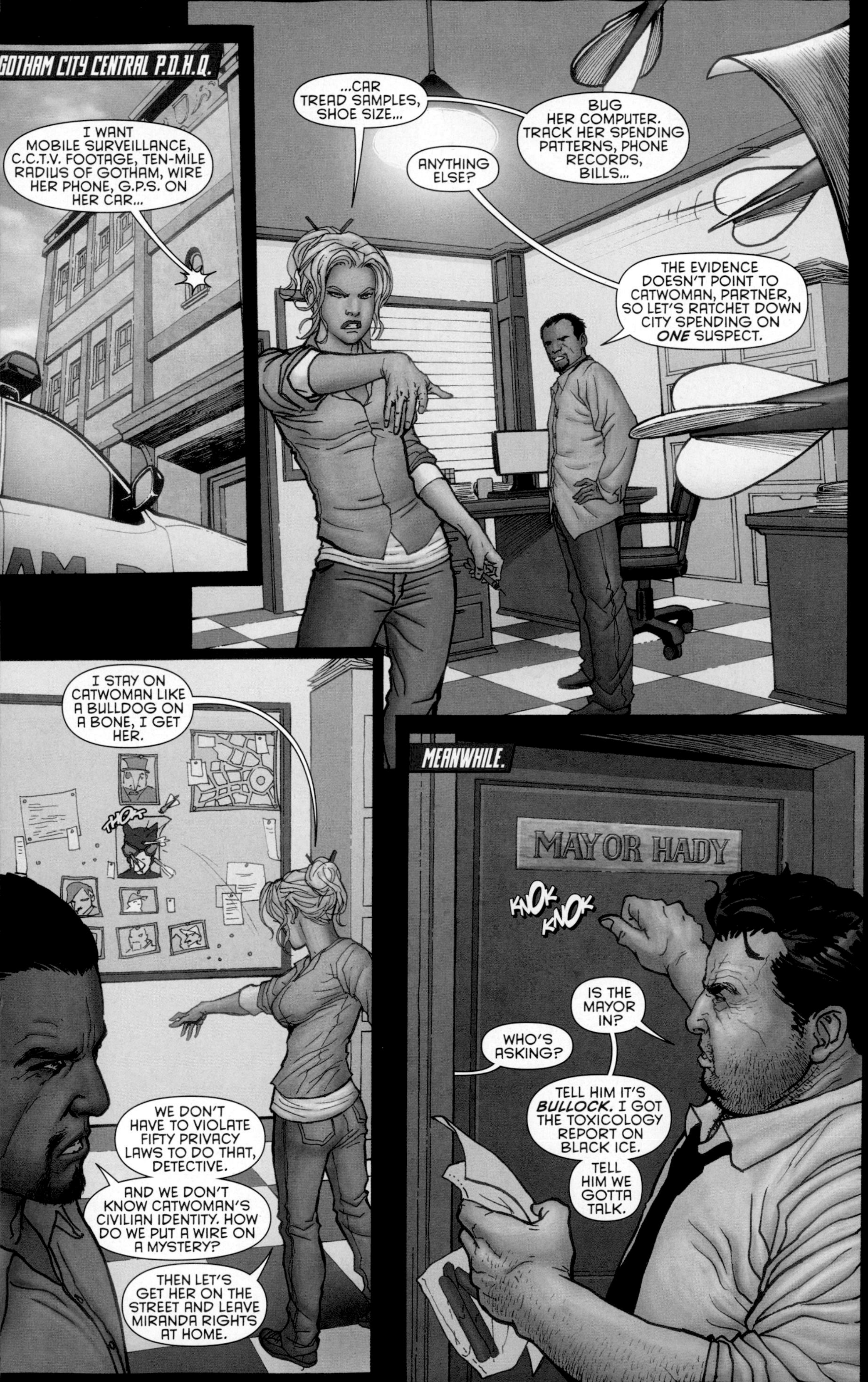
GOTHAM CITY CENTRAL P.D.H.Q.
I WANT MOBILE SURVEILLANCE, C.C.T.V. FOOTAGE, TEN-MILE RADIUS OF GOTHAM, WIRE HER PHONE, G.P.S. ON HER CAR...
...CAR TREAD SAMPLES, SHOE SIZE...
BUG HER COMPUTER. TRACK HER SPENDING PATTERNS, PHONE RECORDS, BILLS...
ANYTHING ELSE?
THE EVIDENCE DOESN'T POINT TO CATWOMAN, PARTNER, SO LET'S RATCHET DOWN CITY SPENDING ON ONE SUSPECT.
I STAY ON CATWOMAN LIKE A BULLDOG ON A BONE, I GET HER.
THOK
WE DON'T HAVE TO VIOLATE FIFTY PRIVACY LAWS TO DO THAT, DETECTIVE.
AND WE DON'T KNOW CATWOMAN'S CIVILIAN IDENTITY. HOW DO WE PUT A WIRE ON A MYSTERY?
THEN LET'S GET HER ON THE STREET AND LEAVE MIRANDA RIGHTS AT HOME.
MEANWHILE.
MAYOR HADY
KNOK KNOK
IS THE MAYOR IN?
WHO'S ASKING?
TELL HIM IT'S BULLOCK. I GOT THE TOXICOLOGY REPORT ON BLACK ICE.
TELL HIM WE GOTTA TALK.

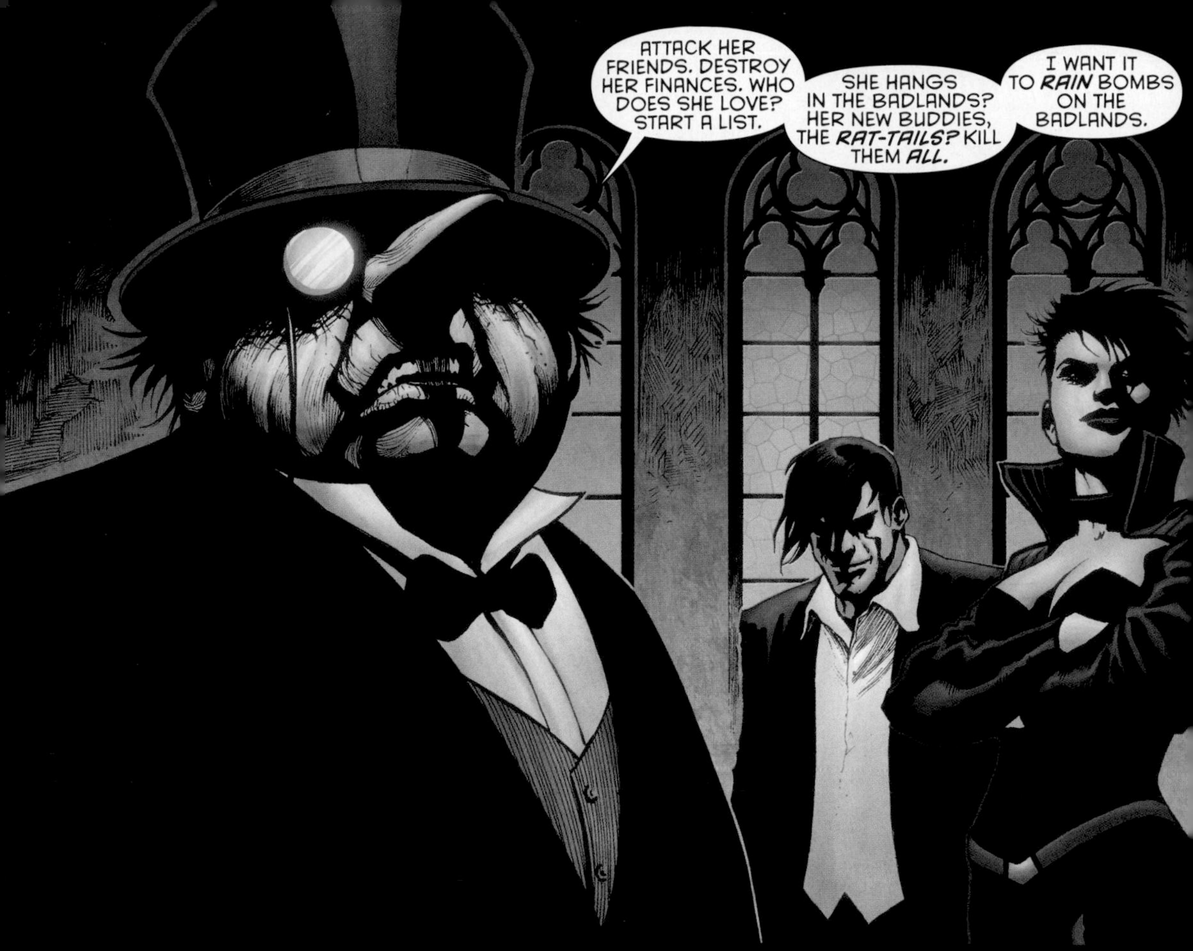
ATTACK HER FRIENDS. DESTROY HER FINANCES. WHO DOES SHE LOVE? START A LIST.
SHE HANGS IN THE BADLANDS? HER NEW BUDDIES, THE *RAT-TAILS?* KILL THEM *ALL.*
I WANT IT TO *RAIN* BOMBS ON THE BADLANDS.

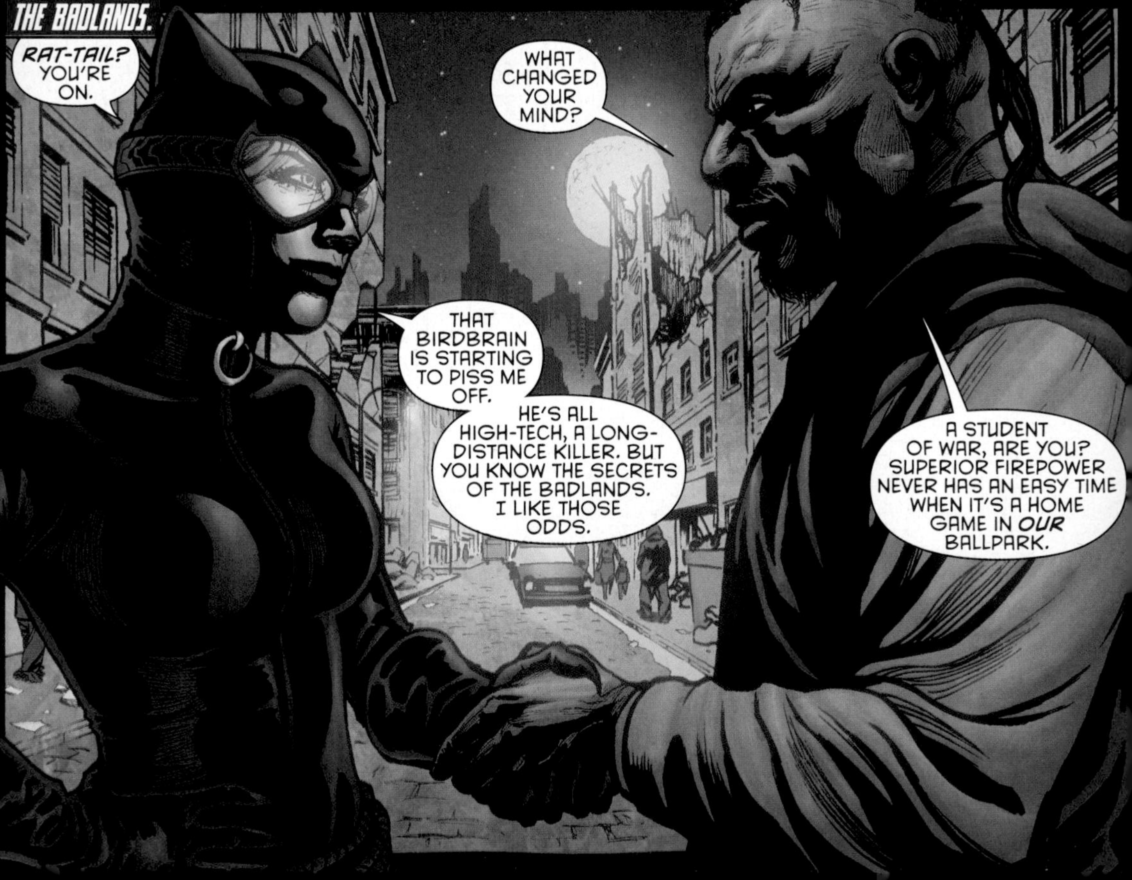
THE BADLANDS.
RAT-TAIL? YOU'RE ON.
WHAT CHANGED YOUR MIND?
THAT BIRDBRAIN IS STARTING TO PISS ME OFF.
HE'S ALL HIGH-TECH, A LONG-DISTANCE KILLER. BUT YOU KNOW THE SECRETS OF THE BADLANDS. I LIKE THOSE ODDS.
A STUDENT OF WAR, ARE YOU? SUPERIOR FIREPOWER NEVER HAS AN EASY TIME WHEN IT'S A HOME GAME IN *OUR* BALLPARK.

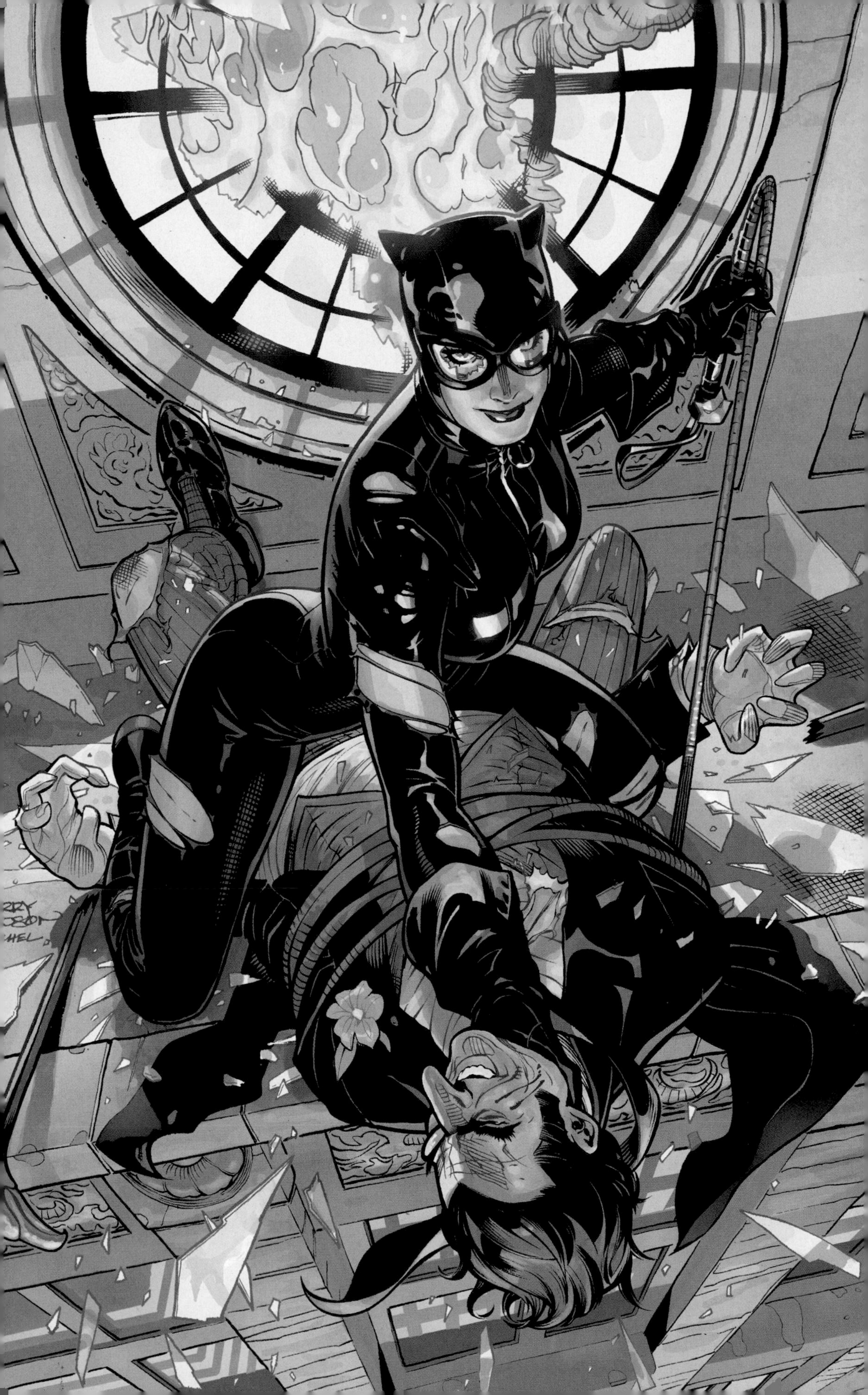

ANN NOCENTI
writer

RAFA SANDOVAL
penciller

JORDI TARRAGONA
inker

SONIA OBACK
colorist

TERRY & RACHEL DODSON
cover artists

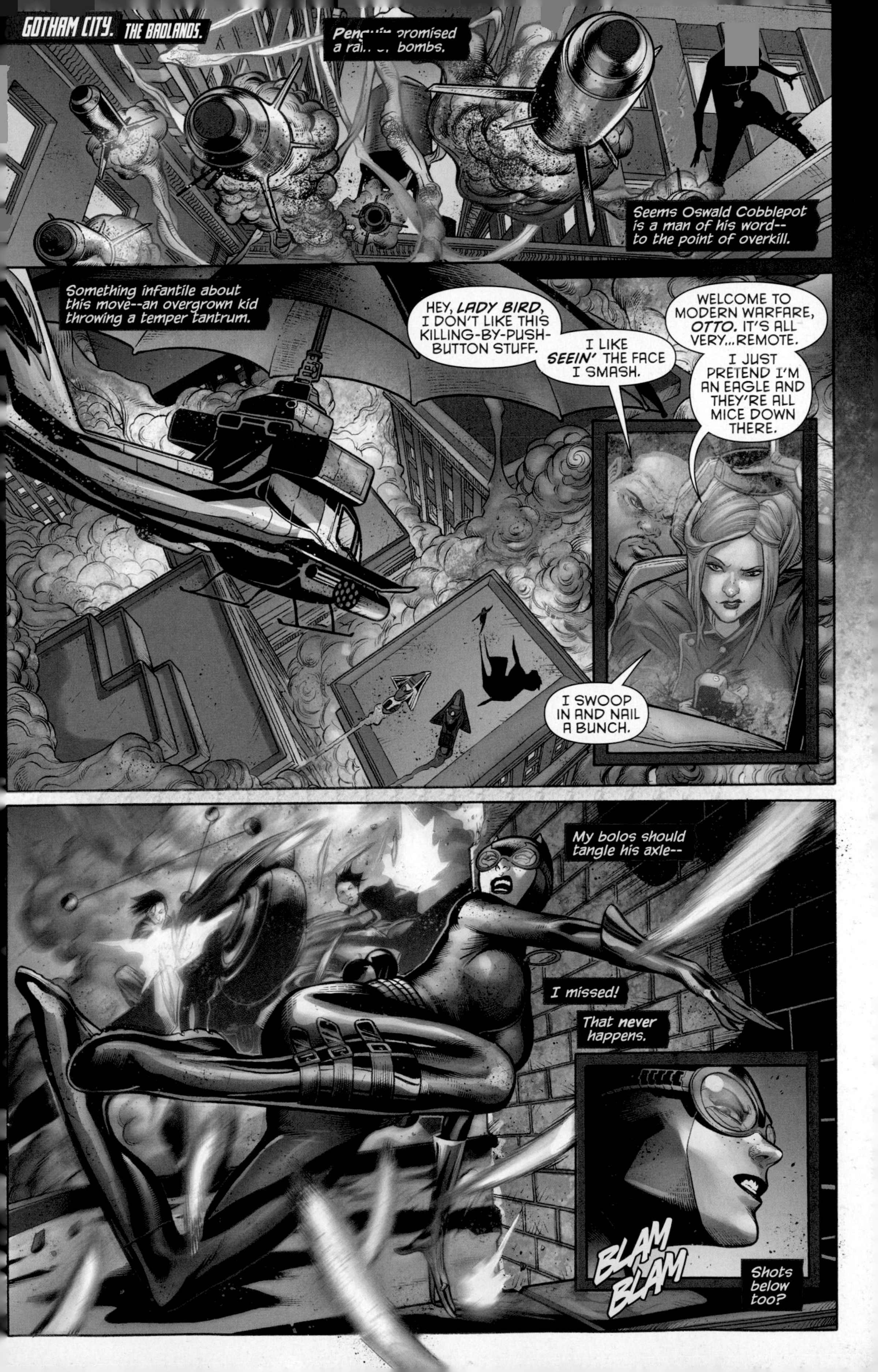
GOTHAM CITY.
THE BADLANDS.
Peng[redacted] promised
a rai[redacted] bombs.
Seems Oswald Cobblepot is a man of his word--to the point of overkill.
Something infantile about this move--an overgrown kid throwing a temper tantrum.
HEY, LADY BIRD, I DON'T LIKE THIS KILLING-BY-PUSH-BUTTON STUFF.
I LIKE SEEIN' THE FACE I SMASH.
WELCOME TO MODERN WARFARE, OTTO. IT'S ALL VERY...REMOTE.
I JUST PRETEND I'M AN EAGLE AND THEY'RE ALL MICE DOWN THERE.
I SWOOP IN AND NAIL A BUNCH.
My bolos should tangle his axle--
I missed!
That never happens.
BLAM BLAM
Shots below too?

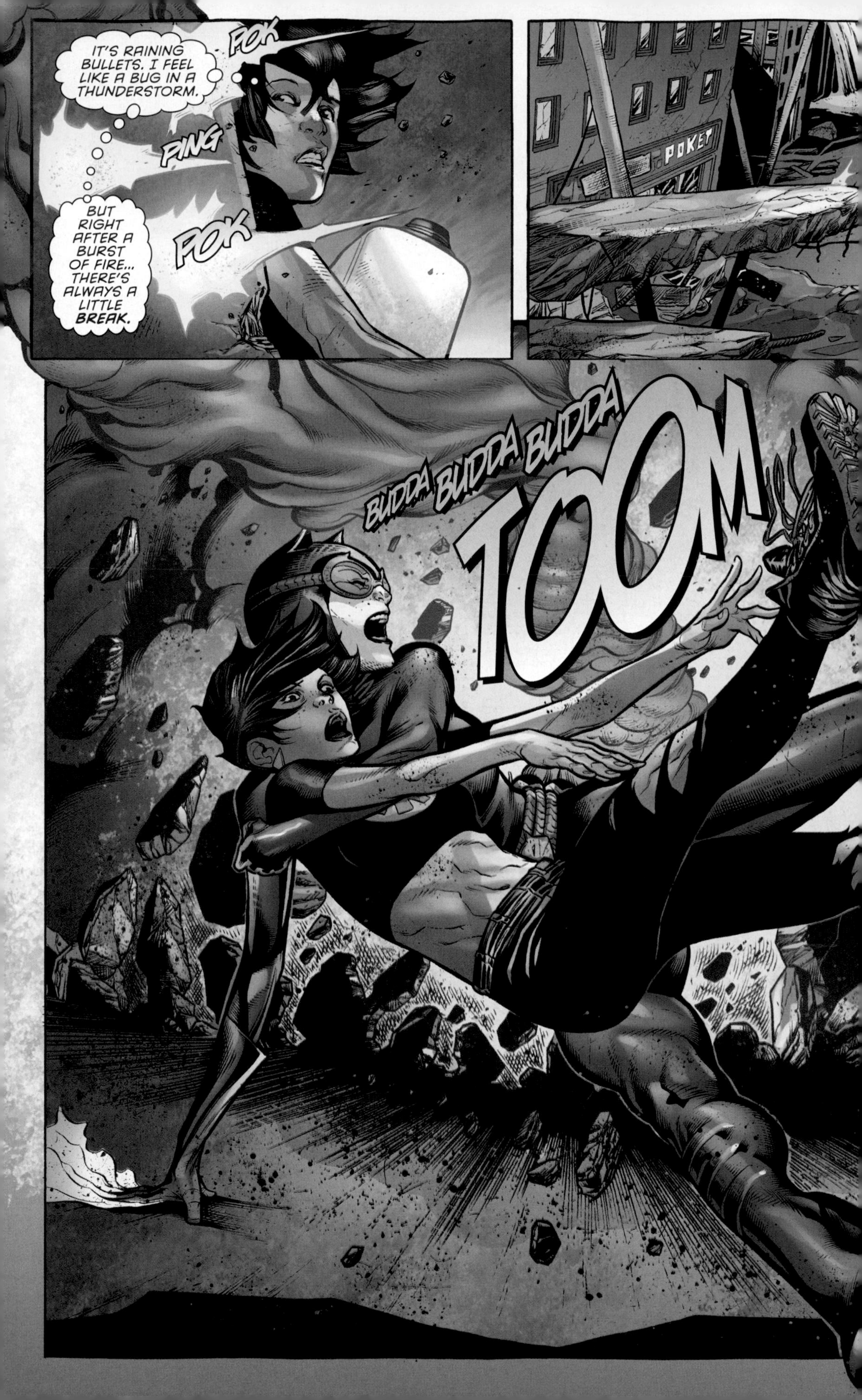
IT'S RAINING BULLETS. I FEEL LIKE A BUG IN A THUNDERSTORM.
POK
PING
POK
BUT RIGHT AFTER A BURST OF FIRE... THERE'S ALWAYS A LITTLE BREAK.
POKET
BUDDA BUDDA BUDDA
TOOM

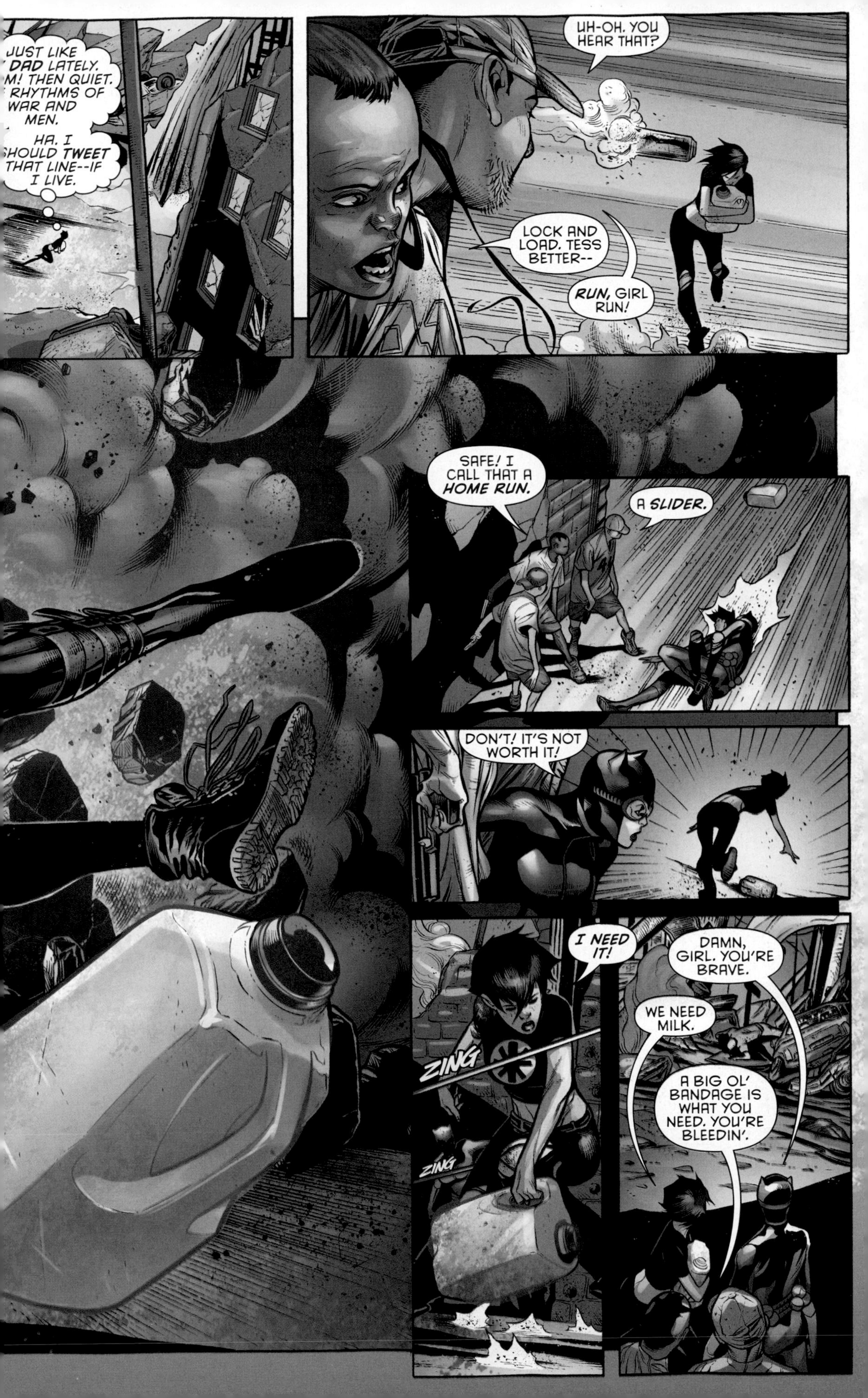
JUST LIKE DAD LATELY. M! THEN QUIET. RHYTHMS OF WAR AND MEN.
HA. I SHOULD TWEET THAT LINE--IF I LIVE.
UH-OH. YOU HEAR THAT?
LOCK AND LOAD. TESS BETTER--
RUN, GIRL RUN!
SAFE! I CALL THAT A HOME RUN.
A SLIDER.
DON'T! IT'S NOT WORTH IT!
I NEED IT!
ZING
ZING
DAMN, GIRL. YOU'RE BRAVE.
WE NEED MILK.
A BIG OL' BANDAGE IS WHAT YOU NEED. YOU'RE BLEEDIN'.

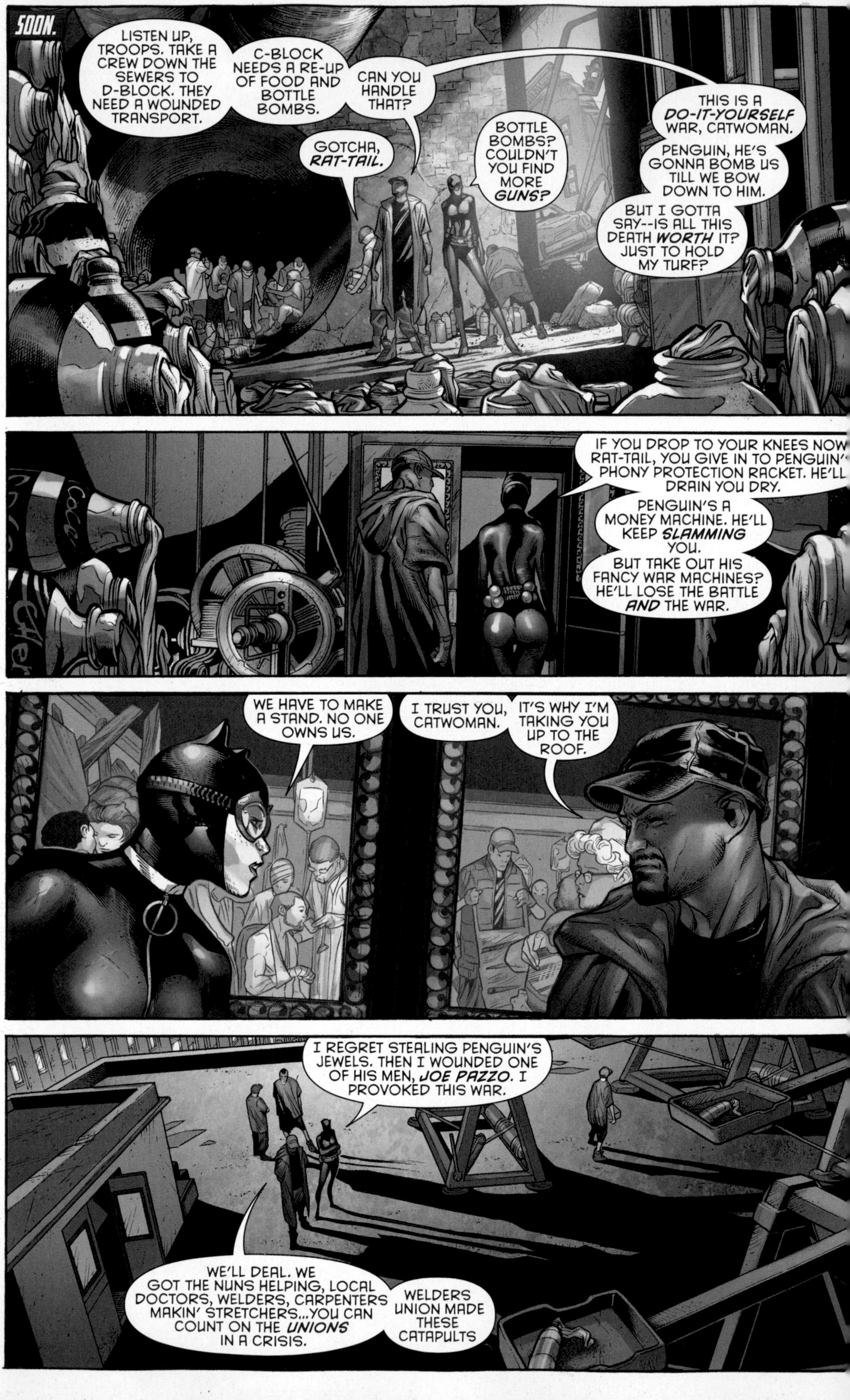

SOON.
LISTEN UP, TROOPS. TAKE A CREW DOWN THE SEWERS TO D-BLOCK. THEY NEED A WOUNDED TRANSPORT.
C-BLOCK NEEDS A RE-UP OF FOOD AND BOTTLE BOMBS.
CAN YOU HANDLE THAT?
GOTCHA, RAT-TAIL.
BOTTLE BOMBS? COULDN'T YOU FIND MORE GUNS?
THIS IS A DO-IT-YOURSELF WAR, CATWOMAN.
PENGUIN, HE'S GONNA BOMB US TILL WE BOW DOWN TO HIM.
BUT I GOTTA SAY--IS ALL THIS DEATH WORTH IT? JUST TO HOLD MY TURF?
IF YOU DROP TO YOUR KNEES NOW RAT-TAIL, YOU GIVE IN TO PENGUIN' PHONY PROTECTION RACKET. HE'LL DRAIN YOU DRY.
PENGUIN'S A MONEY MACHINE. HE'LL KEEP SLAMMING YOU.
BUT TAKE OUT HIS FANCY WAR MACHINES? HE'LL LOSE THE BATTLE AND THE WAR.
WE HAVE TO MAKE A STAND. NO ONE OWNS US.
I TRUST YOU, CATWOMAN.
IT'S WHY I'M TAKING YOU UP TO THE ROOF.
I REGRET STEALING PENGUIN'S JEWELS. THEN I WOUNDED ONE OF HIS MEN, JOE PAZZO. I PROVOKED THIS WAR.
WE'LL DEAL. WE GOT THE NUNS HELPING, LOCAL DOCTORS, WELDERS, CARPENTERS MAKIN' STRETCHERS...YOU CAN COUNT ON THE UNIONS IN A CRISIS.
WELDERS UNION MADE THESE CATAPULTS

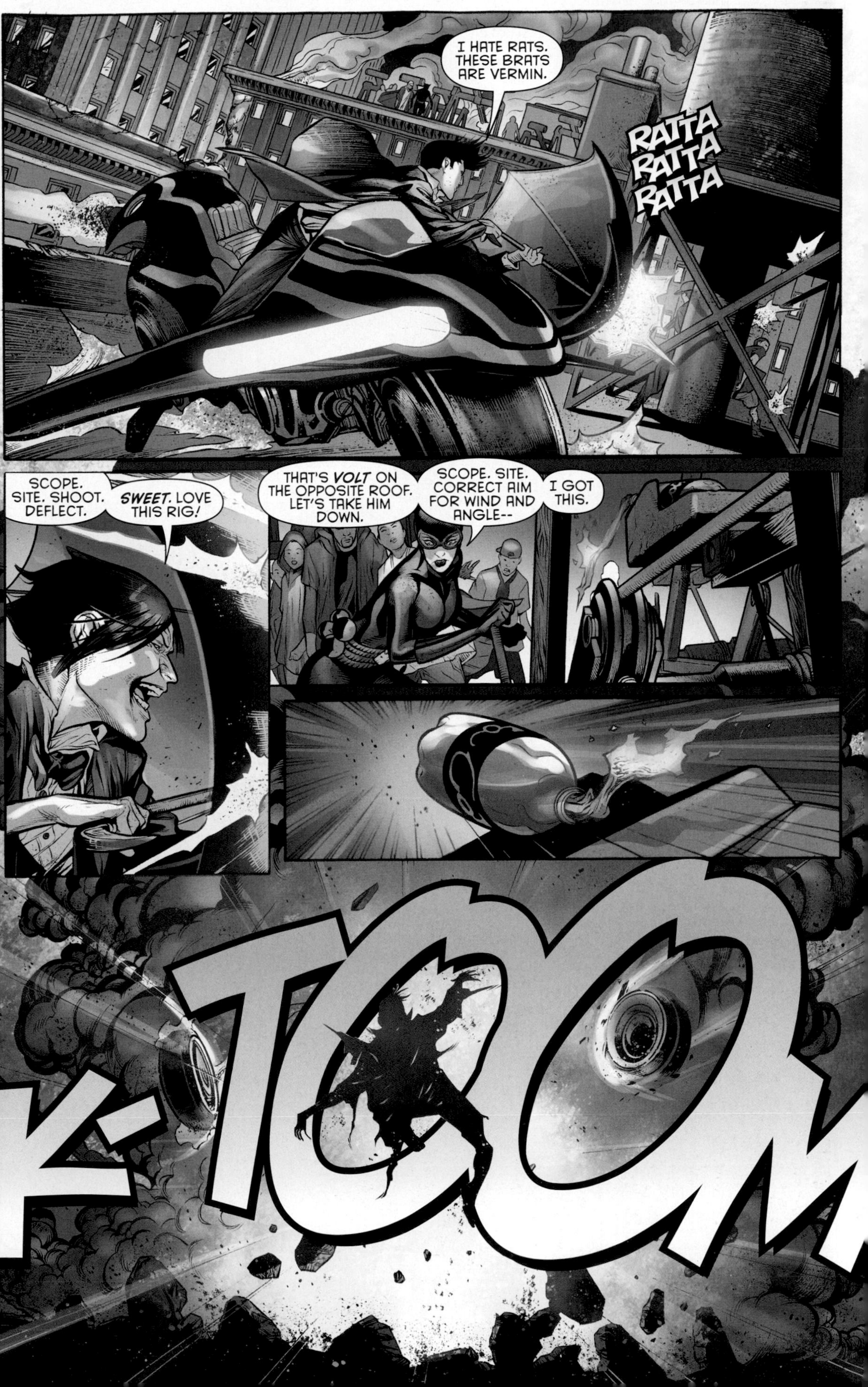
I HATE RATS. THESE BRATS ARE VERMIN.
RATTA RATTA RATTA
SCOPE. SITE. SHOOT. DEFLECT.
SWEET. LOVE THIS RIG!
THAT'S VOLT ON THE OPPOSITE ROOF. LET'S TAKE HIM DOWN.
SCOPE. SITE. CORRECT AIM FOR WIND AND ANGLE--
I GOT THIS.
K-TOOM

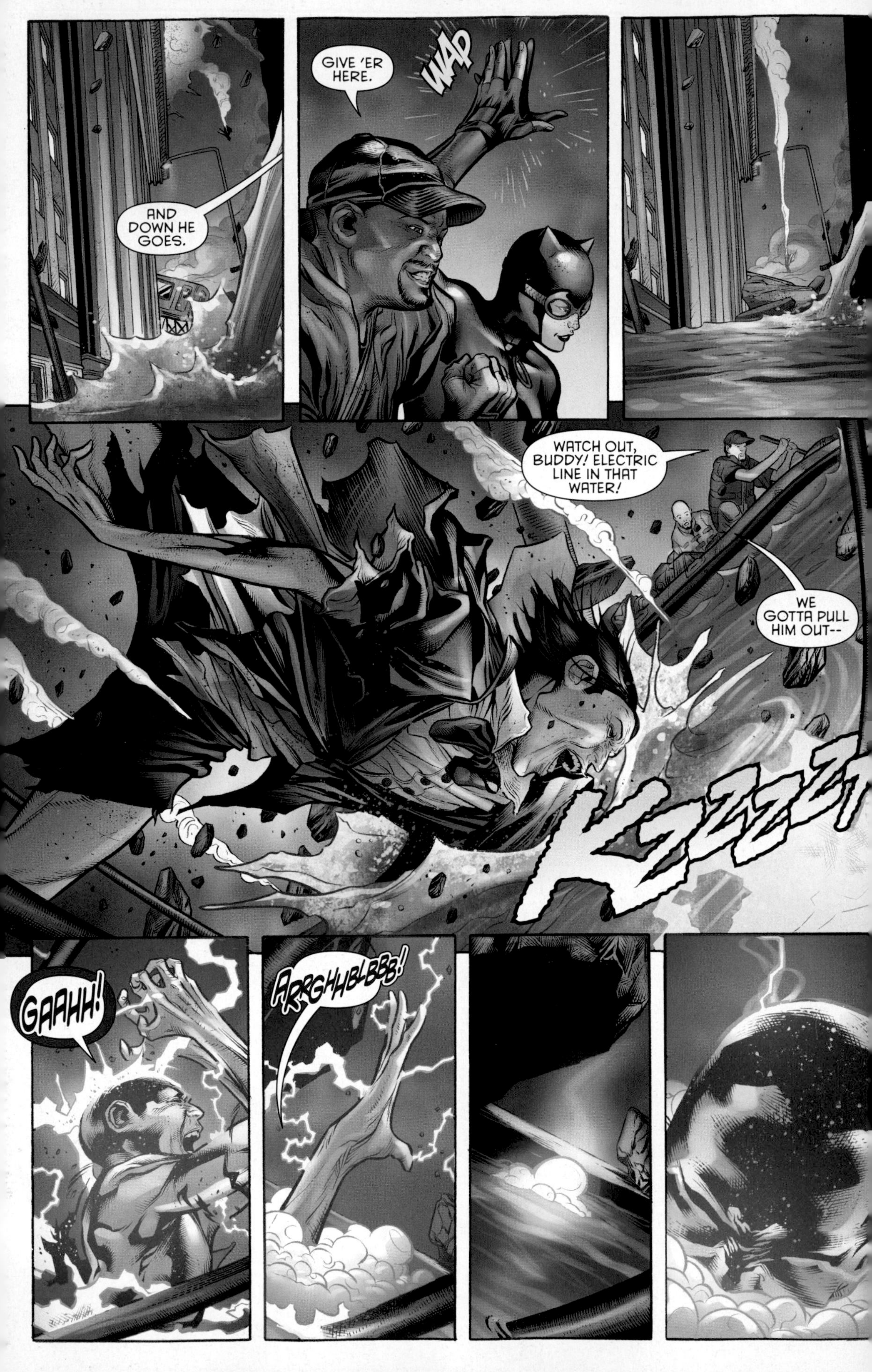
AND DOWN HE GOES.
GIVE 'ER HERE.
WAP
WATCH OUT, BUDDY! ELECTRIC LINE IN THAT WATER!
WE GOTTA PULL HIM OUT--
KZZZZT
GAAHH!
ARRGHHBLBBB!

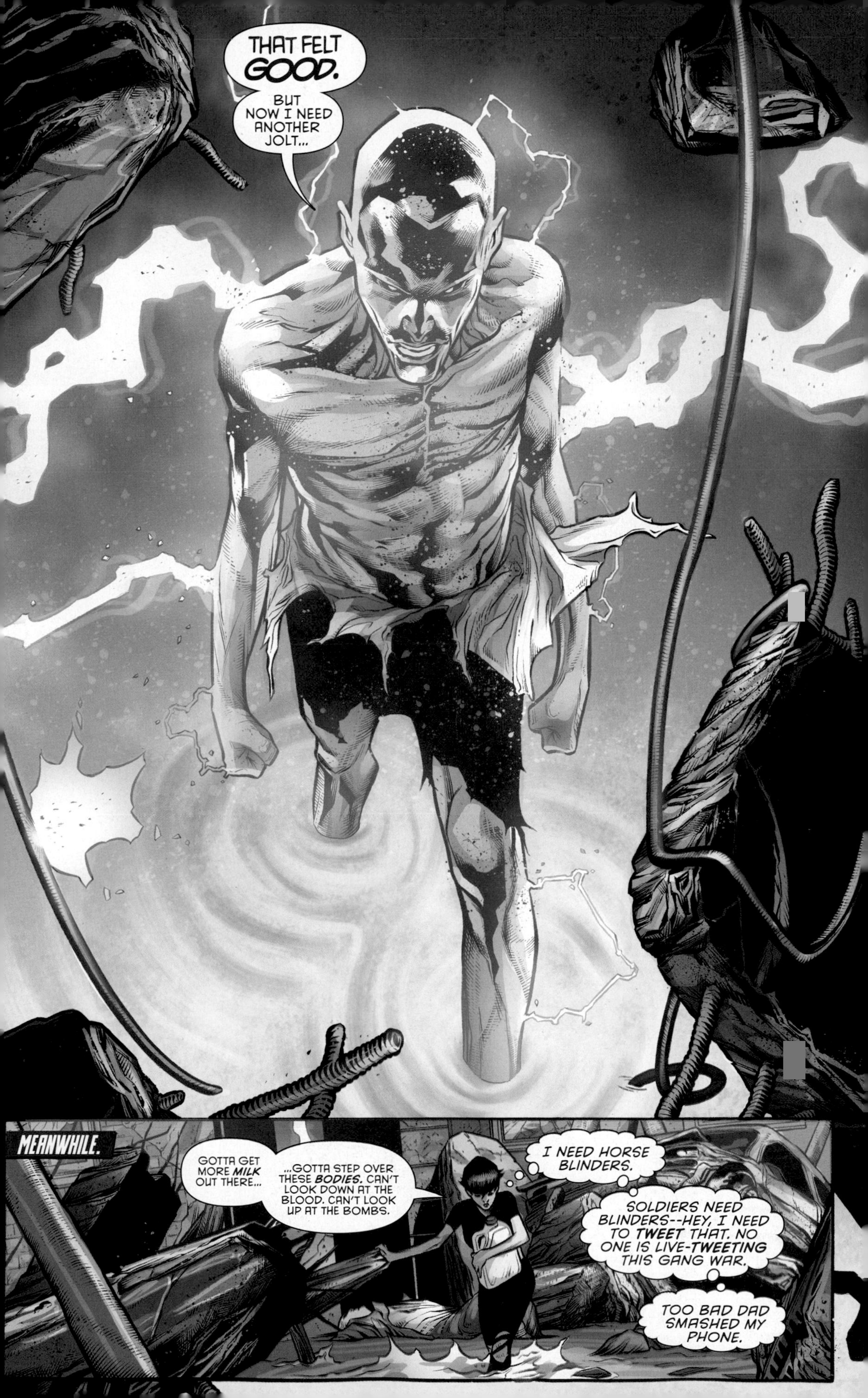
THAT FELT GOOD.
BUT NOW I NEED ANOTHER JOLT...
MEANWHILE.
GOTTA GET MORE MILK OUT THERE...
...GOTTA STEP OVER THESE BODIES. CAN'T LOOK DOWN AT THE BLOOD. CAN'T LOOK UP AT THE BOMBS.
I NEED HORSE BLINDERS.
SOLDIERS NEED BLINDERS--HEY, I NEED TO TWEET THAT. NO ONE IS LIVE-TWEETING THIS GANG WAR.
TOO BAD DAD SMASHED MY PHONE.

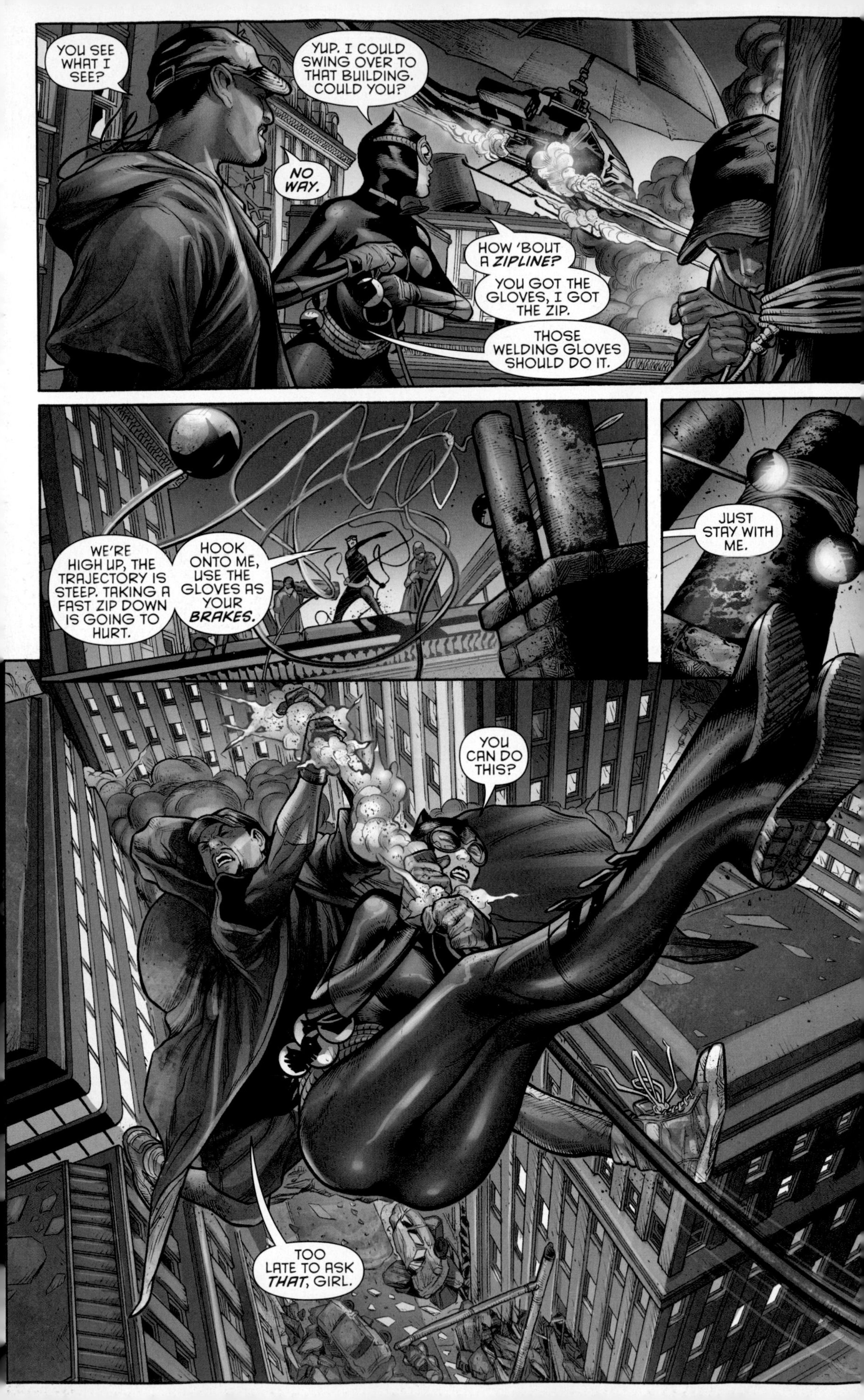
YOU SEE WHAT I SEE?
YUP. I COULD SWING OVER TO THAT BUILDING. COULD YOU?
NO WAY.
HOW 'BOUT A *ZIPLINE?*
YOU GOT THE GLOVES, I GOT THE ZIP.
THOSE WELDING GLOVES SHOULD DO IT.
WE'RE HIGH UP, THE TRAJECTORY IS STEEP. TAKING A FAST ZIP DOWN IS GOING TO HURT.
HOOK ONTO ME, USE THE GLOVES AS YOUR *BRAKES.*
JUST STAY WITH ME.
YOU CAN DO THIS?
TOO LATE TO ASK *THAT*, GIRL.

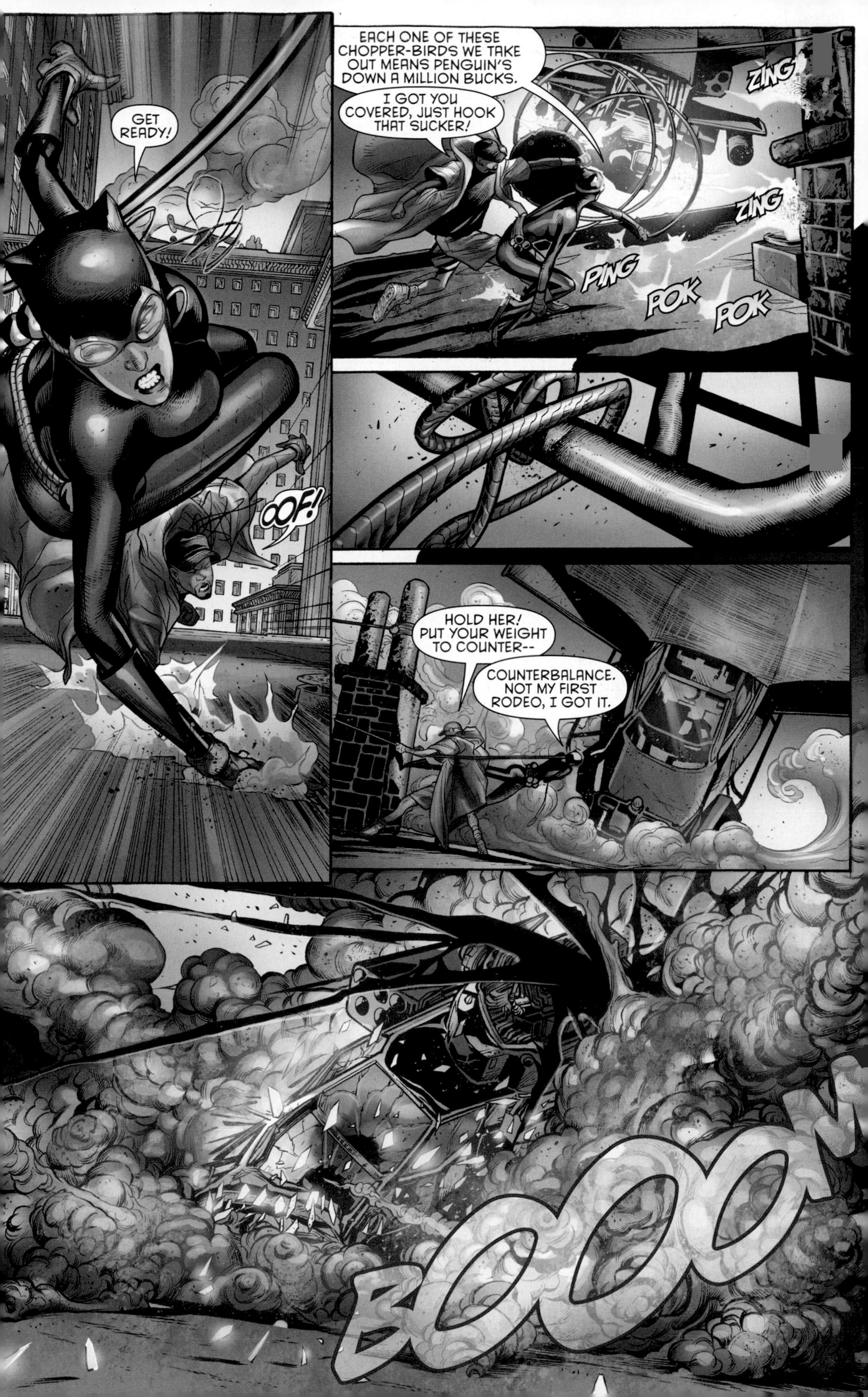
GET READY!
OOF!
EACH ONE OF THESE CHOPPER-BIRDS WE TAKE OUT MEANS PENGUIN'S DOWN A MILLION BUCKS.
I GOT YOU COVERED, JUST HOOK THAT SUCKER!
ZING
ZING
PING
POK
POK
HOLD HER! PUT YOUR WEIGHT TO COUNTER--
COUNTERBALANCE. NOT MY FIRST RODEO, I GOT IT.
BOOOOM

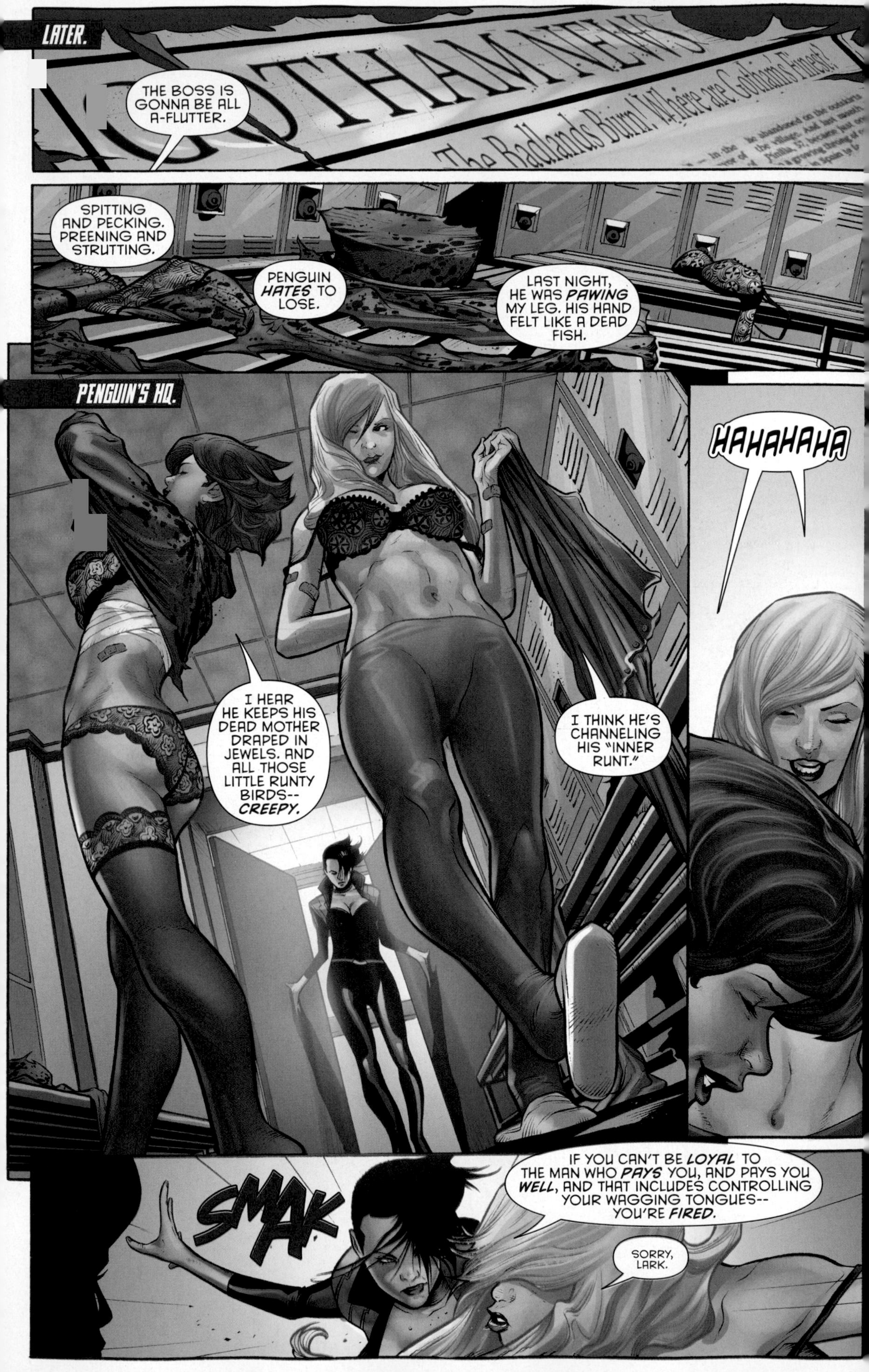

LATER.
The Badlands Burn! Where are Gotham's Finest?
THE BOSS IS GONNA BE ALL A-FLUTTER.
SPITTING AND PECKING. PREENING AND STRUTTING.
PENGUIN HATES TO LOSE.
LAST NIGHT, HE WAS PAWING MY LEG. HIS HAND FELT LIKE A DEAD FISH.
PENGUIN'S HQ.
I HEAR HE KEEPS HIS DEAD MOTHER DRAPED IN JEWELS. AND ALL THOSE LITTLE RUNTY BIRDS-- CREEPY.
I THINK HE'S CHANNELING HIS "INNER RUNT."
HAHAHAHA
SMAK
IF YOU CAN'T BE LOYAL TO THE MAN WHO PAYS YOU, AND PAYS YOU WELL, AND THAT INCLUDES CONTROLLING YOUR WAGGING TONGUES-- YOU'RE FIRED.
SORRY, LARK.

GOTHAM NEWS

GANG WAR in the BADLANDS!

Death toll hits 20. Where is Mayor Hady

GOTHAM CITY MORGUE.

THE BADLANDS IS A CESSPOOL, LIEUTENANT. IT'S NOT WORTH RISKING BOOTS ON THE GROUND.

THESE ARE GANG *MURDERS* WE'RE TALKING ABOUT. PLEASE, *MAYOR HADY*. IF YOU WON'T LET MY MEN GO IN, THEY WILL BE *UNSOLVED* MURDERS.

I'LL AUTHORIZE AERIAL SURVEILLANCE. USE SHARPSHOOTERS, *BULLOCK*. BUT KEEP YOUR MEN OFF THE GROUND TILL THIS IS OVER.

LET THE WORST OF THEM KILL EACH OTHER OFF. THEN WE'LL HEAD IN AND TAKE OUT THE GARBAGE.

YOU'RE GIVING COBBLEPOT A *FREE PASS* TO BOMB THE BADLANDS?

YOU SCREW THIS UP, I AIN'T GOIN' DOWN WITH YOU.

WHERE'S YOUR PAL, *BATMAN?* GET HIM TO TAKE OUT THE GARBAGE.

HE'S GONE ROUND THE BEND, AND YOU KNOW IT.

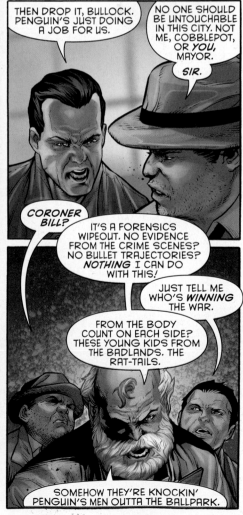

THEN DROP IT, BULLOCK. PENGUIN'S JUST DOING A JOB FOR US.

NO ONE SHOULD BE UNTOUCHABLE IN THIS CITY. NOT ME, COBBLEPOT, OR *YOU*, MAYOR.

SIR.

CORONER BILL?

IT'S A FORENSICS WIPEOUT. NO EVIDENCE FROM THE CRIME SCENES? NO BULLET TRAJECTORIES? *NOTHING* I CAN DO WITH THIS!

JUST TELL ME WHO'S *WINNING* THE WAR.

FROM THE BODY COUNT ON EACH SIDE? THESE YOUNG KIDS FROM THE BADLANDS. THE RAT-TAILS.

SOMEHOW THEY'RE KNOCKIN' PENGUIN'S MEN OUTTA THE BALLPARK.

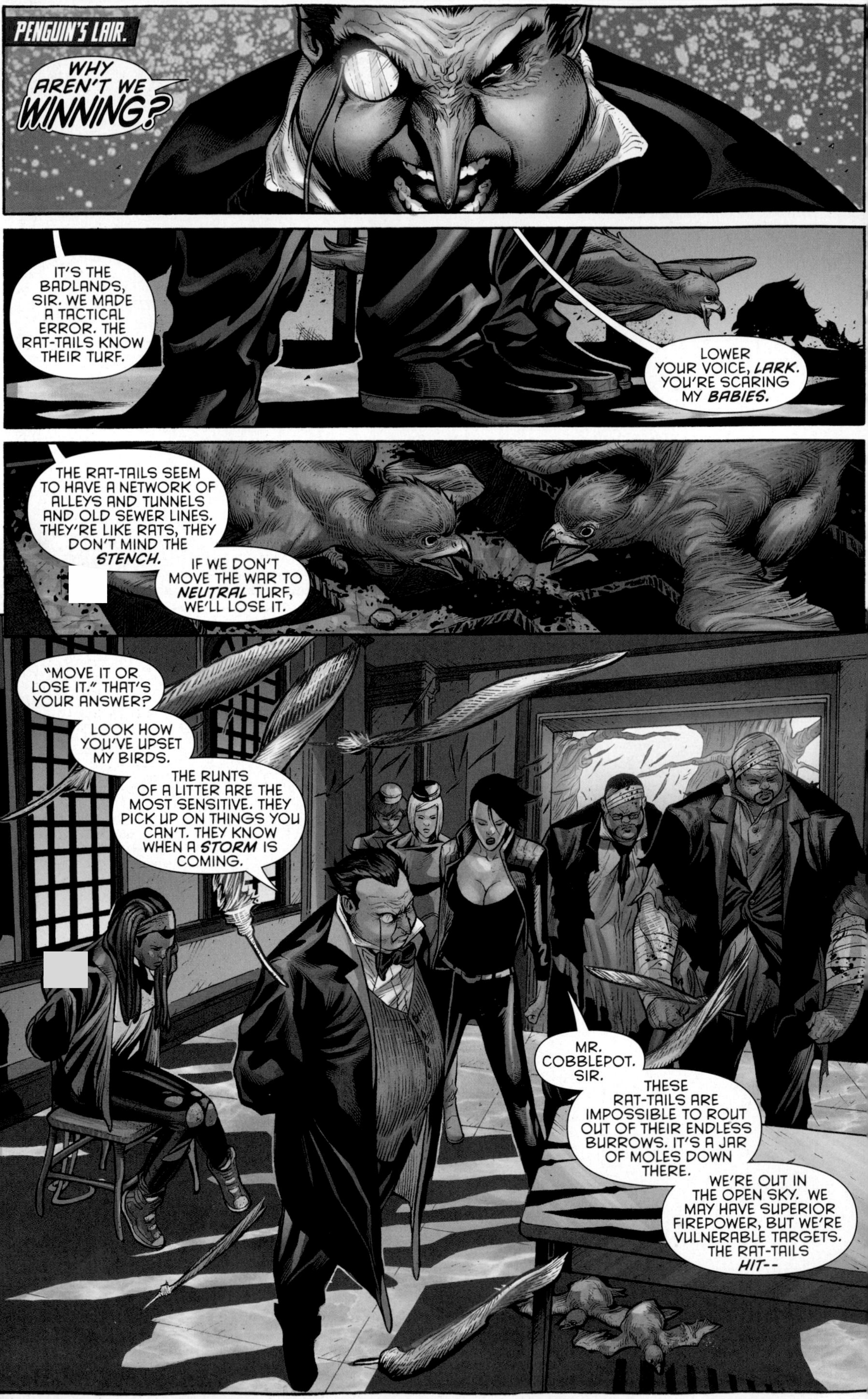
PENGUIN'S LAIR.
WHY AREN'T WE WINNING?
IT'S THE BADLANDS, SIR. WE MADE A TACTICAL ERROR. THE RAT-TAILS KNOW THEIR TURF.
LOWER YOUR VOICE, LARK. YOU'RE SCARING MY BABIES.
THE RAT-TAILS SEEM TO HAVE A NETWORK OF ALLEYS AND TUNNELS AND OLD SEWER LINES. THEY'RE LIKE RATS, THEY DON'T MIND THE STENCH.
IF WE DON'T MOVE THE WAR TO NEUTRAL TURF, WE'LL LOSE IT.
"MOVE IT OR LOSE IT." THAT'S YOUR ANSWER?
LOOK HOW YOU'VE UPSET MY BIRDS.
THE RUNTS OF A LITTER ARE THE MOST SENSITIVE. THEY PICK UP ON THINGS YOU CAN'T. THEY KNOW WHEN A STORM IS COMING.
MR. COBBLEPOT. SIR.
THESE RAT-TAILS ARE IMPOSSIBLE TO ROUT OUT OF THEIR ENDLESS BURROWS. IT'S A JAR OF MOLES DOWN THERE.
WE'RE OUT IN THE OPEN SKY. WE MAY HAVE SUPERIOR FIREPOWER, BUT WE'RE VULNERABLE TARGETS. THE RAT-TAILS HIT--

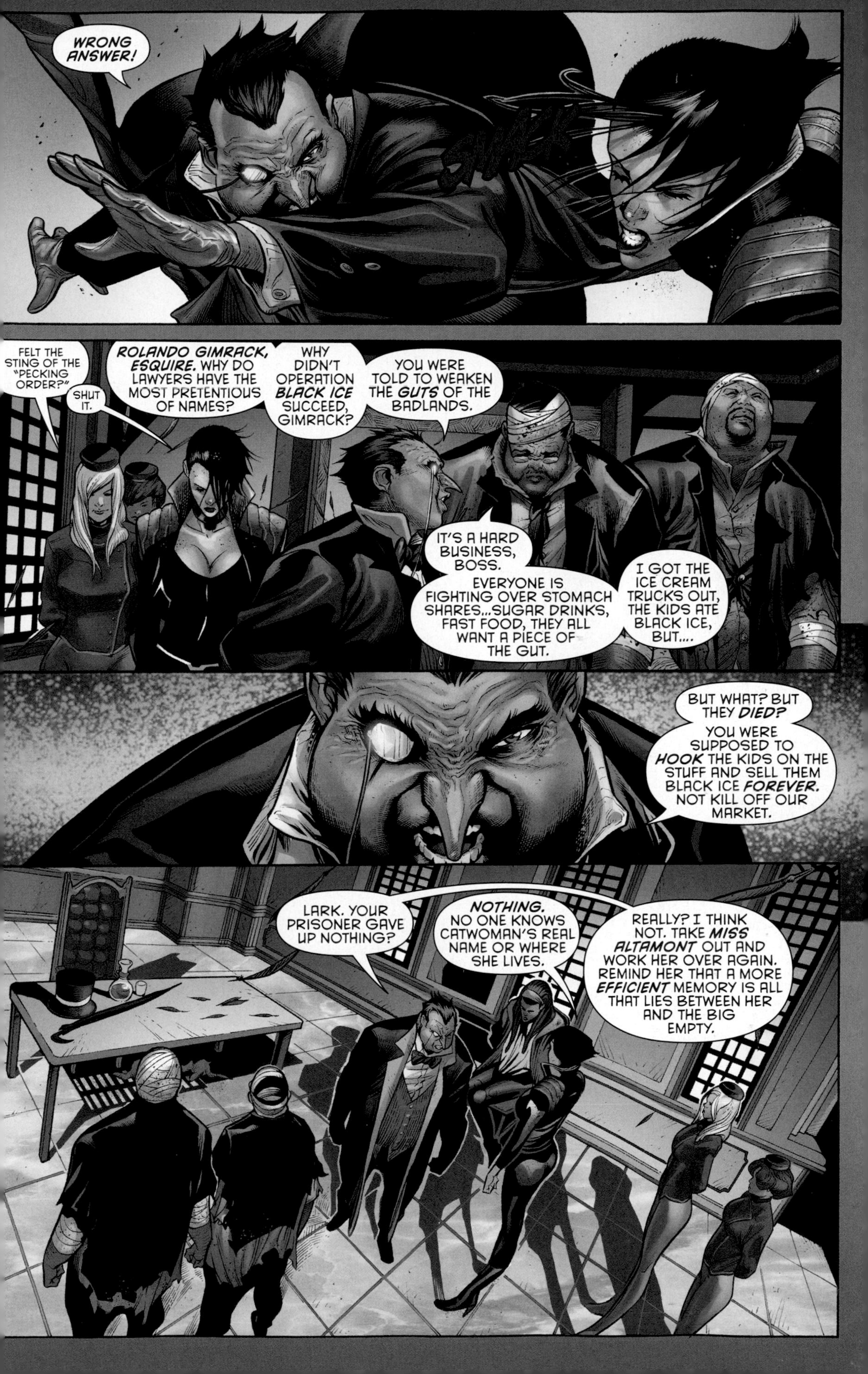
WRONG ANSWER!
SMAK
FELT THE STING OF THE "PECKING ORDER?"
SHUT IT.
ROLANDO GIMRACK, ESQUIRE. WHY DO LAWYERS HAVE THE MOST PRETENTIOUS OF NAMES?
WHY DIDN'T OPERATION BLACK ICE SUCCEED, GIMRACK?
YOU WERE TOLD TO WEAKEN THE GUTS OF THE BADLANDS.
IT'S A HARD BUSINESS, BOSS.
EVERYONE IS FIGHTING OVER STOMACH SHARES...SUGAR DRINKS, FAST FOOD, THEY ALL WANT A PIECE OF THE GUT.
I GOT THE ICE CREAM TRUCKS OUT, THE KIDS ATE BLACK ICE, BUT....
BUT WHAT? BUT THEY DIED?
YOU WERE SUPPOSED TO HOOK THE KIDS ON THE STUFF AND SELL THEM BLACK ICE FOREVER. NOT KILL OFF OUR MARKET.
LARK. YOUR PRISONER GAVE UP NOTHING?
NOTHING. NO ONE KNOWS CATWOMAN'S REAL NAME OR WHERE SHE LIVES.
REALLY? I THINK NOT. TAKE MISS ALTAMONT OUT AND WORK HER OVER AGAIN. REMIND HER THAT A MORE EFFICIENT MEMORY IS ALL THAT LIES BETWEEN HER AND THE BIG EMPTY.

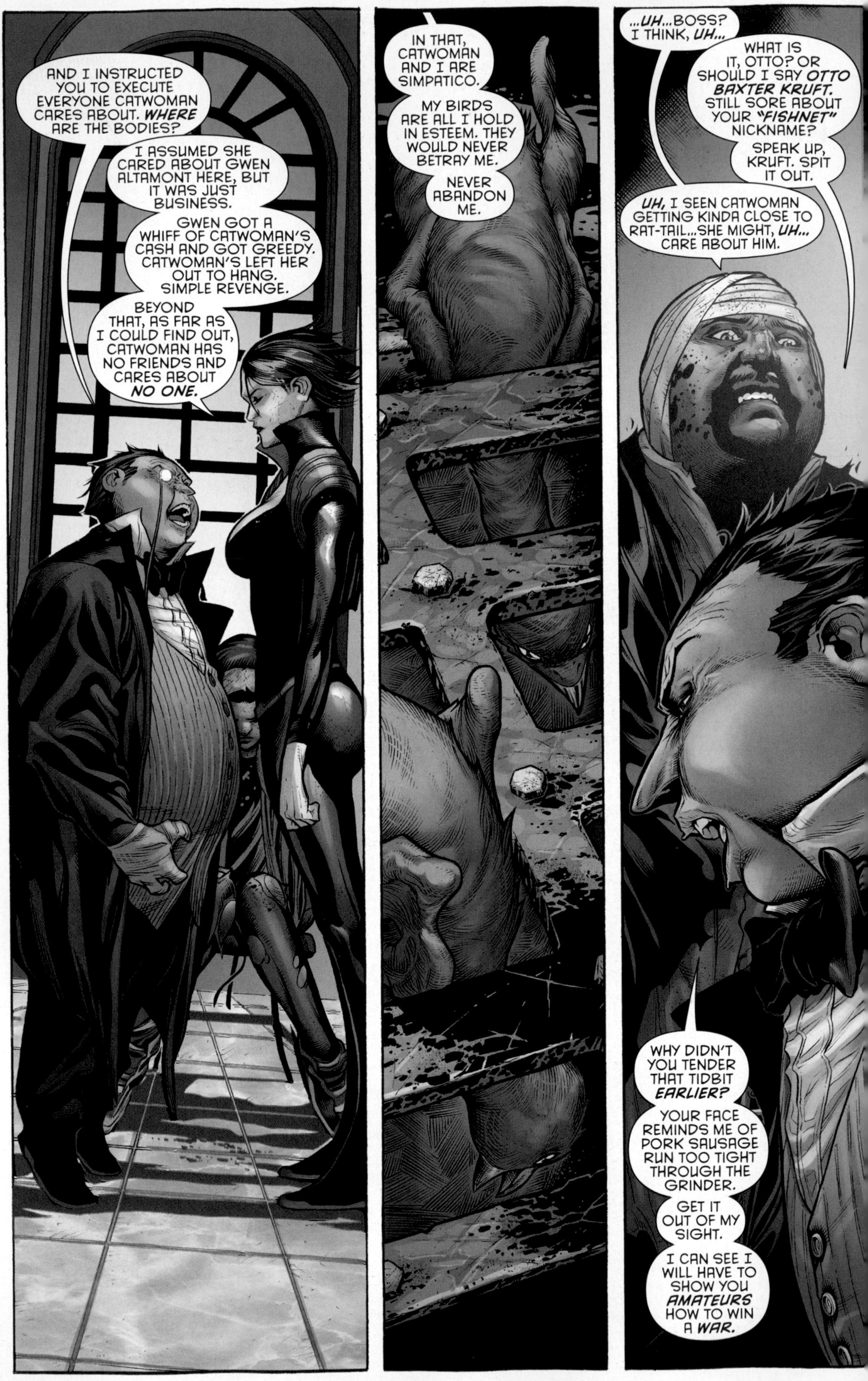
AND I INSTRUCTED YOU TO EXECUTE EVERYONE CATWOMAN CARES ABOUT. WHERE ARE THE BODIES?
I ASSUMED SHE CARED ABOUT GWEN ALTAMONT HERE, BUT IT WAS JUST BUSINESS.
GWEN GOT A WHIFF OF CATWOMAN'S CASH AND GOT GREEDY. CATWOMAN'S LEFT HER OUT TO HANG. SIMPLE REVENGE.
BEYOND THAT, AS FAR AS I COULD FIND OUT, CATWOMAN HAS NO FRIENDS AND CARES ABOUT NO ONE.
IN THAT, CATWOMAN AND I ARE SIMPATICO.
MY BIRDS ARE ALL I HOLD IN ESTEEM. THEY WOULD NEVER BETRAY ME.
NEVER ABANDON ME.
...UH...BOSS? I THINK, UH...
WHAT IS IT, OTTO? OR SHOULD I SAY OTTO BAXTER KRUFT. STILL SORE ABOUT YOUR "FISHNET" NICKNAME?
SPEAK UP, KRUFT. SPIT IT OUT.
UH, I SEEN CATWOMAN GETTING KINDA CLOSE TO RAT-TAIL...SHE MIGHT, UH... CARE ABOUT HIM.
WHY DIDN'T YOU TENDER THAT TIDBIT EARLIER?
YOUR FACE REMINDS ME OF PORK SAUSAGE RUN TOO TIGHT THROUGH THE GRINDER.
GET IT OUT OF MY SIGHT.
I CAN SEE I WILL HAVE TO SHOW YOU AMATEURS HOW TO WIN A WAR.

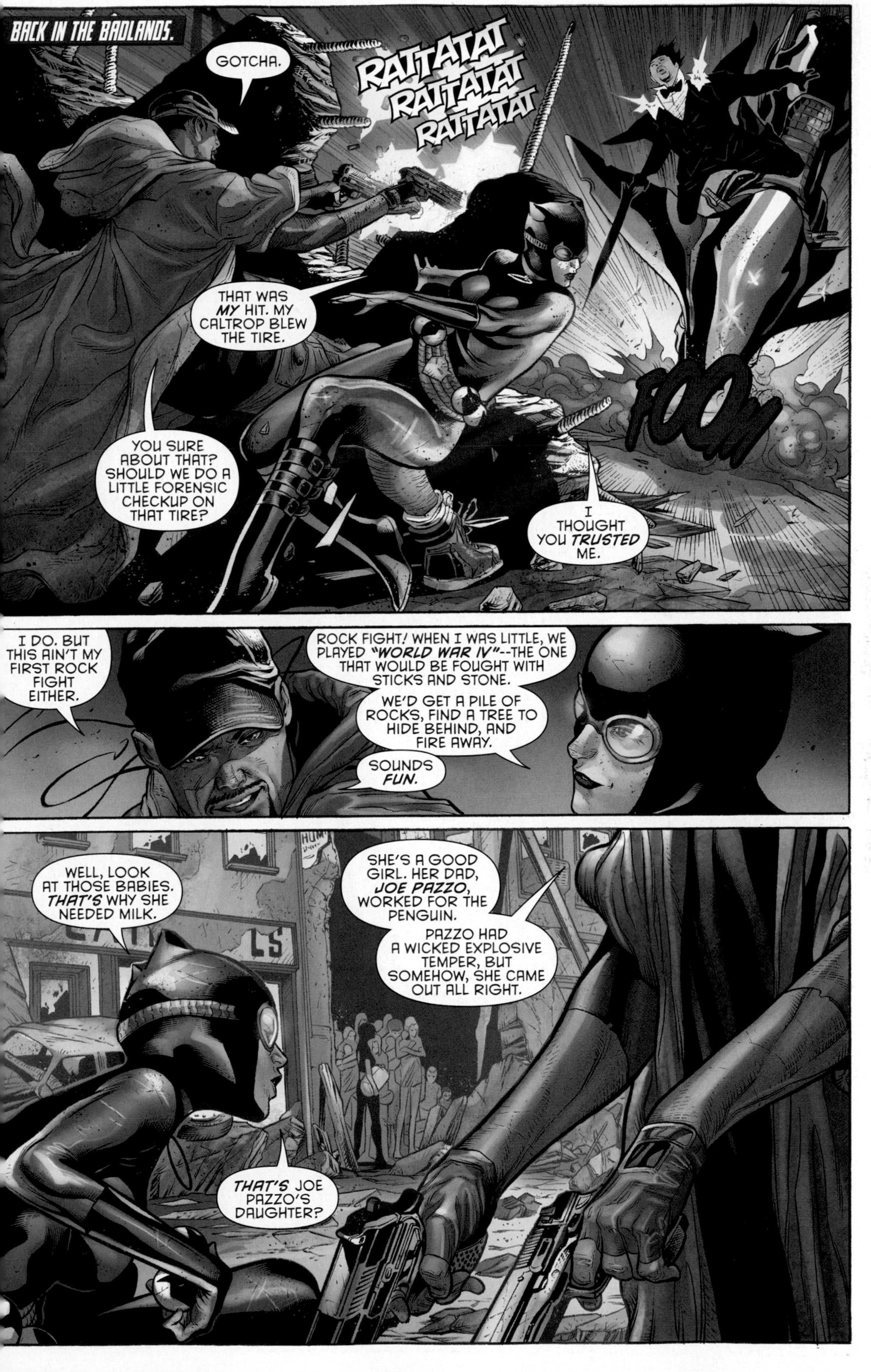
BACK IN THE BADLANDS.
GOTCHA.
RATTATAT RATTATAT RATTATAT
THAT WAS MY HIT. MY CALTROP BLEW THE TIRE.
YOU SURE ABOUT THAT? SHOULD WE DO A LITTLE FORENSIC CHECKUP ON THAT TIRE?
FOOM
I THOUGHT YOU TRUSTED ME.
I DO. BUT THIS AIN'T MY FIRST ROCK FIGHT EITHER.
ROCK FIGHT! WHEN I WAS LITTLE, WE PLAYED "WORLD WAR IV"--THE ONE THAT WOULD BE FOUGHT WITH STICKS AND STONE.
WE'D GET A PILE OF ROCKS, FIND A TREE TO HIDE BEHIND, AND FIRE AWAY.
SOUNDS FUN.
WELL, LOOK AT THOSE BABIES. THAT'S WHY SHE NEEDED MILK.
SHE'S A GOOD GIRL. HER DAD, JOE PAZZO, WORKED FOR THE PENGUIN.
PAZZO HAD A WICKED EXPLOSIVE TEMPER, BUT SOMEHOW, SHE CAME OUT ALL RIGHT.
THAT'S JOE PAZZO'S DAUGHTER?

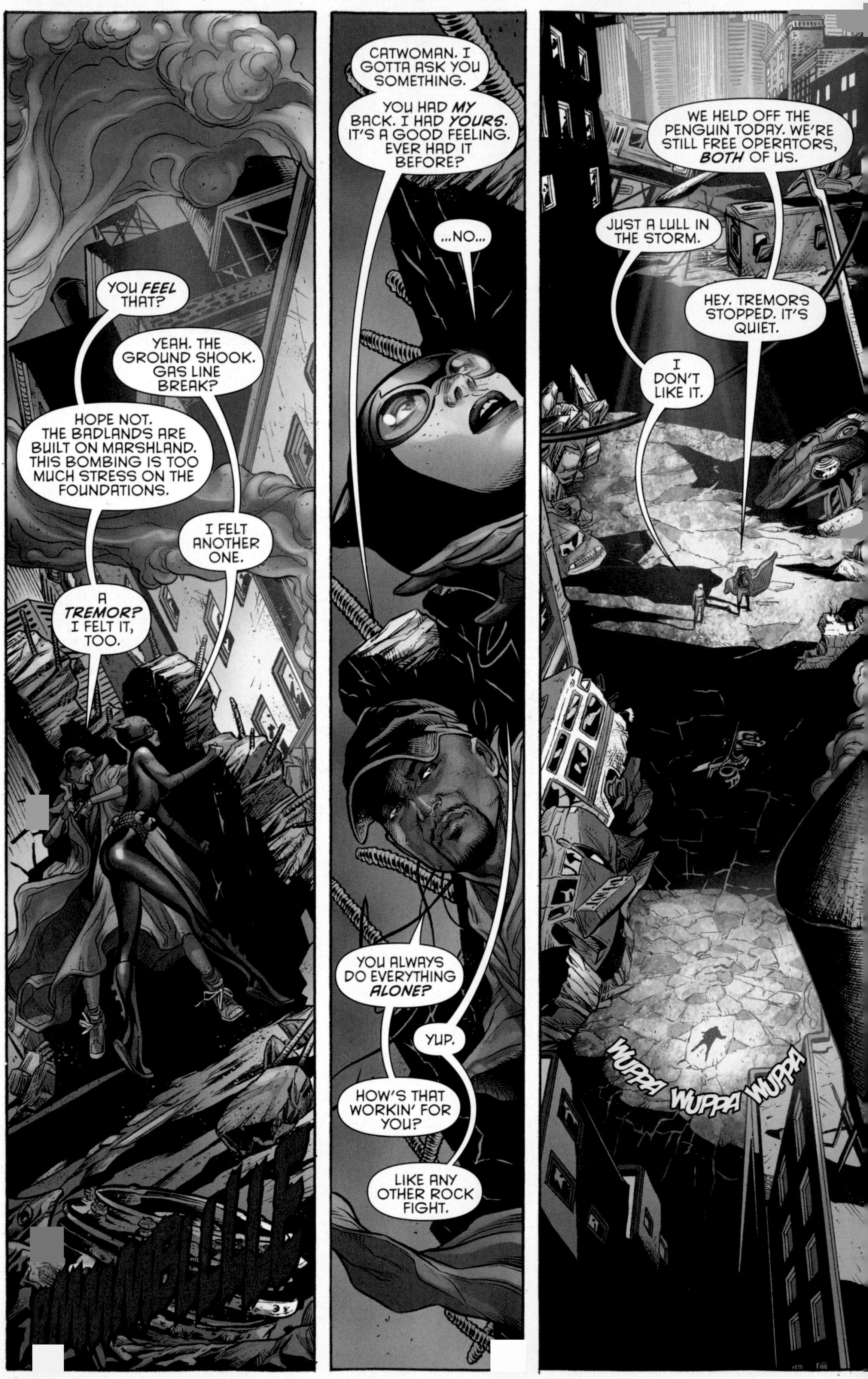
YOU FEEL THAT?
YEAH. THE GROUND SHOOK. GAS LINE BREAK?
HOPE NOT. THE BADLANDS ARE BUILT ON MARSHLAND. THIS BOMBING IS TOO MUCH STRESS ON THE FOUNDATIONS.
I FELT ANOTHER ONE.
A TREMOR? I FELT IT, TOO.
CATWOMAN. I GOTTA ASK YOU SOMETHING.
YOU HAD MY BACK. I HAD YOURS. IT'S A GOOD FEELING. EVER HAD IT BEFORE?
...NO...
YOU ALWAYS DO EVERYTHING ALONE?
YUP.
HOW'S THAT WORKIN' FOR YOU?
LIKE ANY OTHER ROCK FIGHT.
WE HELD OFF THE PENGUIN TODAY. WE'RE STILL FREE OPERATORS, BOTH OF US.
JUST A LULL IN THE STORM.
HEY. TREMORS STOPPED. IT'S QUIET.
I DON'T LIKE IT.
WUPPA WUPPA WUPPA

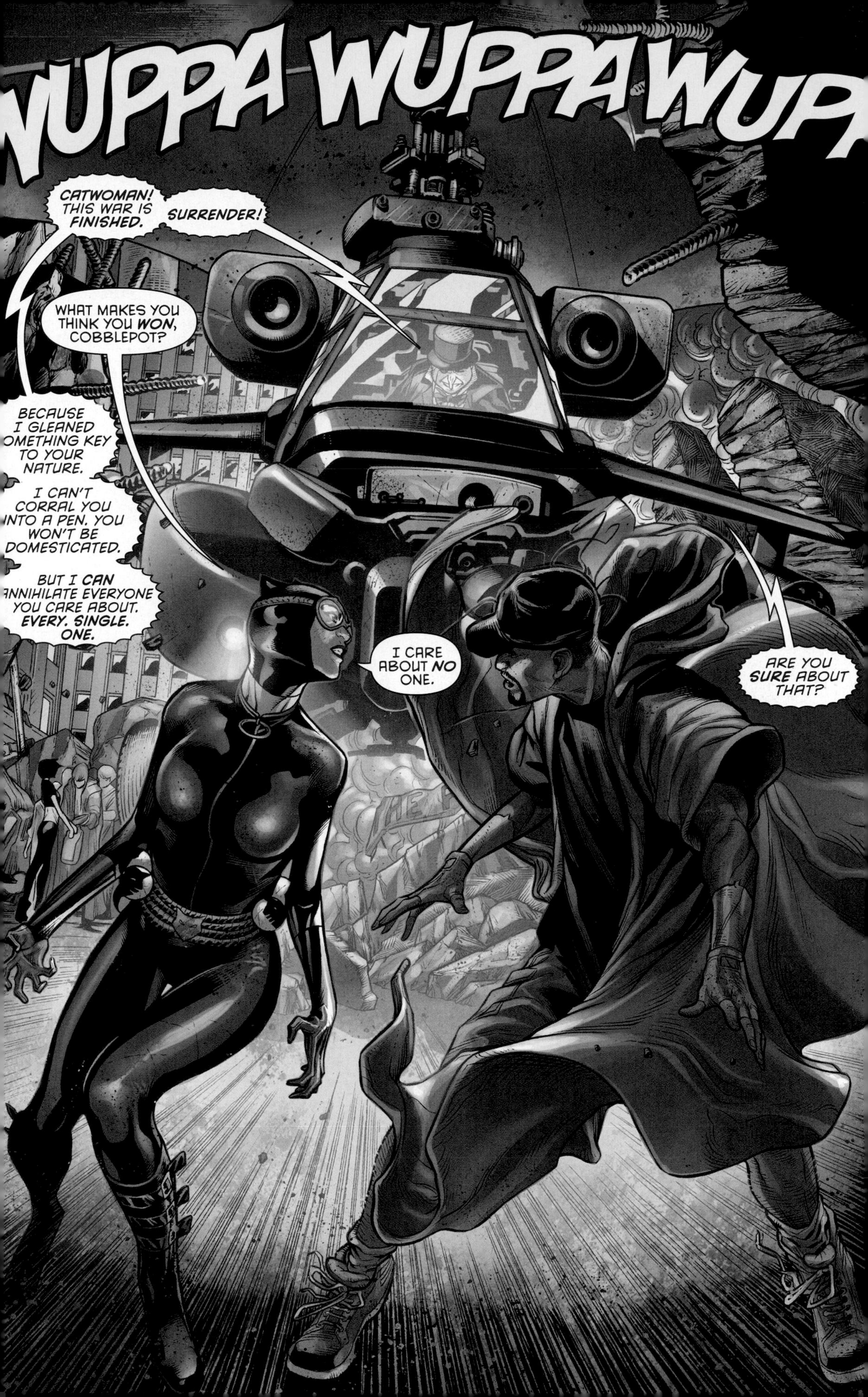
WUPPA WUPPA WUPP
CATWOMAN! THIS WAR IS FINISHED.
SURRENDER!
WHAT MAKES YOU THINK YOU WON, COBBLEPOT?
BECAUSE I GLEANED OMETHING KEY TO YOUR NATURE.
I CAN'T CORRAL YOU INTO A PEN. YOU WON'T BE DOMESTICATED.
BUT I CAN ANNIHILATE EVERYONE YOU CARE ABOUT. EVERY. SINGLE. ONE.
I CARE ABOUT NO ONE.
ARE YOU SURE ABOUT THAT?

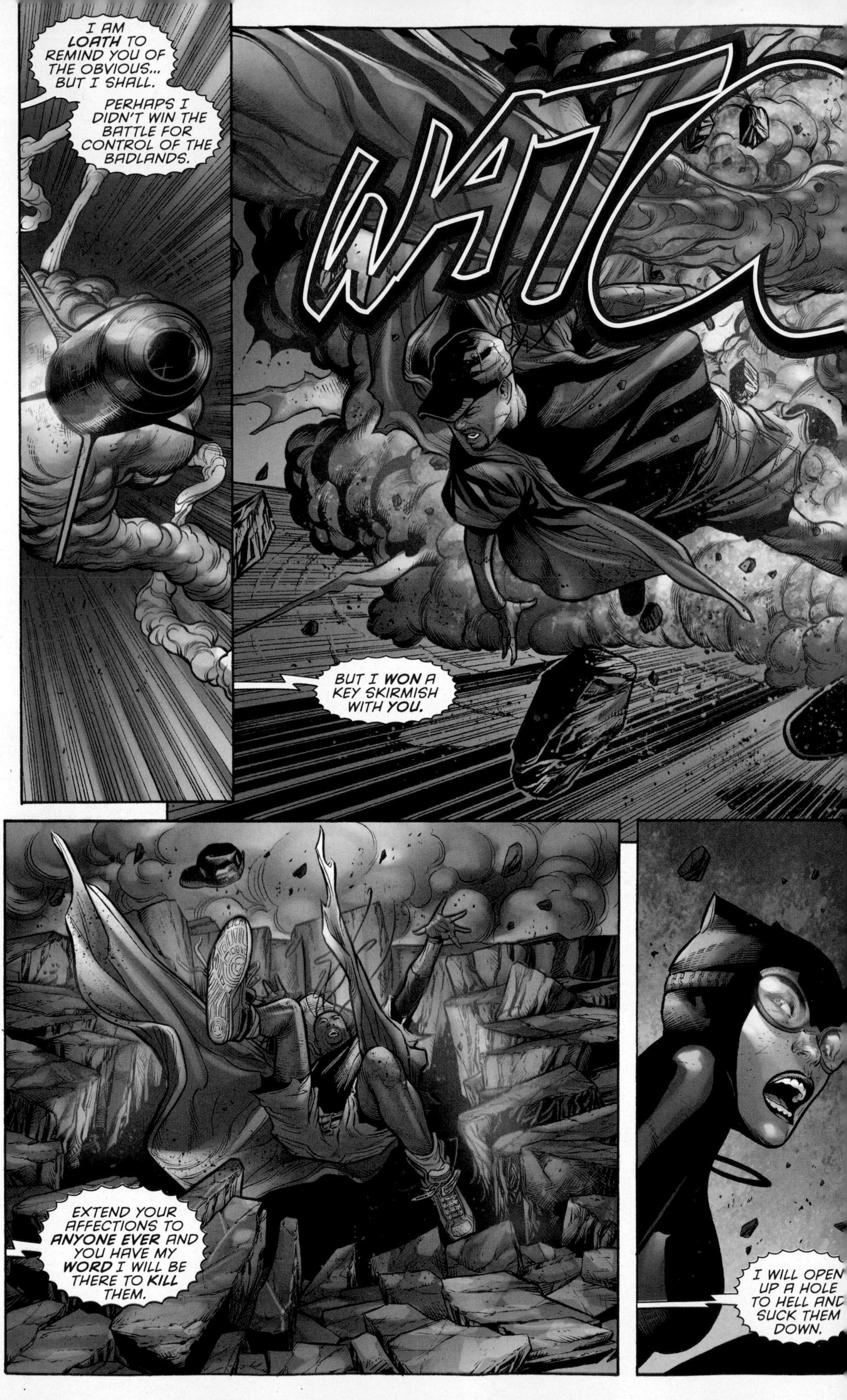
I AM LOATH TO REMIND YOU OF THE OBVIOUS... BUT I SHALL.
PERHAPS I DIDN'T WIN THE BATTLE FOR CONTROL OF THE BADLANDS.
WATC
BUT I WON A KEY SKIRMISH WITH YOU.
EXTEND YOUR AFFECTIONS TO ANYONE EVER AND YOU HAVE MY WORD I WILL BE THERE TO KILL THEM.
I WILL OPEN UP A HOLE TO HELL AND SUCK THEM DOWN.

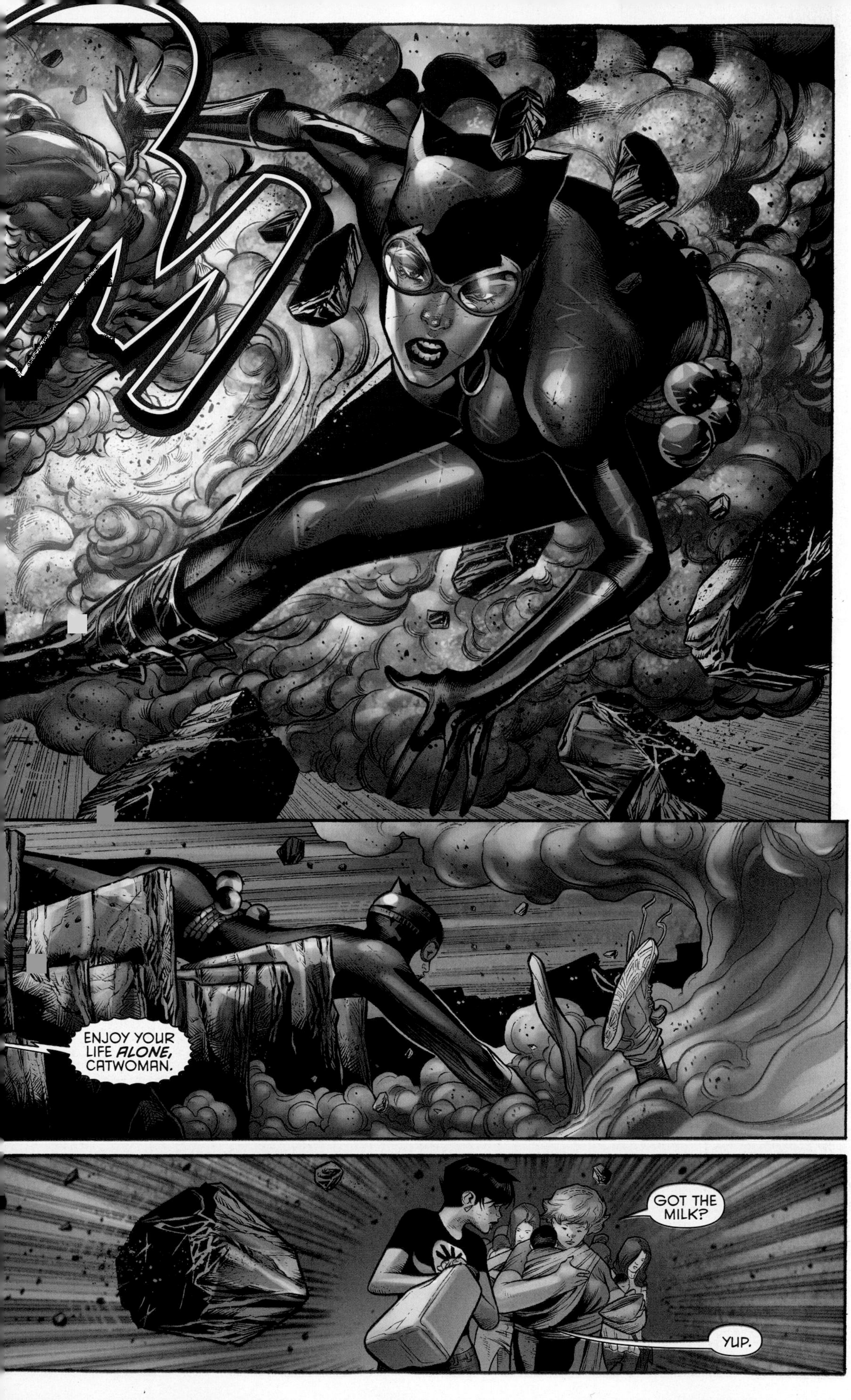
ENJOY YOUR LIFE ALONE, CATWOMAN.
GOT THE MILK?
YUP.

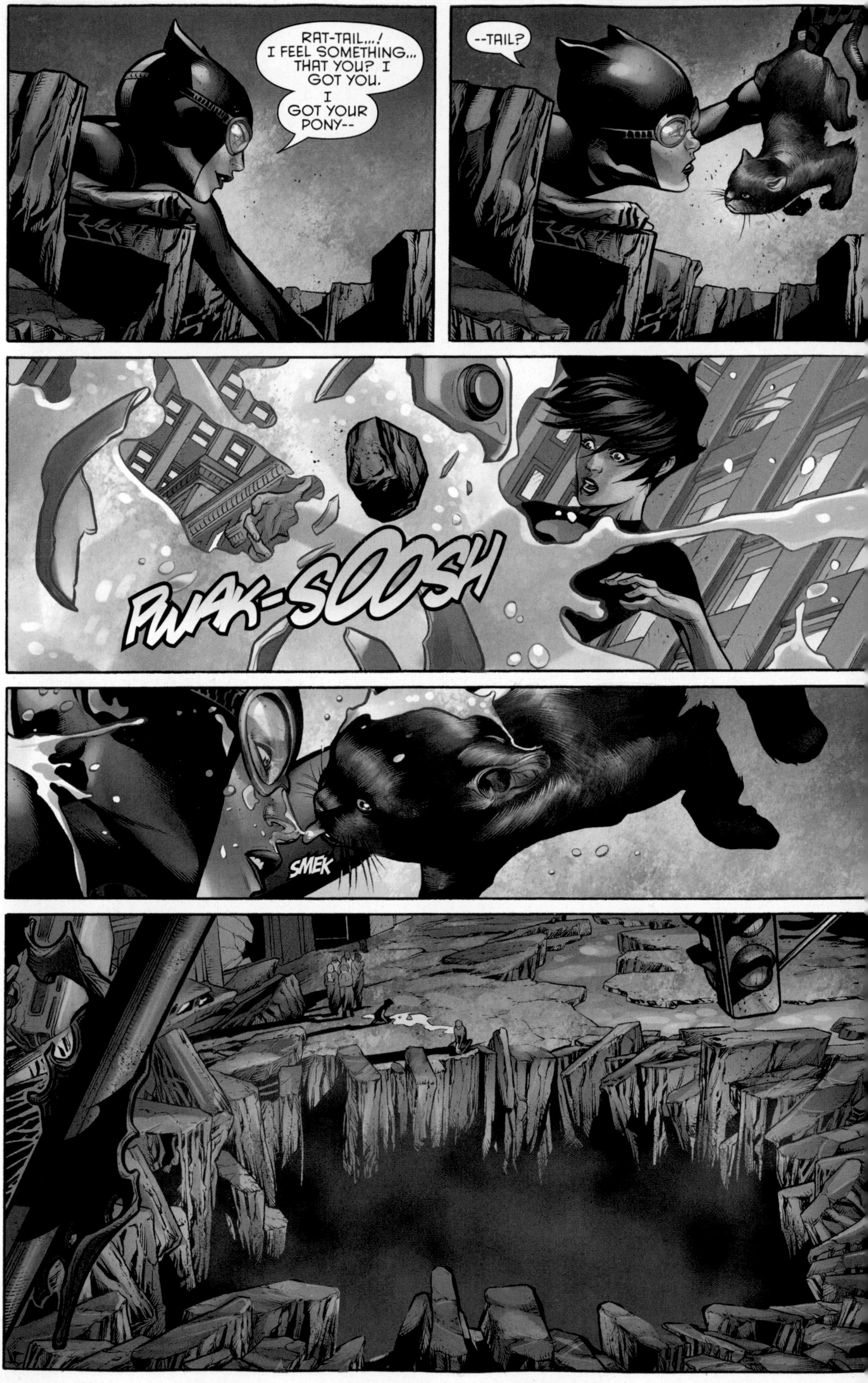
RAT-TAIL...! I FEEL SOMETHING... THAT YOU? I GOT YOU. I GOT YOUR PONY--
--TAIL?
PWAK-SLOOSH
SMEK

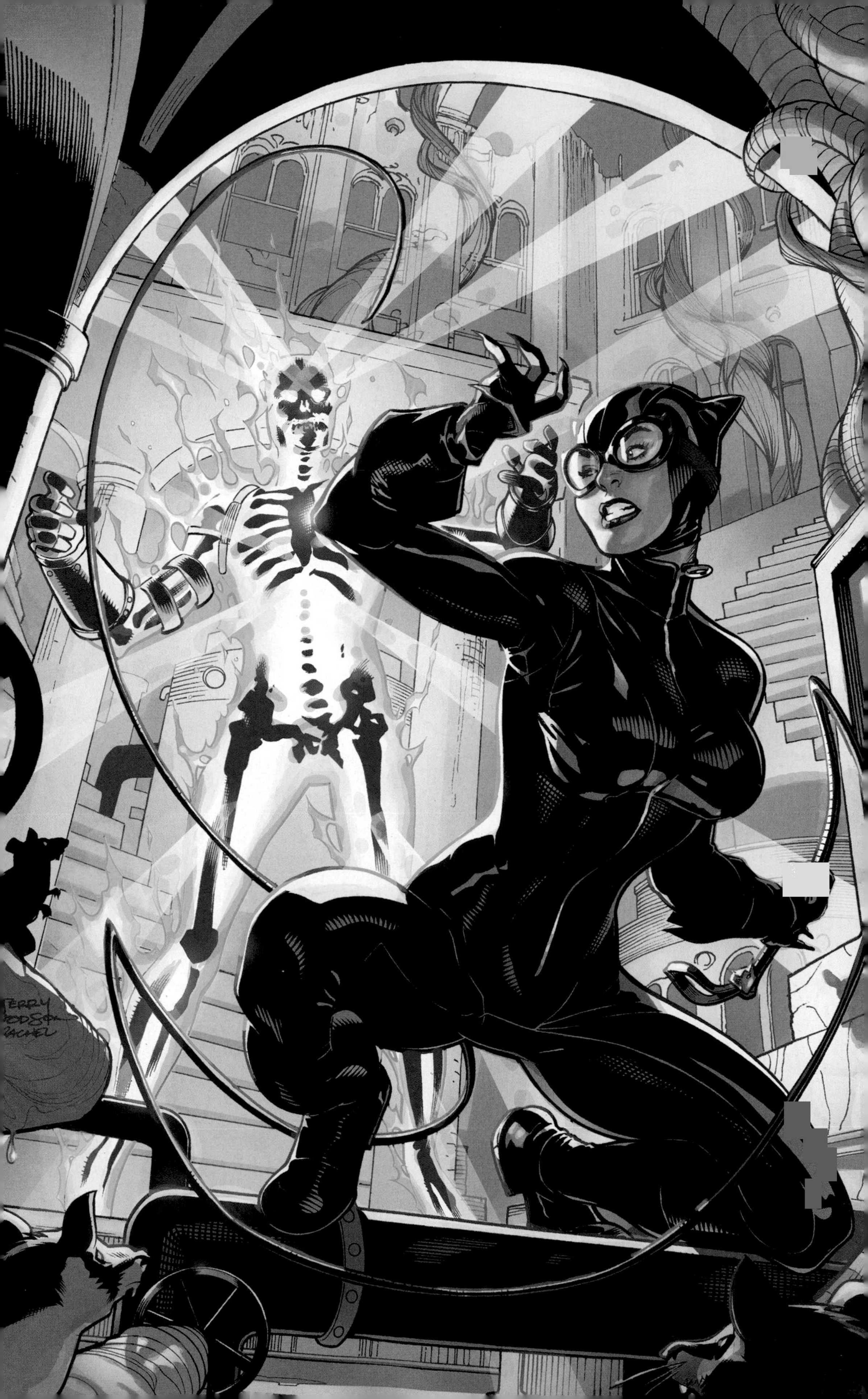
TERRY
DODSON
RACHEL

ANN NOCENTI
writer

RAFA SANDOVAL
penciller

SCOTT McDANIEL
breakdown artist

JORDI TARRAGONA
inker

SONIA OBACK
colorist

TERRY & RACHEL DODSON
cover artists

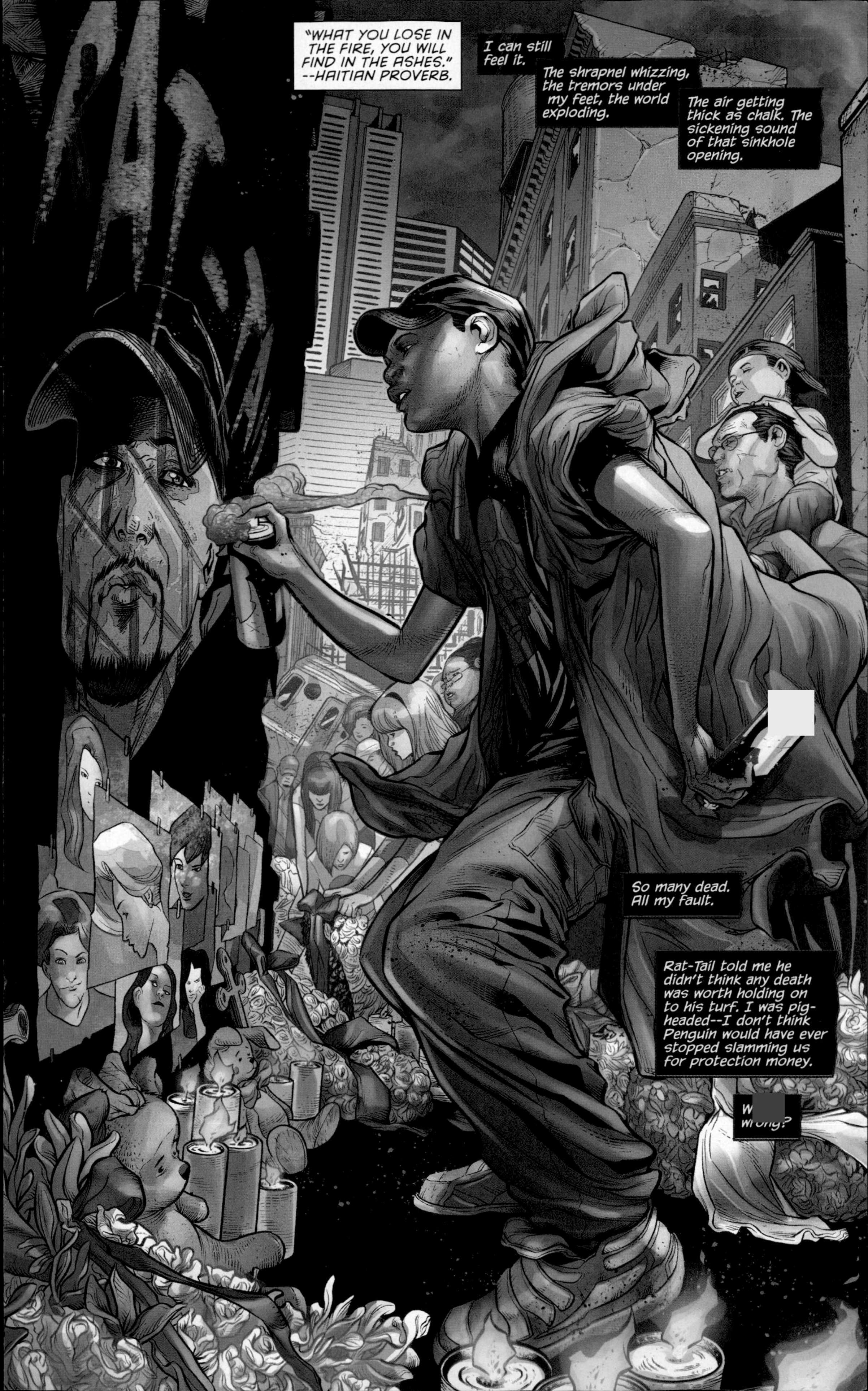
"WHAT YOU LOSE IN THE FIRE, YOU WILL FIND IN THE ASHES." --HAITIAN PROVERB.
I can still feel it.
The shrapnel whizzing, the tremors under my feet, the world exploding.
The air getting thick as chalk. The sickening sound of that sinkhole opening.
So many dead. All my fault.
Rat-Tail told me he didn't think any death was worth holding on to his turf. I was pig-headed--I don't think Penguin would have ever stopped slamming us for protection money.
W[redacted] wrong?

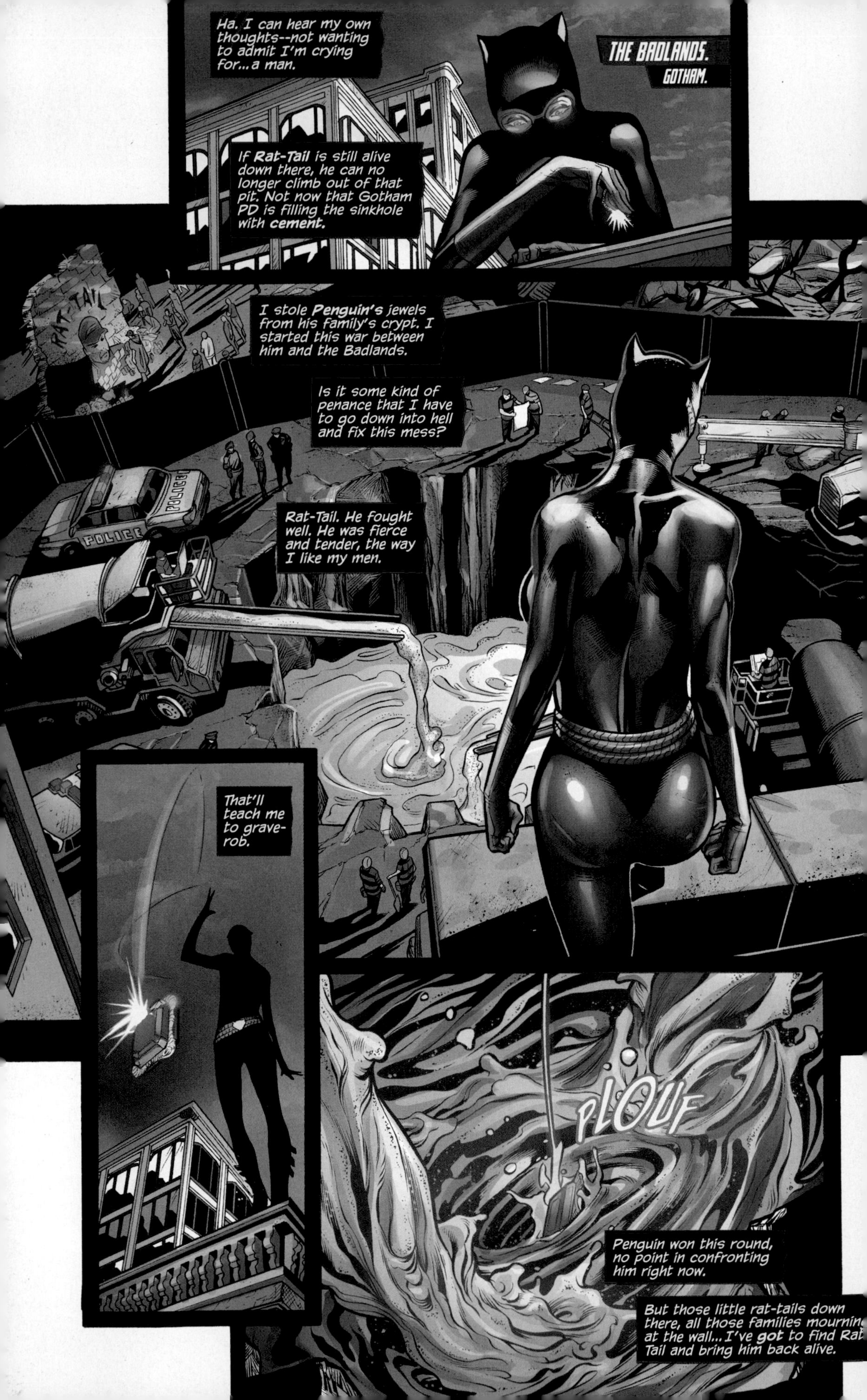

Ha. I can hear my own thoughts--not wanting to admit I'm crying for...a man.
THE BADLANDS.
GOTHAM.
If **Rat-Tail** is still alive down there, he can no longer climb out of that pit. Not now that Gotham PD is filling the sinkhole with **cement.**
RAT-TAIL
I stole **Penguin's** jewels from his family's crypt. I started this war between him and the Badlands.
Is it some kind of penance that I have to go down into hell and fix this mess?
POLICE
POLICE
Rat-Tail. He fought well. He was fierce and tender, the way I like my men.
That'll teach me to grave-rob.
PLOUF
Penguin won this round, no point in confronting him right now.
But those little rat-tails down there, all those families mournin at the wall... I've **got** to find Rat Tail and bring him back alive.

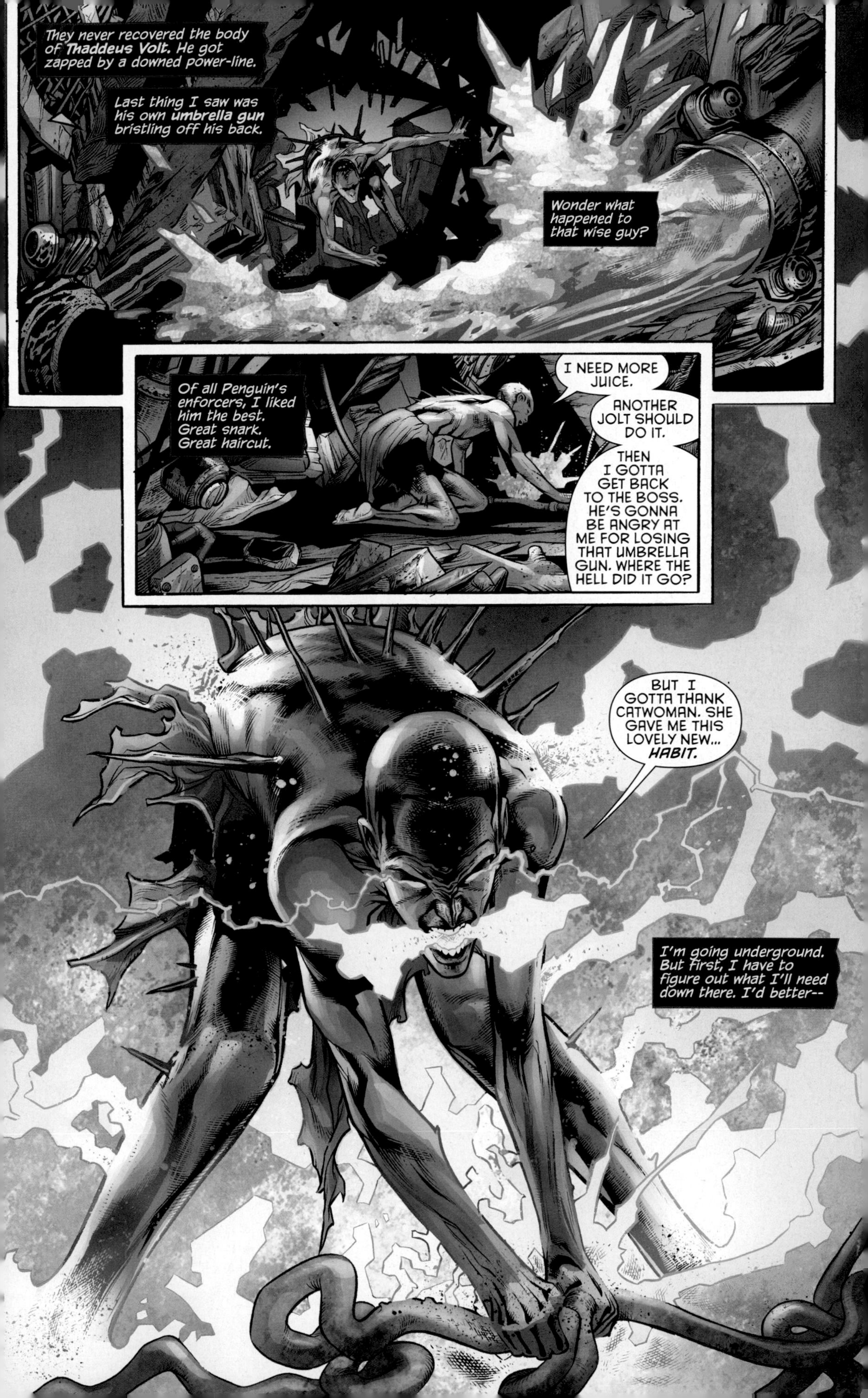
They never recovered the body of **Thaddeus Volt.** He got zapped by a downed power-line.
Last thing I saw was his own **umbrella gun** bristling off his back.
Wonder what happened to that wise guy?
Of all Penguin's enforcers, I liked him the best. Great snark. Great haircut.
I NEED MORE JUICE.
ANOTHER JOLT SHOULD DO IT.
THEN I GOTTA GET BACK TO THE BOSS. HE'S GONNA BE ANGRY AT ME FOR LOSING THAT UMBRELLA GUN. WHERE THE HELL DID IT GO?
BUT I GOTTA THANK CATWOMAN. SHE GAVE ME THIS LOVELY NEW... ***HABIT.***
I'm going underground. But first, I have to figure out what I'll need down there. I'd better--

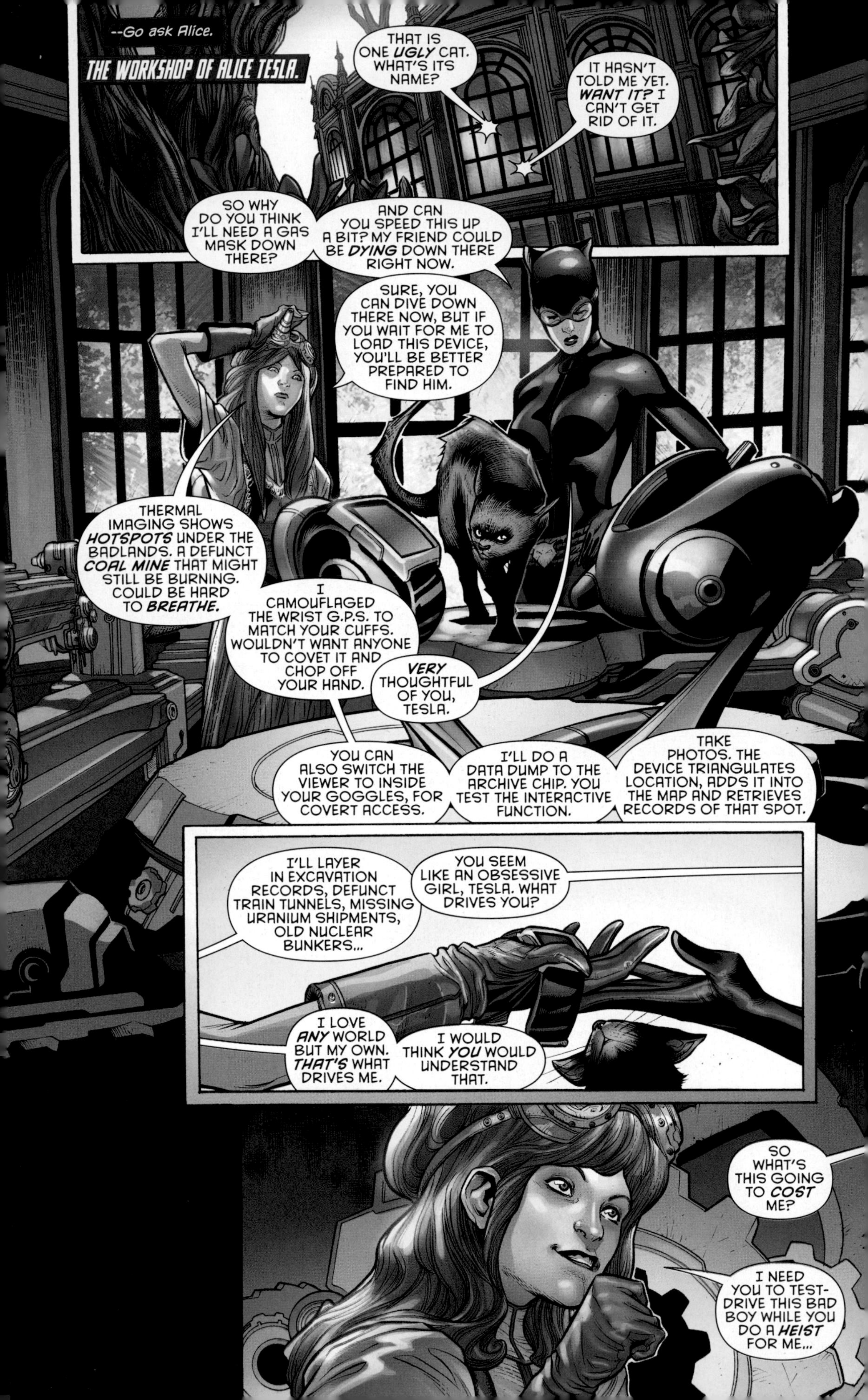
--Go ask Alice.
THE WORKSHOP OF ALICE TESLA.
THAT IS ONE UGLY CAT. WHAT'S ITS NAME?
IT HASN'T TOLD ME YET. WANT IT? I CAN'T GET RID OF IT.
SO WHY DO YOU THINK I'LL NEED A GAS MASK DOWN THERE?
AND CAN YOU SPEED THIS UP A BIT? MY FRIEND COULD BE DYING DOWN THERE RIGHT NOW.
SURE, YOU CAN DIVE DOWN THERE NOW, BUT IF YOU WAIT FOR ME TO LOAD THIS DEVICE, YOU'LL BE BETTER PREPARED TO FIND HIM.
THERMAL IMAGING SHOWS HOTSPOTS UNDER THE BADLANDS. A DEFUNCT COAL MINE THAT MIGHT STILL BE BURNING. COULD BE HARD TO BREATHE.
I CAMOUFLAGED THE WRIST G.P.S. TO MATCH YOUR CUFFS. WOULDN'T WANT ANYONE TO COVET IT AND CHOP OFF YOUR HAND.
VERY THOUGHTFUL OF YOU, TESLA.
YOU CAN ALSO SWITCH THE VIEWER TO INSIDE YOUR GOGGLES, FOR COVERT ACCESS.
I'LL DO A DATA DUMP TO THE ARCHIVE CHIP. YOU TEST THE INTERACTIVE FUNCTION.
TAKE PHOTOS. THE DEVICE TRIANGULATES LOCATION, ADDS IT INTO THE MAP AND RETRIEVES RECORDS OF THAT SPOT.
I'LL LAYER IN EXCAVATION RECORDS, DEFUNCT TRAIN TUNNELS, MISSING URANIUM SHIPMENTS, OLD NUCLEAR BUNKERS...
YOU SEEM LIKE AN OBSESSIVE GIRL, TESLA. WHAT DRIVES YOU?
I LOVE ANY WORLD BUT MY OWN. THAT'S WHAT DRIVES ME.
I WOULD THINK YOU WOULD UNDERSTAND THAT.
SO WHAT'S THIS GOING TO COST ME?
I NEED YOU TO TEST-DRIVE THIS BAD BOY WHILE YOU DO A HEIST FOR ME...

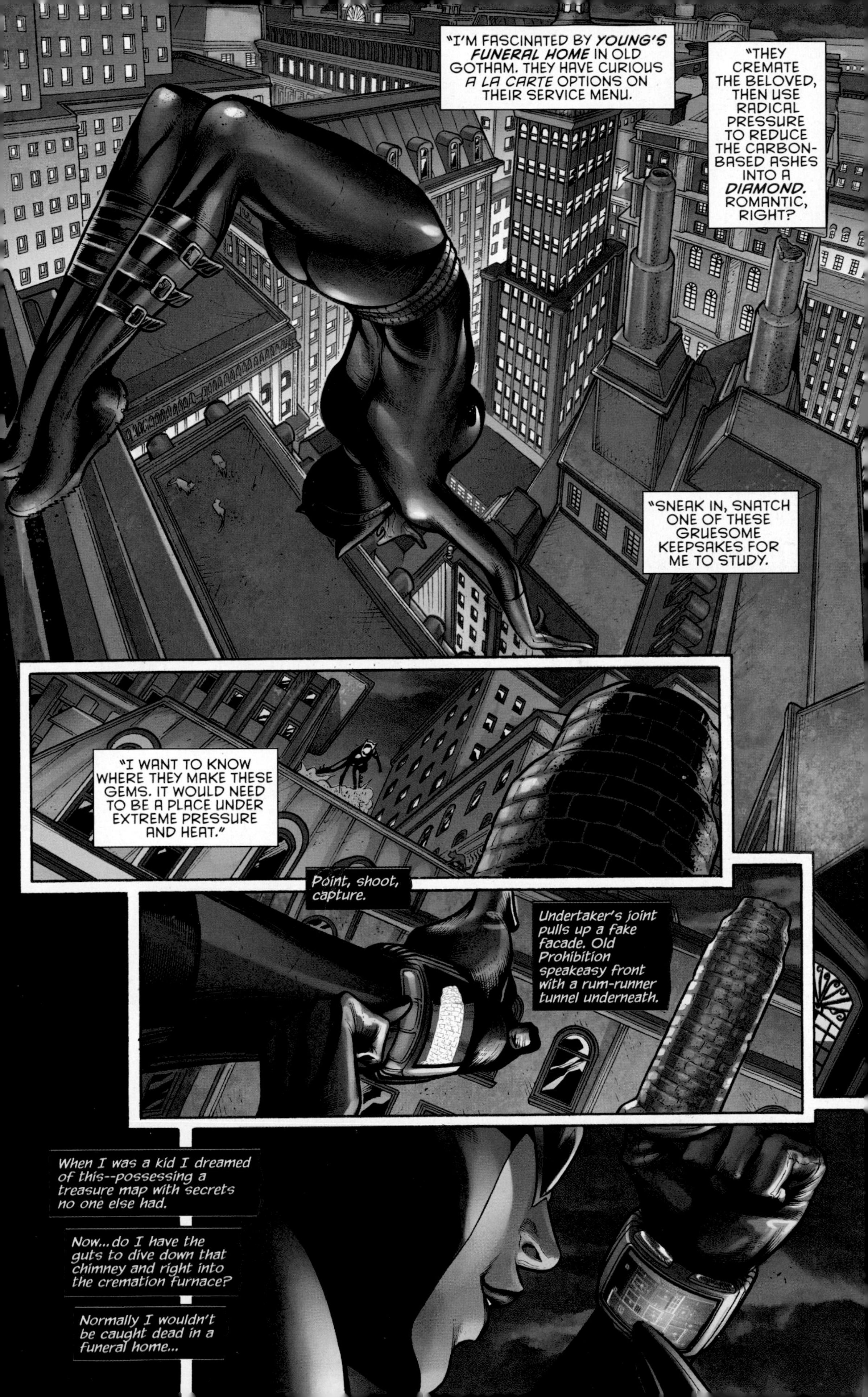
"I'M FASCINATED BY *YOUNG'S FUNERAL HOME* IN OLD GOTHAM. THEY HAVE CURIOUS *A LA CARTE* OPTIONS ON THEIR SERVICE MENU.
"THEY CREMATE THE BELOVED, THEN USE RADICAL PRESSURE TO REDUCE THE CARBON-BASED ASHES INTO A *DIAMOND.* ROMANTIC, RIGHT?
"SNEAK IN, SNATCH ONE OF THESE GRUESOME KEEPSAKES FOR ME TO STUDY.
"I WANT TO KNOW WHERE THEY MAKE THESE GEMS. IT WOULD NEED TO BE A PLACE UNDER EXTREME PRESSURE AND HEAT."
Point, shoot, capture.
Undertaker's joint pulls up a fake facade. Old Prohibition speakeasy front with a rum-runner tunnel underneath.
When I was a kid I dreamed of this--possessing a treasure map with secrets no one else had.
Now...do I have the guts to dive down that chimney and right into the cremation furnace?
Normally I wouldn't be caught dead in a funeral home...

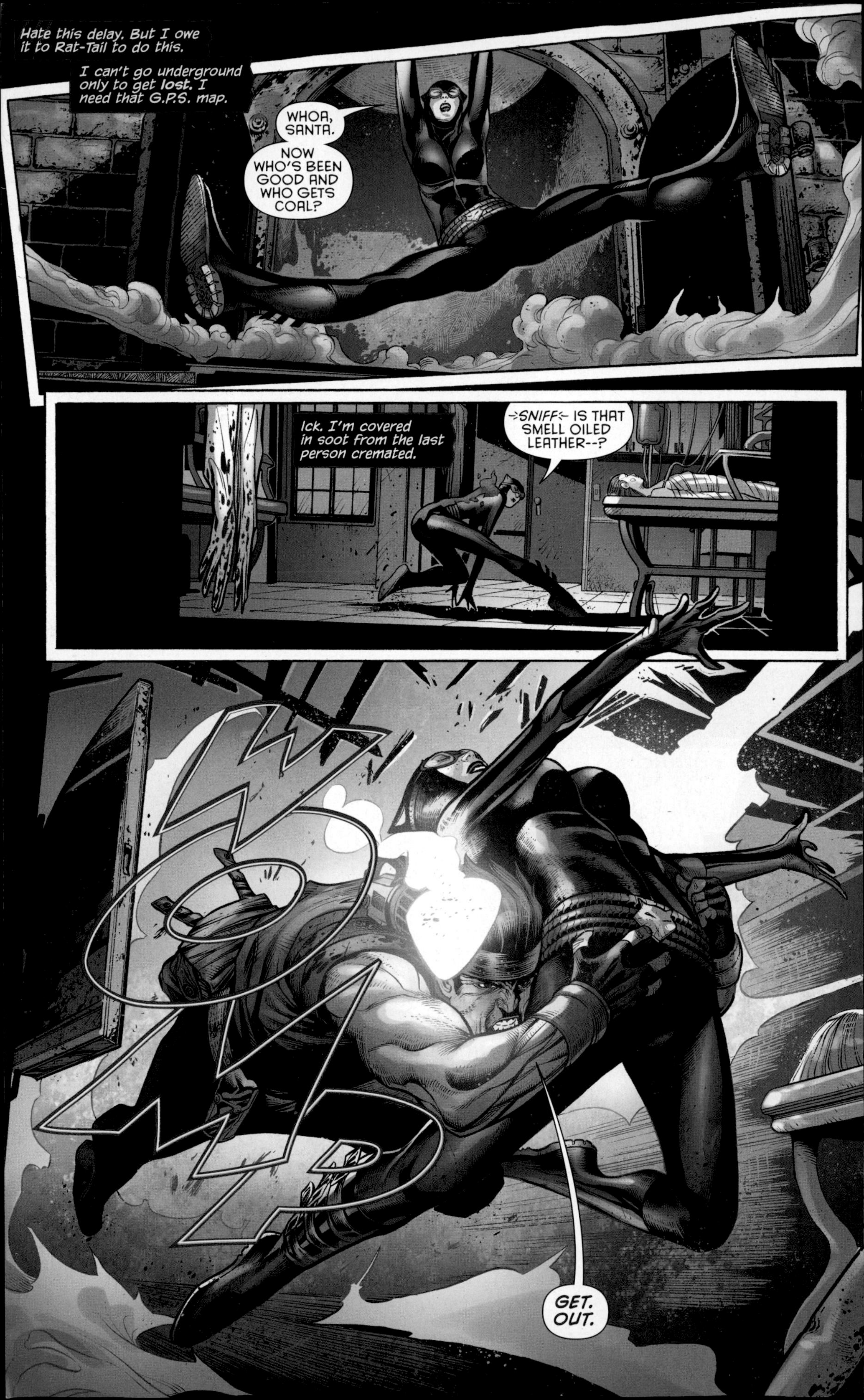
Hate this delay. But I owe it to Rat-Tail to do this.
I can't go underground only to get **lost**. I need that G.P.S. map.
WHOA, SANTA.
NOW WHO'S BEEN GOOD AND WHO GETS COAL?
Ick. I'm covered in soot from the last person cremated.
⇒SNIFF⇐ IS THAT SMELL OILED LEATHER--?
GET. OUT.

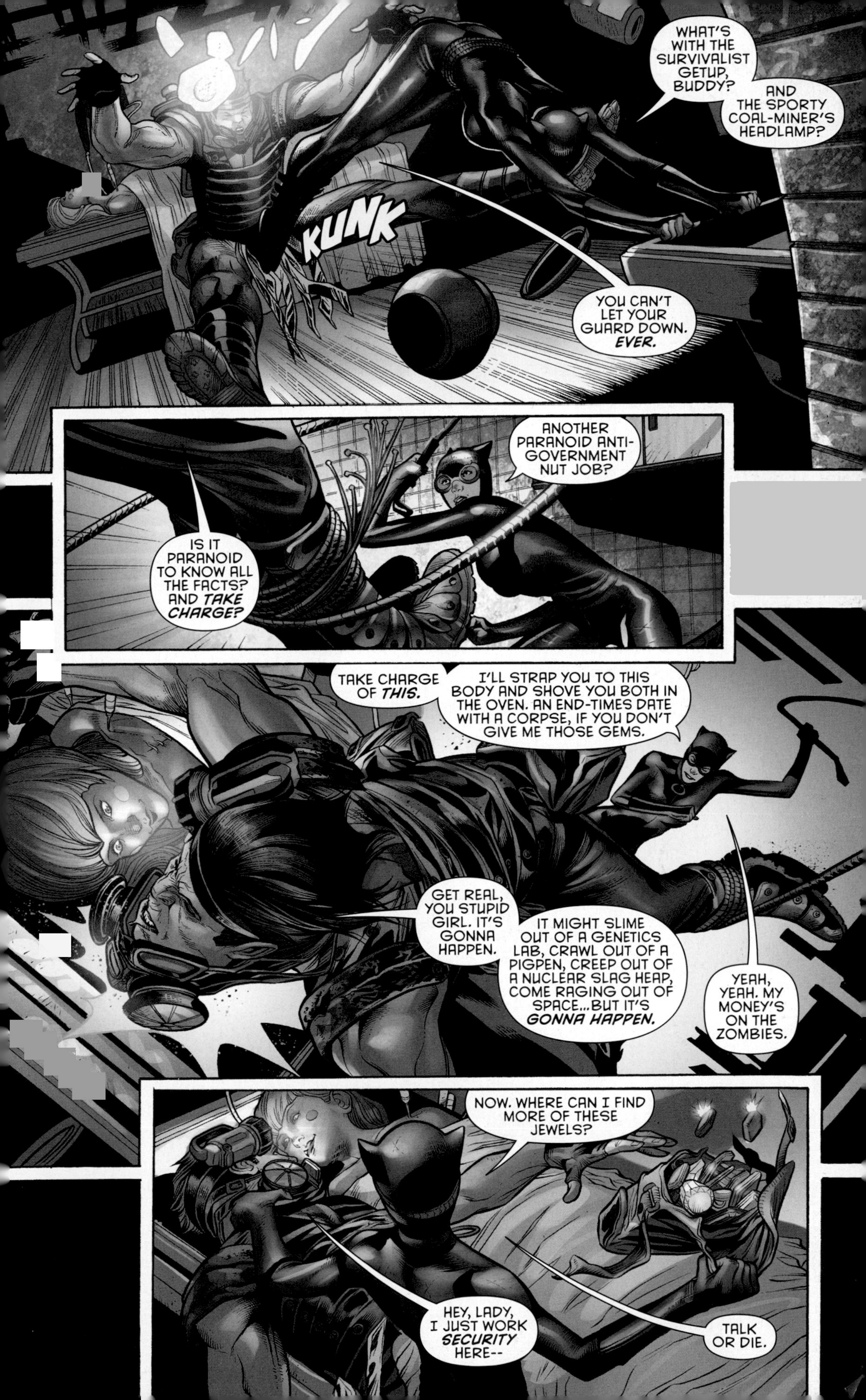

WHAT'S WITH THE SURVIVALIST GETUP, BUDDY?
AND THE SPORTY COAL-MINER'S HEADLAMP?
KUNK
YOU CAN'T LET YOUR GUARD DOWN. EVER.
ANOTHER PARANOID ANTI-GOVERNMENT NUT JOB?
IS IT PARANOID TO KNOW ALL THE FACTS? AND TAKE CHARGE?
TAKE CHARGE OF THIS.
I'LL STRAP YOU TO THIS BODY AND SHOVE YOU BOTH IN THE OVEN. AN END-TIMES DATE WITH A CORPSE, IF YOU DON'T GIVE ME THOSE GEMS.
GET REAL, YOU STUPID GIRL. IT'S GONNA HAPPEN.
IT MIGHT SLIME OUT OF A GENETICS LAB, CRAWL OUT OF A PIGPEN, CREEP OUT OF A NUCLEAR SLAG HEAP, COME RAGING OUT OF SPACE...BUT IT'S GONNA HAPPEN.
YEAH, YEAH. MY MONEY'S ON THE ZOMBIES.
NOW. WHERE CAN I FIND MORE OF THESE JEWELS?
HEY, LADY, I JUST WORK SECURITY HERE--
TALK OR DIE.

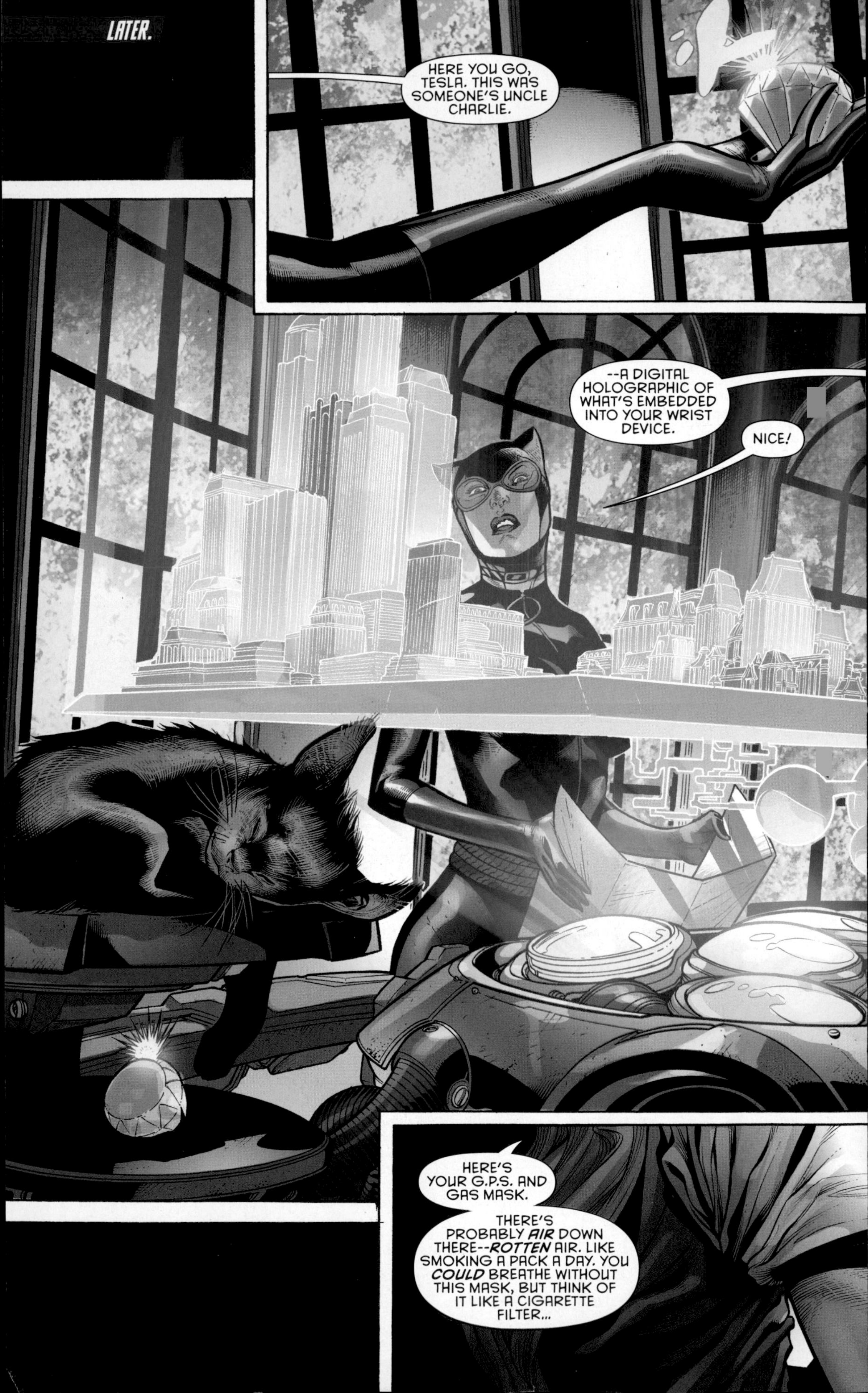
LATER.
HERE YOU GO, TESLA. THIS WAS SOMEONE'S UNCLE CHARLIE.
--A DIGITAL HOLOGRAPHIC OF WHAT'S EMBEDDED INTO YOUR WRIST DEVICE.
NICE!
HERE'S YOUR G.P.S. AND GAS MASK.
THERE'S PROBABLY *AIR* DOWN THERE--*ROTTEN* AIR. LIKE SMOKING A PACK A DAY. YOU *COULD* BREATHE WITHOUT THIS MASK, BUT THINK OF IT LIKE A CIGARETTE FILTER...

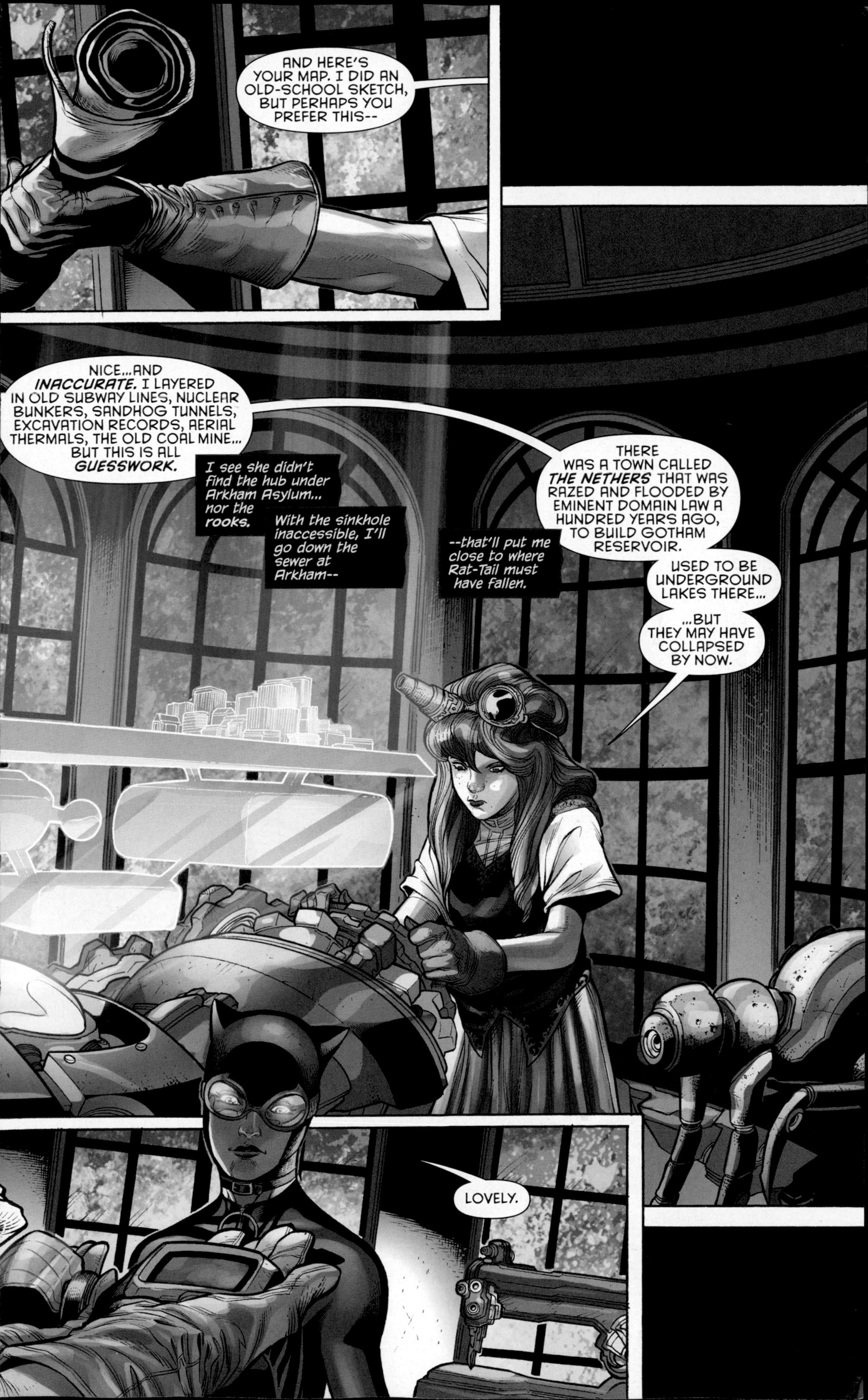
AND HERE'S YOUR MAP. I DID AN OLD-SCHOOL SKETCH, BUT PERHAPS YOU PREFER THIS--
NICE...AND INACCURATE. I LAYERED IN OLD SUBWAY LINES, NUCLEAR BUNKERS, SANDHOG TUNNELS, EXCAVATION RECORDS, AERIAL THERMALS, THE OLD COAL MINE... BUT THIS IS ALL GUESSWORK.
I see she didn't find the hub under Arkham Asylum... nor the rooks.
With the sinkhole inaccessible, I'll go down the sewer at Arkham--
--that'll put me close to where Rat-Tail must have fallen.
THERE WAS A TOWN CALLED THE NETHERS THAT WAS RAZED AND FLOODED BY EMINENT DOMAIN LAW A HUNDRED YEARS AGO, TO BUILD GOTHAM RESERVOIR.
USED TO BE UNDERGROUND LAKES THERE...
...BUT THEY MAY HAVE COLLAPSED BY NOW.
LOVELY.

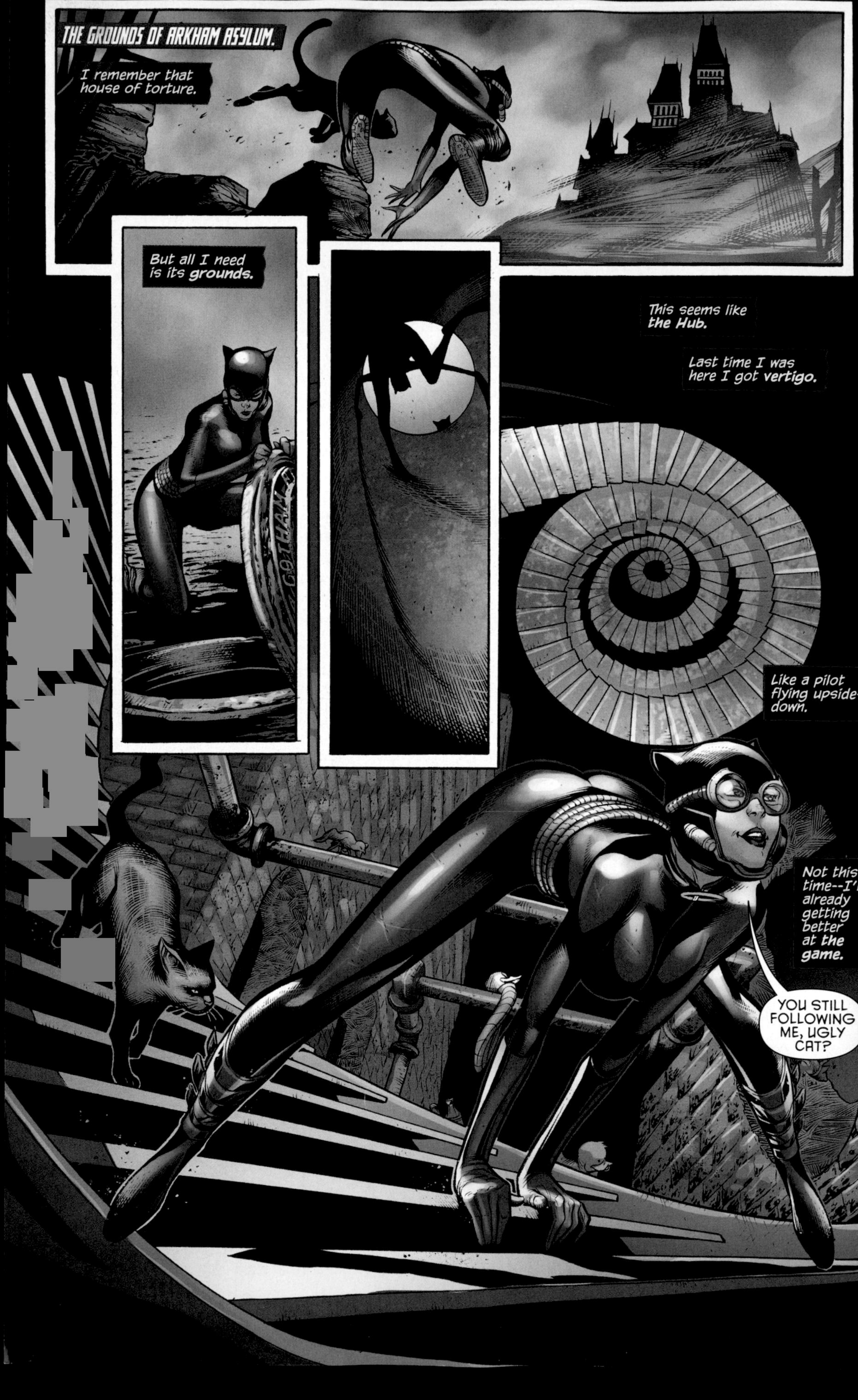
THE GROUNDS OF ARKHAM ASYLUM.
I remember that house of torture.
But all I need is its grounds.
GOTHAM
This seems like the Hub.
Last time I was here I got vertigo.
Like a pilot flying upside down.
Not this time--I'm already getting better at the game.
YOU STILL FOLLOWING ME, UGLY CAT?

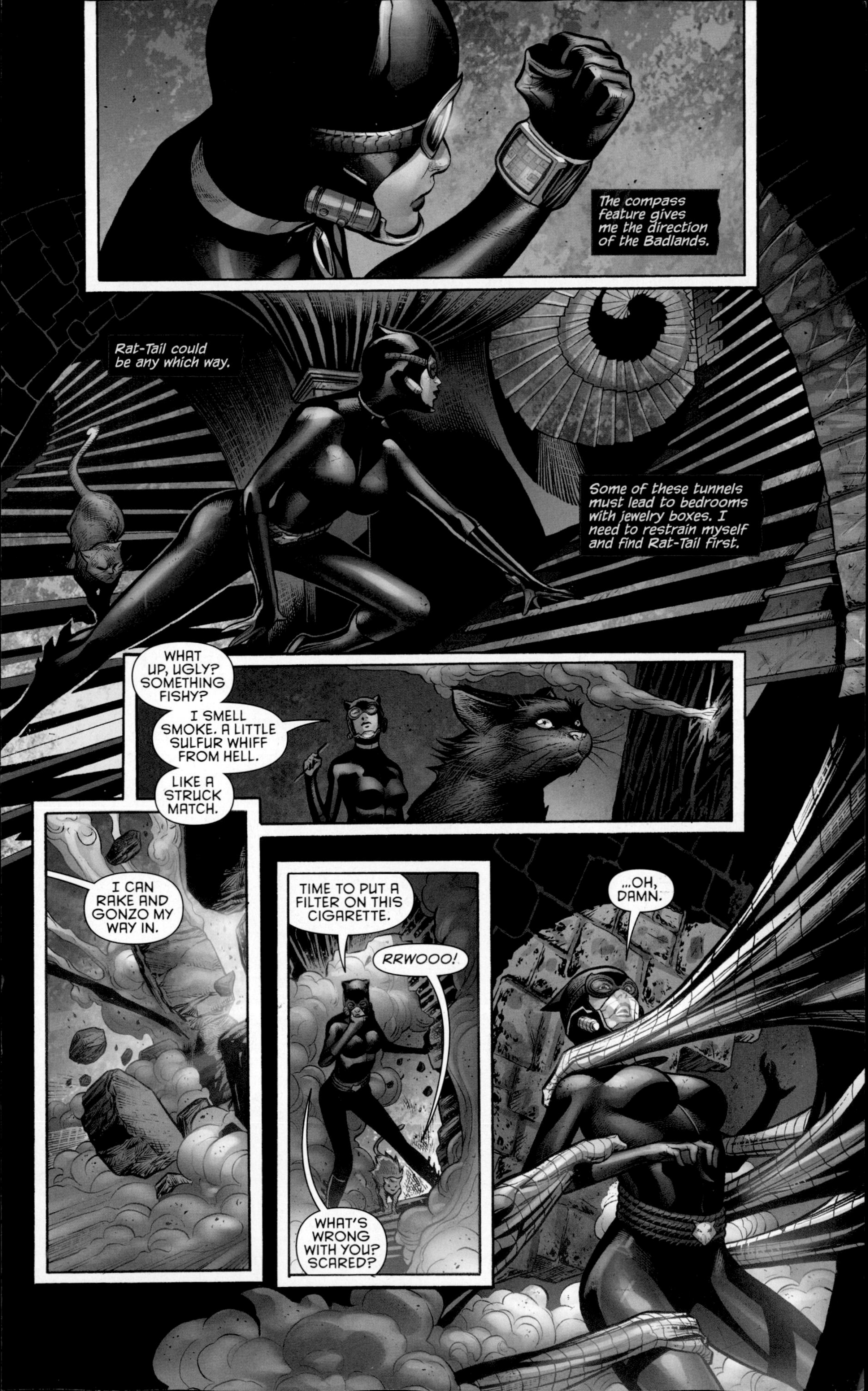
The compass feature gives me the direction of the Badlands.
Rat-Tail could be any which way.
Some of these tunnels must lead to bedrooms with jewelry boxes. I need to restrain myself and find Rat-Tail first.
WHAT UP, UGLY? SOMETHING FISHY?
I SMELL SMOKE. A LITTLE SULFUR WHIFF FROM HELL.
LIKE A STRUCK MATCH.
I CAN RAKE AND GONZO MY WAY IN.
TIME TO PUT A FILTER ON THIS CIGARETTE.
RRWOOO!
WHAT'S WRONG WITH YOU? SCARED?
...OH, DAMN.

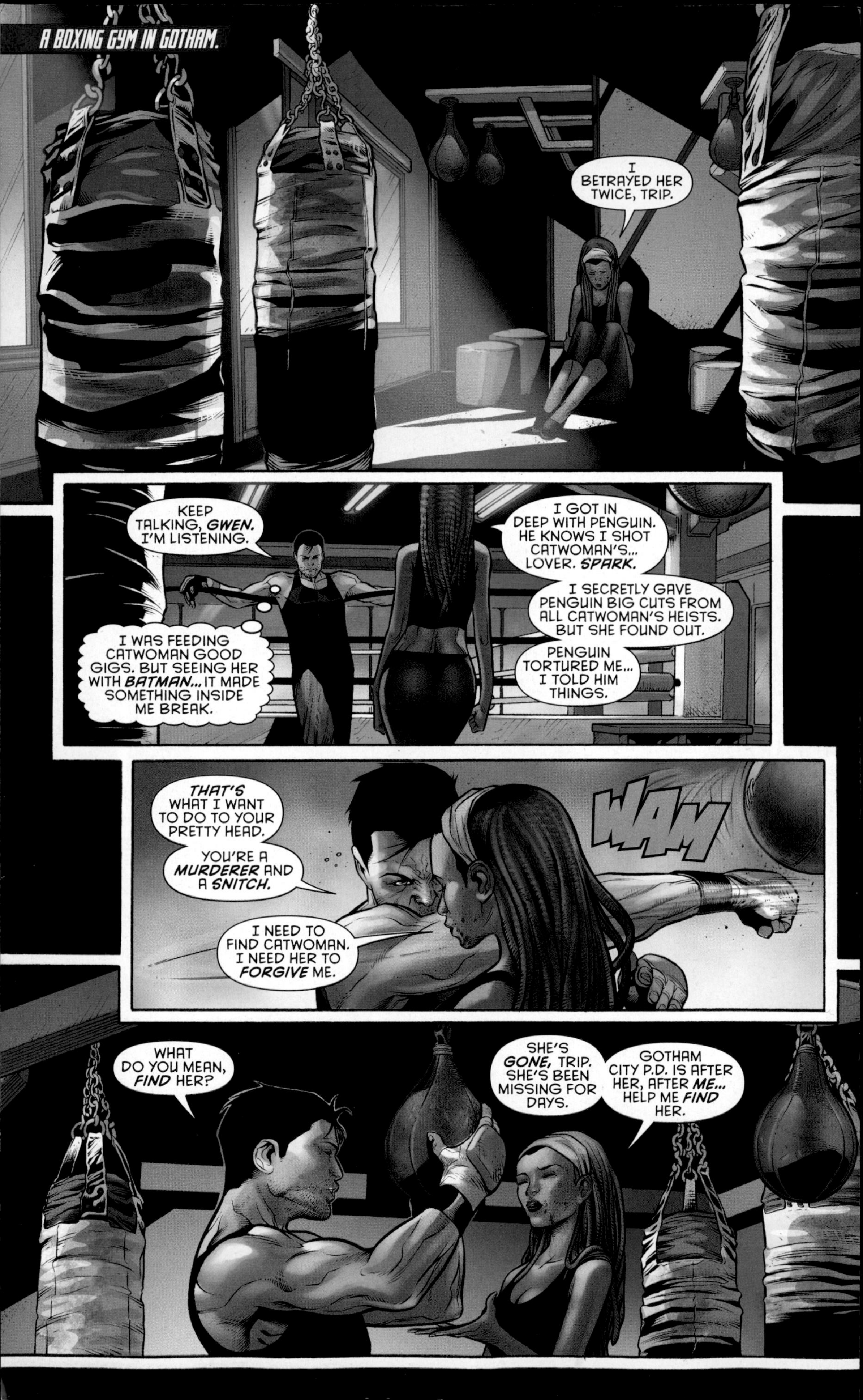
A BOXING GYM IN GOTHAM.
I BETRAYED HER TWICE, TRIP.
KEEP TALKING, GWEN. I'M LISTENING.
I GOT IN DEEP WITH PENGUIN. HE KNOWS I SHOT CATWOMAN'S... LOVER. SPARK.
I SECRETLY GAVE PENGUIN BIG CUTS FROM ALL CATWOMAN'S HEISTS. BUT SHE FOUND OUT.
PENGUIN TORTURED ME... I TOLD HIM THINGS.
I WAS FEEDING CATWOMAN GOOD GIGS. BUT SEEING HER WITH BATMAN... IT MADE SOMETHING INSIDE ME BREAK.
THAT'S WHAT I WANT TO DO TO YOUR PRETTY HEAD.
YOU'RE A MURDERER AND A SNITCH.
WAM
I NEED TO FIND CATWOMAN. I NEED HER TO FORGIVE ME.
WHAT DO YOU MEAN, FIND HER?
SHE'S GONE, TRIP. SHE'S BEEN MISSING FOR DAYS.
GOTHAM CITY P.D. IS AFTER HER, AFTER ME... HELP ME FIND HER.

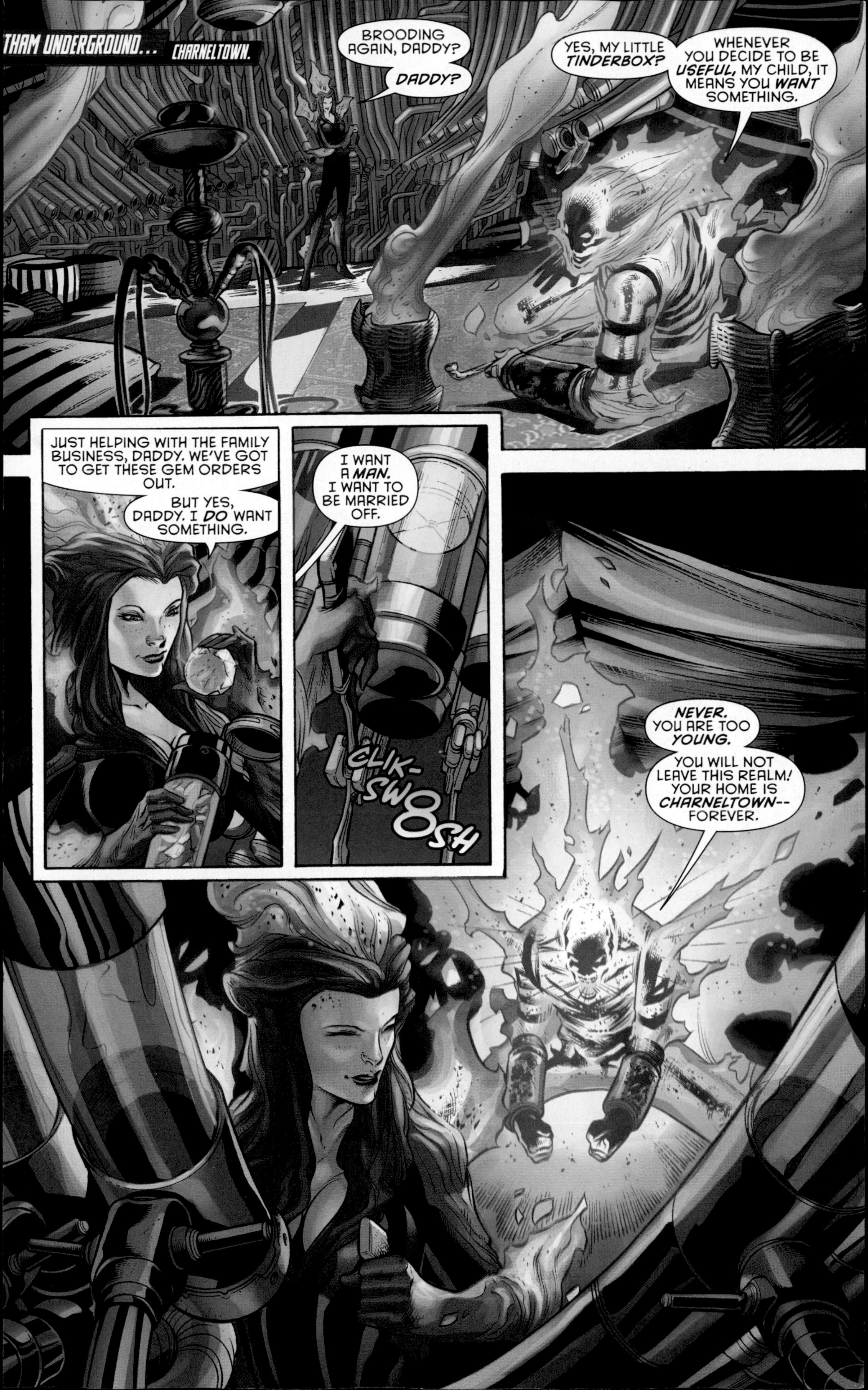
THAM UNDERGROUND... CHARNELTOWN.
BROODING AGAIN, DADDY?
DADDY?
YES, MY LITTLE TINDERBOX?
WHENEVER YOU DECIDE TO BE USEFUL, MY CHILD, IT MEANS YOU WANT SOMETHING.
JUST HELPING WITH THE FAMILY BUSINESS, DADDY. WE'VE GOT TO GET THESE GEM ORDERS OUT.
BUT YES, DADDY. I DO WANT SOMETHING.
I WANT A MAN. I WANT TO BE MARRIED OFF.
CLIK-SW8OSH
NEVER. YOU ARE TOO YOUNG.
YOU WILL NOT LEAVE THIS REALM! YOUR HOME IS CHARNELTOWN--FOREVER.

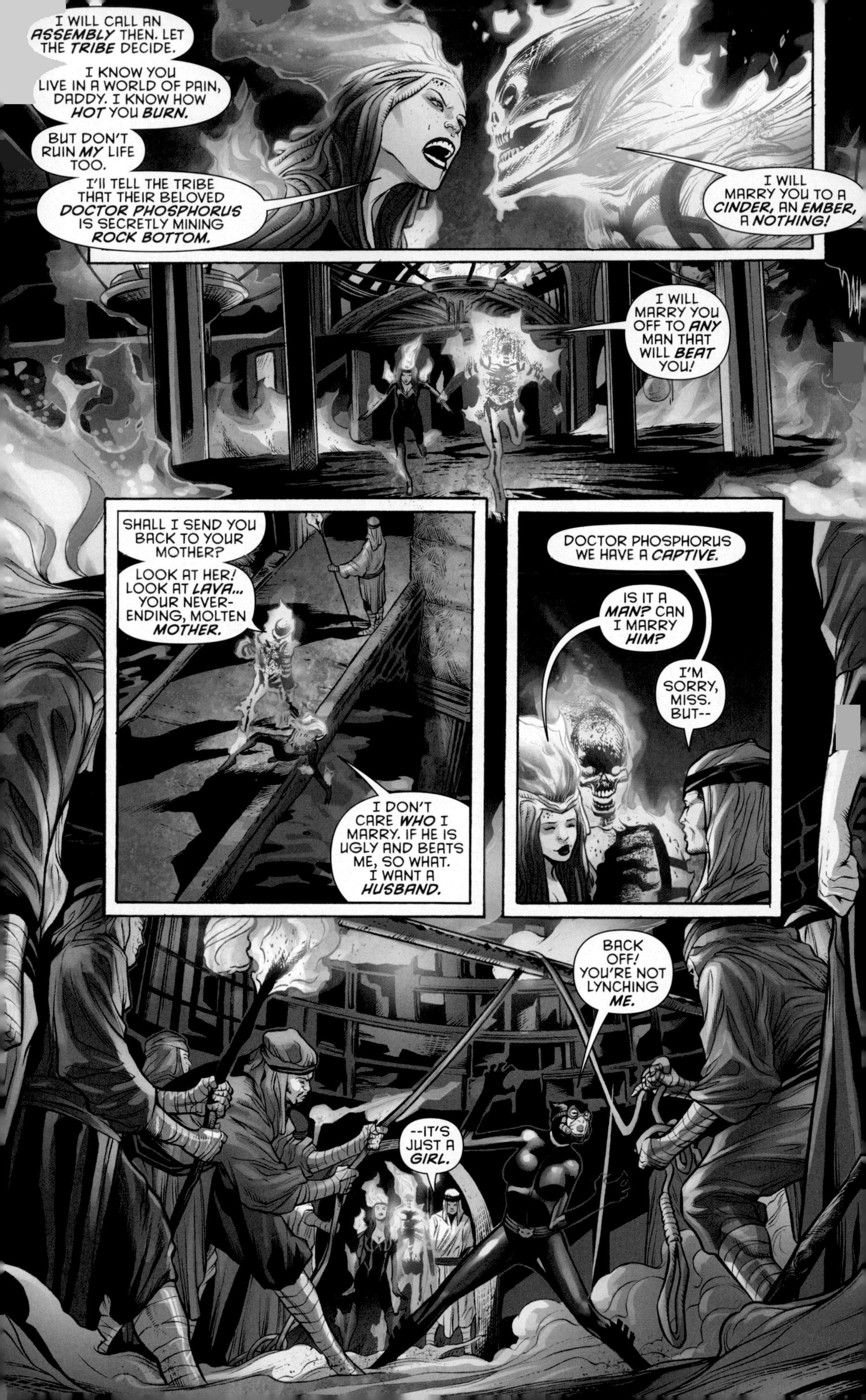
I WILL CALL AN ASSEMBLY THEN. LET THE TRIBE DECIDE.
I KNOW YOU LIVE IN A WORLD OF PAIN, DADDY. I KNOW HOW HOT YOU BURN.
BUT DON'T RUIN MY LIFE TOO.
I'LL TELL THE TRIBE THAT THEIR BELOVED DOCTOR PHOSPHORUS IS SECRETLY MINING ROCK BOTTOM.
I WILL MARRY YOU TO A CINDER, AN EMBER, A NOTHING!
I WILL MARRY YOU OFF TO ANY MAN THAT WILL BEAT YOU!
SHALL I SEND YOU BACK TO YOUR MOTHER?
LOOK AT HER! LOOK AT LAVA... YOUR NEVER-ENDING, MOLTEN MOTHER.
I DON'T CARE WHO I MARRY. IF HE IS UGLY AND BEATS ME, SO WHAT. I WANT A HUSBAND.
DOCTOR PHOSPHORUS WE HAVE A CAPTIVE.
IS IT A MAN? CAN I MARRY HIM?
I'M SORRY, MISS. BUT--
--IT'S JUST A GIRL.
BACK OFF! YOU'RE NOT LYNCHING ME.

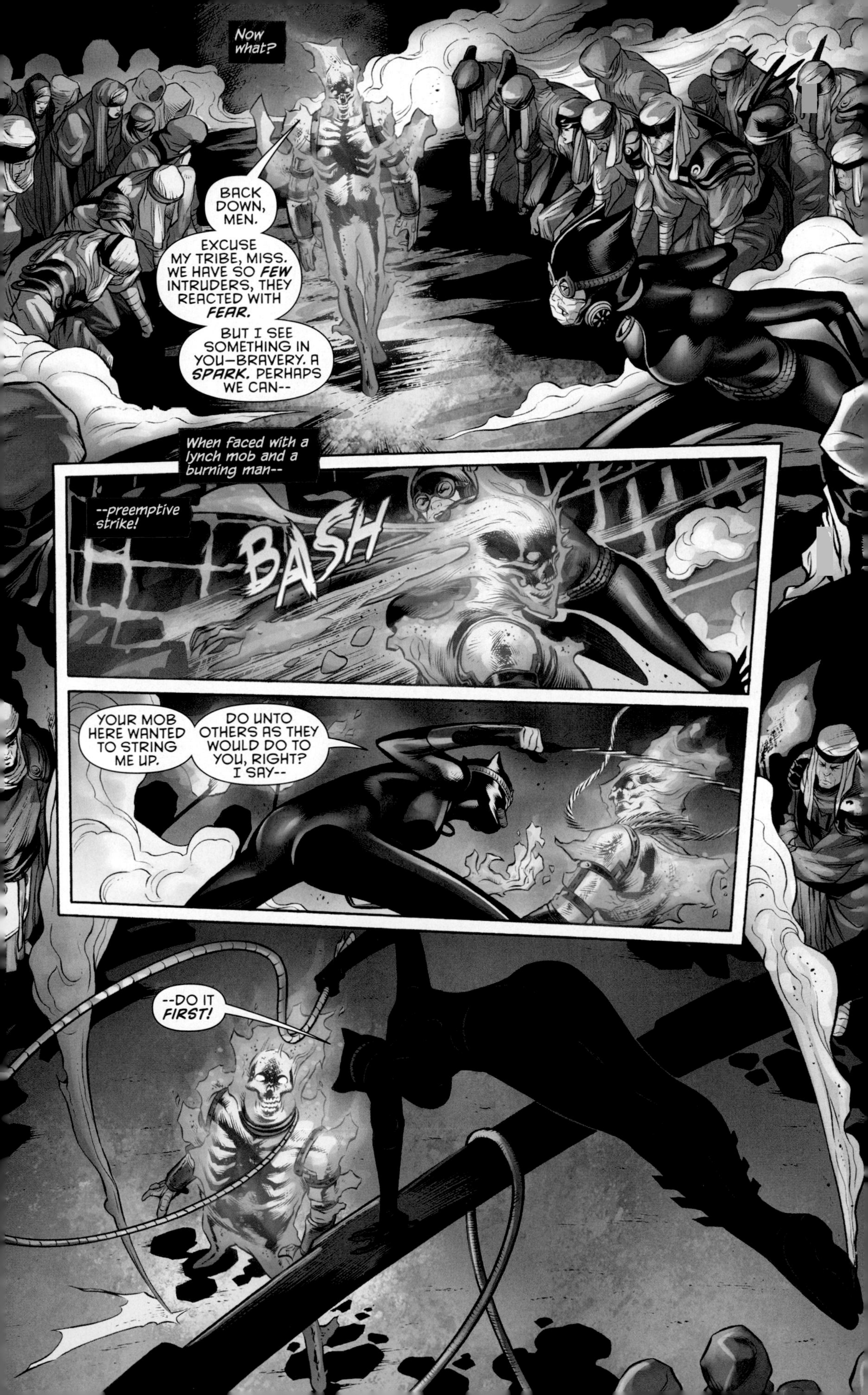
Now what?
BACK DOWN, MEN.
EXCUSE MY TRIBE, MISS. WE HAVE SO FEW INTRUDERS, THEY REACTED WITH FEAR.
BUT I SEE SOMETHING IN YOU—BRAVERY. A SPARK. PERHAPS WE CAN--
When faced with a lynch mob and a burning man--
--preemptive strike!
BASH
YOUR MOB HERE WANTED TO STRING ME UP.
DO UNTO OTHERS AS THEY WOULD DO TO YOU, RIGHT? I SAY--
--DO IT FIRST!

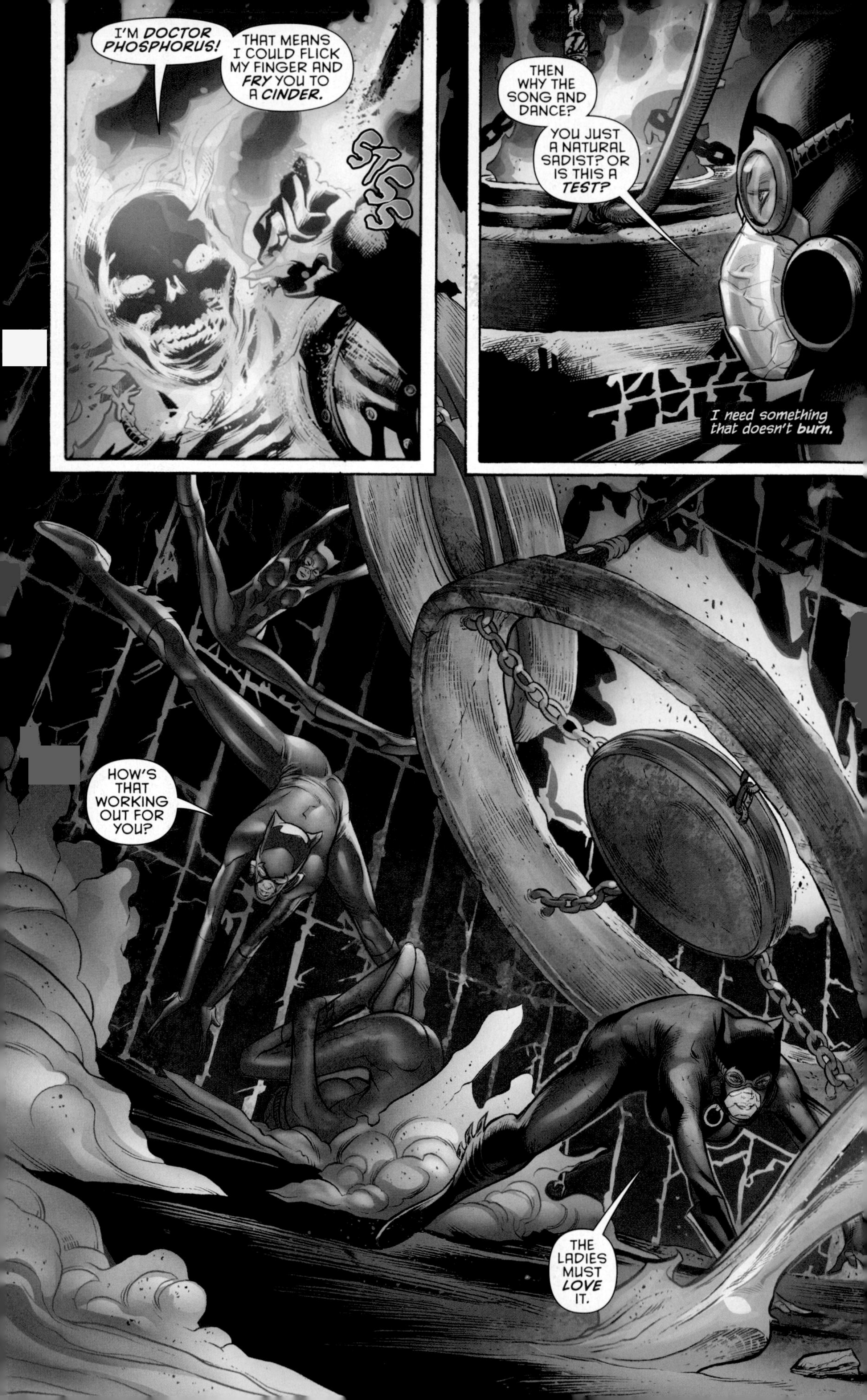

I'M DOCTOR PHOSPHORUS!
THAT MEANS I COULD FLICK MY FINGER AND FRY YOU TO A CINDER.
STSS
THEN WHY THE SONG AND DANCE?
YOU JUST A NATURAL SADIST? OR IS THIS A TEST?
I need something that doesn't burn.
HOW'S THAT WORKING OUT FOR YOU?
THE LADIES MUST LOVE IT.

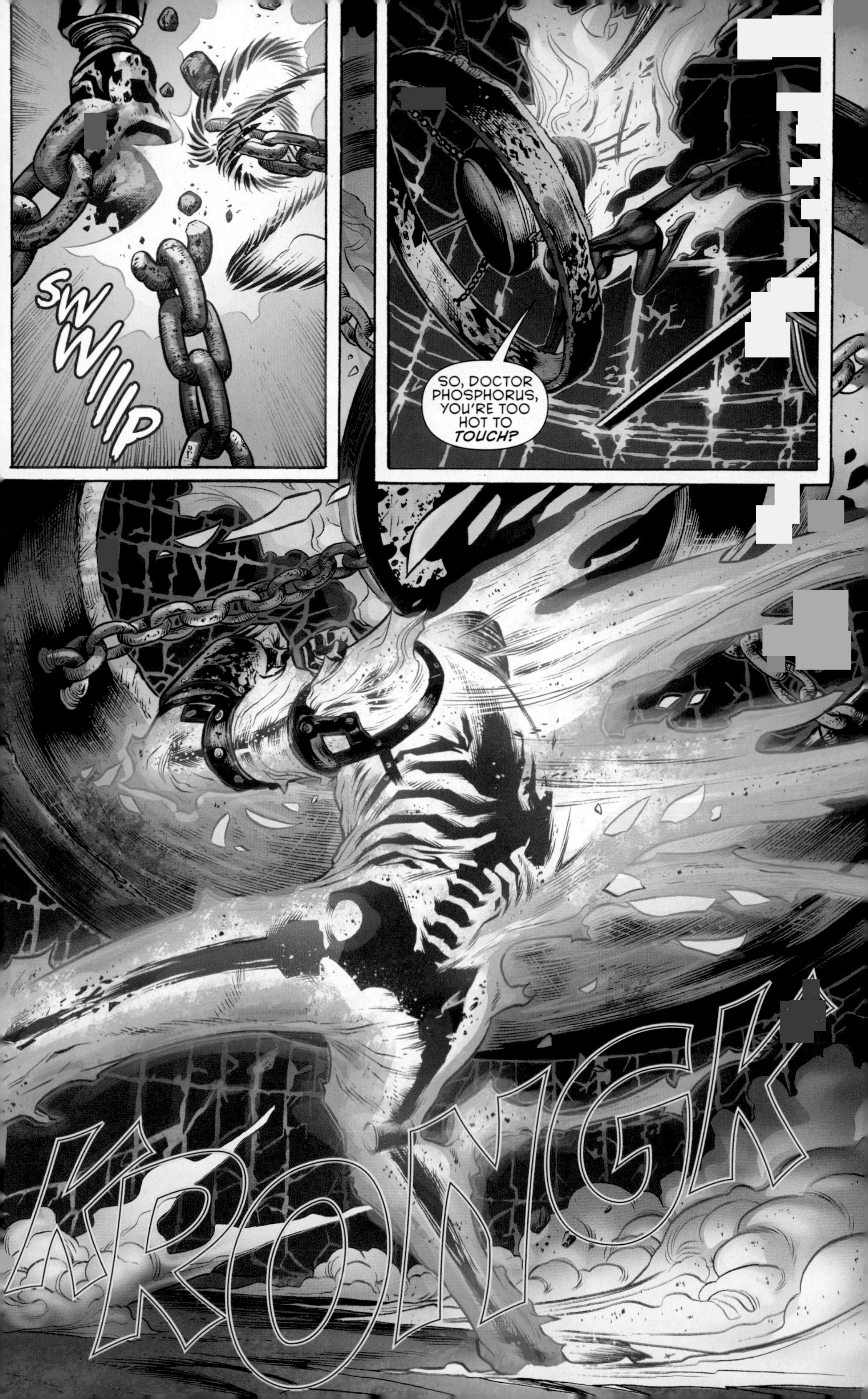
SWWIIIP
SO, DOCTOR PHOSPHORUS, YOU'RE TOO HOT TO *TOUCH?*
KRONNGK

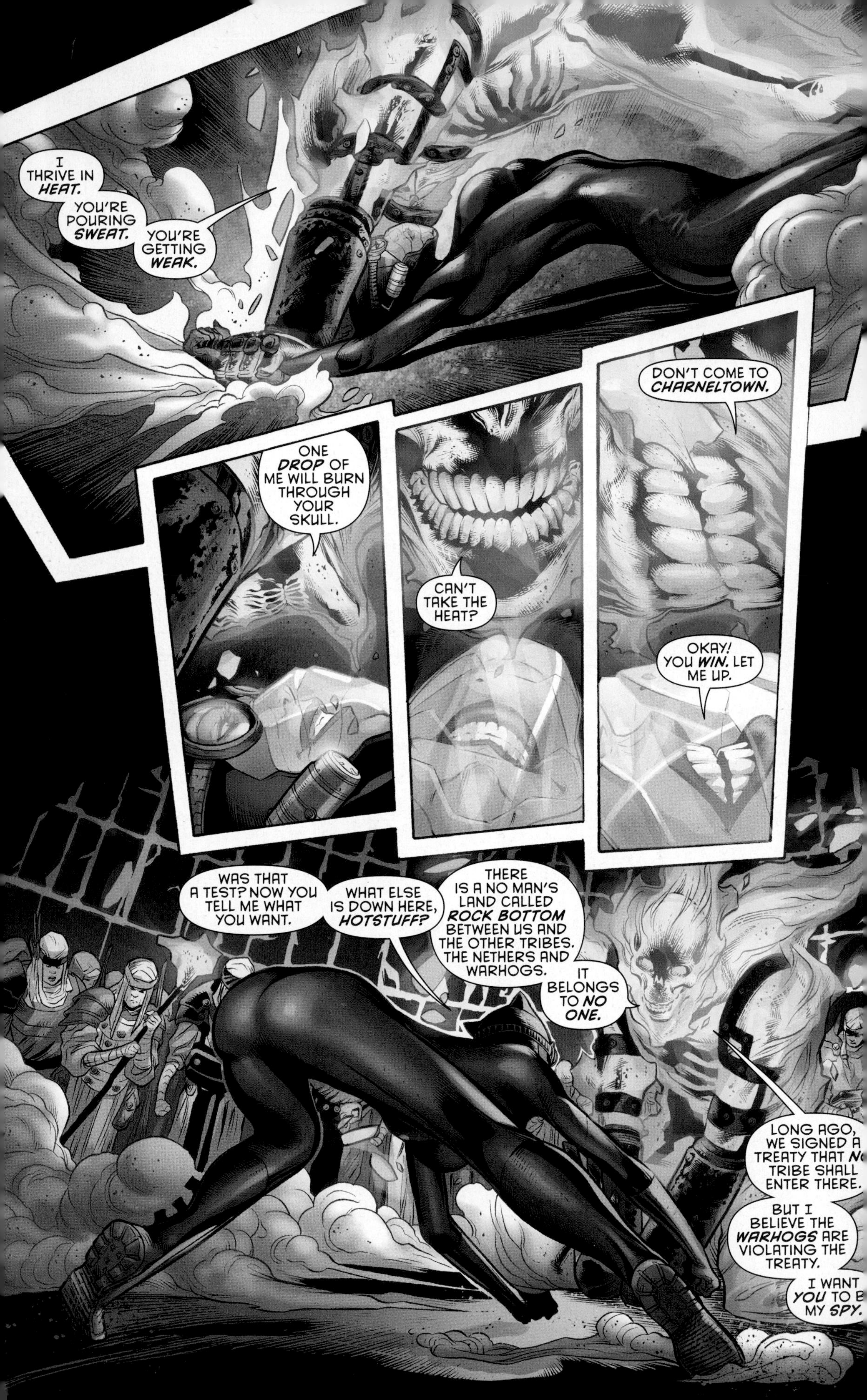
I THRIVE IN HEAT.
YOU'RE POURING SWEAT.
YOU'RE GETTING WEAK.
ONE DROP OF ME WILL BURN THROUGH YOUR SKULL.
CAN'T TAKE THE HEAT?
DON'T COME TO CHARNELTOWN.
OKAY! YOU WIN. LET ME UP.
WAS THAT A TEST? NOW YOU TELL ME WHAT YOU WANT.
WHAT ELSE IS DOWN HERE, HOTSTUFF?
THERE IS A NO MAN'S LAND CALLED ROCK BOTTOM BETWEEN US AND THE OTHER TRIBES. THE NETHERS AND WARHOGS.
IT BELONGS TO NO ONE.
LONG AGO, WE SIGNED A TREATY THAT NO TRIBE SHALL ENTER THERE.
BUT I BELIEVE THE WARHOGS ARE VIOLATING THE TREATY.
I WANT YOU TO BE MY SPY.

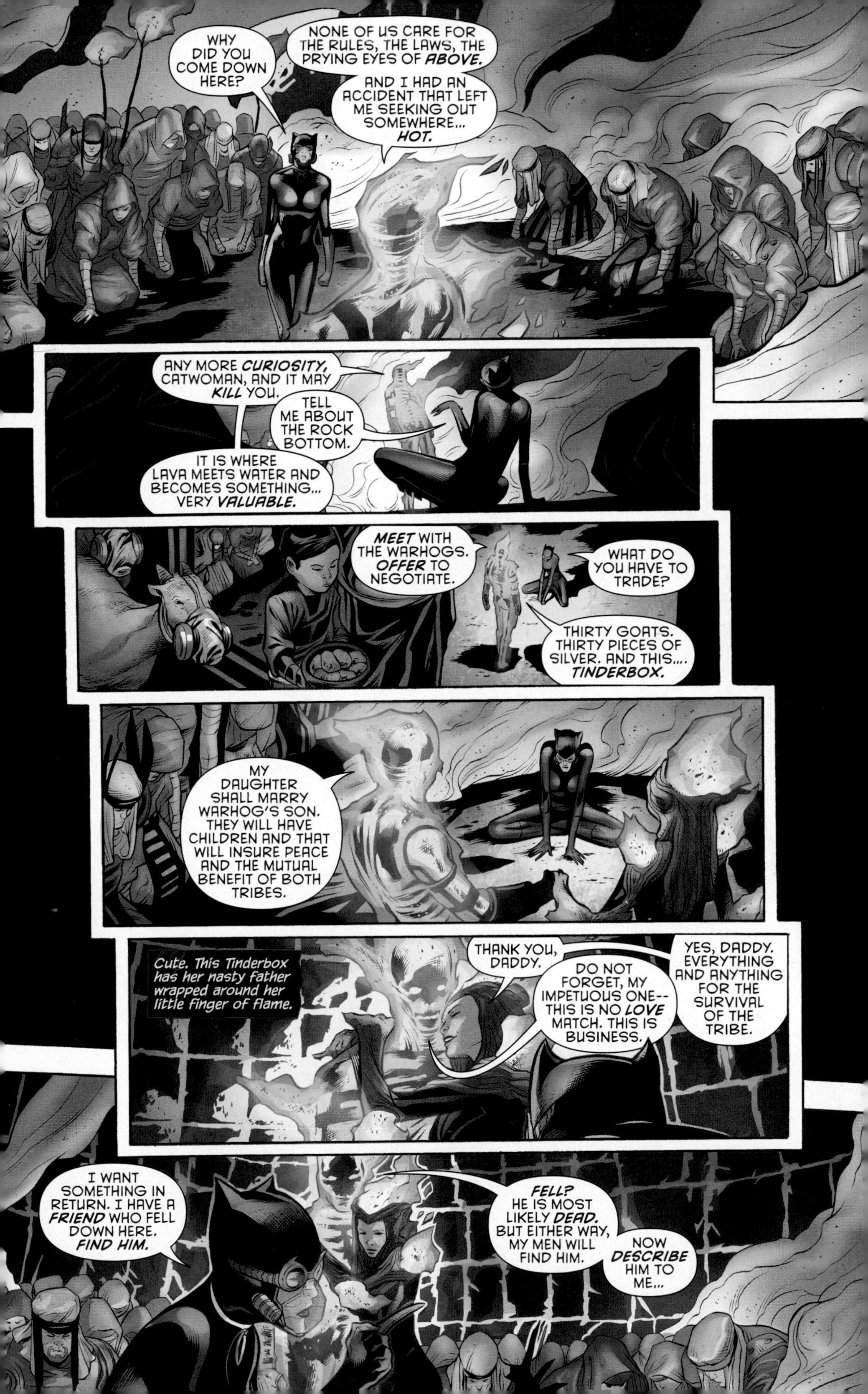
WHY DID YOU COME DOWN HERE?
NONE OF US CARE FOR THE RULES, THE LAWS, THE PRYING EYES OF ABOVE.
AND I HAD AN ACCIDENT THAT LEFT ME SEEKING OUT SOMEWHERE... HOT.
ANY MORE CURIOSITY, CATWOMAN, AND IT MAY KILL YOU.
TELL ME ABOUT THE ROCK BOTTOM.
IT IS WHERE LAVA MEETS WATER AND BECOMES SOMETHING... VERY VALUABLE.
MEET WITH THE WARHOGS. OFFER TO NEGOTIATE.
WHAT DO YOU HAVE TO TRADE?
THIRTY GOATS. THIRTY PIECES OF SILVER. AND THIS.... TINDERBOX.
MY DAUGHTER SHALL MARRY WARHOG'S SON. THEY WILL HAVE CHILDREN AND THAT WILL INSURE PEACE AND THE MUTUAL BENEFIT OF BOTH TRIBES.
Cute. This Tinderbox has her nasty father wrapped around her little finger of flame.
THANK YOU, DADDY.
DO NOT FORGET, MY IMPETUOUS ONE-- THIS IS NO LOVE MATCH. THIS IS BUSINESS.
YES, DADDY. EVERYTHING AND ANYTHING FOR THE SURVIVAL OF THE TRIBE.
I WANT SOMETHING IN RETURN. I HAVE A FRIEND WHO FELL DOWN HERE. FIND HIM.
FELL? HE IS MOST LIKELY DEAD. BUT EITHER WAY, MY MEN WILL FIND HIM.
NOW DESCRIBE HIM TO ME...

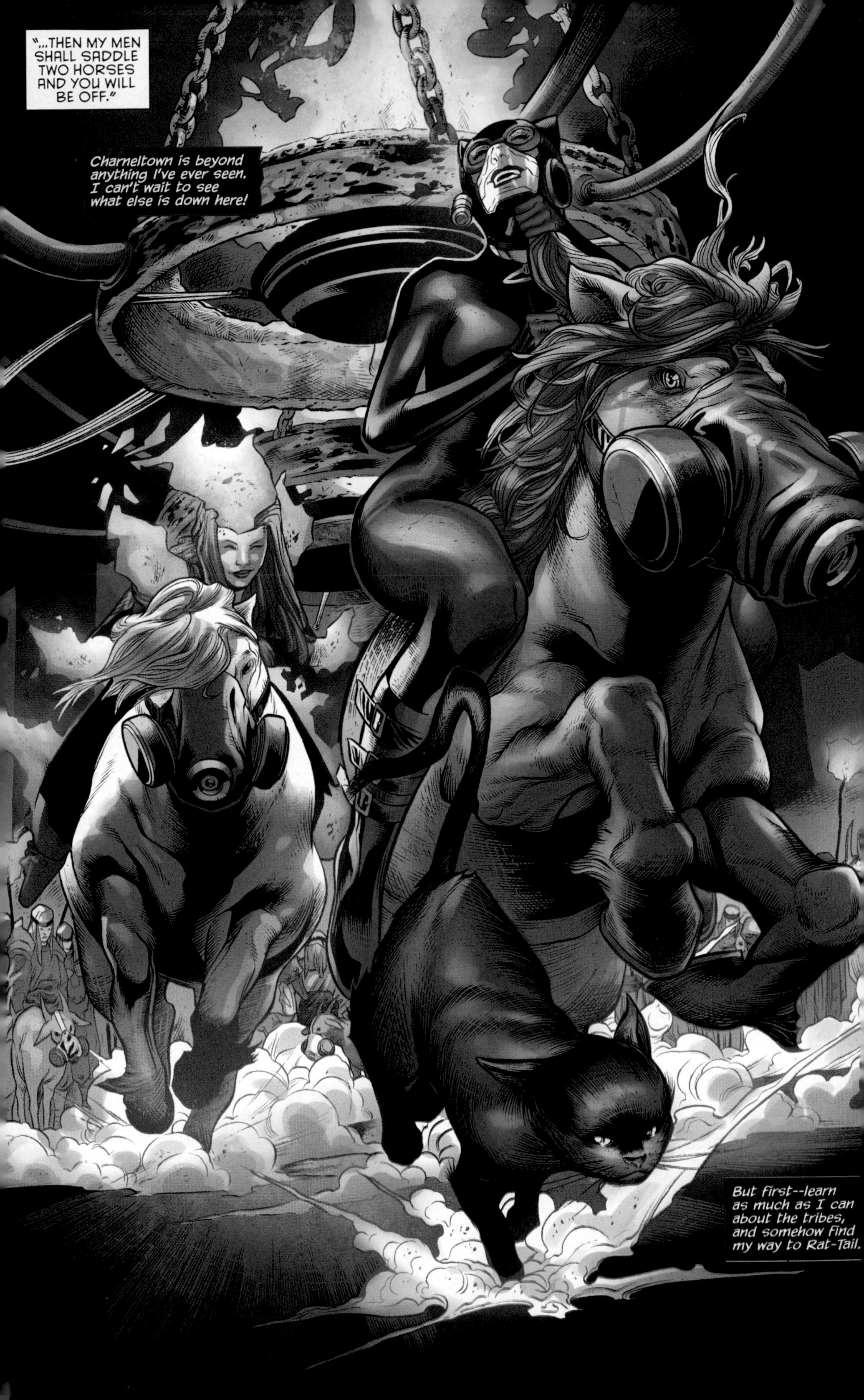
"...THEN MY MEN SHALL SADDLE TWO HORSES AND YOU WILL BE OFF."
Charneltown is beyond anything I've ever seen. I can't wait to see what else is down here!
But first--learn as much as I can about the tribes, and somehow find my way to Rat-Tail.

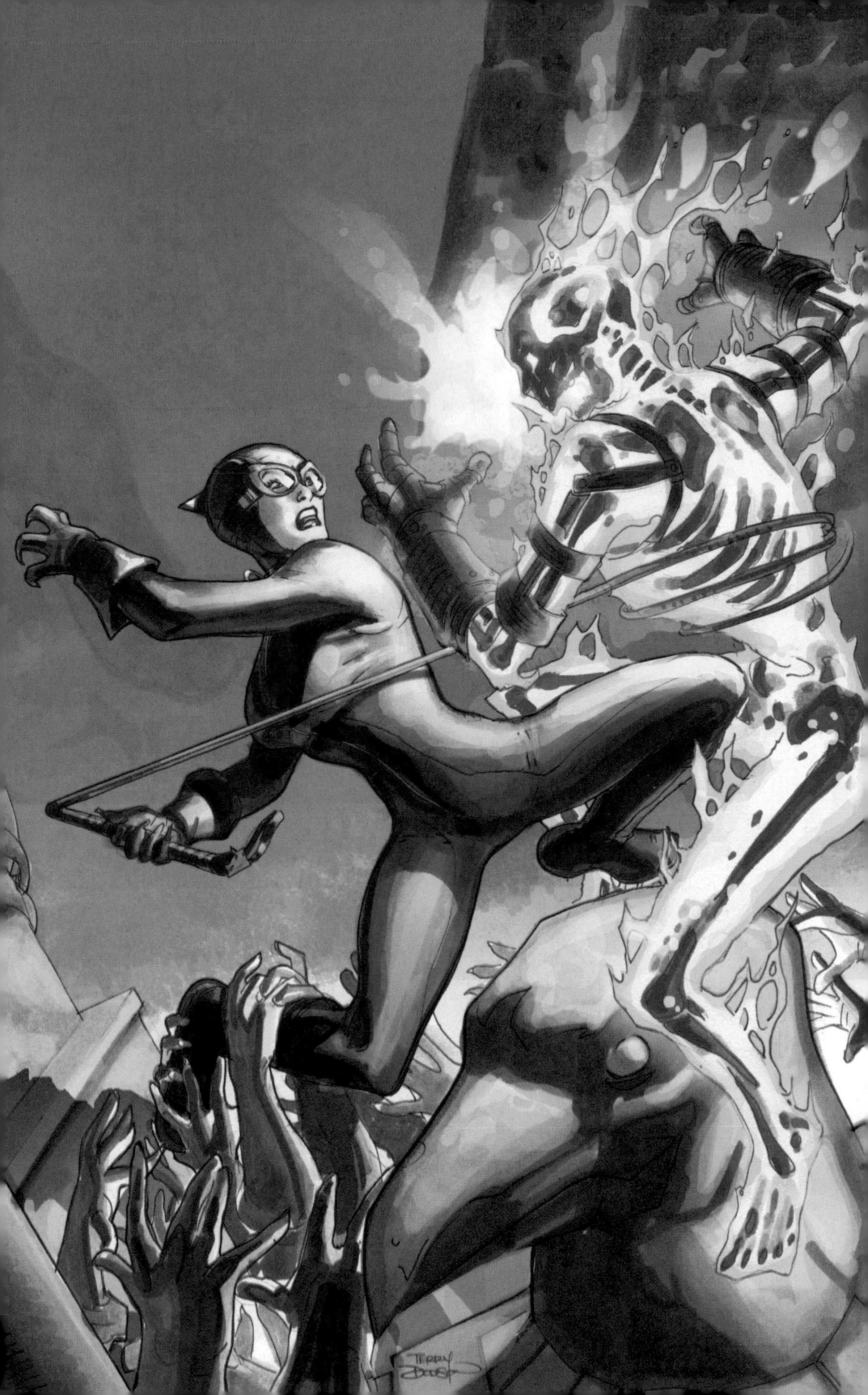

ANN NOCENTI
co-plotter & scripter

SCOTT McDANIEL
co-plotter & breakdown artist

RAFA SANDOVAL
penciller

JORDI TARRAGONA
inker

SONIA OBACK
colorist

TERRY & RACHEL DODSON
cover artists

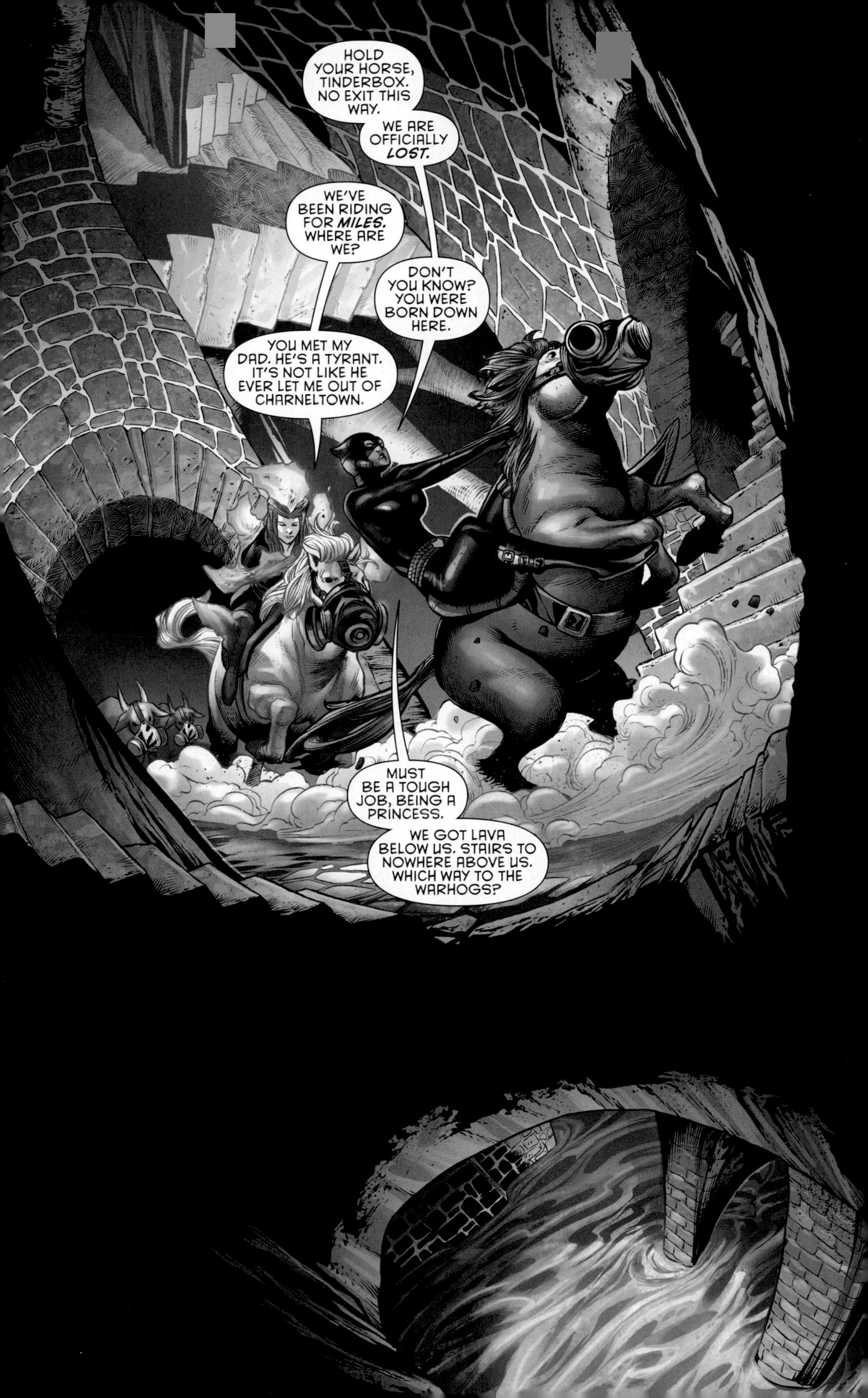
HOLD YOUR HORSE, TINDERBOX. NO EXIT THIS WAY.
WE ARE OFFICIALLY *LOST.*
WE'VE BEEN RIDING FOR *MILES.* WHERE ARE WE?
DON'T YOU KNOW? YOU WERE BORN DOWN HERE.
YOU MET MY DAD. HE'S A TYRANT. IT'S NOT LIKE HE EVER LET ME OUT OF CHARNELTOWN.
MUST BE A TOUGH JOB, BEING A PRINCESS.
WE GOT LAVA BELOW US. STAIRS TO NOWHERE ABOVE US. WHICH WAY TO THE WARHOGS?

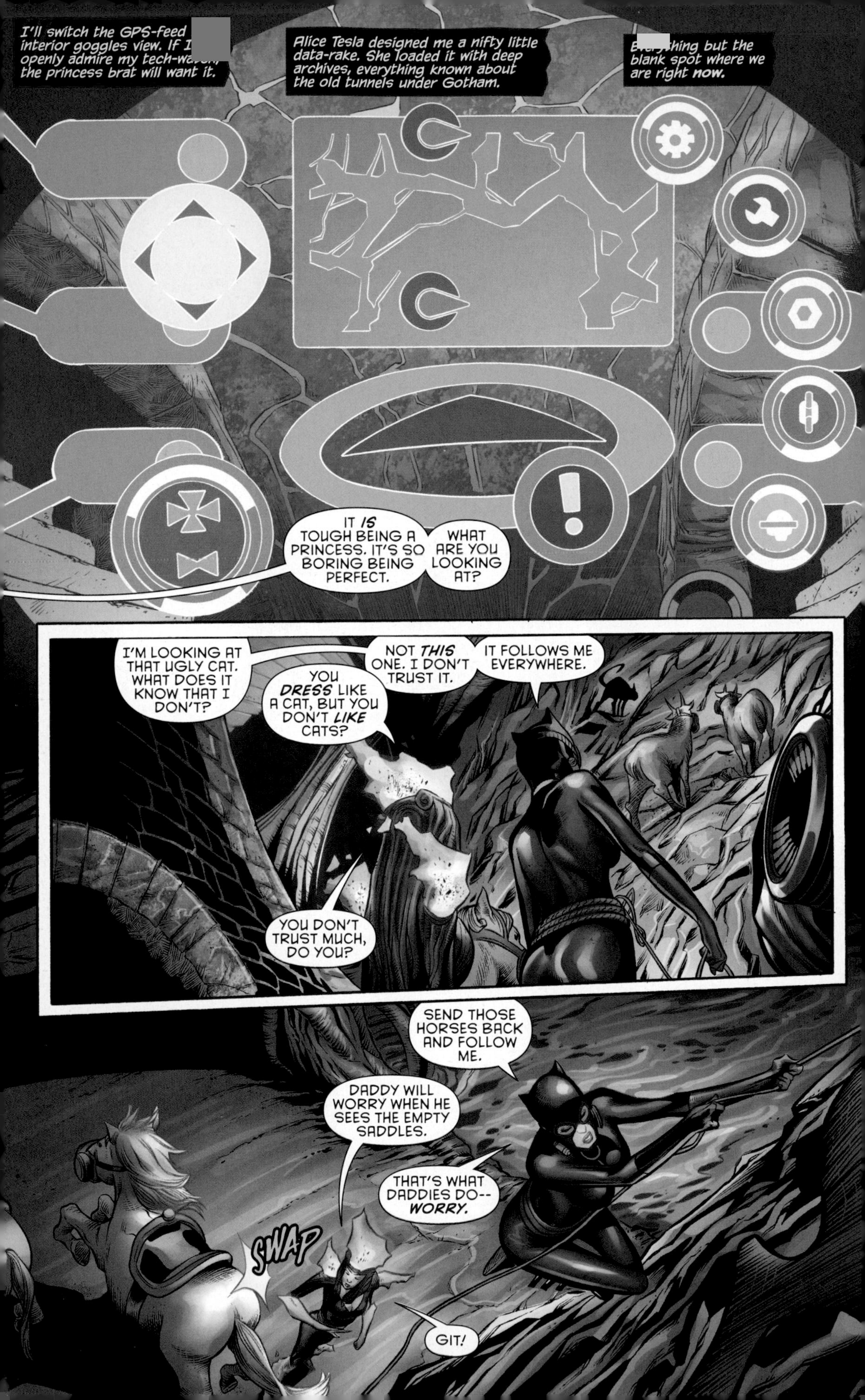
I'll switch the GPS-feed [redacted] interior goggles view. If I [redacted] openly admire my tech-wa[redacted], the princess brat will want it.
Alice Tesla designed me a nifty little data-rake. She loaded it with deep archives, everything known about the old tunnels under Gotham.
[redacted]thing but the blank spot where we are right ***now.***
IT ***IS*** TOUGH BEING A PRINCESS. IT'S SO BORING BEING PERFECT.
WHAT ARE YOU LOOKING AT?
I'M LOOKING AT THAT UGLY CAT. WHAT DOES IT KNOW THAT I DON'T?
NOT ***THIS*** ONE. I DON'T TRUST IT.
IT FOLLOWS ME EVERYWHERE.
YOU ***DRESS*** LIKE A CAT, BUT YOU DON'T ***LIKE*** CATS?
YOU DON'T TRUST MUCH, DO YOU?
SEND THOSE HORSES BACK AND FOLLOW ME.
DADDY WILL WORRY WHEN HE SEES THE EMPTY SADDLES.
THAT'S WHAT DADDIES DO-- ***WORRY.***
SWAP
GIT!

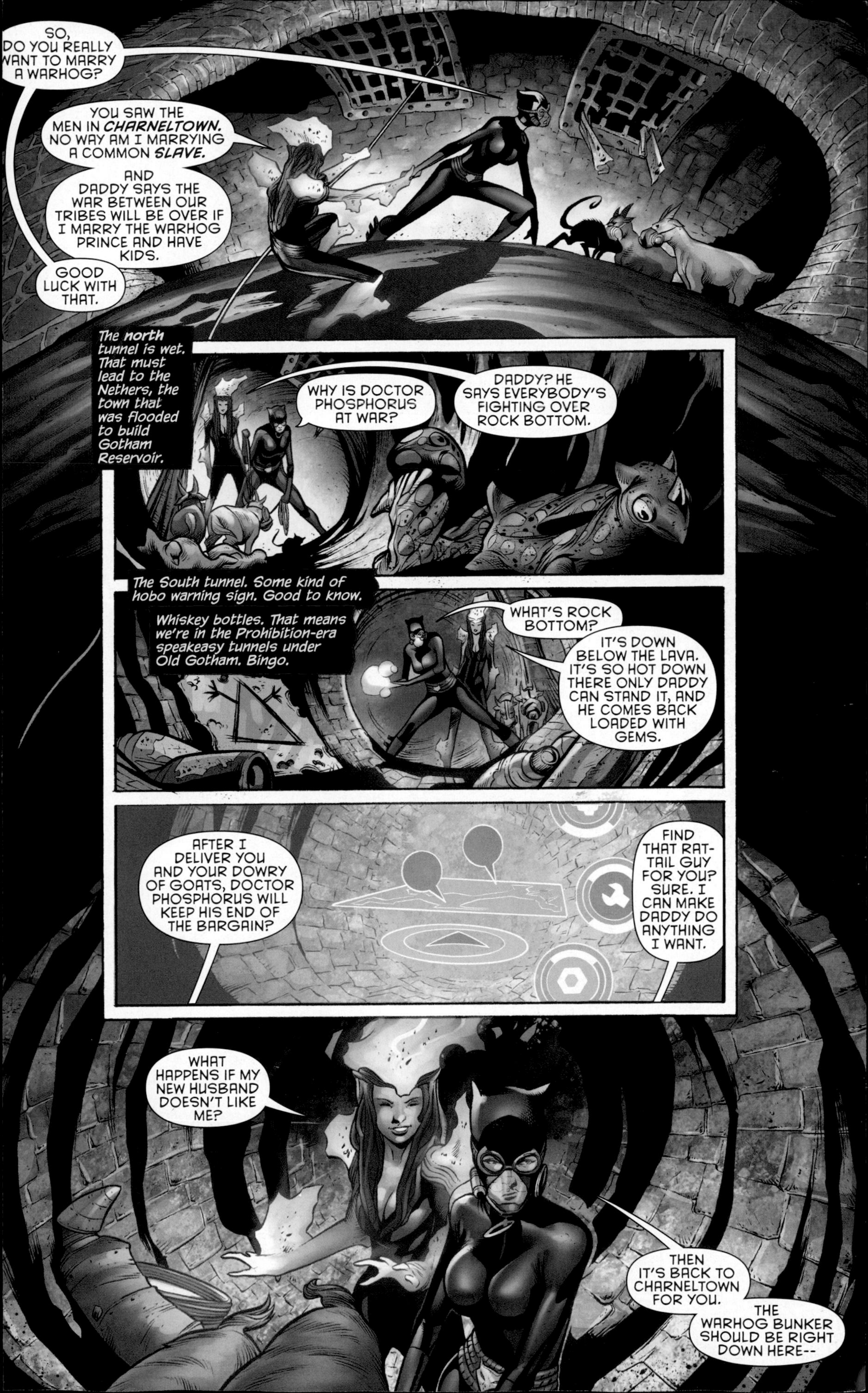
SO, DO YOU REALLY WANT TO MARRY A WARHOG?
YOU SAW THE MEN IN CHARNELTOWN. NO WAY AM I MARRYING A COMMON SLAVE.
AND DADDY SAYS THE WAR BETWEEN OUR TRIBES WILL BE OVER IF I MARRY THE WARHOG PRINCE AND HAVE KIDS.
GOOD LUCK WITH THAT.
The north tunnel is wet. That must lead to the Nethers, the town that was flooded to build Gotham Reservoir.
WHY IS DOCTOR PHOSPHORUS AT WAR?
DADDY? HE SAYS EVERYBODY'S FIGHTING OVER ROCK BOTTOM.
The South tunnel. Some kind of hobo warning sign. Good to know.
Whiskey bottles. That means we're in the Prohibition-era speakeasy tunnels under Old Gotham. Bingo.
WHAT'S ROCK BOTTOM?
IT'S DOWN BELOW THE LAVA. IT'S SO HOT DOWN THERE ONLY DADDY CAN STAND IT, AND HE COMES BACK LOADED WITH GEMS.
AFTER I DELIVER YOU AND YOUR DOWRY OF GOATS, DOCTOR PHOSPHORUS WILL KEEP HIS END OF THE BARGAIN?
FIND THAT RAT-TAIL GUY FOR YOU? SURE. I CAN MAKE DADDY DO ANYTHING I WANT.
WHAT HAPPENS IF MY NEW HUSBAND DOESN'T LIKE ME?
THEN IT'S BACK TO CHARNELTOWN FOR YOU.
THE WARHOG BUNKER SHOULD BE RIGHT DOWN HERE--

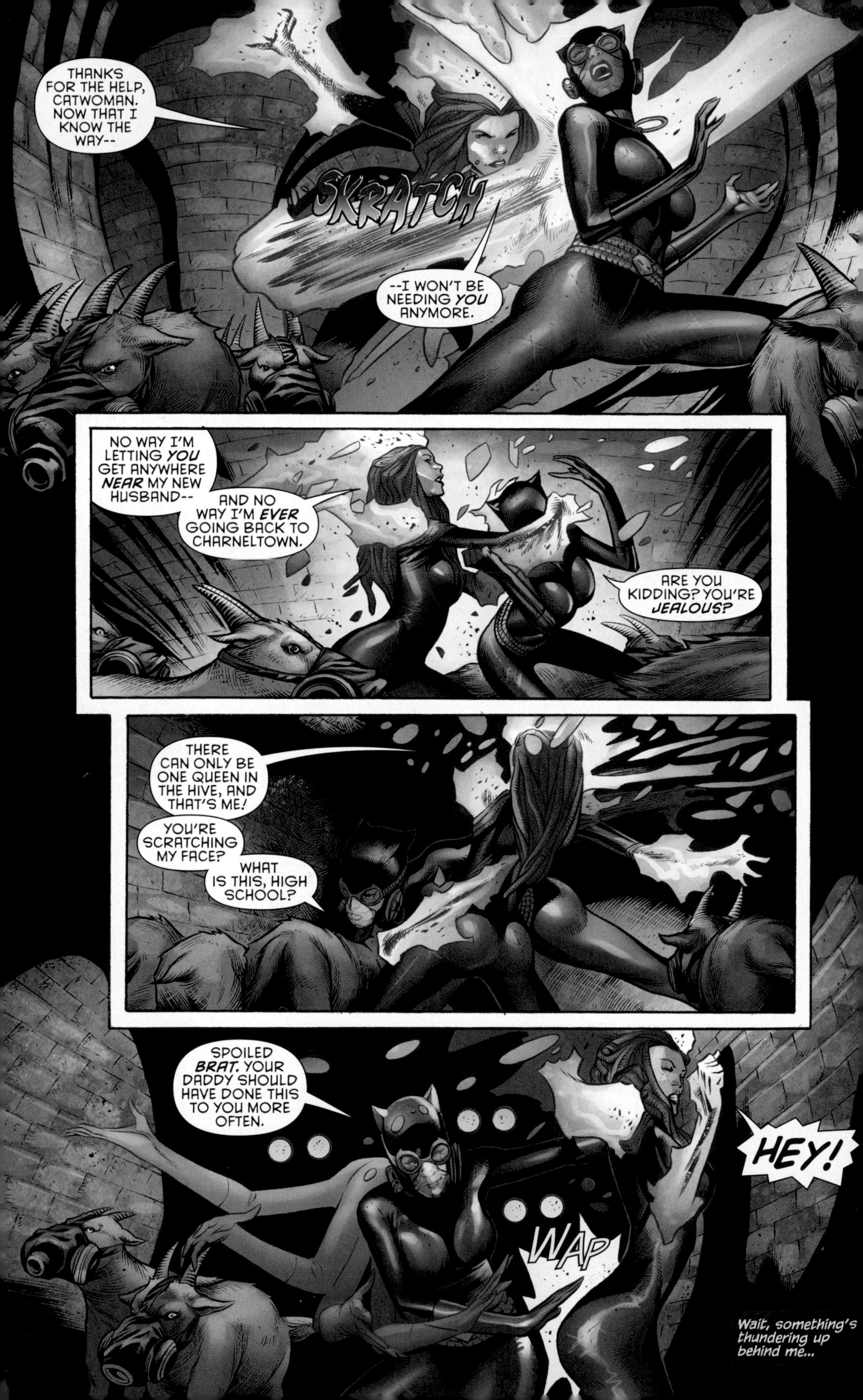
THANKS FOR THE HELP, CATWOMAN. NOW THAT I KNOW THE WAY--
SKRATCH
--I WON'T BE NEEDING YOU ANYMORE.
NO WAY I'M LETTING YOU GET ANYWHERE NEAR MY NEW HUSBAND--
AND NO WAY I'M EVER GOING BACK TO CHARNELTOWN.
ARE YOU KIDDING? YOU'RE JEALOUS?
THERE CAN ONLY BE ONE QUEEN IN THE HIVE, AND THAT'S ME!
YOU'RE SCRATCHING MY FACE?
WHAT IS THIS, HIGH SCHOOL?
SPOILED BRAT. YOUR DADDY SHOULD HAVE DONE THIS TO YOU MORE OFTEN.
HEY!
WAP
Wait, something's thundering up behind me...

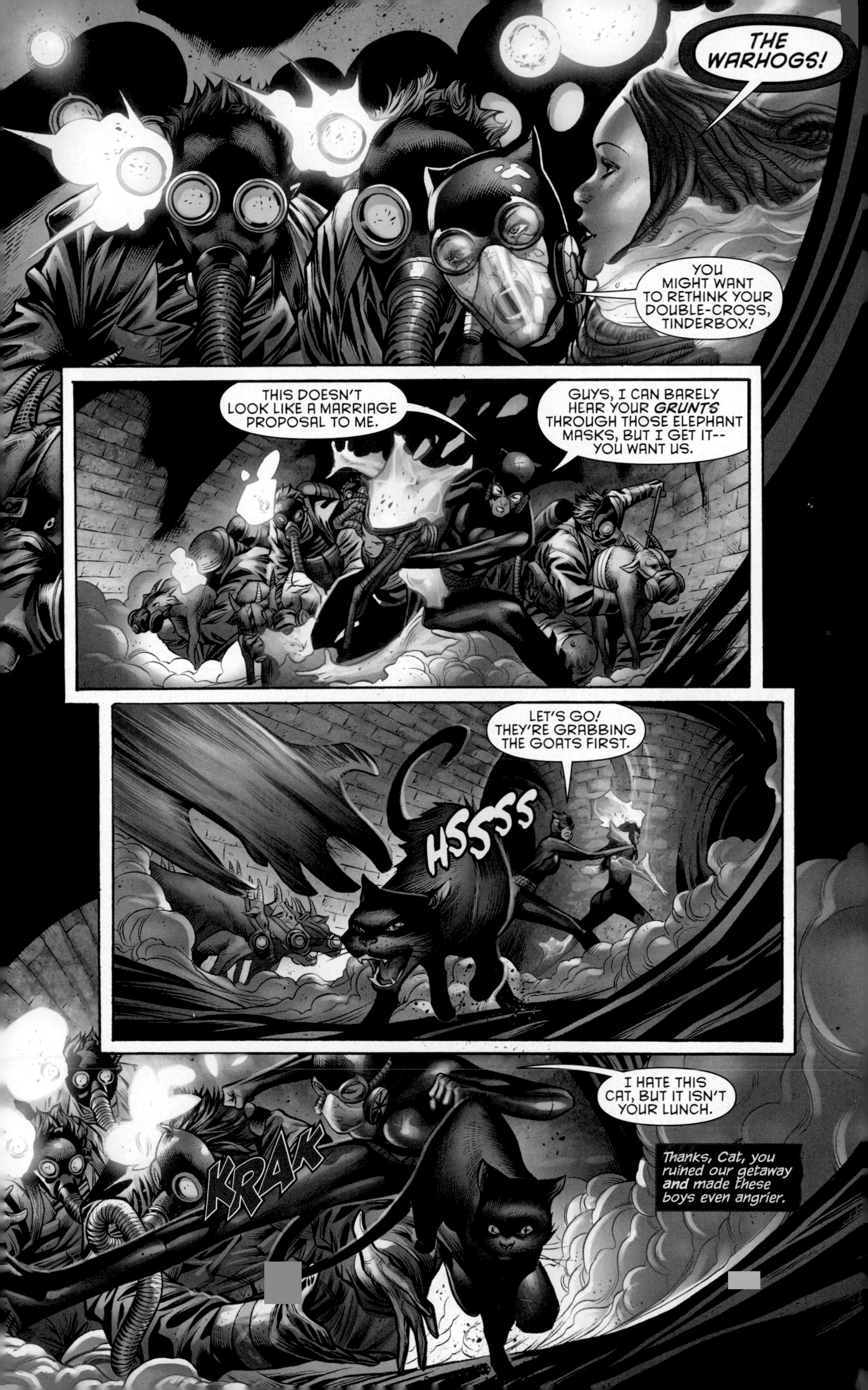
THE WARHOGS!
YOU MIGHT WANT TO RETHINK YOUR DOUBLE-CROSS, TINDERBOX!
THIS DOESN'T LOOK LIKE A MARRIAGE PROPOSAL TO ME.
GUYS, I CAN BARELY HEAR YOUR *GRUNTS* THROUGH THOSE ELEPHANT MASKS, BUT I GET IT-- YOU WANT US.
LET'S GO! THEY'RE GRABBING THE GOATS FIRST.
HSSSS
I HATE THIS CAT, BUT IT ISN'T YOUR LUNCH.
KRAK
Thanks, Cat, you ruined our getaway ***and*** *made these boys even angrier.*

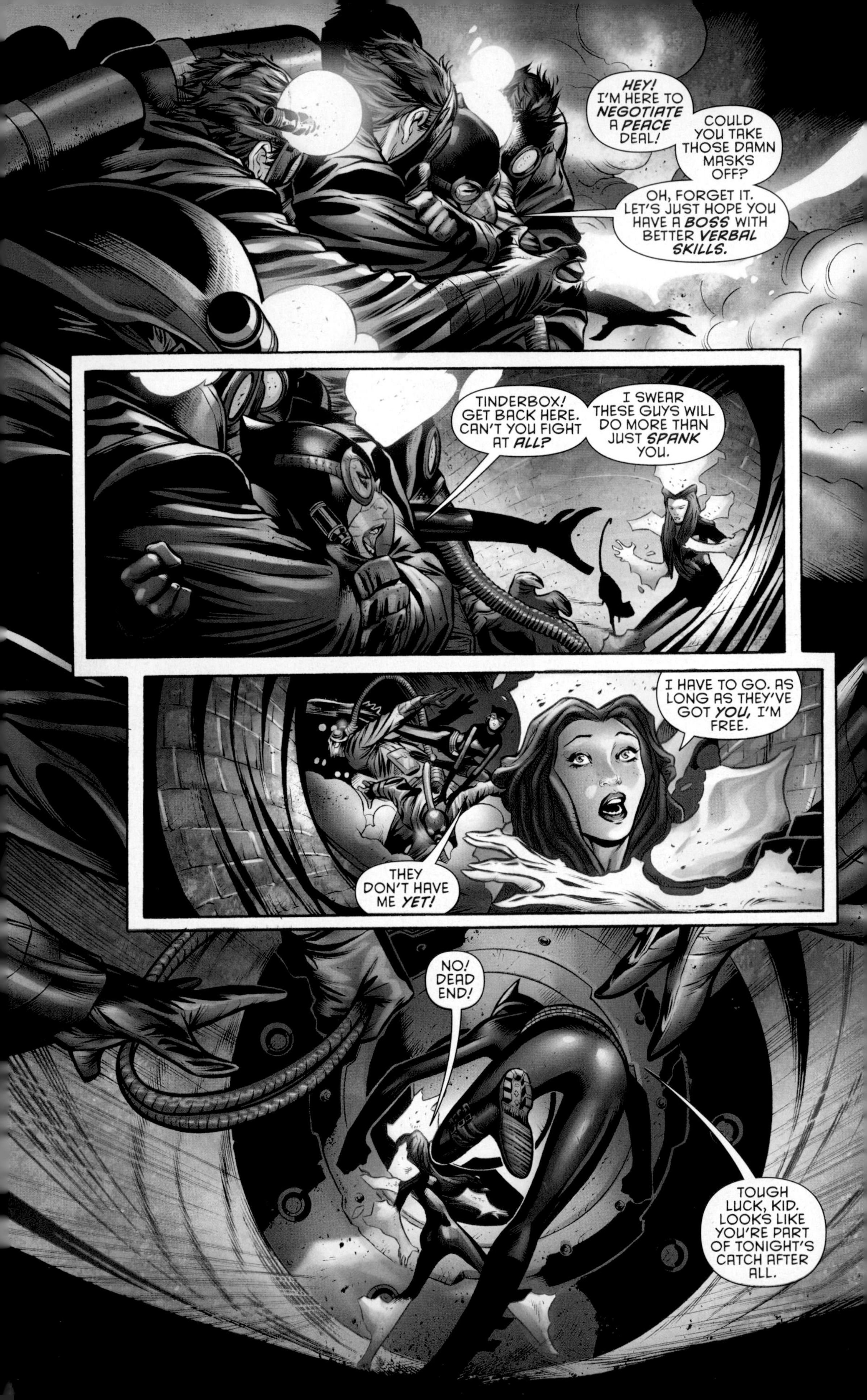
HEY! I'M HERE TO NEGOTIATE A PEACE DEAL!
COULD YOU TAKE THOSE DAMN MASKS OFF?
OH, FORGET IT. LET'S JUST HOPE YOU HAVE A BOSS WITH BETTER VERBAL SKILLS.
TINDERBOX! GET BACK HERE. CAN'T YOU FIGHT AT ALL?
I SWEAR THESE GUYS WILL DO MORE THAN JUST SPANK YOU.
I HAVE TO GO. AS LONG AS THEY'VE GOT YOU, I'M FREE.
THEY DON'T HAVE ME YET!
NO! DEAD END!
TOUGH LUCK, KID. LOOKS LIKE YOU'RE PART OF TONIGHT'S CATCH AFTER ALL.

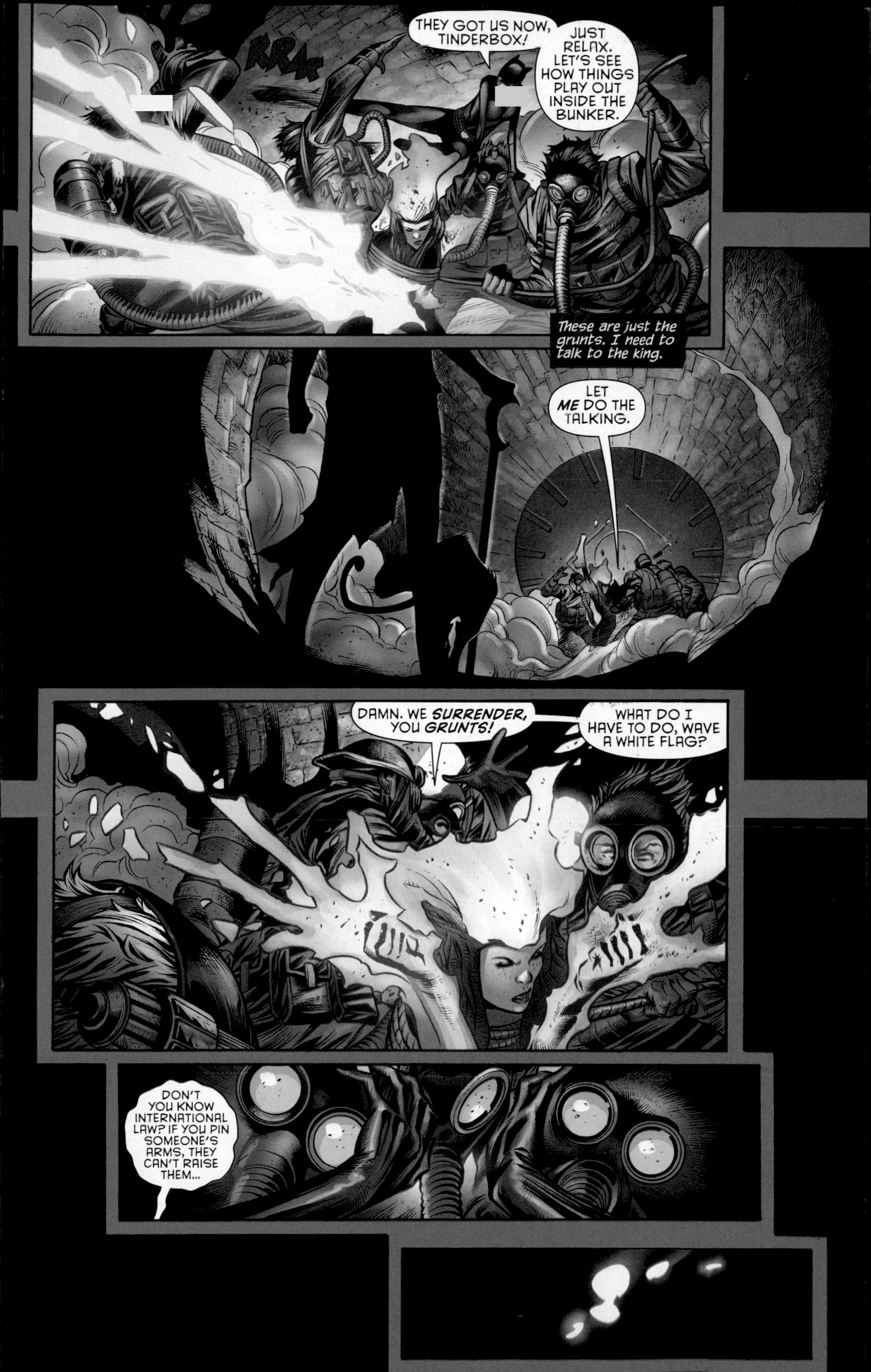
THEY GOT US NOW, TINDERBOX!
JUST RELAX. LET'S SEE HOW THINGS PLAY OUT INSIDE THE BUNKER.
These are just the grunts. I need to talk to the king.
LET *ME* DO THE TALKING.
DAMN. WE *SURRENDER,* YOU *GRUNTS!*
WHAT DO I HAVE TO DO, WAVE A WHITE FLAG?
DON'T YOU KNOW INTERNATIONAL LAW? IF YOU PIN SOMEONE'S ARMS, THEY CAN'T RAISE THEM...

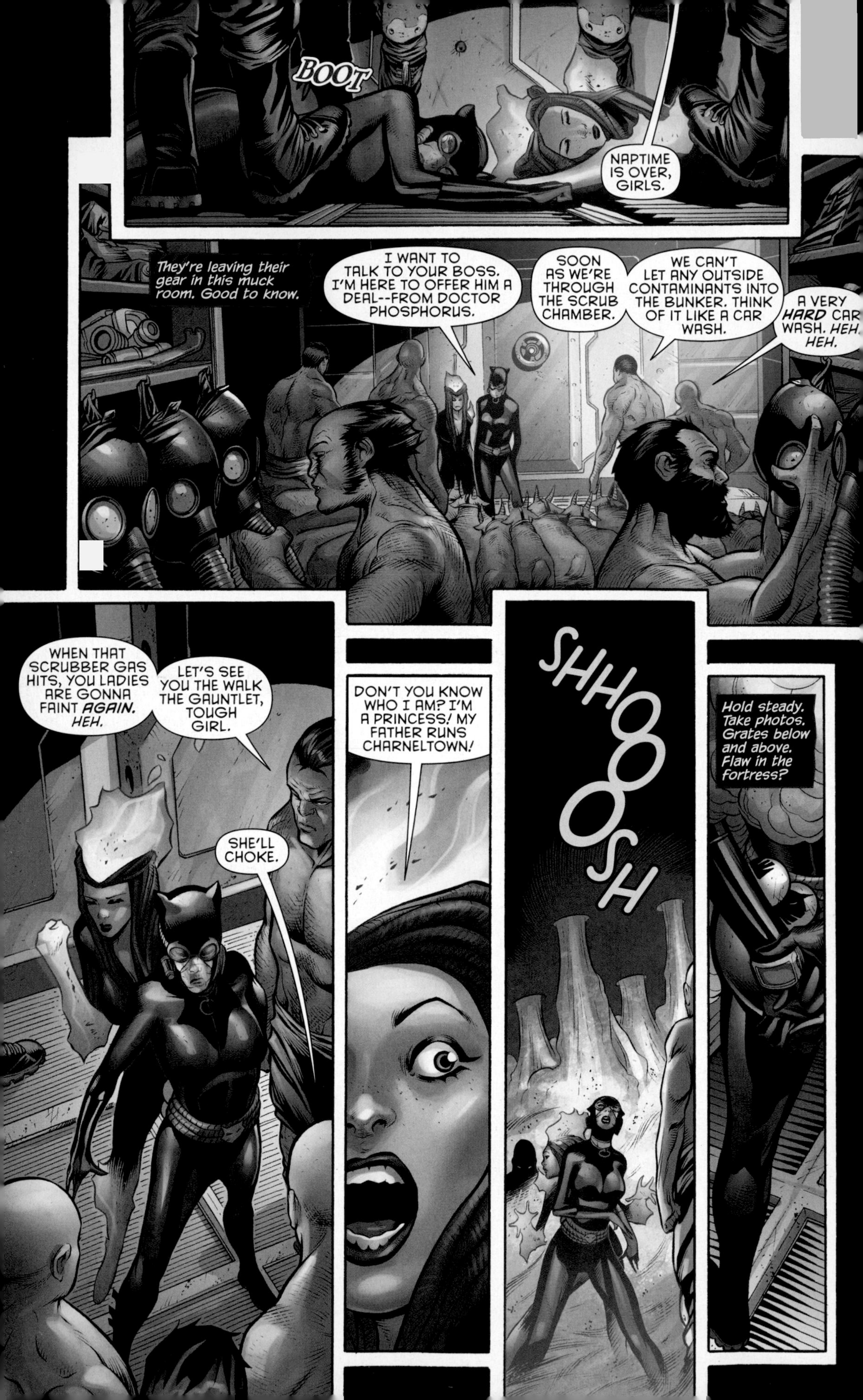
BOOT
NAPTIME IS OVER, GIRLS.
They're leaving their gear in this muck room. Good to know.
I WANT TO TALK TO YOUR BOSS. I'M HERE TO OFFER HIM A DEAL--FROM DOCTOR PHOSPHORUS.
SOON AS WE'RE THROUGH THE SCRUB CHAMBER.
WE CAN'T LET ANY OUTSIDE CONTAMINANTS INTO THE BUNKER. THINK OF IT LIKE A CAR WASH.
A VERY HARD CAR WASH. HEH. HEH.
WHEN THAT SCRUBBER GAS HITS, YOU LADIES ARE GONNA FAINT AGAIN. HEH.
LET'S SEE YOU THE WALK THE GAUNTLET, TOUGH GIRL.
SHE'LL CHOKE.
DON'T YOU KNOW WHO I AM? I'M A PRINCESS! MY FATHER RUNS CHARNELTOWN!
SHHOOOOSH
Hold steady. Take photos. Grates below and above. Flaw in the fortress?

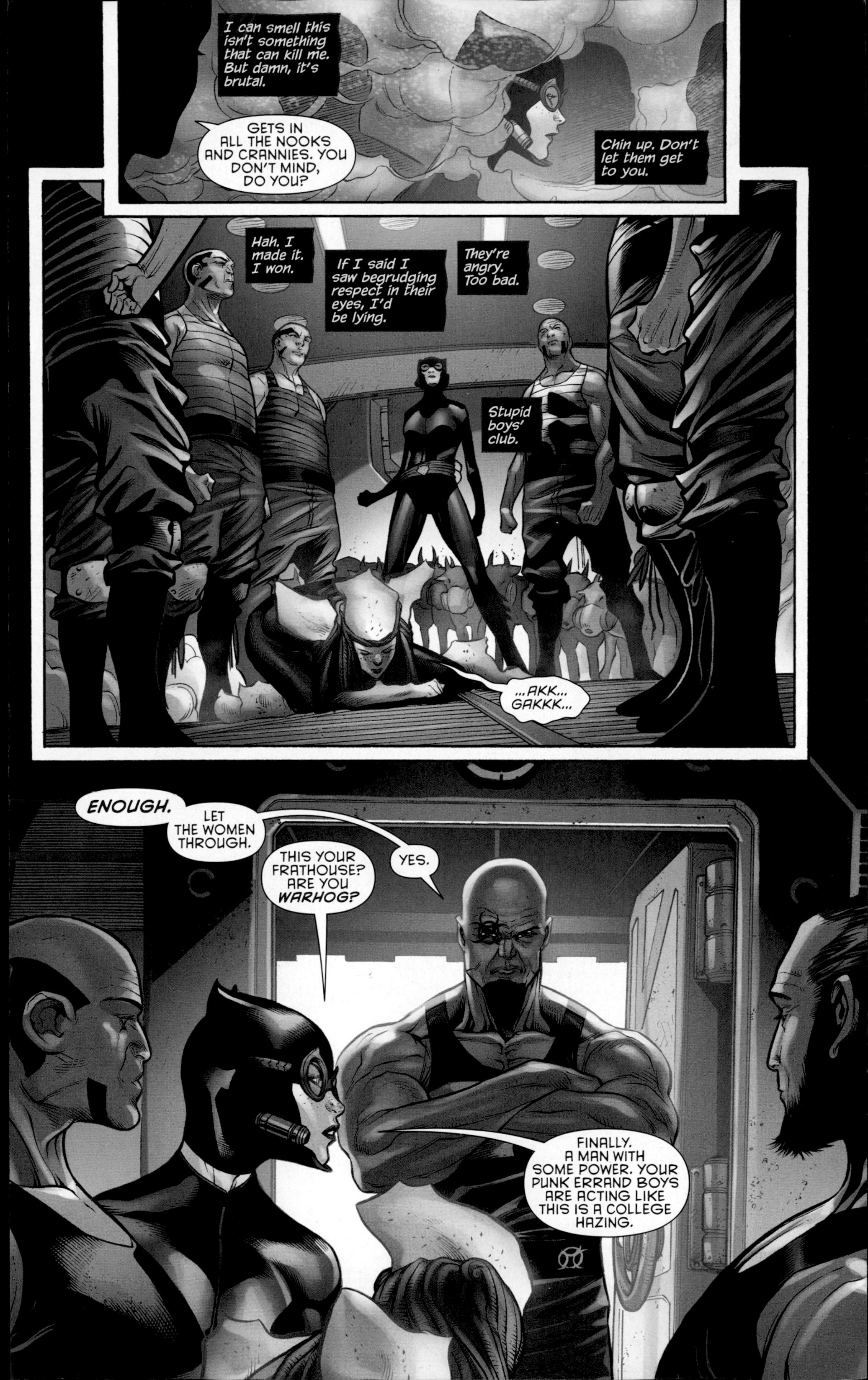
I can smell this isn't something that can kill me. But damn, it's brutal.
GETS IN ALL THE NOOKS AND CRANNIES. YOU DON'T MIND, DO YOU?
Chin up. Don't let them get to you.
Hah. I made it. I won.
If I said I saw begrudging respect in their eyes, I'd be lying.
They're angry. Too bad.
Stupid boys' club.
...AKK... GAKKK...
ENOUGH.
LET THE WOMEN THROUGH.
THIS YOUR FRATHOUSE? ARE YOU WARHOG?
YES.
FINALLY. A MAN WITH SOME POWER. YOUR PUNK ERRAND BOYS ARE ACTING LIKE THIS IS A COLLEGE HAZING.

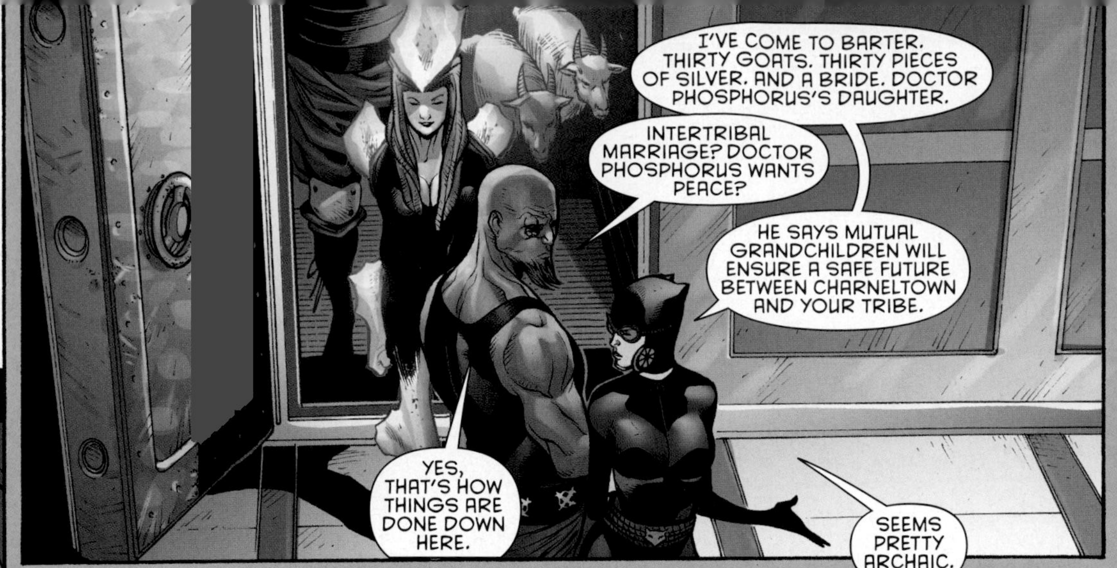
I'VE COME TO BARTER. THIRTY GOATS. THIRTY PIECES OF SILVER. AND A BRIDE. DOCTOR PHOSPHORUS'S DAUGHTER.
INTERTRIBAL MARRIAGE? DOCTOR PHOSPHORUS WANTS PEACE?
HE SAYS MUTUAL GRANDCHILDREN WILL ENSURE A SAFE FUTURE BETWEEN CHARNELTOWN AND YOUR TRIBE.
YES, THAT'S HOW THINGS ARE DONE DOWN HERE.
SEEMS PRETTY ARCHAIC.
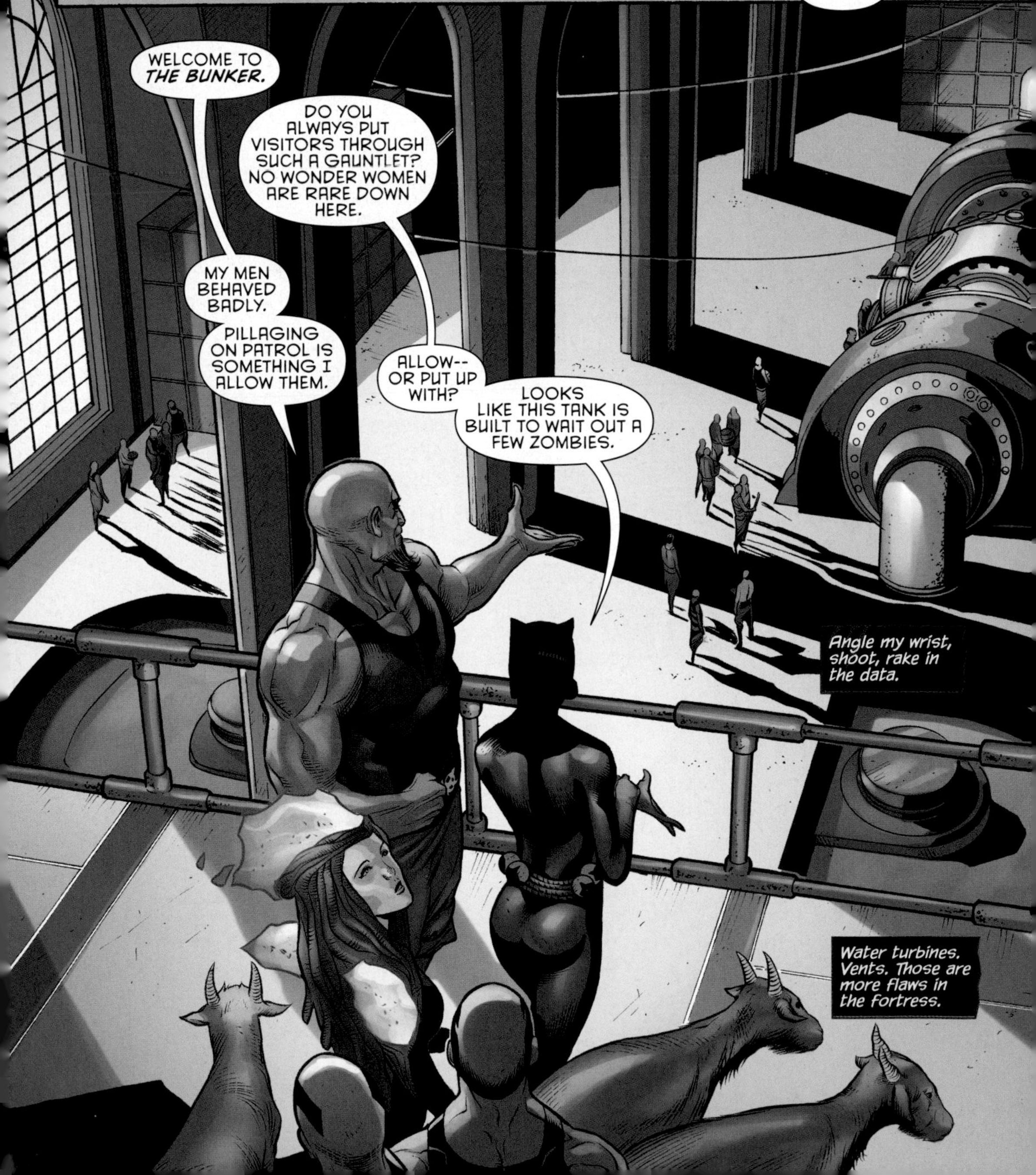
WELCOME TO *THE BUNKER.*
DO YOU ALWAYS PUT VISITORS THROUGH SUCH A GAUNTLET? NO WONDER WOMEN ARE RARE DOWN HERE.
MY MEN BEHAVED BADLY.
PILLAGING ON PATROL IS SOMETHING I ALLOW THEM.
ALLOW-- OR PUT UP WITH?
LOOKS LIKE THIS TANK IS BUILT TO WAIT OUT A FEW ZOMBIES.
Angle my wrist, shoot, rake in the data.
Water turbines. Vents. Those are more flaws in the fortress.

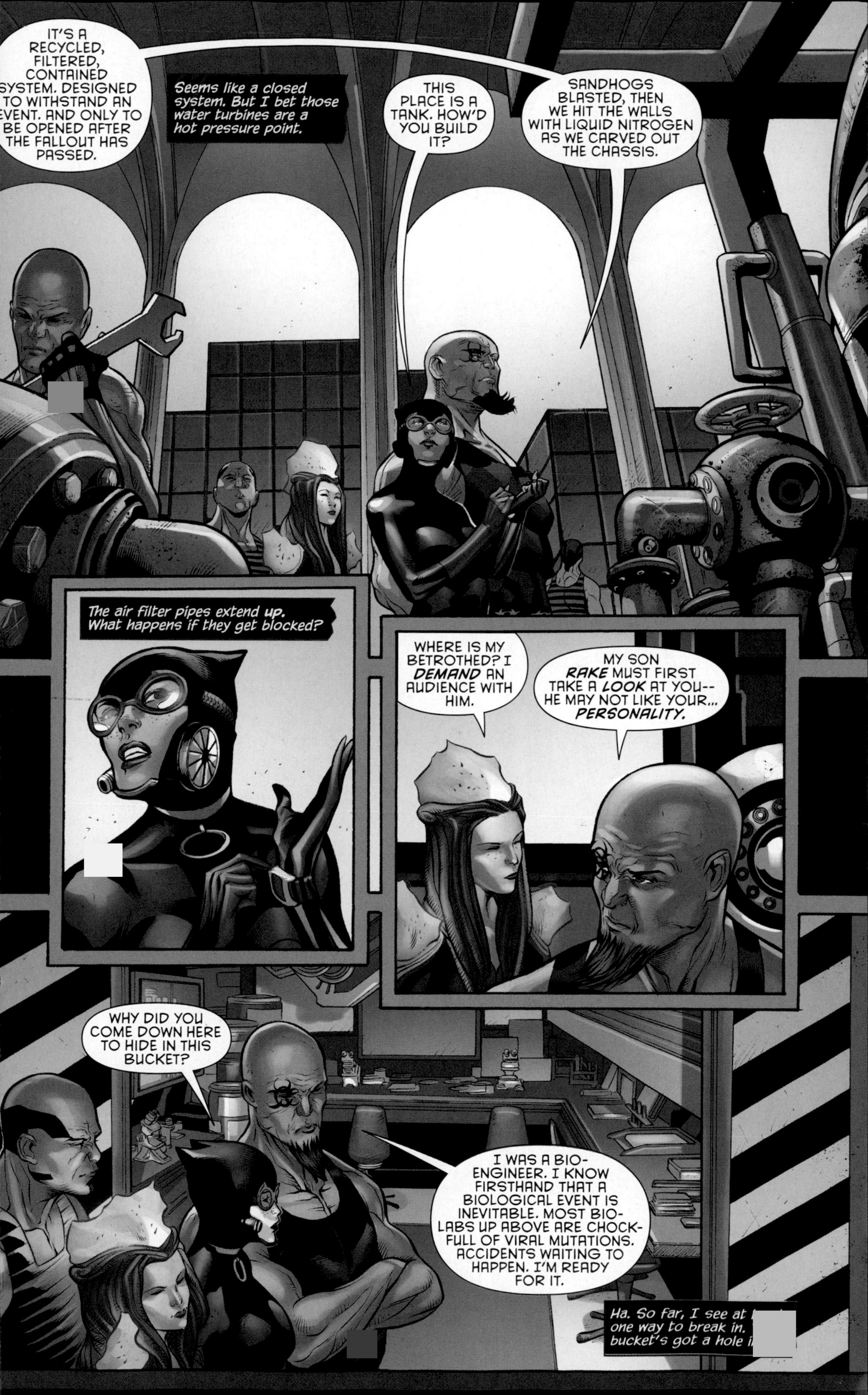

IT'S A RECYCLED, FILTERED, CONTAINED SYSTEM. DESIGNED TO WITHSTAND AN EVENT. AND ONLY TO BE OPENED AFTER THE FALLOUT HAS PASSED.
Seems like a closed system. But I bet those water turbines are a hot pressure point.
THIS PLACE IS A TANK. HOW'D YOU BUILD IT?
SANDHOGS BLASTED, THEN WE HIT THE WALLS WITH LIQUID NITROGEN AS WE CARVED OUT THE CHASSIS.
The air filter pipes extend up. What happens if they get blocked?
WHERE IS MY BETROTHED? I DEMAND AN AUDIENCE WITH HIM.
MY SON RAKE MUST FIRST TAKE A LOOK AT YOU-- HE MAY NOT LIKE YOUR... PERSONALITY.
WHY DID YOU COME DOWN HERE TO HIDE IN THIS BUCKET?
I WAS A BIO-ENGINEER. I KNOW FIRSTHAND THAT A BIOLOGICAL EVENT IS INEVITABLE. MOST BIO-LABS UP ABOVE ARE CHOCK-FULL OF VIRAL MUTATIONS. ACCIDENTS WAITING TO HAPPEN. I'M READY FOR IT.
Ha. So far, I see at one way to break in. bucket's got a hole i

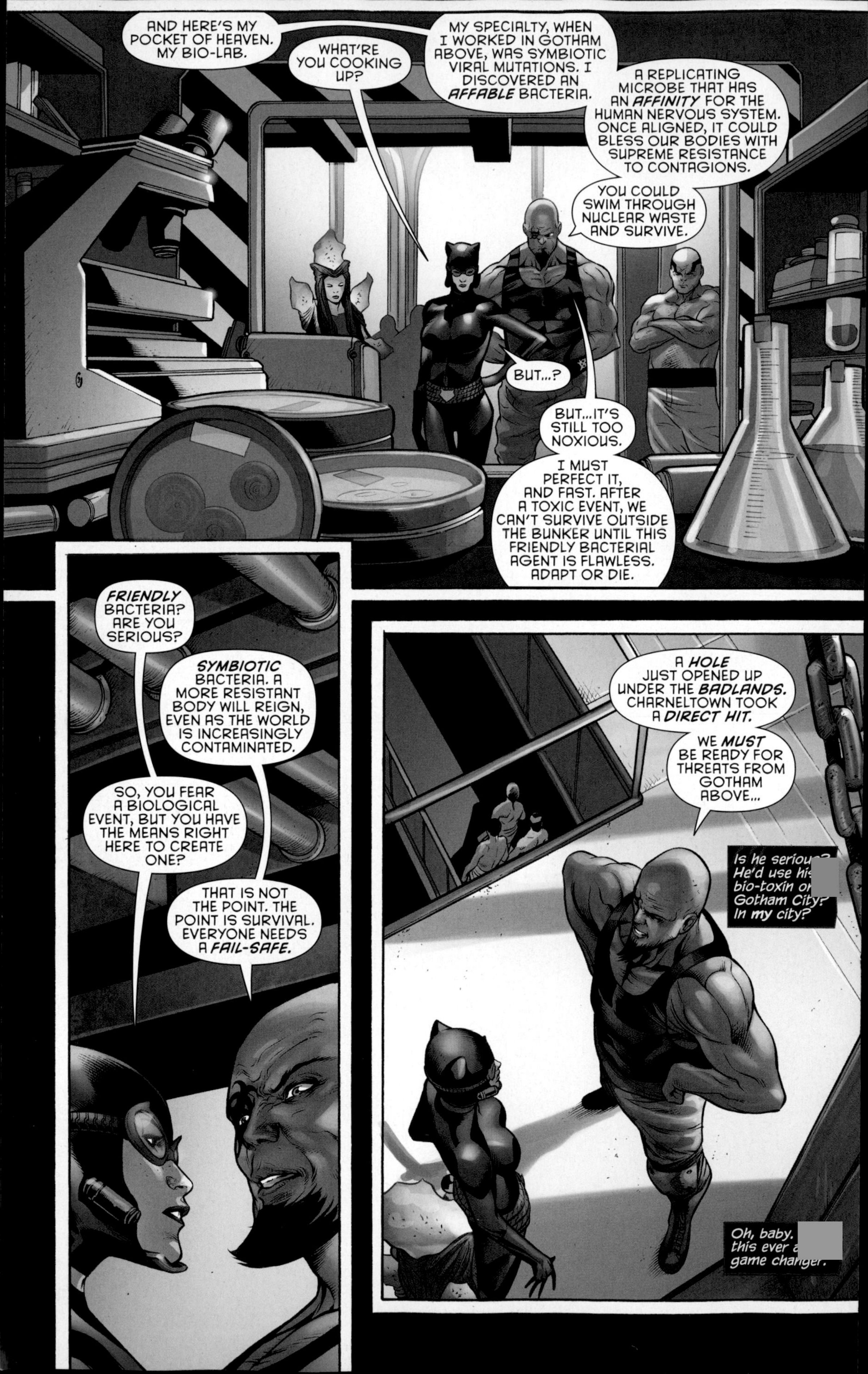

AND HERE'S MY POCKET OF HEAVEN. MY BIO-LAB.
WHAT'RE YOU COOKING UP?
MY SPECIALTY, WHEN I WORKED IN GOTHAM ABOVE, WAS SYMBIOTIC VIRAL MUTATIONS. I DISCOVERED AN *AFFABLE* BACTERIA.
A REPLICATING MICROBE THAT HAS AN *AFFINITY* FOR THE HUMAN NERVOUS SYSTEM. ONCE ALIGNED, IT COULD BLESS OUR BODIES WITH SUPREME RESISTANCE TO CONTAGIONS.
YOU COULD SWIM THROUGH NUCLEAR WASTE AND SURVIVE.
BUT...?
BUT...IT'S STILL TOO NOXIOUS.
I MUST PERFECT IT, AND FAST. AFTER A TOXIC EVENT, WE CAN'T SURVIVE OUTSIDE THE BUNKER UNTIL THIS FRIENDLY BACTERIAL AGENT IS FLAWLESS. ADAPT OR DIE.
FRIENDLY BACTERIA? ARE YOU SERIOUS?
SYMBIOTIC BACTERIA. A MORE RESISTANT BODY WILL REIGN, EVEN AS THE WORLD IS INCREASINGLY CONTAMINATED.
SO, YOU FEAR A BIOLOGICAL EVENT, BUT YOU HAVE THE MEANS RIGHT HERE TO CREATE ONE?
THAT IS NOT THE POINT. THE POINT IS SURVIVAL. EVERYONE NEEDS A *FAIL-SAFE.*
A *HOLE* JUST OPENED UP UNDER THE *BADLANDS.* CHARNELTOWN TOOK A *DIRECT HIT.*
WE *MUST* BE READY FOR THREATS FROM GOTHAM ABOVE...
Is he seriou
He'd use hi
bio-toxin o
Gotham City?
*In **my** city?*
Oh, baby.
this ever a
game changer.

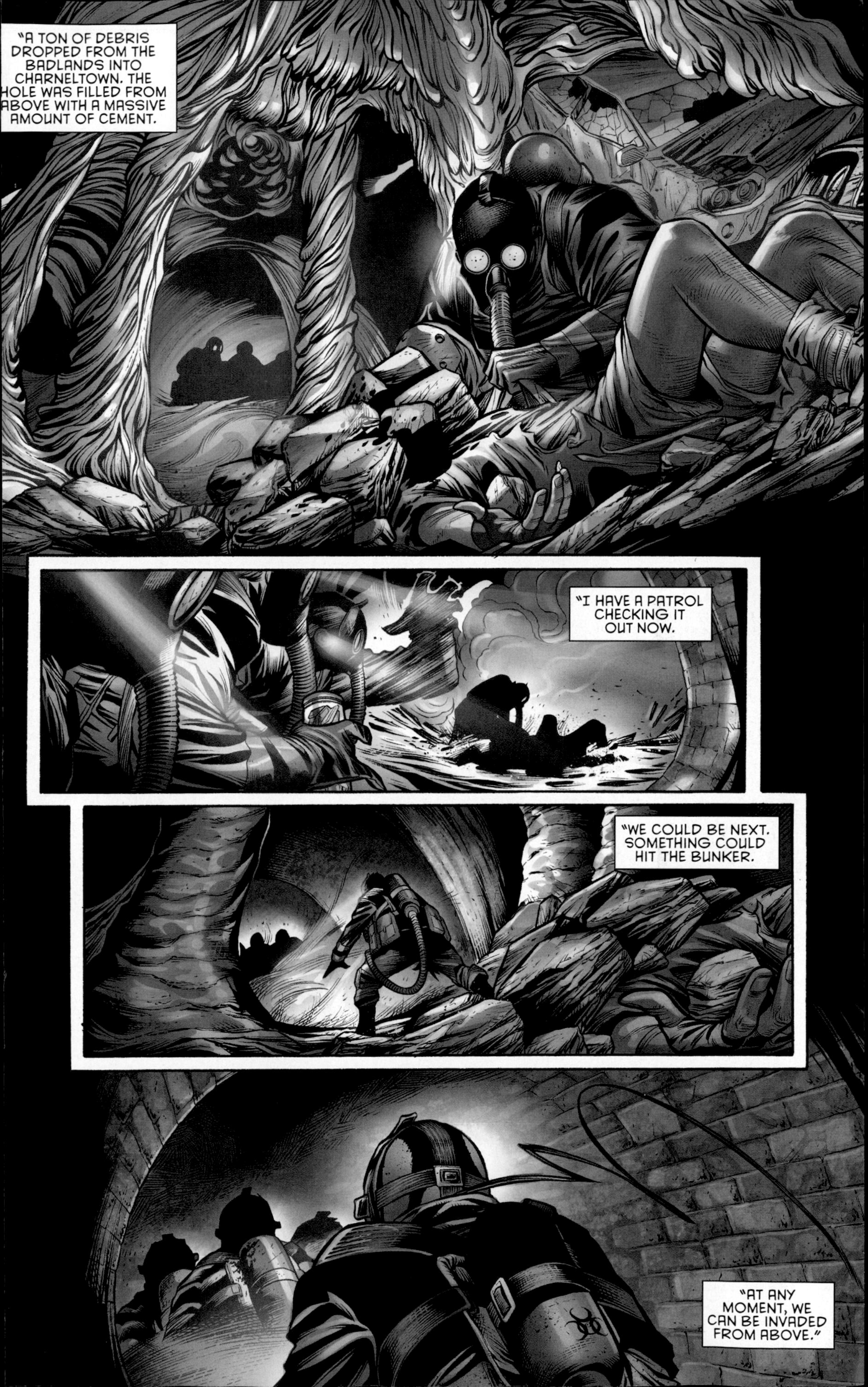
"A TON OF DEBRIS DROPPED FROM THE BADLANDS INTO CHARNELTOWN. THE HOLE WAS FILLED FROM ABOVE WITH A MASSIVE AMOUNT OF CEMENT.
"I HAVE A PATROL CHECKING IT OUT NOW.
"WE COULD BE NEXT. SOMETHING COULD HIT THE BUNKER.
"AT ANY MOMENT, WE CAN BE INVADED FROM ABOVE."

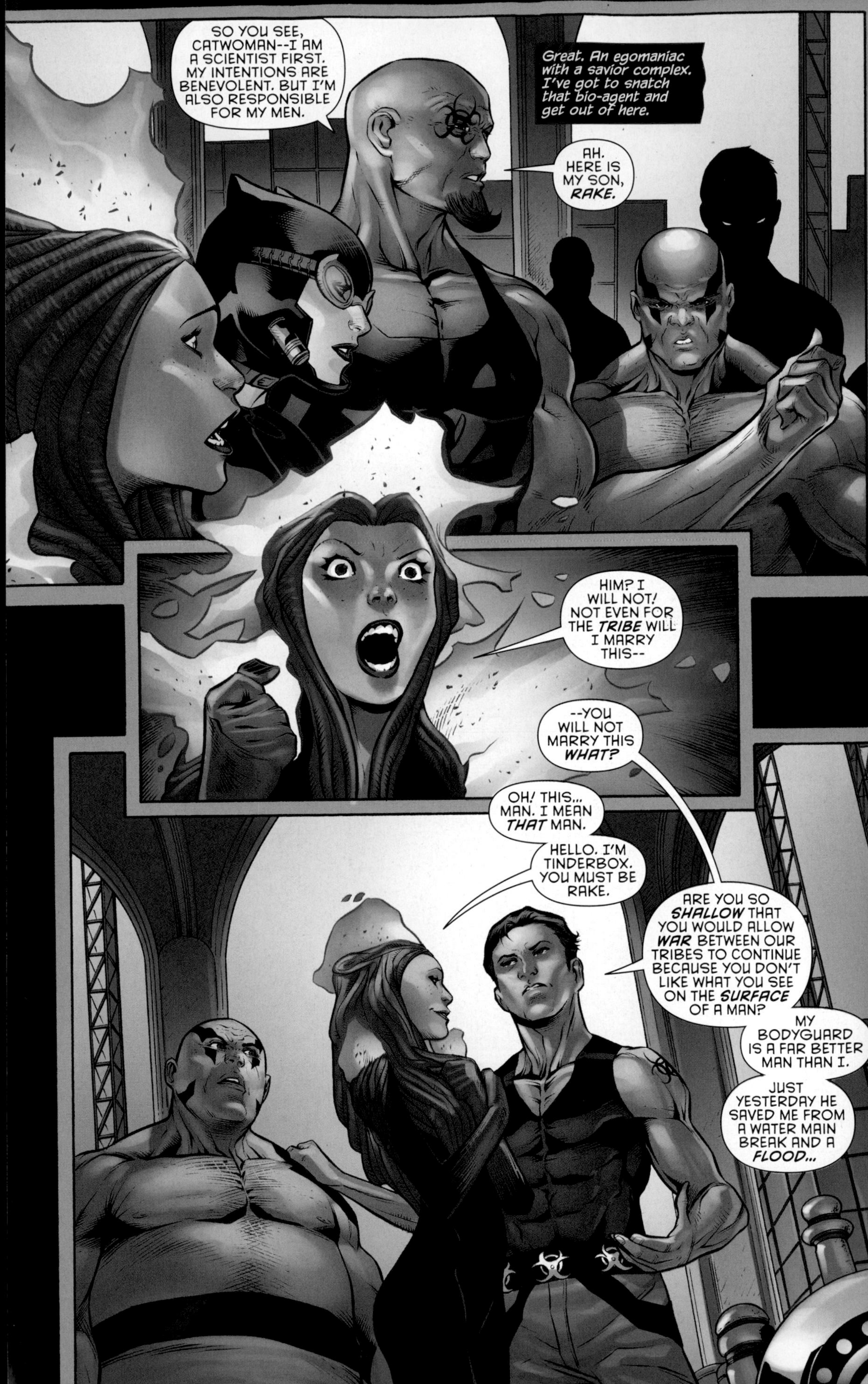
SO YOU SEE, CATWOMAN--I AM A SCIENTIST FIRST. MY INTENTIONS ARE BENEVOLENT. BUT I'M ALSO RESPONSIBLE FOR MY MEN.
Great. An egomaniac with a savior complex. I've got to snatch that bio-agent and get out of here.
AH. HERE IS MY SON, RAKE.
HIM? I WILL NOT! NOT EVEN FOR THE TRIBE WILL I MARRY THIS--
--YOU WILL NOT MARRY THIS WHAT?
OH! THIS... MAN. I MEAN THAT MAN.
HELLO. I'M TINDERBOX. YOU MUST BE RAKE.
ARE YOU SO SHALLOW THAT YOU WOULD ALLOW WAR BETWEEN OUR TRIBES TO CONTINUE BECAUSE YOU DON'T LIKE WHAT YOU SEE ON THE SURFACE OF A MAN?
MY BODYGUARD IS A FAR BETTER MAN THAN I.
JUST YESTERDAY HE SAVED ME FROM A WATER MAIN BREAK AND A FLOOD...

"...OVER IN THE NETHERS."

MY SPIES TELL ME THERE'S GOING TO BE A WEDDING--AND *WE* WEREN'T INVITED.

DOCTOR PHOSPHORUS IS MAKING PEACE WITH WARHOG BY CONJOINING THEIR BRATS RAKE AND TINDERBOX.

WE CAN'T HAVE *THAT.* THAT WOULDN'T BE GOOD FOR NETHERS. AND EVERYBODY DESERVES A SHOT AT ROCK BOTTOM.

YOU WANT ME TO PET YOU? YOU ABANDONED ME TOO LONG THIS TIME.

YOU'RE LUCKY I DON'T KICK YOU.

PRRR

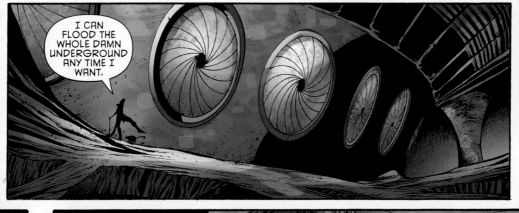

I CAN FLOOD THE WHOLE DAMN UNDERGROUND ANY TIME I WANT.

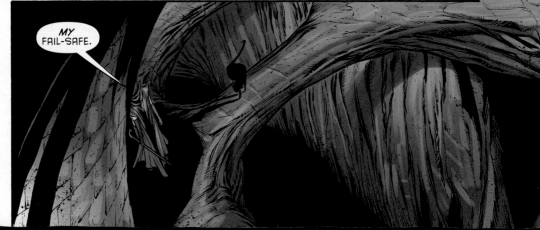

MY FAIL-SAFE.

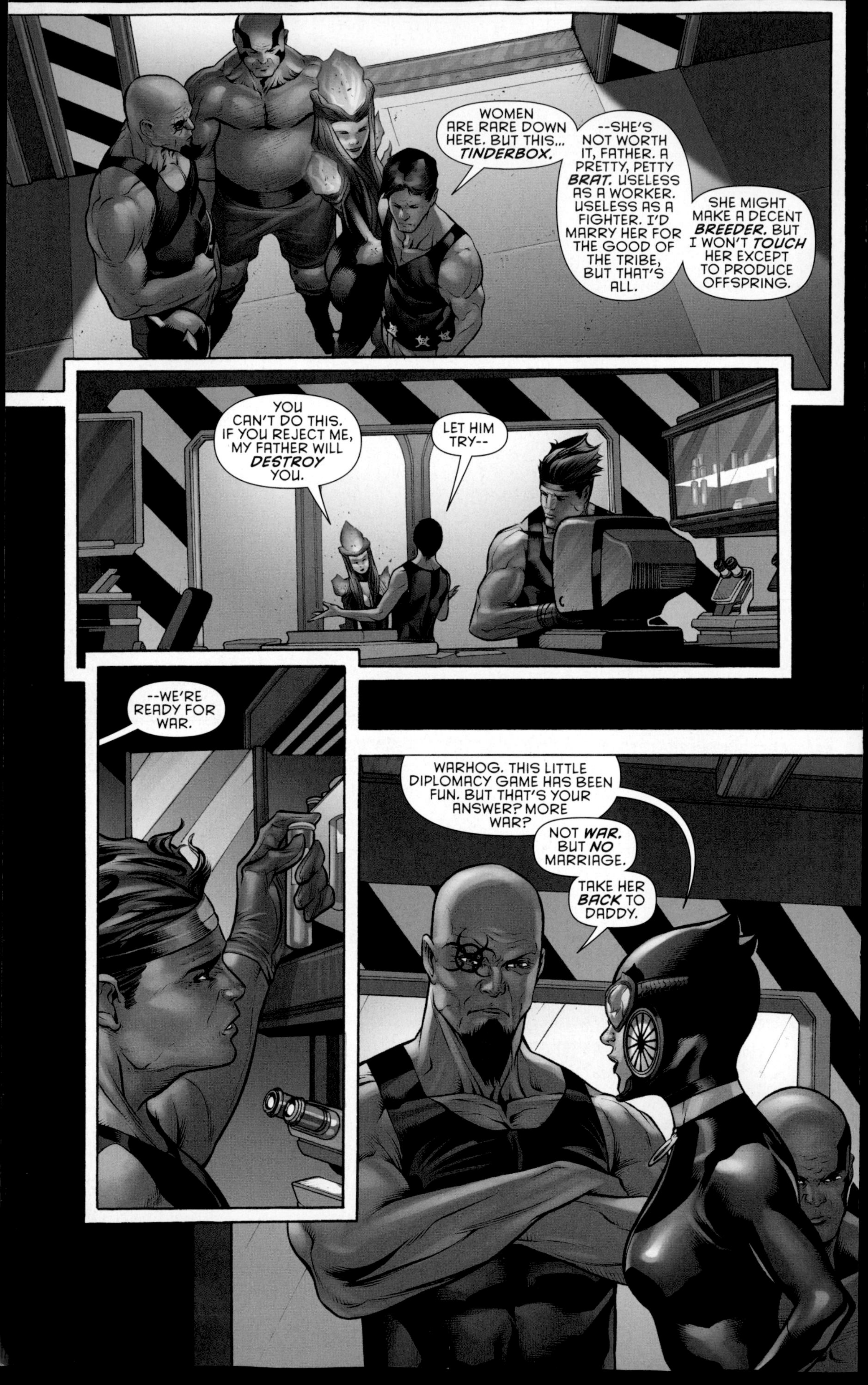
WOMEN ARE RARE DOWN HERE. BUT THIS... TINDERBOX.
--SHE'S NOT WORTH IT, FATHER. A PRETTY, PETTY BRAT. USELESS AS A WORKER. USELESS AS A FIGHTER. I'D MARRY HER FOR THE GOOD OF THE TRIBE, BUT THAT'S ALL.
SHE MIGHT MAKE A DECENT BREEDER. BUT I WON'T TOUCH HER EXCEPT TO PRODUCE OFFSPRING.
YOU CAN'T DO THIS. IF YOU REJECT ME, MY FATHER WILL DESTROY YOU.
LET HIM TRY--
--WE'RE READY FOR WAR.
WARHOG. THIS LITTLE DIPLOMACY GAME HAS BEEN FUN. BUT THAT'S YOUR ANSWER? MORE WAR?
NOT WAR. BUT NO MARRIAGE.
TAKE HER BACK TO DADDY.

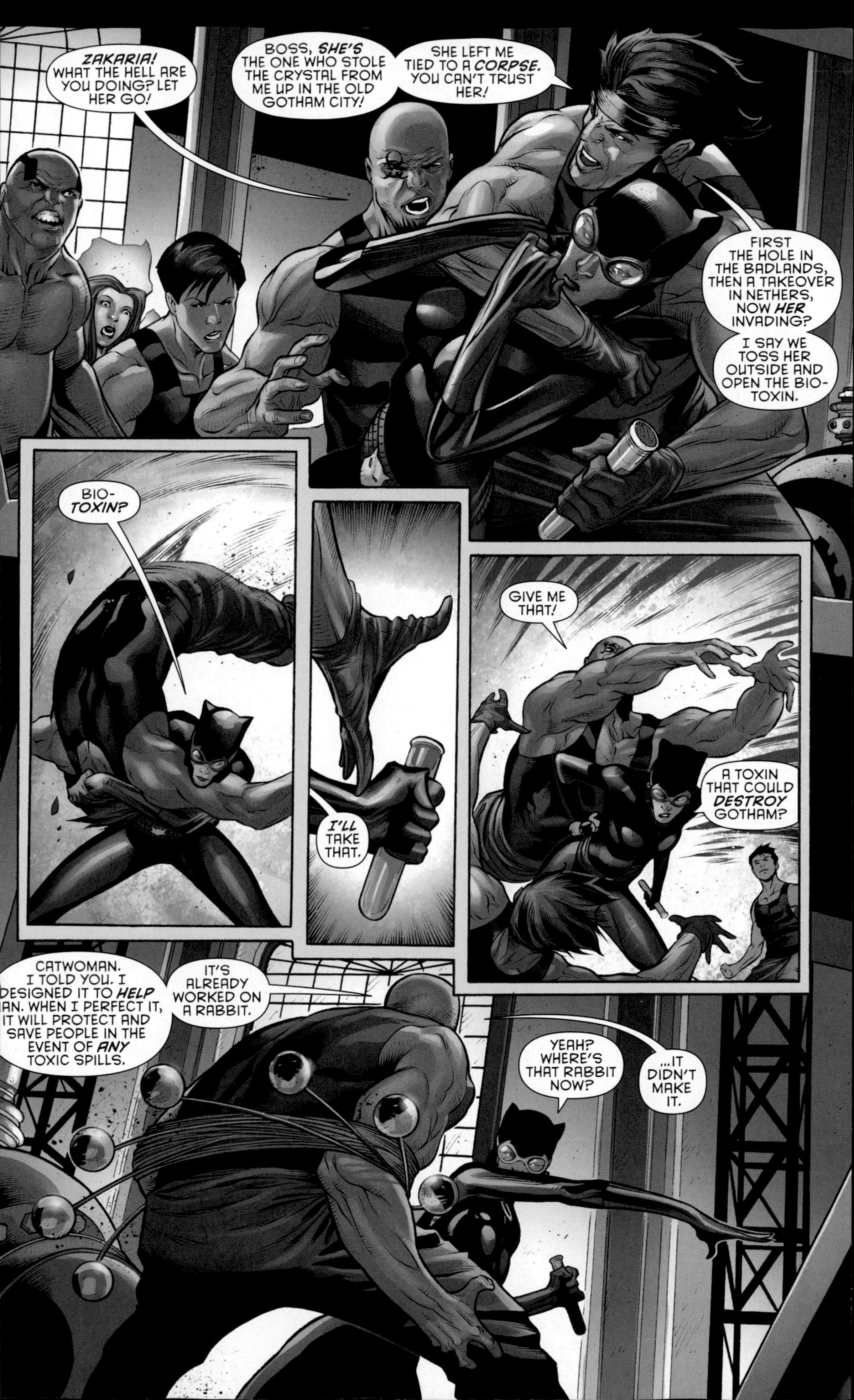
ZAKARIA! WHAT THE HELL ARE YOU DOING? LET HER GO!
BOSS, SHE'S THE ONE WHO STOLE THE CRYSTAL FROM ME UP IN THE OLD GOTHAM CITY!
SHE LEFT ME TIED TO A CORPSE. YOU CAN'T TRUST HER!
FIRST THE HOLE IN THE BADLANDS, THEN A TAKEOVER IN NETHERS, NOW HER INVADING?
I SAY WE TOSS HER OUTSIDE AND OPEN THE BIO-TOXIN.
BIO-TOXIN?
I'LL TAKE THAT.
GIVE ME THAT!
A TOXIN THAT COULD DESTROY GOTHAM?
CATWOMAN. I TOLD YOU. I DESIGNED IT TO HELP MAN. WHEN I PERFECT IT, IT WILL PROTECT AND SAVE PEOPLE IN THE EVENT OF ANY TOXIC SPILLS.
IT'S ALREADY WORKED ON A RABBIT.
YEAH? WHERE'S THAT RABBIT NOW?
...IT DIDN'T MAKE IT.

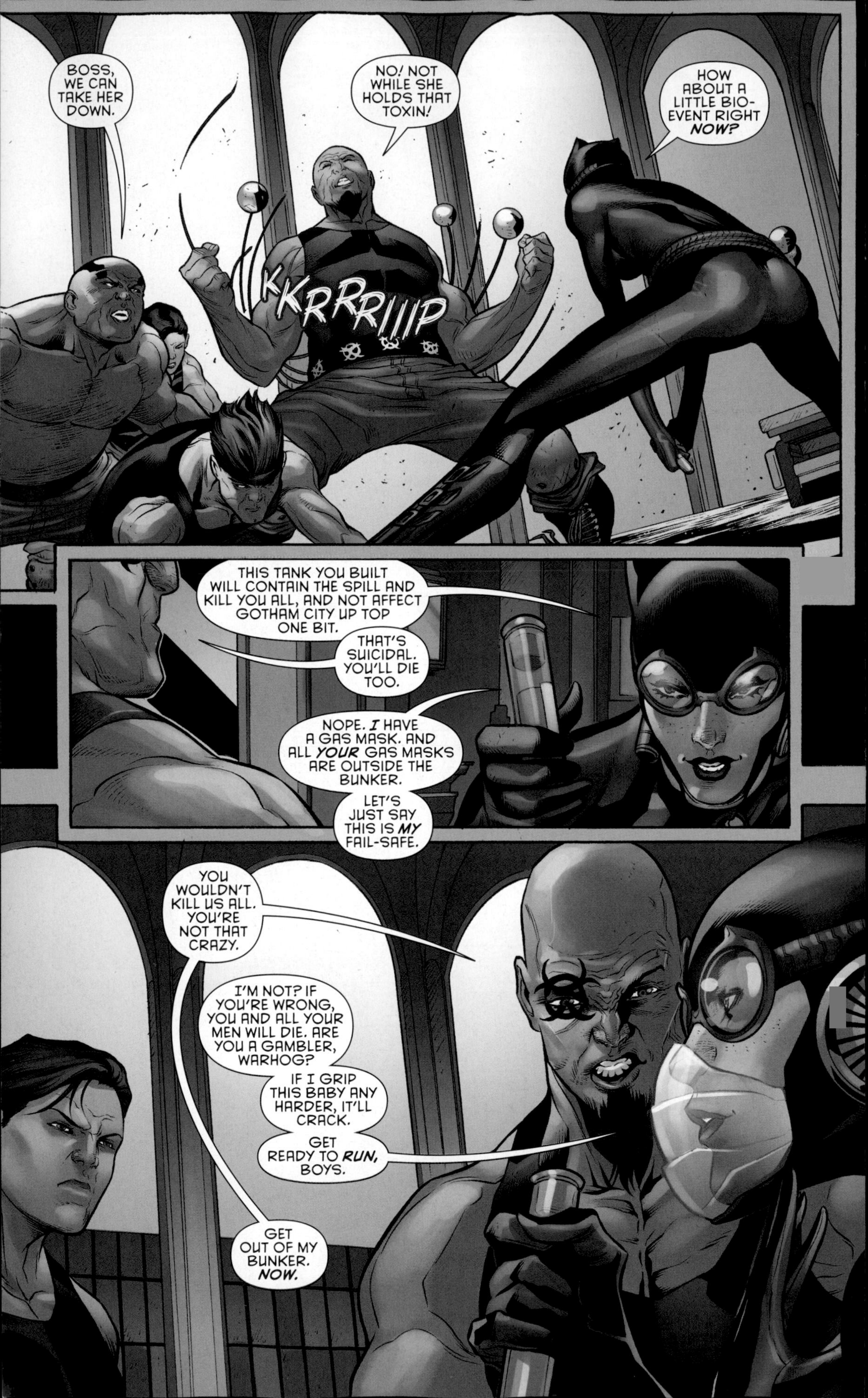
BOSS, WE CAN TAKE HER DOWN.
NO! NOT WHILE SHE HOLDS THAT TOXIN!
HOW ABOUT A LITTLE BIO-EVENT RIGHT *NOW?*
KKRRRIIIP
THIS TANK YOU BUILT WILL CONTAIN THE SPILL AND KILL YOU ALL, AND NOT AFFECT GOTHAM CITY UP TOP ONE BIT.
THAT'S SUICIDAL. YOU'LL DIE TOO.
NOPE. *I* HAVE A GAS MASK. AND ALL *YOUR* GAS MASKS ARE OUTSIDE THE BUNKER.
LET'S JUST SAY THIS IS *MY* FAIL-SAFE.
YOU WOULDN'T KILL US ALL. YOU'RE NOT THAT CRAZY.
I'M NOT? IF YOU'RE WRONG, YOU AND ALL YOUR MEN WILL DIE. ARE YOU A GAMBLER, WARHOG?
IF I GRIP THIS BABY ANY HARDER, IT'LL CRACK.
GET READY TO *RUN,* BOYS.
GET OUT OF MY BUNKER. *NOW.*

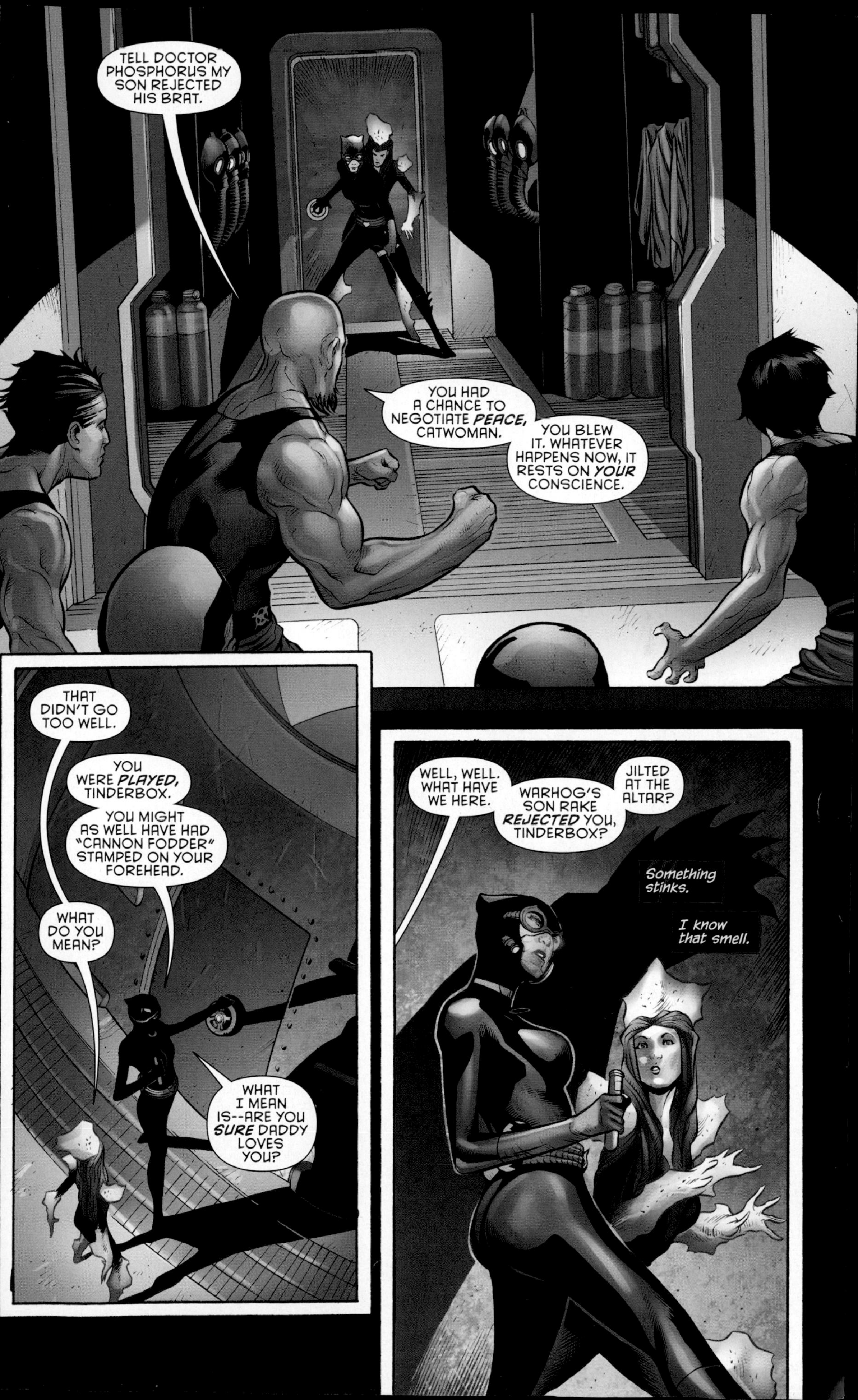
TELL DOCTOR PHOSPHORUS MY SON REJECTED HIS BRAT.
YOU HAD A CHANCE TO NEGOTIATE PEACE, CATWOMAN.
YOU BLEW IT. WHATEVER HAPPENS NOW, IT RESTS ON YOUR CONSCIENCE.
THAT DIDN'T GO TOO WELL.
YOU WERE PLAYED, TINDERBOX.
YOU MIGHT AS WELL HAVE HAD "CANNON FODDER" STAMPED ON YOUR FOREHEAD.
WHAT DO YOU MEAN?
WHAT I MEAN IS--ARE YOU SURE DADDY LOVES YOU?
WELL, WELL. WHAT HAVE WE HERE.
WARHOG'S SON RAKE REJECTED YOU, TINDERBOX?
JILTED AT THE ALTAR?
Something stinks.
I know that smell.

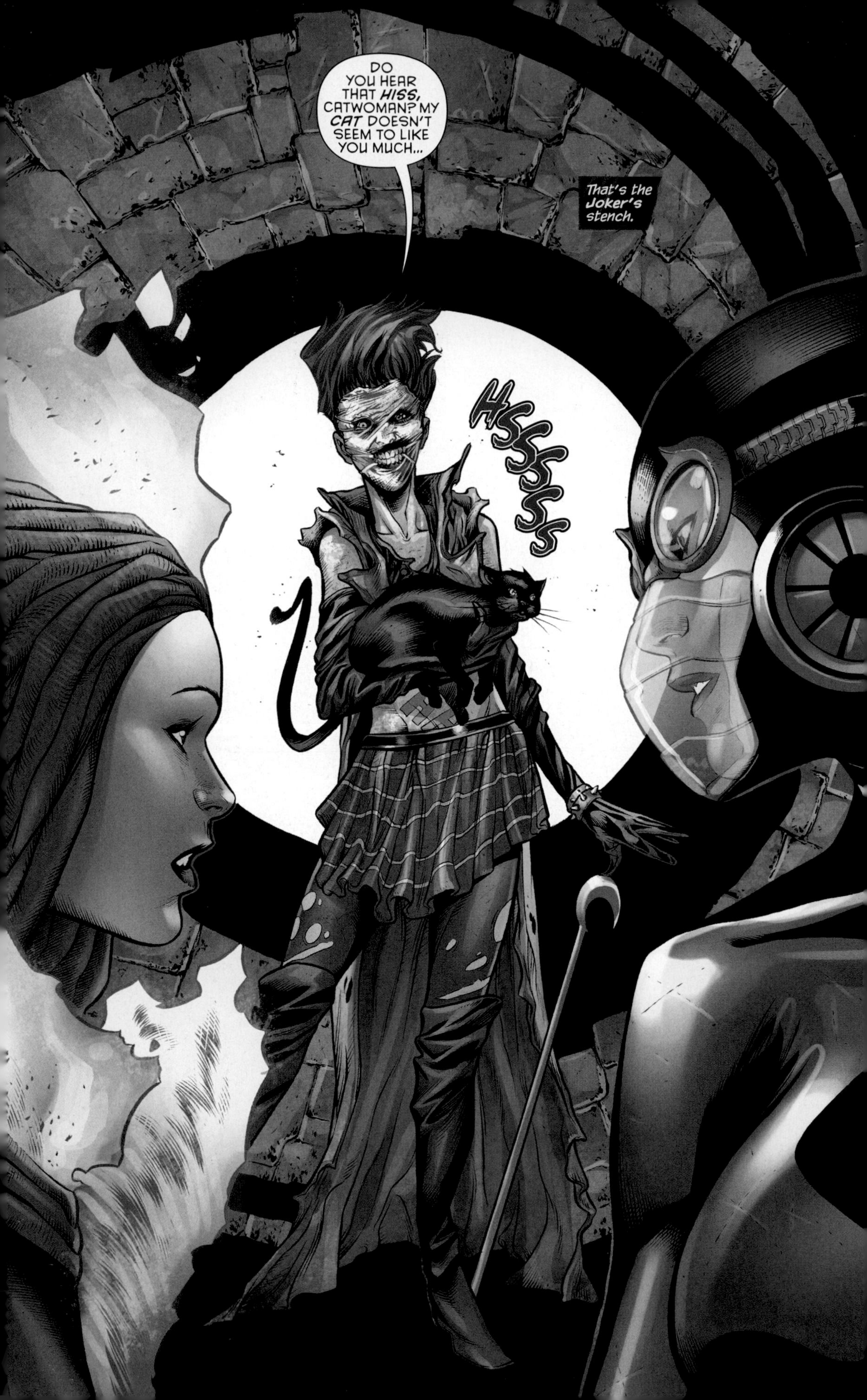
DO YOU HEAR THAT HISS, CATWOMAN? MY CAT DOESN'T SEEM TO LIKE YOU MUCH...
That's the Joker's stench.
HSSSSSS

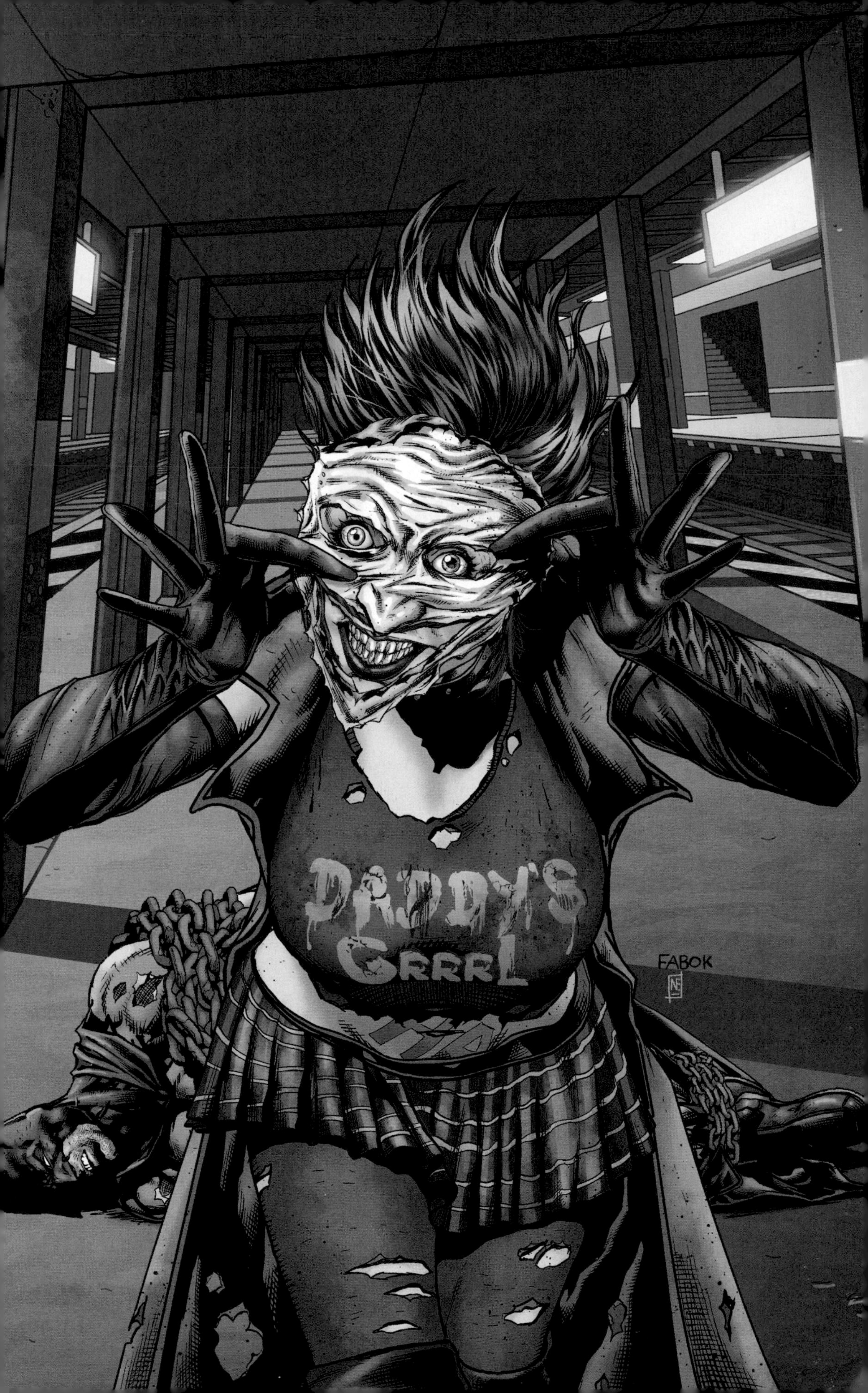
DADDY'S
GRRRL
FABOK

ANN NOCENTI
writer

GEORGES JEANTY
penciller

DEXTER VINES
inker

MICHELLE MADSEN
colorist

JASON FABOK with NATHAN FAIRBAIRN
cover artists

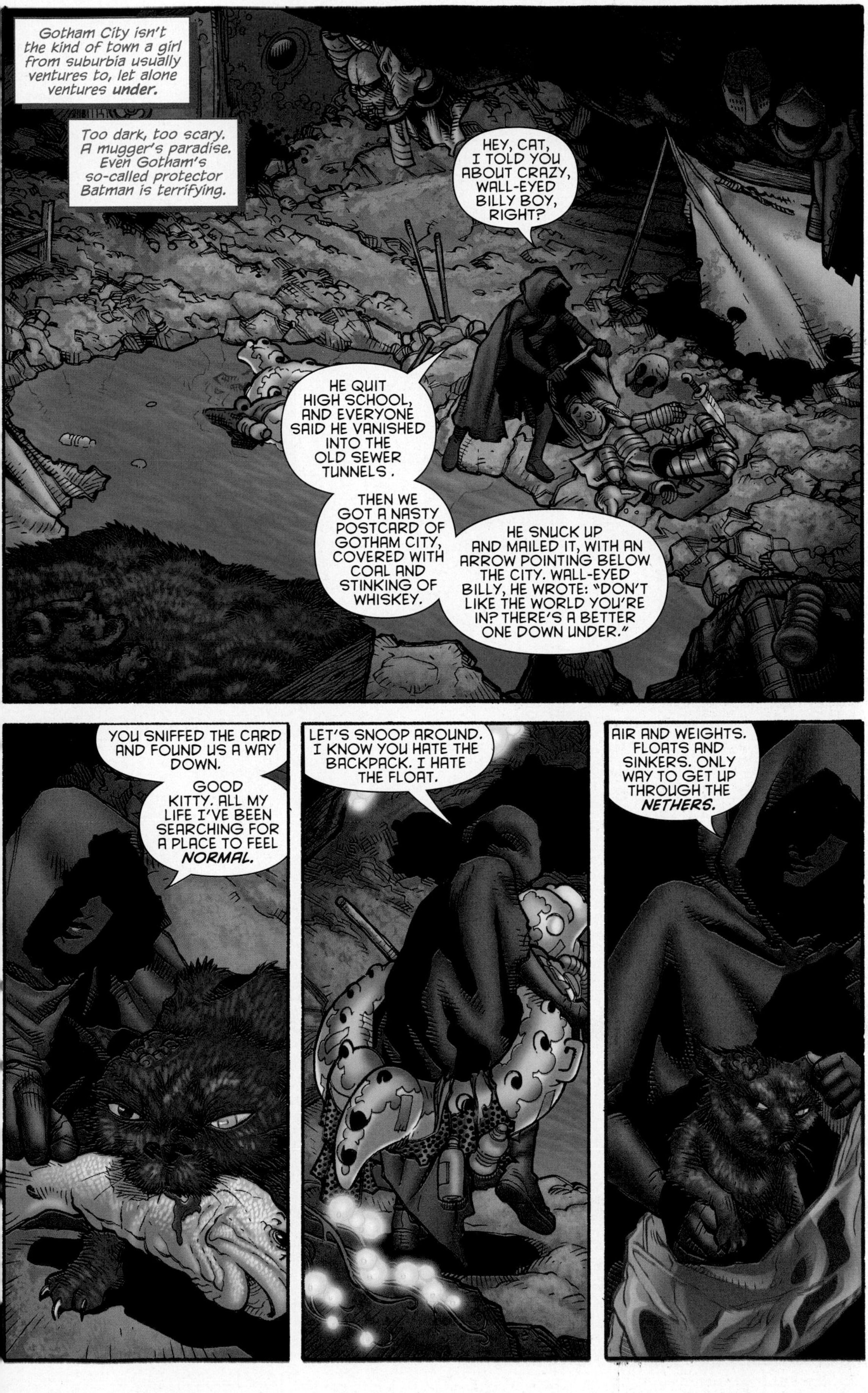
Gotham City isn't the kind of town a girl from suburbia usually ventures to, let alone ventures **under.**
Too dark, too scary. A mugger's paradise. Even Gotham's so-called protector Batman is terrifying.
HEY, CAT, I TOLD YOU ABOUT CRAZY, WALL-EYED BILLY BOY, RIGHT?
HE QUIT HIGH SCHOOL, AND EVERYONE SAID HE VANISHED INTO THE OLD SEWER TUNNELS .
THEN WE GOT A NASTY POSTCARD OF GOTHAM CITY, COVERED WITH COAL AND STINKING OF WHISKEY.
HE SNUCK UP AND MAILED IT, WITH AN ARROW POINTING BELOW THE CITY. WALL-EYED BILLY, HE WROTE: "DON'T LIKE THE WORLD YOU'RE IN? THERE'S A BETTER ONE DOWN UNDER."
YOU SNIFFED THE CARD AND FOUND US A WAY DOWN.
GOOD KITTY. ALL MY LIFE I'VE BEEN SEARCHING FOR A PLACE TO FEEL **NORMAL.**
LET'S SNOOP AROUND. I KNOW YOU HATE THE BACKPACK. I HATE THE FLOAT.
AIR AND WEIGHTS. FLOATS AND SINKERS. ONLY WAY TO GET UP THROUGH THE **NETHERS.**

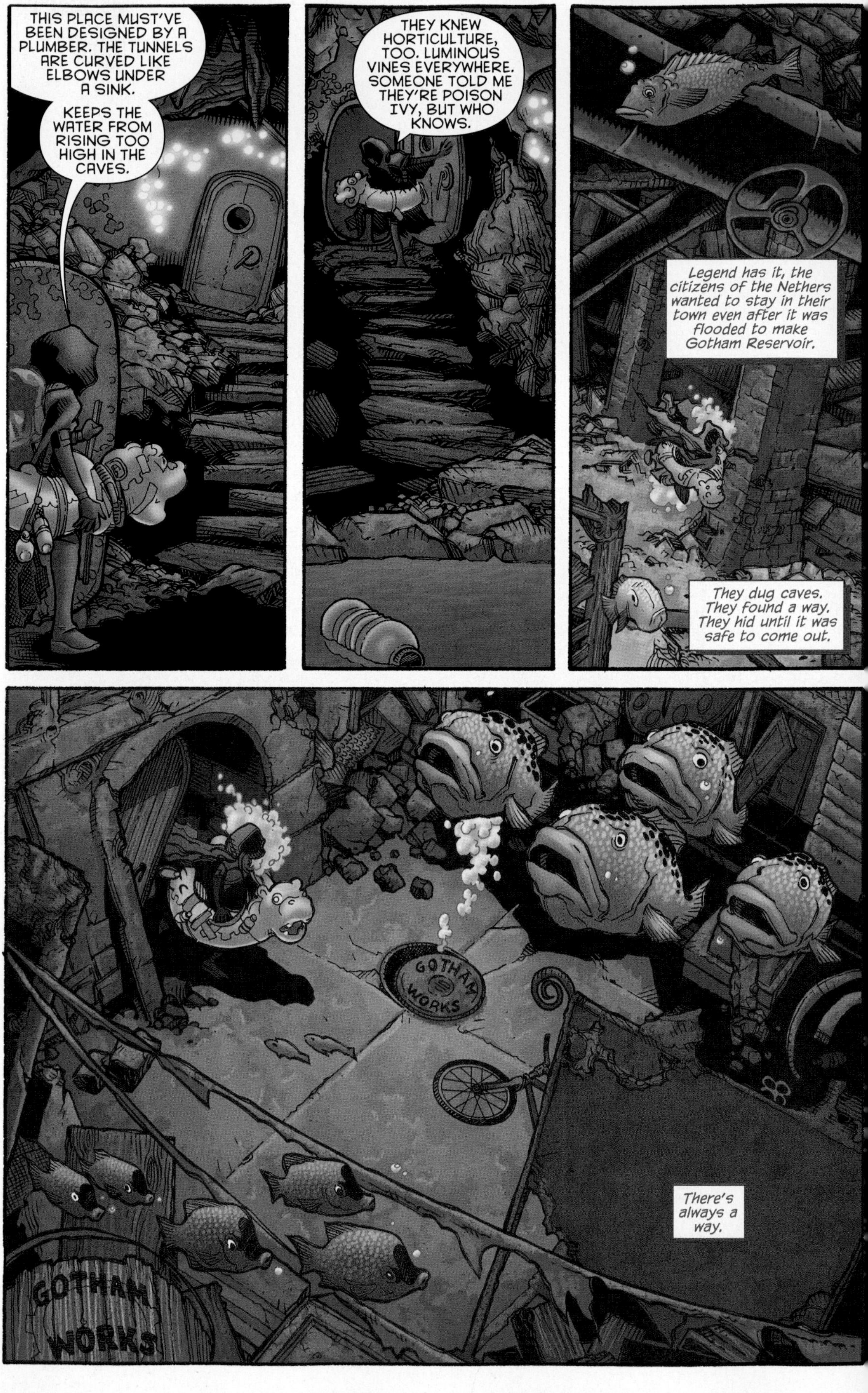
THIS PLACE MUST'VE BEEN DESIGNED BY A PLUMBER. THE TUNNELS ARE CURVED LIKE ELBOWS UNDER A SINK.
KEEPS THE WATER FROM RISING TOO HIGH IN THE CAVES.
THEY KNEW HORTICULTURE, TOO. LUMINOUS VINES EVERYWHERE. SOMEONE TOLD ME THEY'RE POISON IVY, BUT WHO KNOWS.
Legend has it, the citizens of the Nethers wanted to stay in their town even after it was flooded to make Gotham Reservoir.
They dug caves. They found a way. They hid until it was safe to come out.
GOTHAM WORKS
There's always a way.
GOTHAM WORKS

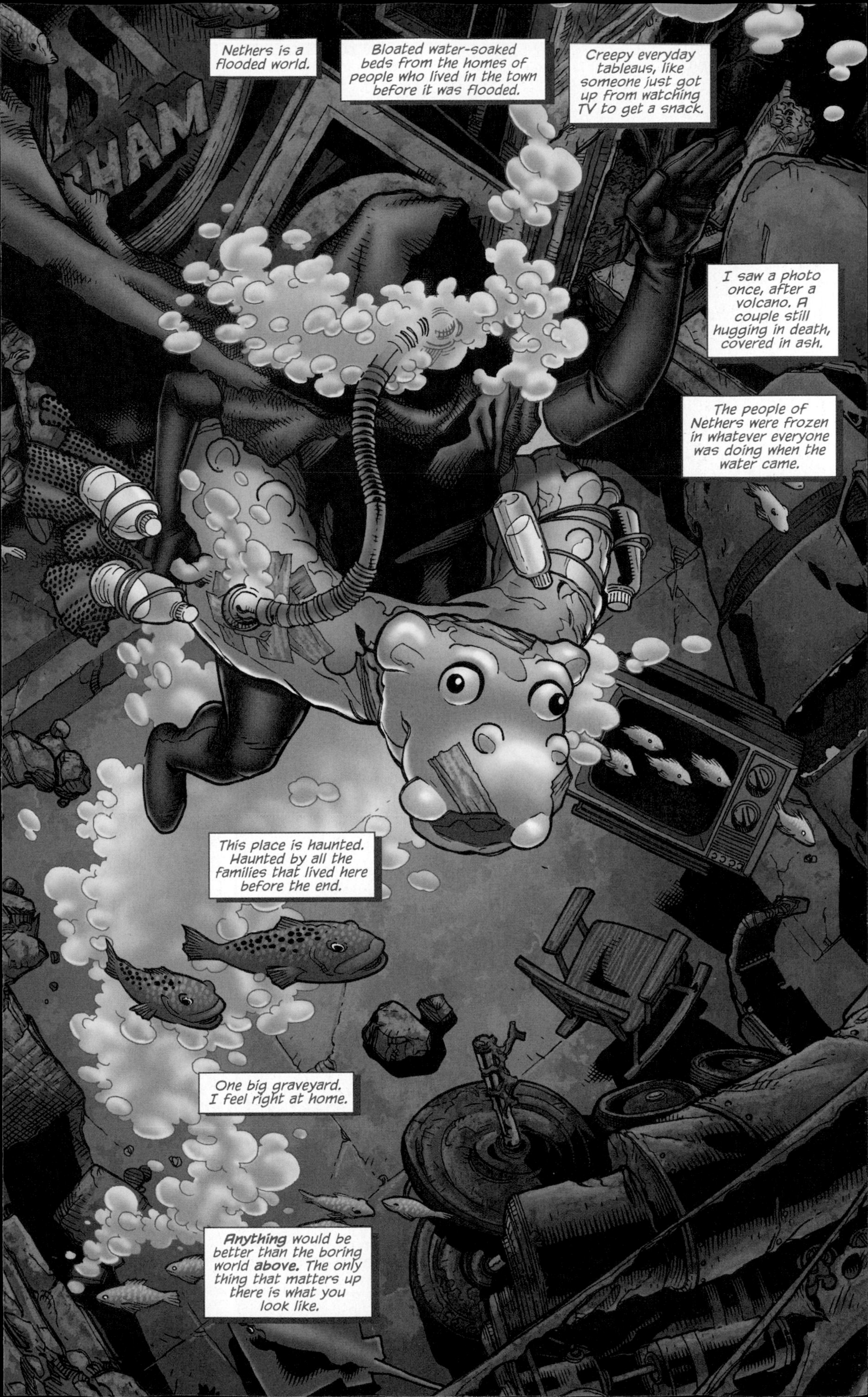

Nethers is a flooded world.
Bloated water-soaked beds from the homes of people who lived in the town before it was flooded.
Creepy everyday tableaus, like someone just got up from watching TV to get a snack.
I saw a photo once, after a volcano. A couple still hugging in death, covered in ash.
The people of Nethers were frozen in whatever everyone was doing when the water came.
This place is haunted. Haunted by all the families that lived here before the end.
One big graveyard. I feel right at home.
Anything would be better than the boring world above. The only thing that matters up there is what you look like.

Wish you'd quit squirming, Cat. You got enough air in that bag to make it to the top.

Hmmm. I want that *half-moon* of metal.

I've seen people up there *trading* metal for stuff.

Got it.

Ooops. My tube is deflating. No more air.

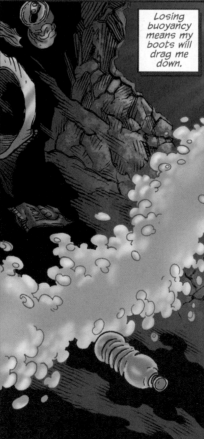

Losing buoyancy means my boots will drag me down.

Time to go up.

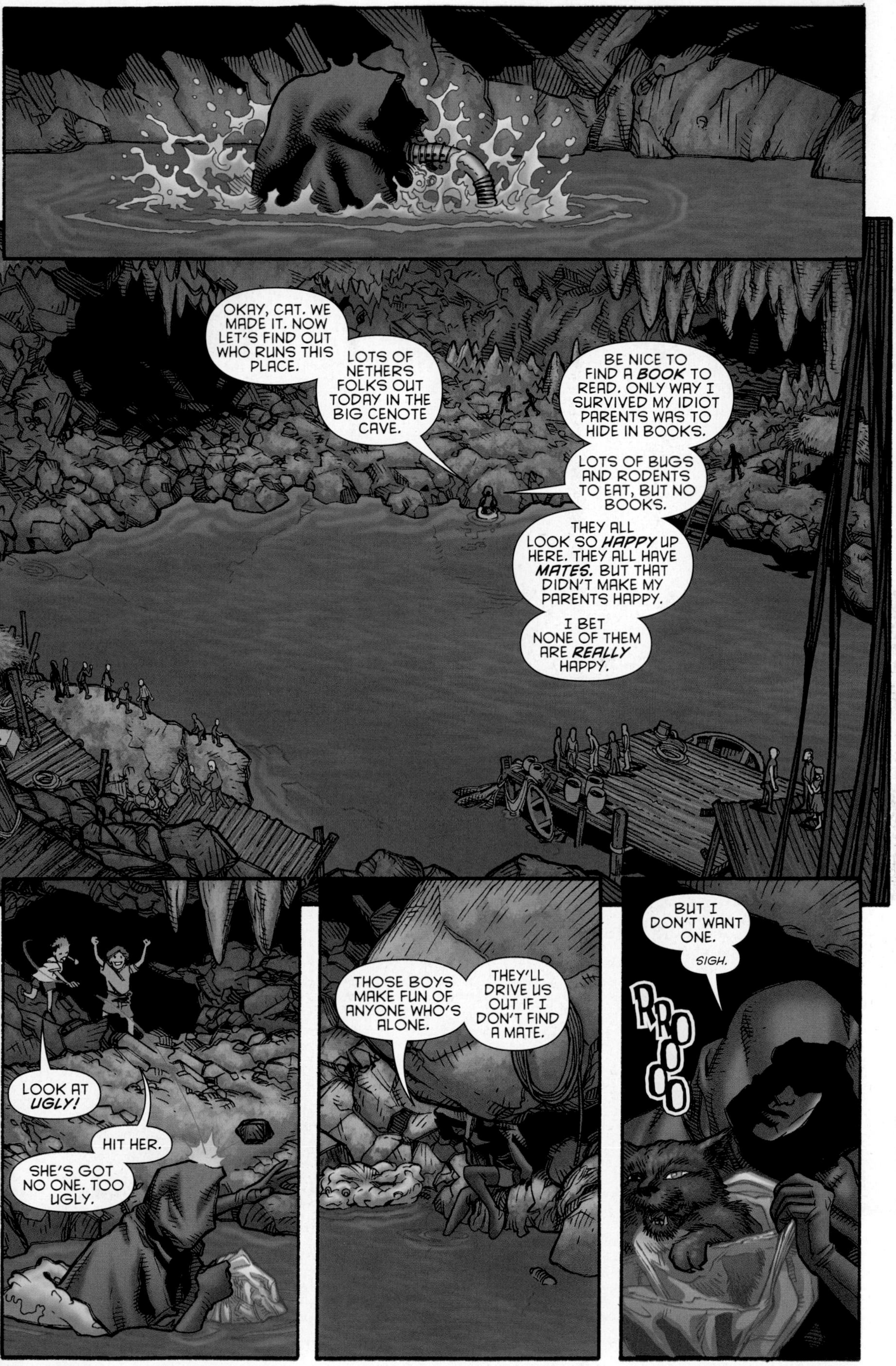
OKAY, CAT. WE MADE IT. NOW LET'S FIND OUT WHO RUNS THIS PLACE.
LOTS OF NETHERS FOLKS OUT TODAY IN THE BIG CENOTE CAVE.
BE NICE TO FIND A BOOK TO READ. ONLY WAY I SURVIVED MY IDIOT PARENTS WAS TO HIDE IN BOOKS.
LOTS OF BUGS AND RODENTS TO EAT, BUT NO BOOKS.
THEY ALL LOOK SO HAPPY UP HERE. THEY ALL HAVE MATES. BUT THAT DIDN'T MAKE MY PARENTS HAPPY.
I BET NONE OF THEM ARE REALLY HAPPY.
LOOK AT UGLY!
HIT HER.
SHE'S GOT NO ONE. TOO UGLY.
THOSE BOYS MAKE FUN OF ANYONE WHO'S ALONE.
THEY'LL DRIVE US OUT IF I DON'T FIND A MATE.
BUT I DON'T WANT ONE.
SIGH.
RROOOO

HOLD ON, CAT, LET ME SEE HOW I LOOK FIRST?

I WANT TO LOOK MY BEST.

SIGH.

I LOOK SO GOOD. BETTER THAN EVER.

IN FACT, I'M *BEAUTIFUL*.

ALL THOSE BEAUTY TREATMENTS I GAVE MYSELF WHEN I WAS YOUNG...REALLY PAID OFF, DON'T YOU THINK, CAT?

I had a bony body when I was young. Anorexic.

I was gaunt, pale, hollow-eyed--as erotic as bones.

Ugly is beautiful, I thought. Ugly is the new beautiful.

Why couldn't my father see that? He was always pushing me to dress **pretty**. *Pretty is so... shallow.*

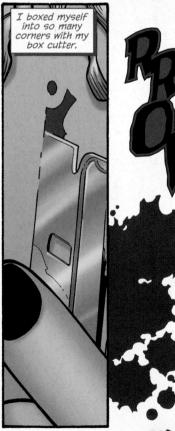

I boxed myself into so many corners with my box cutter.

RROW

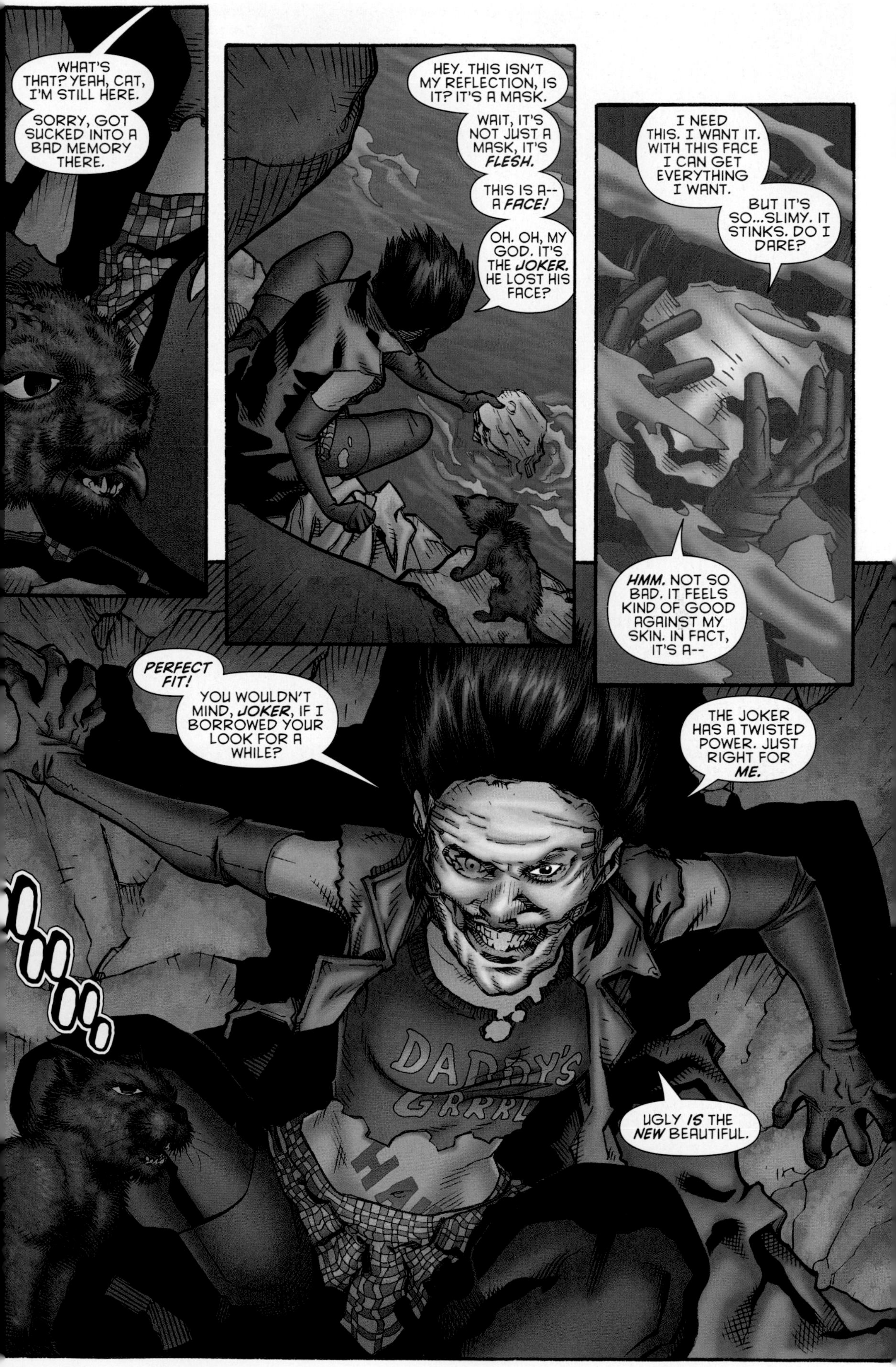
WHAT'S THAT? YEAH, CAT, I'M STILL HERE.
SORRY, GOT SUCKED INTO A BAD MEMORY THERE.
HEY. THIS ISN'T MY REFLECTION, IS IT? IT'S A MASK.
WAIT, IT'S NOT JUST A MASK, IT'S *FLESH.*
THIS IS A-- A *FACE!*
OH. OH, MY GOD. IT'S THE *JOKER.* HE LOST HIS FACE?
I NEED THIS. I WANT IT. WITH THIS FACE I CAN GET EVERYTHING I WANT.
BUT IT'S SO...SLIMY. IT STINKS. DO I DARE?
HMM. NOT SO BAD. IT FEELS KIND OF GOOD AGAINST MY SKIN. IN FACT, IT'S A--
PERFECT FIT!
YOU WOULDN'T MIND, *JOKER*, IF I BORROWED YOUR LOOK FOR A WHILE?
THE JOKER HAS A TWISTED POWER. JUST RIGHT FOR *ME.*
UGLY *IS* THE *NEW* BEAUTIFUL.

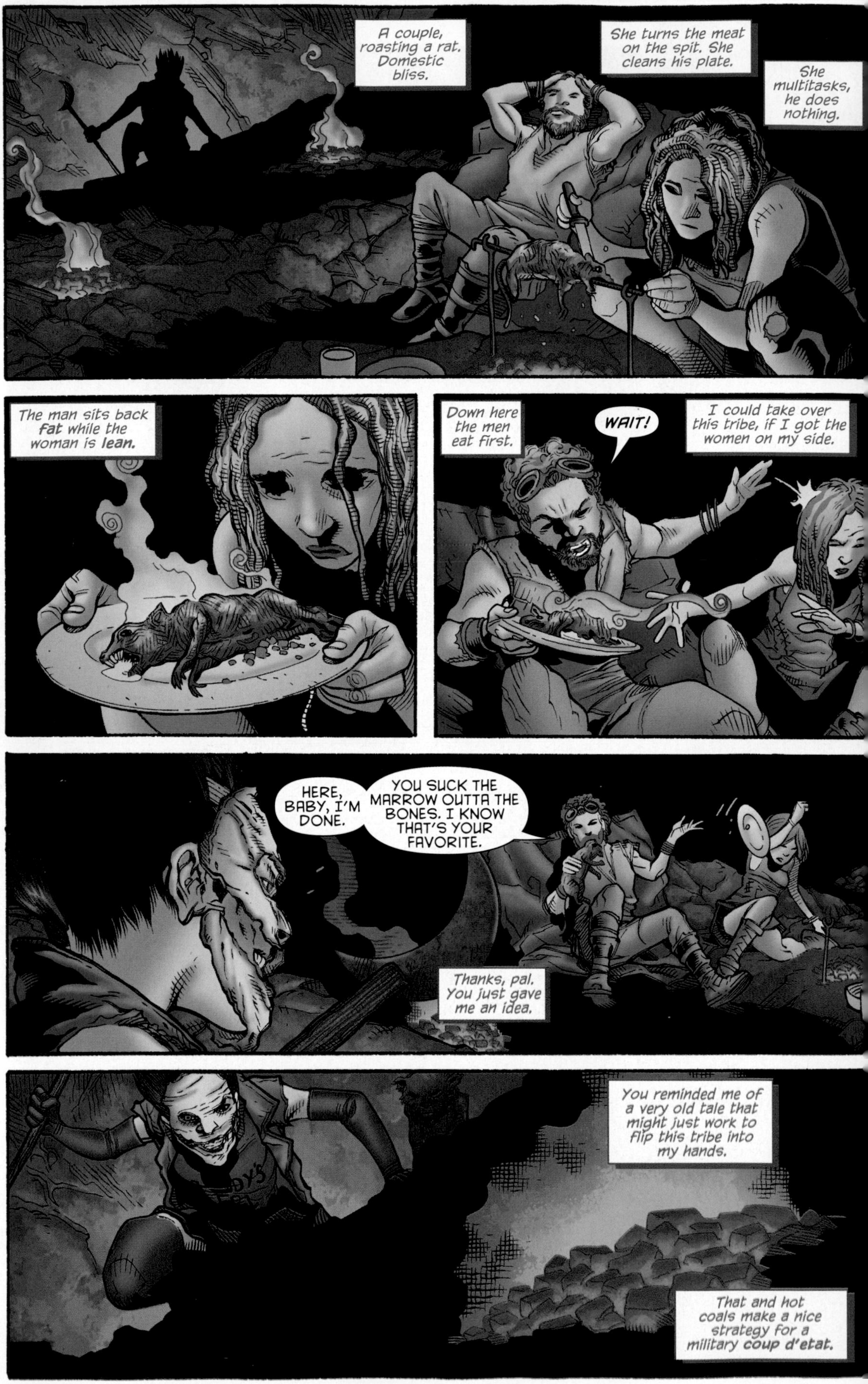
A couple, roasting a rat. Domestic bliss.
She turns the meat on the spit. She cleans his plate.
She multitasks, he does nothing.
The man sits back **fat** while the woman is **lean.**
Down here the men eat first.
WAIT!
I could take over this tribe, if I got the women on my side.
HERE, BABY, I'M DONE.
YOU SUCK THE MARROW OUTTA THE BONES. I KNOW THAT'S YOUR FAVORITE.
Thanks, pal. You just gave me an idea.
You reminded me of a very old tale that might just work to flip this tribe into my hands.
That and hot coals make a nice strategy for a military **coup d'etat.**

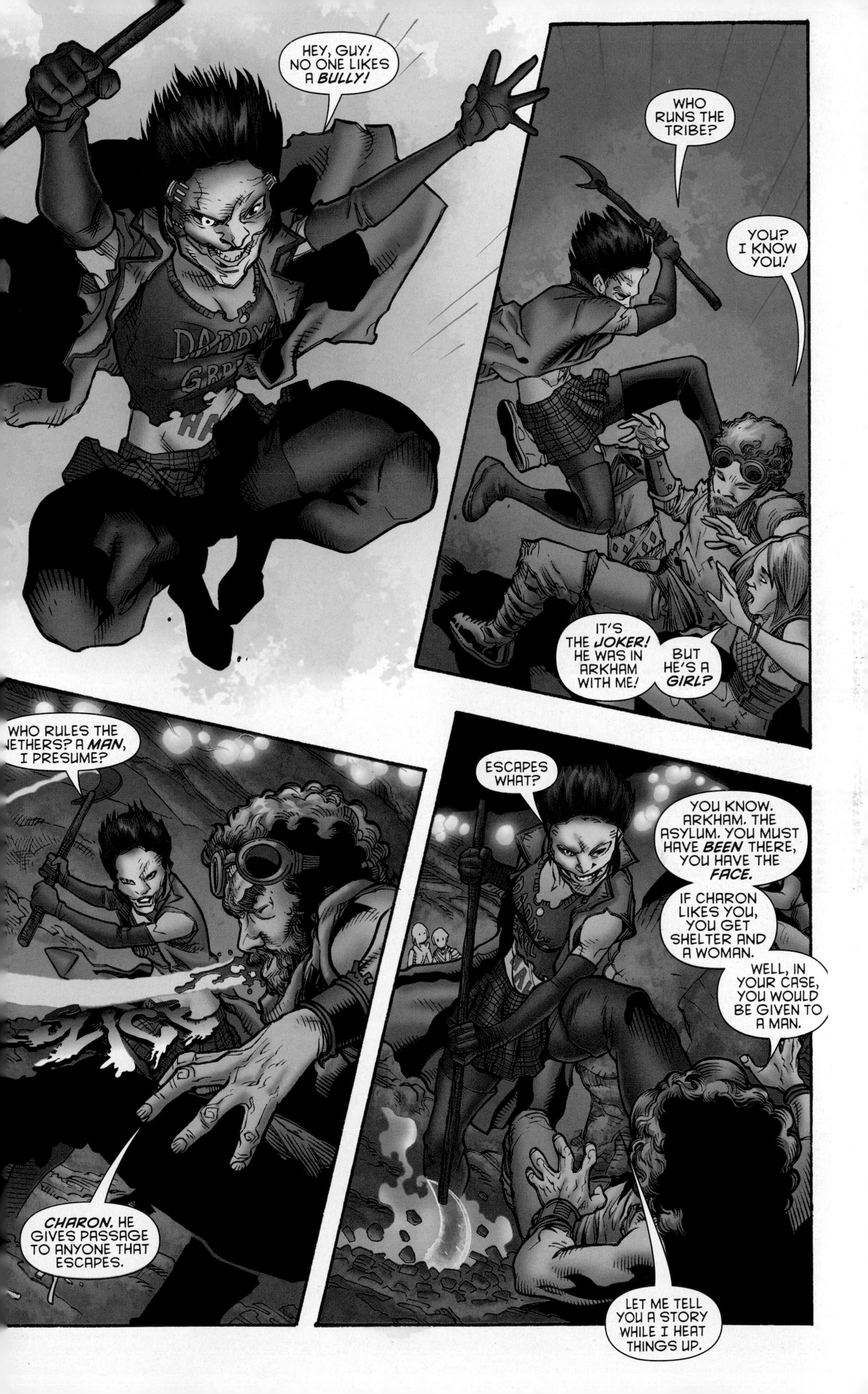

HEY, GUY! NO ONE LIKES A *BULLY!*
WHO RUNS THE TRIBE?
YOU? I KNOW YOU!
IT'S THE *JOKER!* HE WAS IN ARKHAM WITH ME!
BUT HE'S A *GIRL?*
WHO RULES THE NETHERS? A *MAN*, I PRESUME?
CHARON. HE GIVES PASSAGE TO ANYONE THAT ESCAPES.
ESCAPES WHAT?
YOU KNOW. ARKHAM. THE ASYLUM. YOU MUST HAVE *BEEN* THERE, YOU HAVE THE *FACE.*
IF CHARON LIKES YOU, YOU GET SHELTER AND A WOMAN.
WELL, IN YOUR CASE, YOU WOULD BE GIVEN TO A MAN.
LET ME TELL YOU A STORY WHILE I HEAT THINGS UP.

I ONCE READ A GREEK PLAY CALLED *LYSISTRATA.*

THE MEN WERE ALWAYS AT WAR. *ENDLESS* WAR.

THE WOMEN HAD A BRIGHT IDEA. WITHHOLD ALL SERVICES FROM THE MEN UNTIL THEY STOP WARRING AND TREAT WOMEN AS EQUALS.

LET ME GIVE YOU A *NEW* FACE TO GO WITH THE WAY THINGS ARE GOING TO BE AROUND HERE.

DO AS SHE SAYS. YOU REMEMBER HOW JOKER RAN THINGS ON THE INSIDE. YOU BETTER LET HER DO IT--

PLEASE, MISS JOKER, NOT *THAT* FACE, DON'T GIVE ME THAT FACE!

DOCTOR'S ORDERS.

AND YOUR *WIFE'S.* SHE KNOWS WHAT'S BEST.

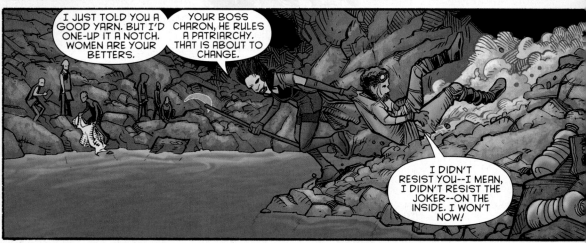

I JUST TOLD YOU A GOOD YARN. BUT I'D ONE-UP IT A NOTCH. WOMEN ARE YOUR BETTERS.

YOUR BOSS CHARON, HE RULES A PATRIARCHY. THAT IS ABOUT TO CHANGE.

I DIDN'T RESIST YOU--I MEAN, I DIDN'T RESIST THE JOKER--ON THE INSIDE. I WON'T NOW!

FROM NOW ON, YOUR WIFE EATS FIRST. *SHE* GETS THE MEAT, *YOU* GET THE MARROW.

TAKE ME TO CHARON. IT'S TIME FOR THE WOMEN TO RULE THE TRIBE.

Arkham Asylum? They're all nutters down here? That makes things easy.

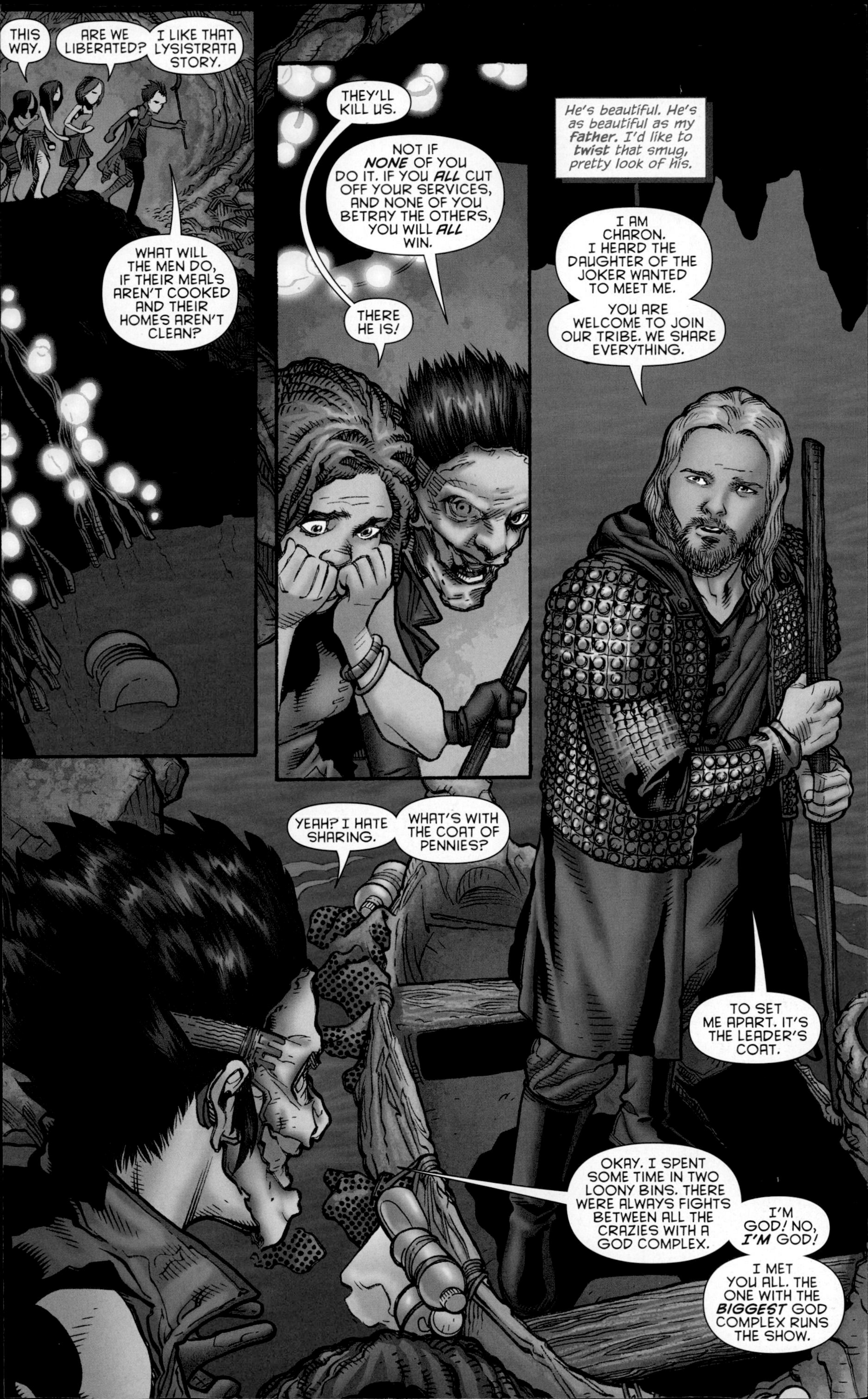
THIS WAY.
ARE WE LIBERATED?
I LIKE THAT LYSISTRATA STORY.
WHAT WILL THE MEN DO, IF THEIR MEALS AREN'T COOKED AND THEIR HOMES AREN'T CLEAN?
THEY'LL KILL US.
NOT IF NONE OF YOU DO IT. IF YOU ALL CUT OFF YOUR SERVICES, AND NONE OF YOU BETRAY THE OTHERS, YOU WILL ALL WIN.
THERE HE IS!
He's beautiful. He's as beautiful as my father. I'd like to twist that smug, pretty look of his.
I AM CHARON. I HEARD THE DAUGHTER OF THE JOKER WANTED TO MEET ME.
YOU ARE WELCOME TO JOIN OUR TRIBE. WE SHARE EVERYTHING.
YEAH? I HATE SHARING.
WHAT'S WITH THE COAT OF PENNIES?
TO SET ME APART. IT'S THE LEADER'S COAT.
OKAY. I SPENT SOME TIME IN TWO LOONY BINS. THERE WERE ALWAYS FIGHTS BETWEEN ALL THE CRAZIES WITH A GOD COMPLEX.
I'M GOD! NO, I'M GOD!
I MET YOU ALL. THE ONE WITH THE BIGGEST GOD COMPLEX RUNS THE SHOW.

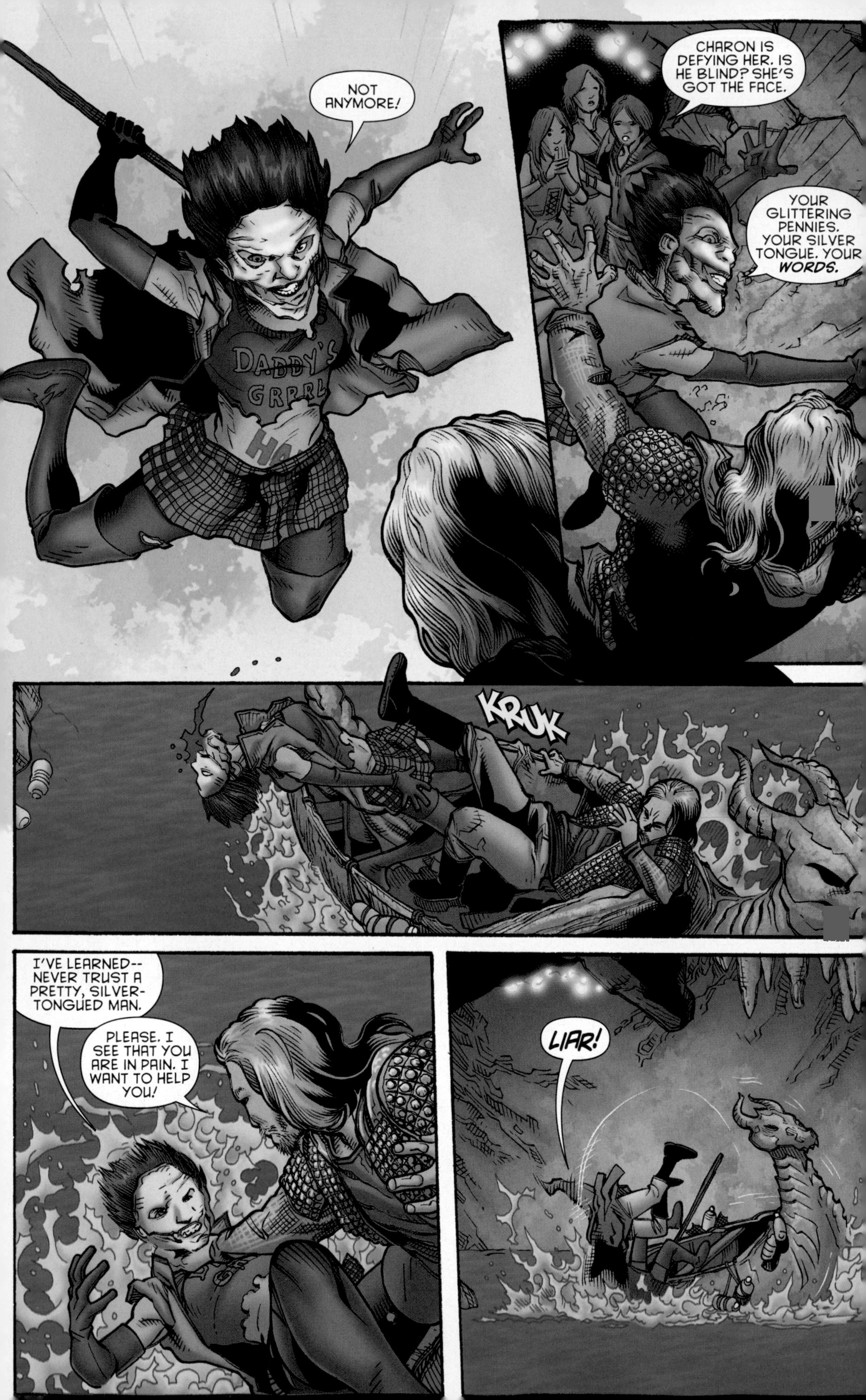
NOT ANYMORE!
CHARON IS DEFYING HER. IS HE BLIND? SHE'S GOT THE FACE.
YOUR GLITTERING PENNIES. YOUR SILVER TONGUE. YOUR WORDS.
DADDY'S GRRRL
KRUK
I'VE LEARNED-- NEVER TRUST A PRETTY, SILVER-TONGUED MAN.
PLEASE. I SEE THAT YOU ARE IN PAIN. I WANT TO HELP YOU!
LIAR!

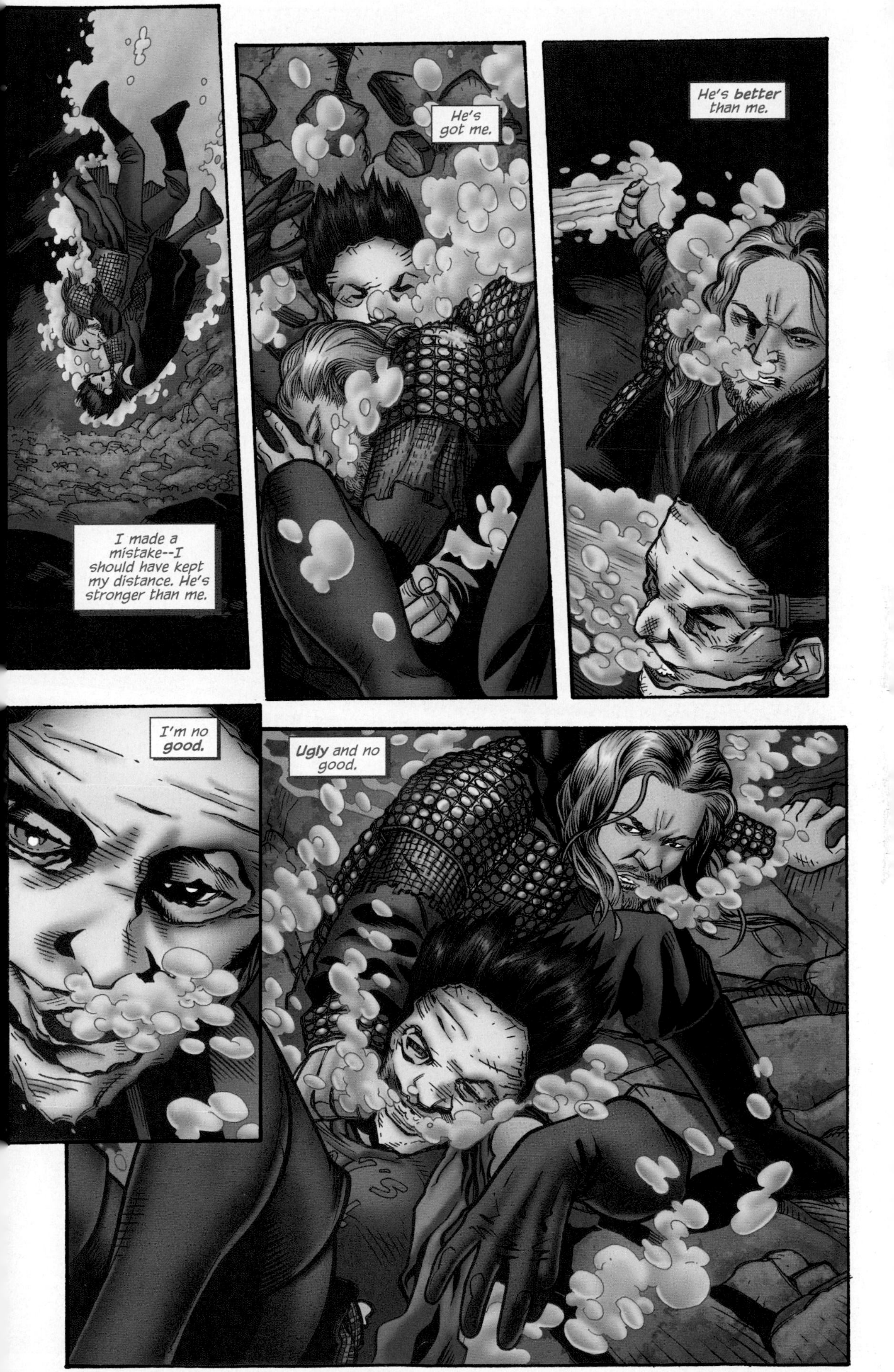

I made a mistake--I should have kept my distance. He's stronger than me.
He's got me.
He's better than me.
I'm no good.
Ugly and no good.

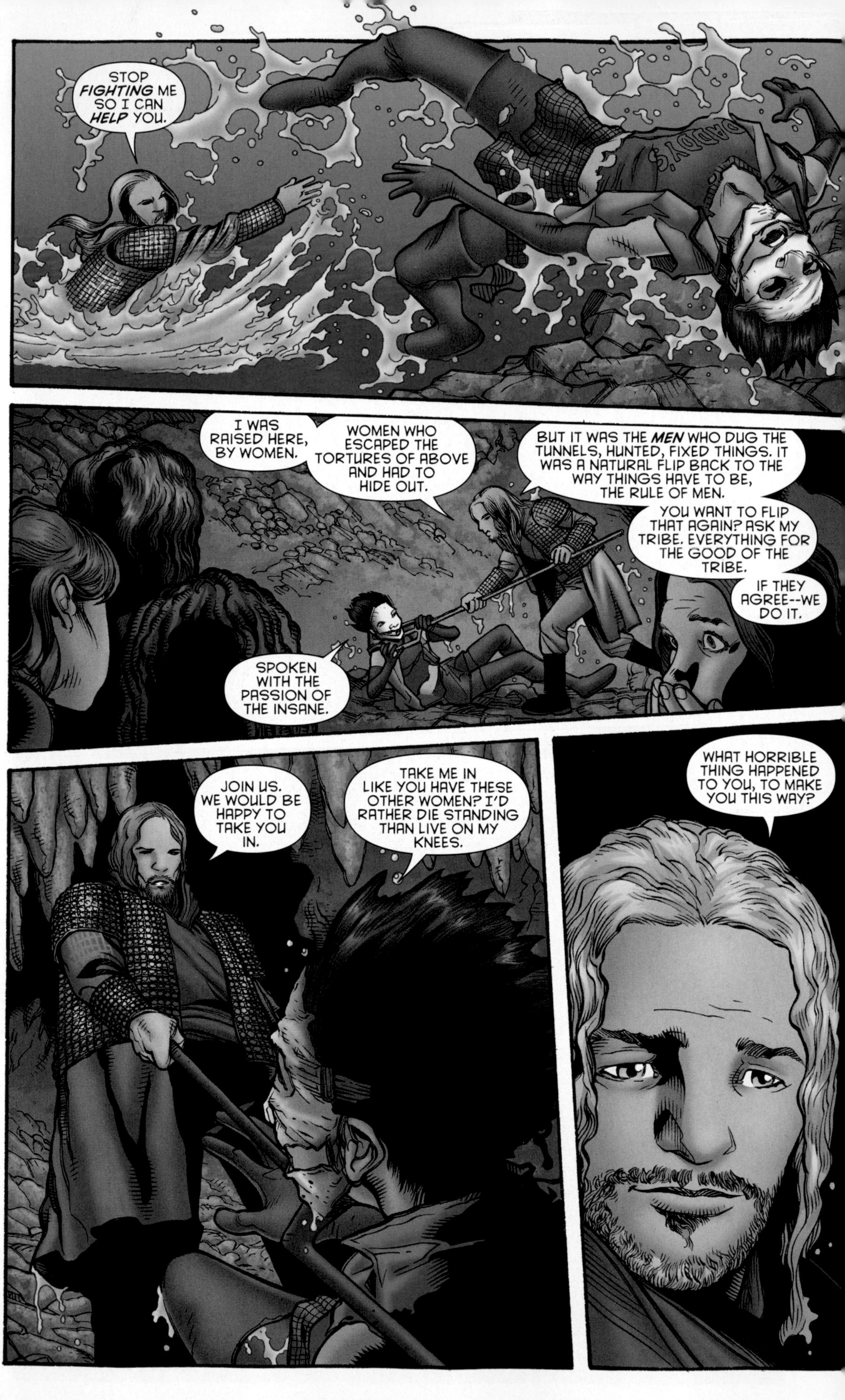
STOP FIGHTING ME SO I CAN HELP YOU.
I WAS RAISED HERE, BY WOMEN.
WOMEN WHO ESCAPED THE TORTURES OF ABOVE AND HAD TO HIDE OUT.
BUT IT WAS THE MEN WHO DUG THE TUNNELS, HUNTED, FIXED THINGS. IT WAS A NATURAL FLIP BACK TO THE WAY THINGS HAVE TO BE, THE RULE OF MEN.
SPOKEN WITH THE PASSION OF THE INSANE.
YOU WANT TO FLIP THAT AGAIN? ASK MY TRIBE. EVERYTHING FOR THE GOOD OF THE TRIBE.
IF THEY AGREE--WE DO IT.
JOIN US. WE WOULD BE HAPPY TO TAKE YOU IN.
TAKE ME IN LIKE YOU HAVE THESE OTHER WOMEN? I'D RATHER DIE STANDING THAN LIVE ON MY KNEES.
WHAT HORRIBLE THING HAPPENED TO YOU, TO MAKE YOU THIS WAY?

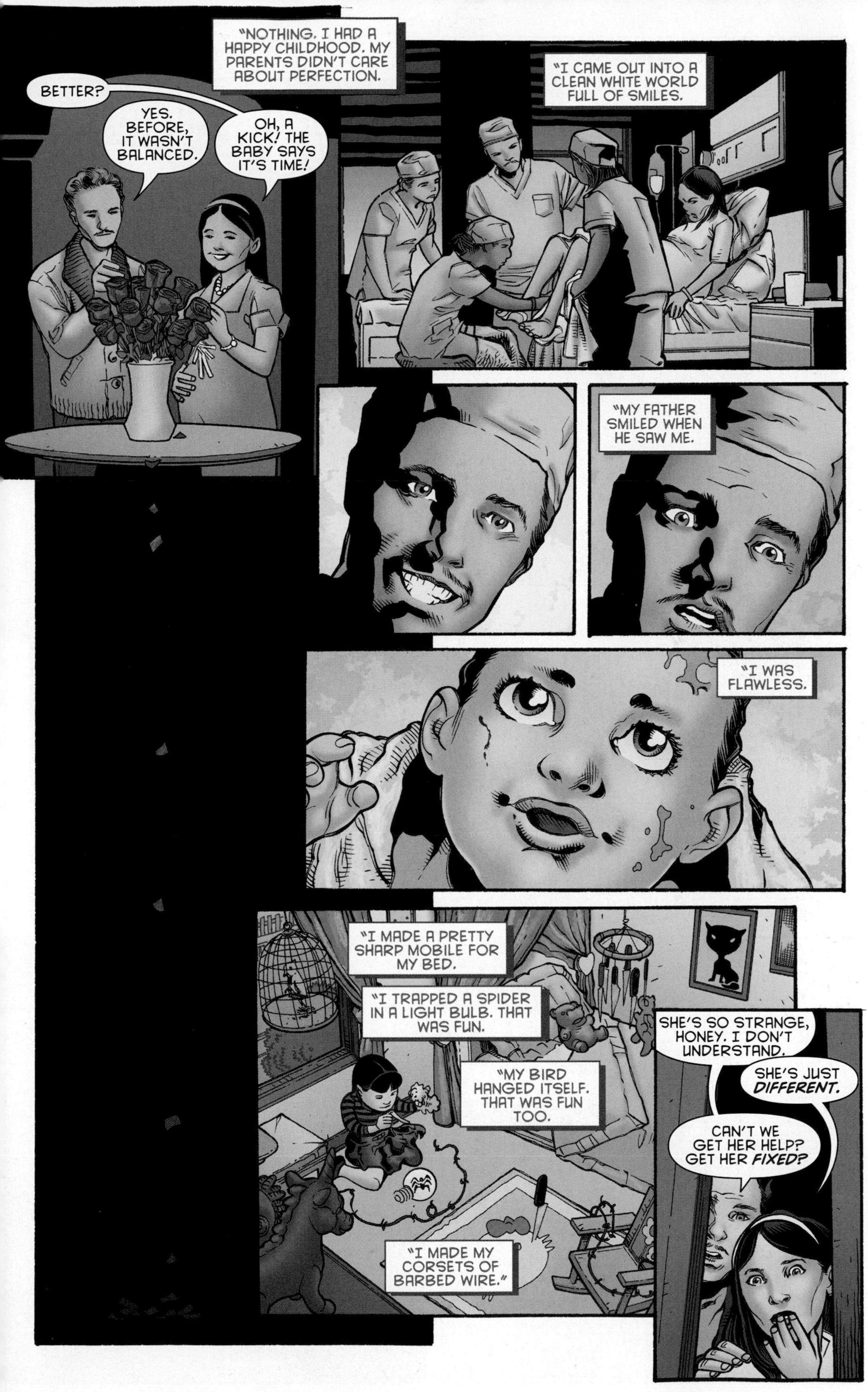
"NOTHING. I HAD A HAPPY CHILDHOOD. MY PARENTS DIDN'T CARE ABOUT PERFECTION.
BETTER?
YES. BEFORE, IT WASN'T BALANCED.
OH, A KICK! THE BABY SAYS IT'S TIME!
"I CAME OUT INTO A CLEAN WHITE WORLD FULL OF SMILES.
"MY FATHER SMILED WHEN HE SAW ME.
"I WAS FLAWLESS.
"I MADE A PRETTY SHARP MOBILE FOR MY BED.
"I TRAPPED A SPIDER IN A LIGHT BULB. THAT WAS FUN.
"MY BIRD HANGED ITSELF. THAT WAS FUN TOO.
"I MADE MY CORSETS OF BARBED WIRE."
SHE'S SO STRANGE, HONEY. I DON'T UNDERSTAND.
SHE'S JUST *DIFFERENT*.
CAN'T WE GET HER HELP? GET HER *FIXED*?

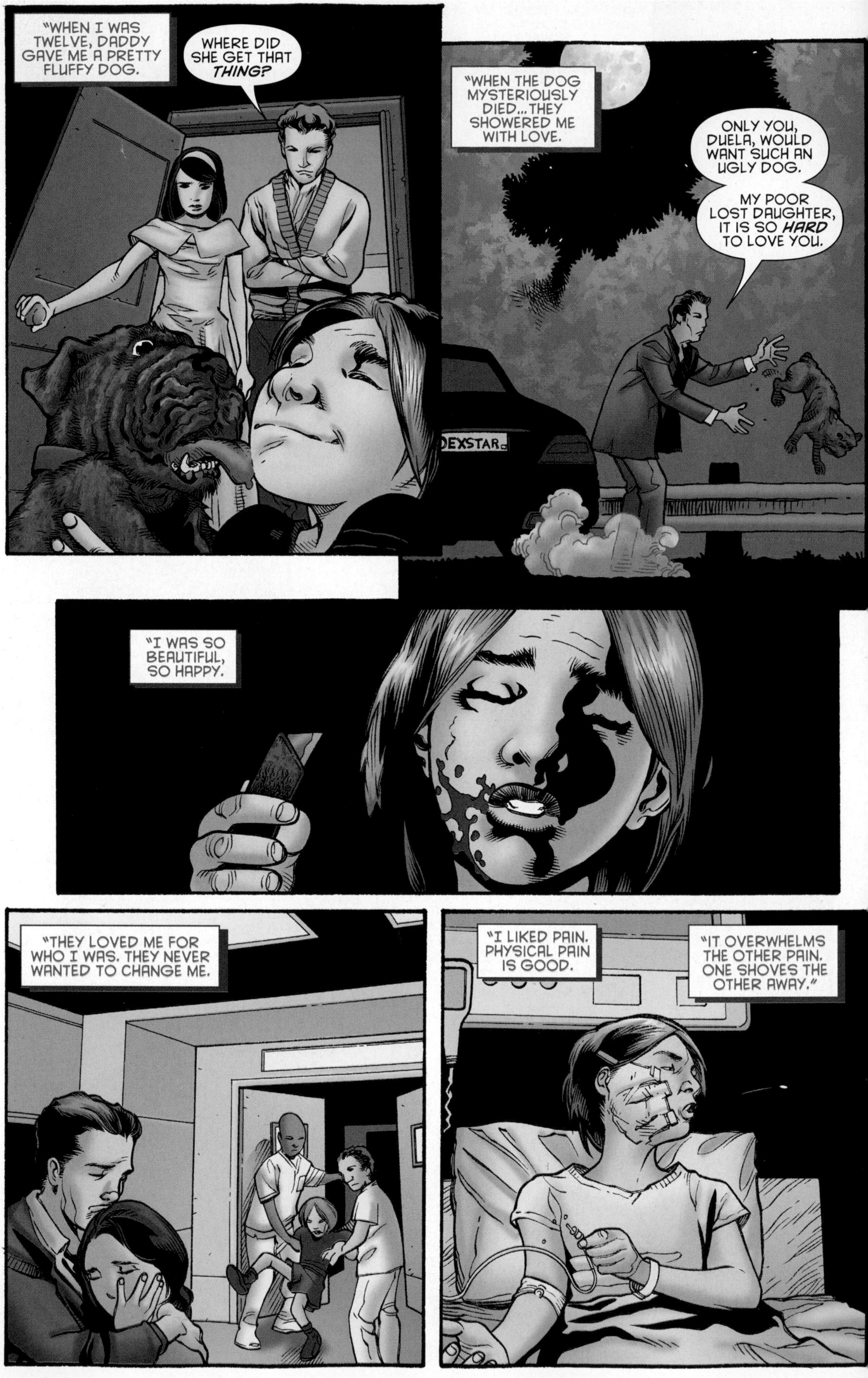
"WHEN I WAS TWELVE, DADDY GAVE ME A PRETTY FLUFFY DOG.
WHERE DID SHE GET THAT *THING?*
"WHEN THE DOG MYSTERIOUSLY DIED... THEY SHOWERED ME WITH LOVE.
ONLY YOU, DUELA, WOULD WANT SUCH AN UGLY DOG.
MY POOR LOST DAUGHTER, IT IS SO *HARD* TO LOVE YOU.
DEXSTAR
"I WAS SO BEAUTIFUL, SO HAPPY.
"THEY LOVED ME FOR WHO I WAS. THEY NEVER WANTED TO CHANGE ME.
"I LIKED PAIN. PHYSICAL PAIN IS GOOD.
"IT OVERWHELMS THE OTHER PAIN. ONE SHOVES THE OTHER AWAY."

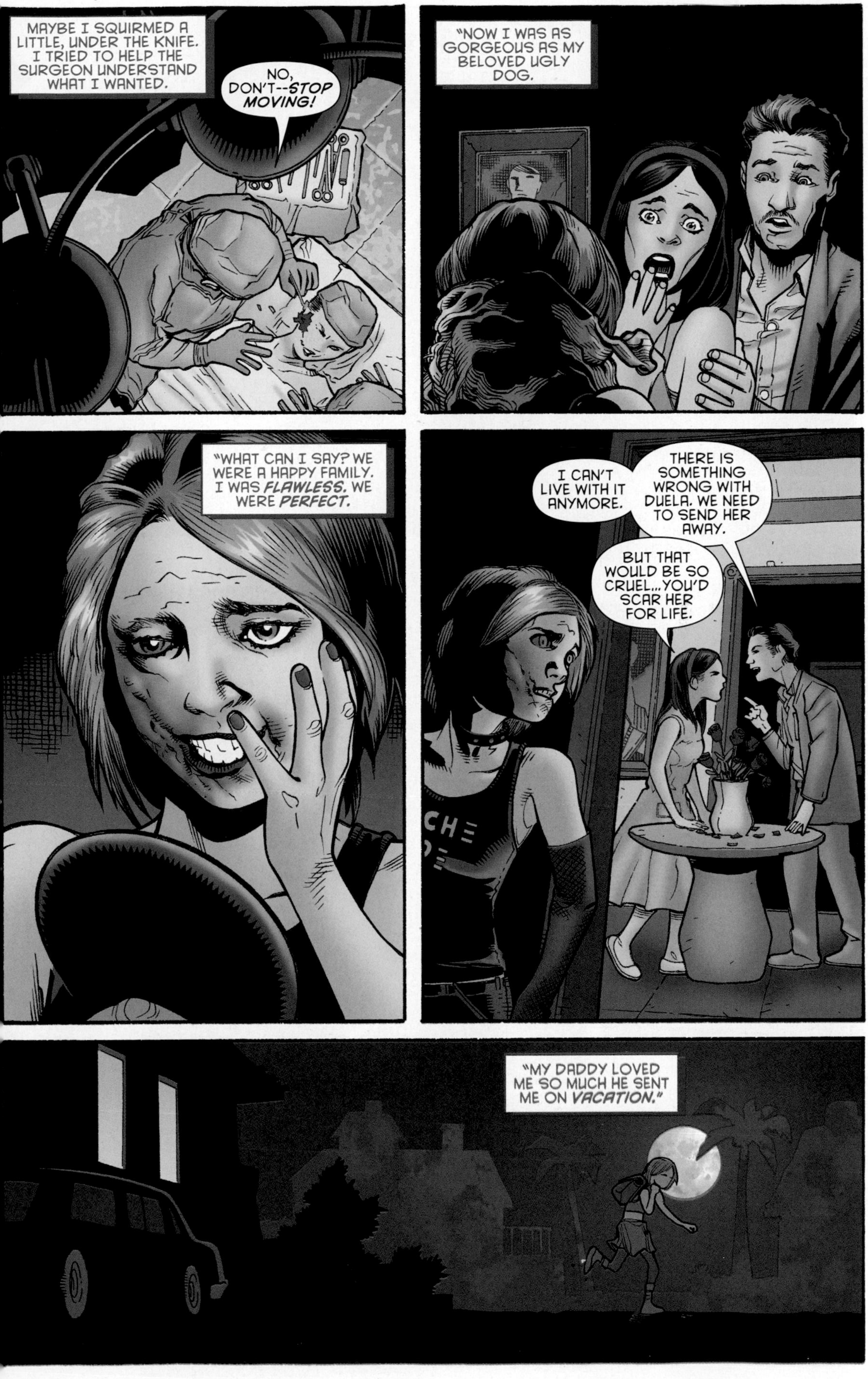
MAYBE I SQUIRMED A LITTLE, UNDER THE KNIFE. I TRIED TO HELP THE SURGEON UNDERSTAND WHAT I WANTED.
NO, DON'T--STOP MOVING!
"NOW I WAS AS GORGEOUS AS MY BELOVED UGLY DOG.
"WHAT CAN I SAY? WE WERE A HAPPY FAMILY. I WAS FLAWLESS. WE WERE PERFECT.
I CAN'T LIVE WITH IT ANYMORE.
THERE IS SOMETHING WRONG WITH DUELA. WE NEED TO SEND HER AWAY.
BUT THAT WOULD BE SO CRUEL...YOU'D SCAR HER FOR LIFE.
"MY DADDY LOVED ME SO MUCH HE SENT ME ON VACATION."

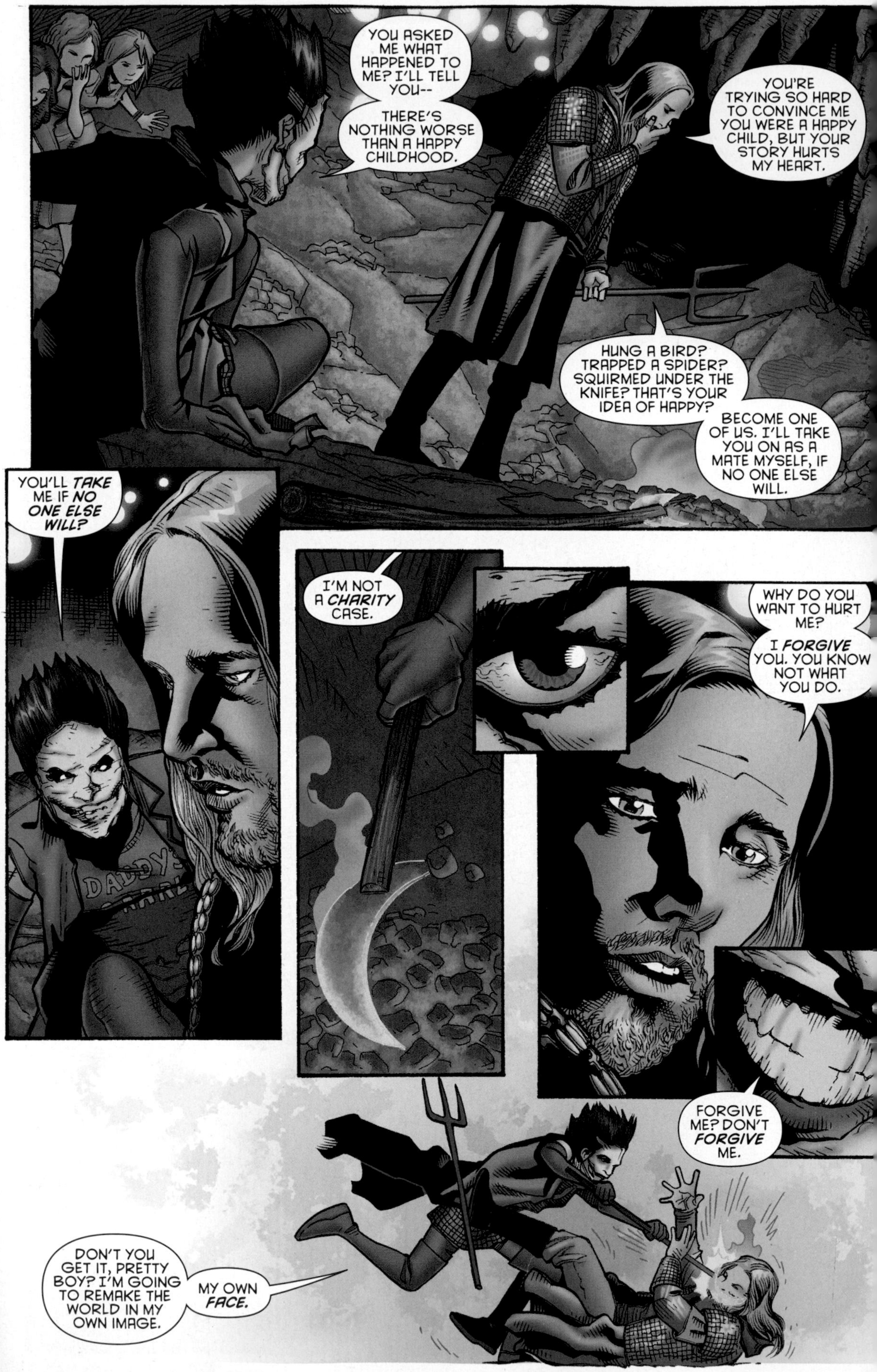
YOU ASKED ME WHAT HAPPENED TO ME? I'LL TELL YOU--
THERE'S NOTHING WORSE THAN A HAPPY CHILDHOOD.
YOU'RE TRYING SO HARD TO CONVINCE ME YOU WERE A HAPPY CHILD, BUT YOUR STORY HURTS MY HEART.
HUNG A BIRD? TRAPPED A SPIDER? SQUIRMED UNDER THE KNIFE? THAT'S YOUR IDEA OF HAPPY?
BECOME ONE OF US. I'LL TAKE YOU ON AS A MATE MYSELF, IF NO ONE ELSE WILL.
YOU'LL *TAKE* ME IF *NO ONE ELSE WILL?*
I'M NOT A *CHARITY* CASE.
WHY DO YOU WANT TO HURT ME?
I *FORGIVE* YOU. YOU KNOW NOT WHAT YOU DO.
FORGIVE ME? DON'T *FORGIVE* ME.
DON'T YOU GET IT, PRETTY BOY? I'M GOING TO REMAKE THE WORLD IN MY OWN IMAGE.
MY OWN *FACE.*

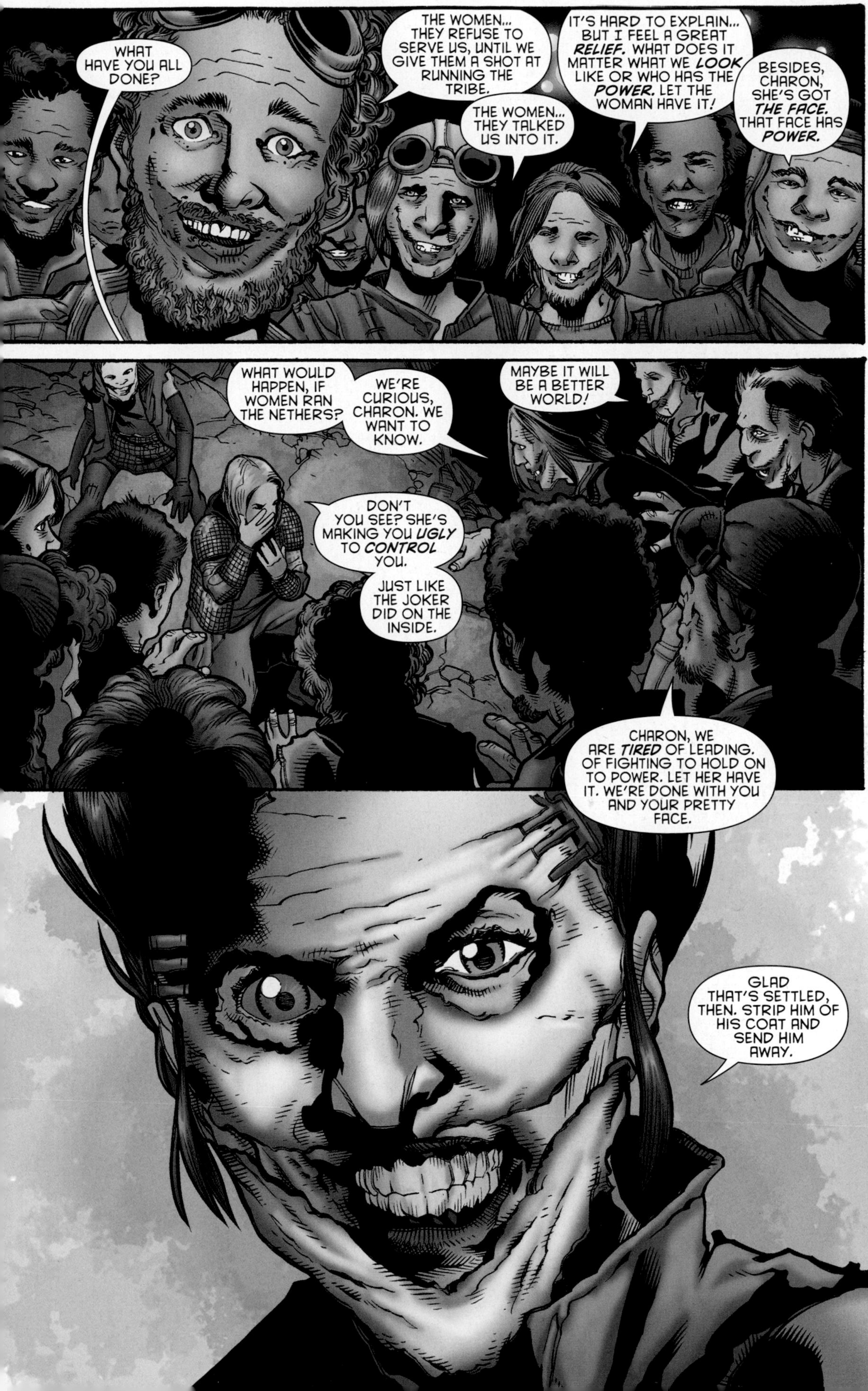

WHAT HAVE YOU ALL DONE?
THE WOMEN... THEY REFUSE TO SERVE US, UNTIL WE GIVE THEM A SHOT AT RUNNING THE TRIBE.
THE WOMEN... THEY TALKED US INTO IT.
IT'S HARD TO EXPLAIN... BUT I FEEL A GREAT RELIEF. WHAT DOES IT MATTER WHAT WE LOOK LIKE OR WHO HAS THE POWER. LET THE WOMAN HAVE IT!
BESIDES, CHARON, SHE'S GOT THE FACE. THAT FACE HAS POWER.
WHAT WOULD HAPPEN, IF WOMEN RAN THE NETHERS?
WE'RE CURIOUS, CHARON. WE WANT TO KNOW.
MAYBE IT WILL BE A BETTER WORLD!
DON'T YOU SEE? SHE'S MAKING YOU UGLY TO CONTROL YOU.
JUST LIKE THE JOKER DID ON THE INSIDE.
CHARON, WE ARE TIRED OF LEADING. OF FIGHTING TO HOLD ON TO POWER. LET HER HAVE IT. WE'RE DONE WITH YOU AND YOUR PRETTY FACE.
GLAD THAT'S SETTLED, THEN. STRIP HIM OF HIS COAT AND SEND HIM AWAY.

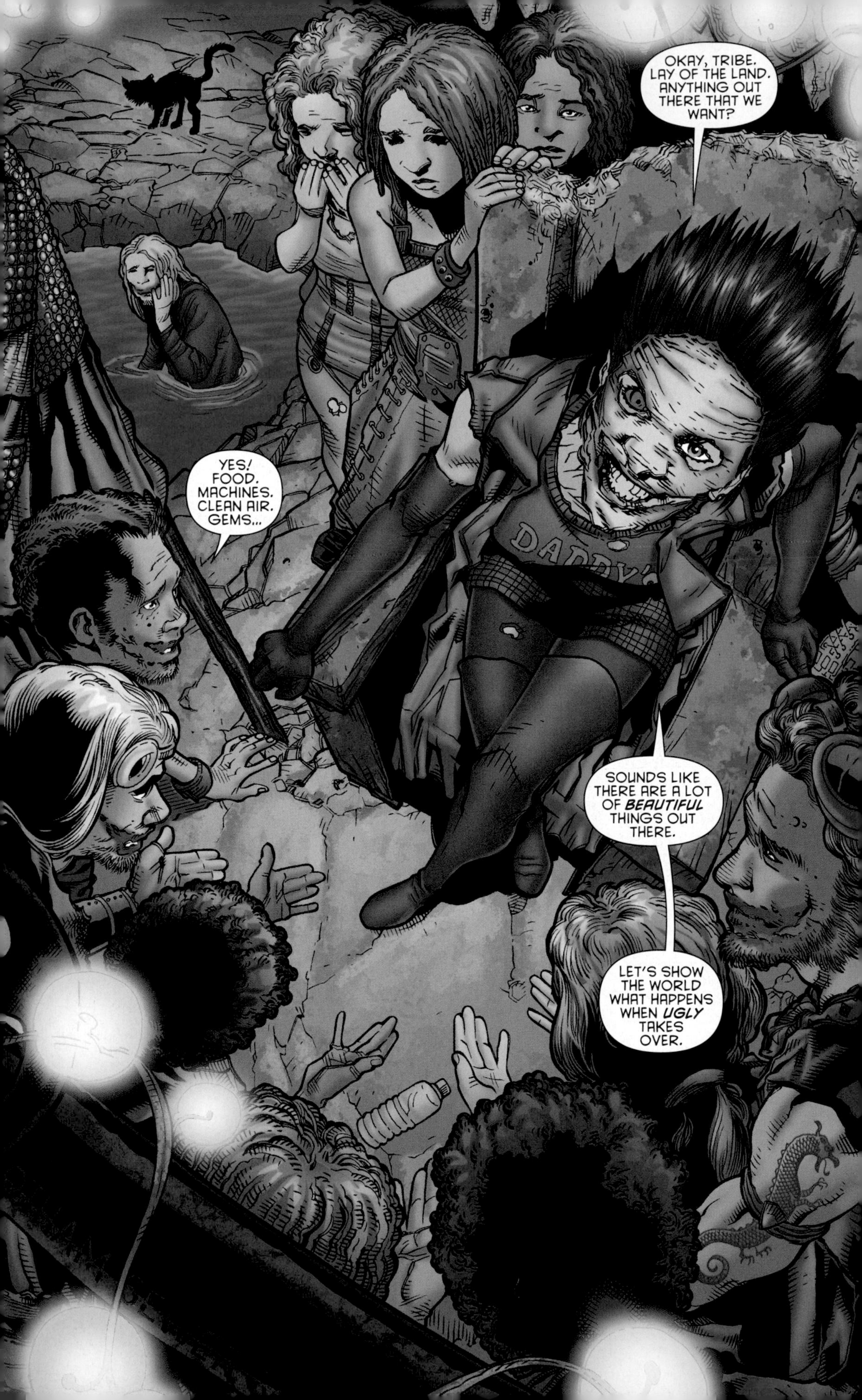
OKAY, TRIBE. LAY OF THE LAND. ANYTHING OUT THERE THAT WE WANT?
YES! FOOD. MACHINES. CLEAN AIR. GEMS...
SOUNDS LIKE THERE ARE A LOT OF *BEAUTIFUL* THINGS OUT THERE.
LET'S SHOW THE WORLD WHAT HAPPENS WHEN *UGLY* TAKES OVER.
DADDY'S

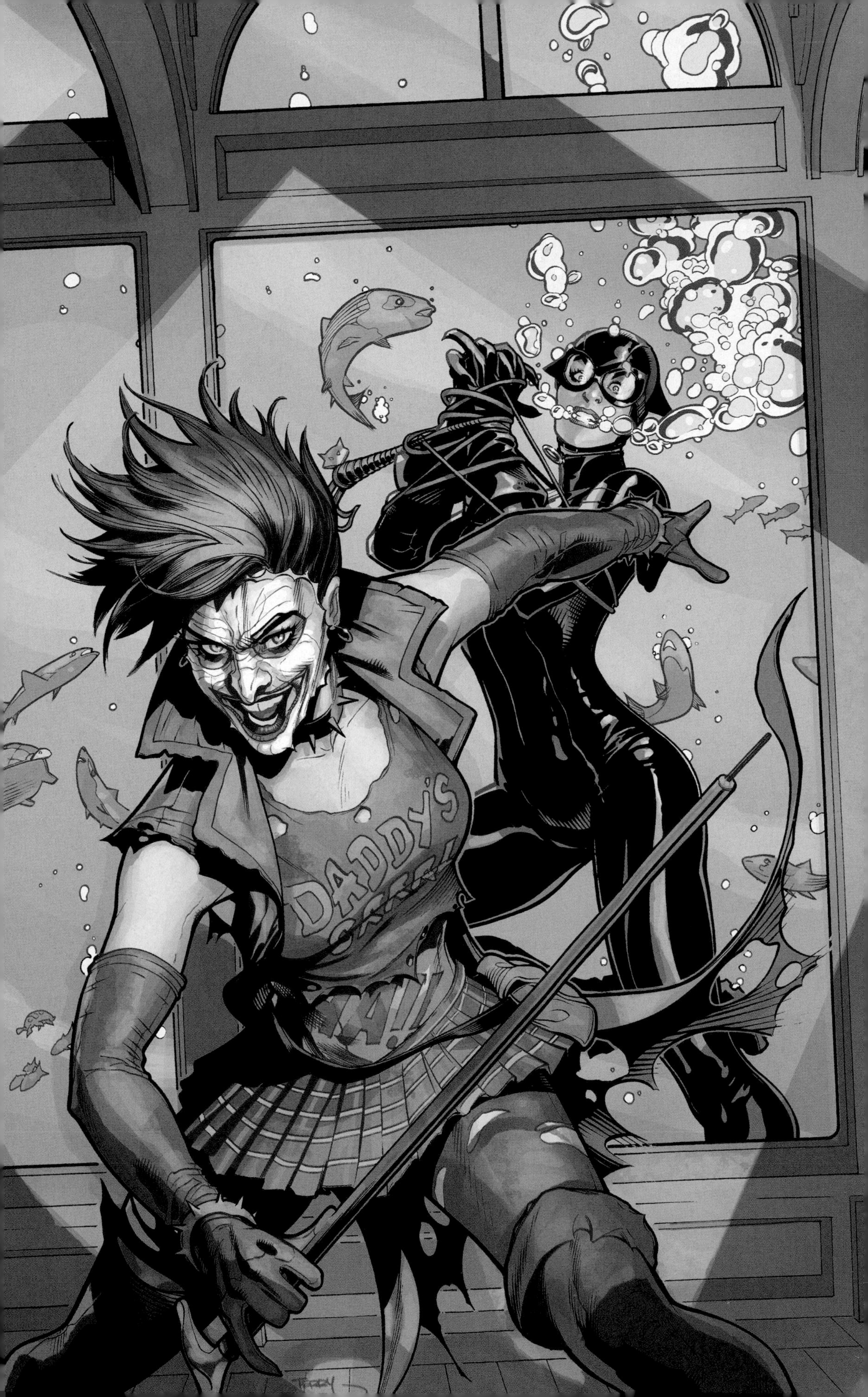
DADDY'S

ANN NOCENTI
writer

RAFA SANDOVAL
penciller

JORDI TARRAGONA
inker

SONIA OBACK
colorist

TERRY & RACHEL DODSON
cover artists

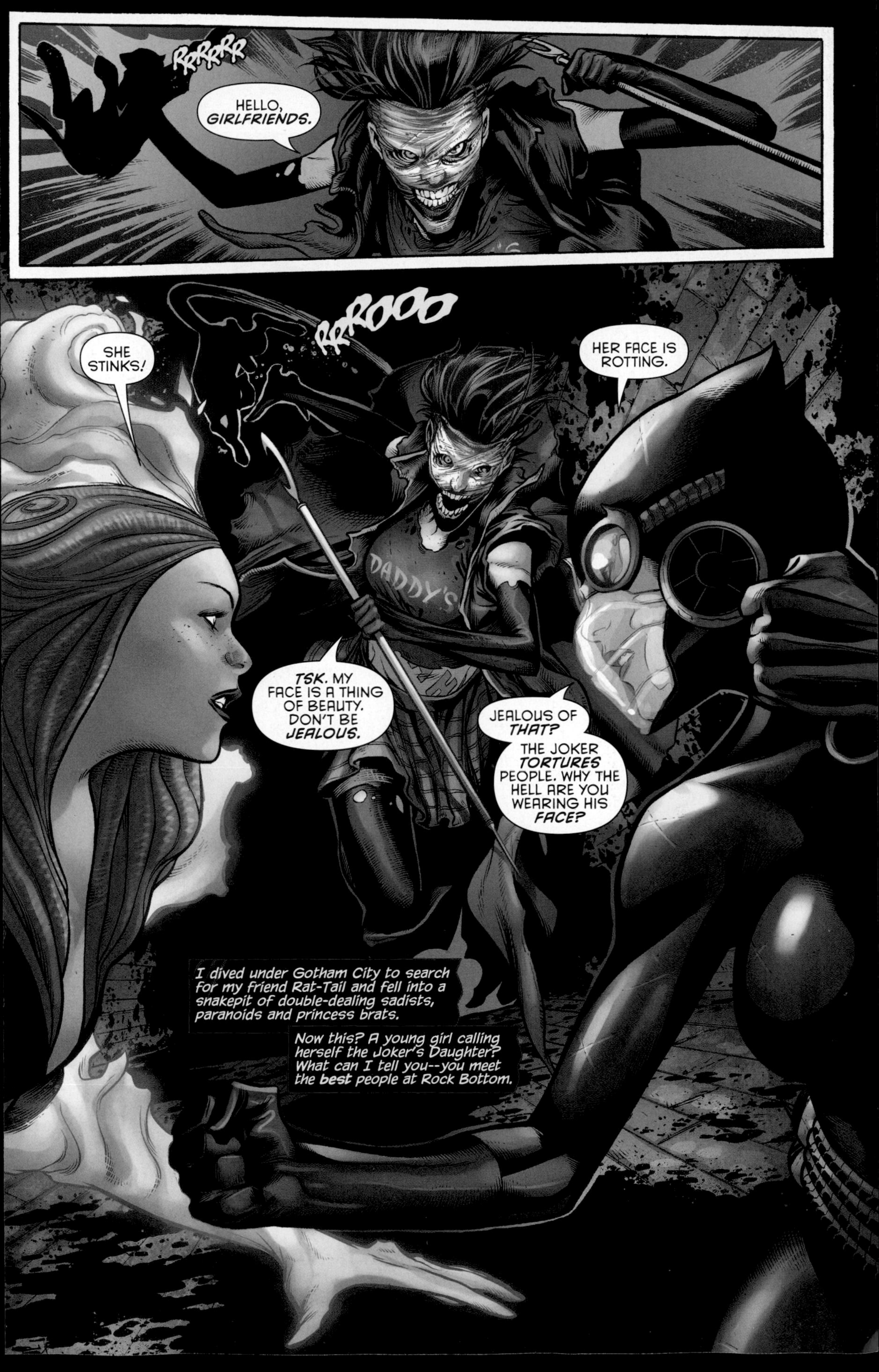
RRRRRR
HELLO, *GIRLFRIENDS.*
RRROOO
SHE STINKS!
HER FACE IS ROTTING.
DADDY'S
TSK. MY FACE IS A THING OF BEAUTY. DON'T BE *JEALOUS.*
JEALOUS OF *THAT?*
THE JOKER *TORTURES* PEOPLE. WHY THE HELL ARE YOU WEARING HIS *FACE?*
I dived under Gotham City to search for my friend Rat-Tail and fell into a snakepit of double-dealing sadists, paranoids and princess brats.
*Now this? A young girl calling herself the Joker's Daughter? What can I tell you--you meet the **best** people at Rock Bottom.*

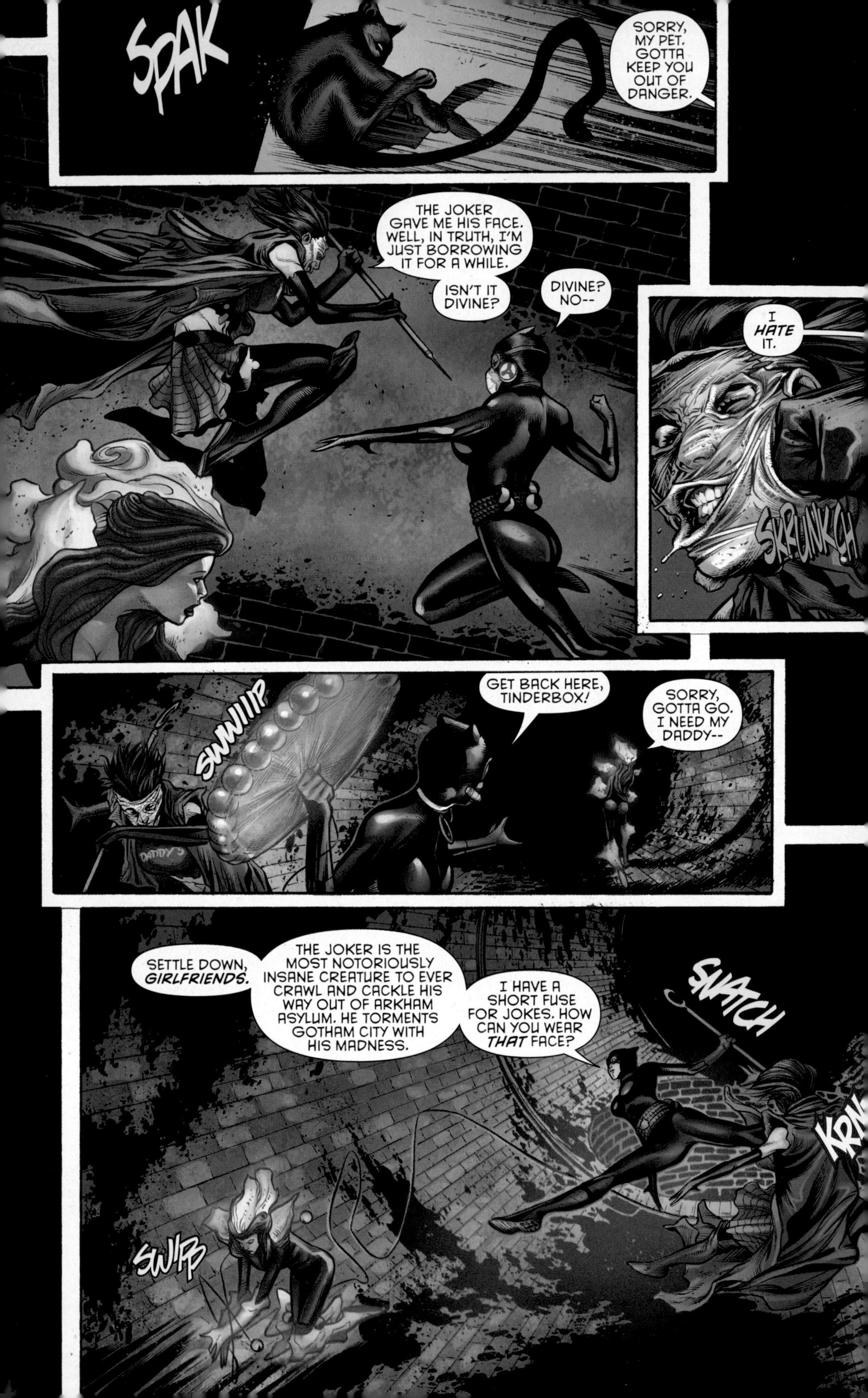
SPAK
SORRY, MY PET. GOTTA KEEP YOU OUT OF DANGER.
THE JOKER GAVE ME HIS FACE. WELL, IN TRUTH, I'M JUST BORROWING IT FOR A WHILE.
ISN'T IT DIVINE?
DIVINE? NO--
I *HATE* IT.
SKRUNKCH
GET BACK HERE, TINDERBOX!
SWIIIP
SORRY, GOTTA GO. I NEED MY DADDY--
DADDY'S
SETTLE DOWN, *GIRLFRIENDS.*
THE JOKER IS THE MOST NOTORIOUSLY INSANE CREATURE TO EVER CRAWL AND CACKLE HIS WAY OUT OF ARKHAM ASYLUM. HE TORMENTS GOTHAM CITY WITH HIS MADNESS.
I HAVE A SHORT FUSE FOR JOKES. HOW CAN YOU WEAR *THAT* FACE?
SNATCH
KRN
SWIPP

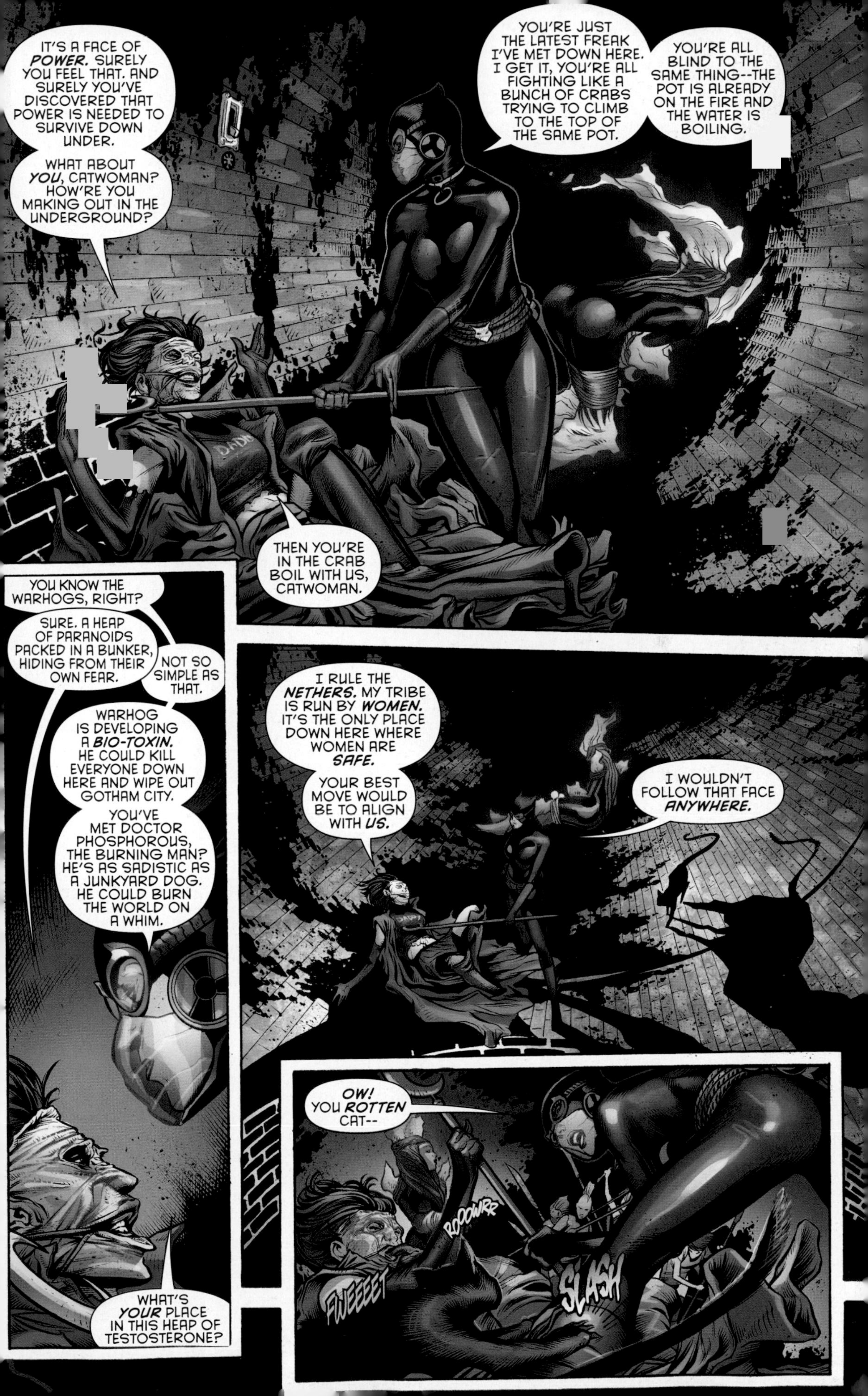
IT'S A FACE OF POWER. SURELY YOU FEEL THAT. AND SURELY YOU'VE DISCOVERED THAT POWER IS NEEDED TO SURVIVE DOWN UNDER.
WHAT ABOUT YOU, CATWOMAN? HOW'RE YOU MAKING OUT IN THE UNDERGROUND?
YOU'RE JUST THE LATEST FREAK I'VE MET DOWN HERE. I GET IT, YOU'RE ALL FIGHTING LIKE A BUNCH OF CRABS TRYING TO CLIMB TO THE TOP OF THE SAME POT.
YOU'RE ALL BLIND TO THE SAME THING--THE POT IS ALREADY ON THE FIRE AND THE WATER IS BOILING.
THEN YOU'RE IN THE CRAB BOIL WITH US, CATWOMAN.
YOU KNOW THE WARHOGS, RIGHT?
SURE. A HEAP OF PARANOIDS PACKED IN A BUNKER, HIDING FROM THEIR OWN FEAR.
NOT SO SIMPLE AS THAT.
WARHOG IS DEVELOPING A BIO-TOXIN. HE COULD KILL EVERYONE DOWN HERE AND WIPE OUT GOTHAM CITY.
YOU'VE MET DOCTOR PHOSPHOROUS, THE BURNING MAN? HE'S AS SADISTIC AS A JUNKYARD DOG. HE COULD BURN THE WORLD ON A WHIM.
WHAT'S YOUR PLACE IN THIS HEAP OF TESTOSTERONE?
I RULE THE NETHERS. MY TRIBE IS RUN BY WOMEN. IT'S THE ONLY PLACE DOWN HERE WHERE WOMEN ARE SAFE.
YOUR BEST MOVE WOULD BE TO ALIGN WITH US.
I WOULDN'T FOLLOW THAT FACE ANYWHERE.
OW! YOU ROTTEN CAT--
RROOWRR
FWEEEEET
SLASH

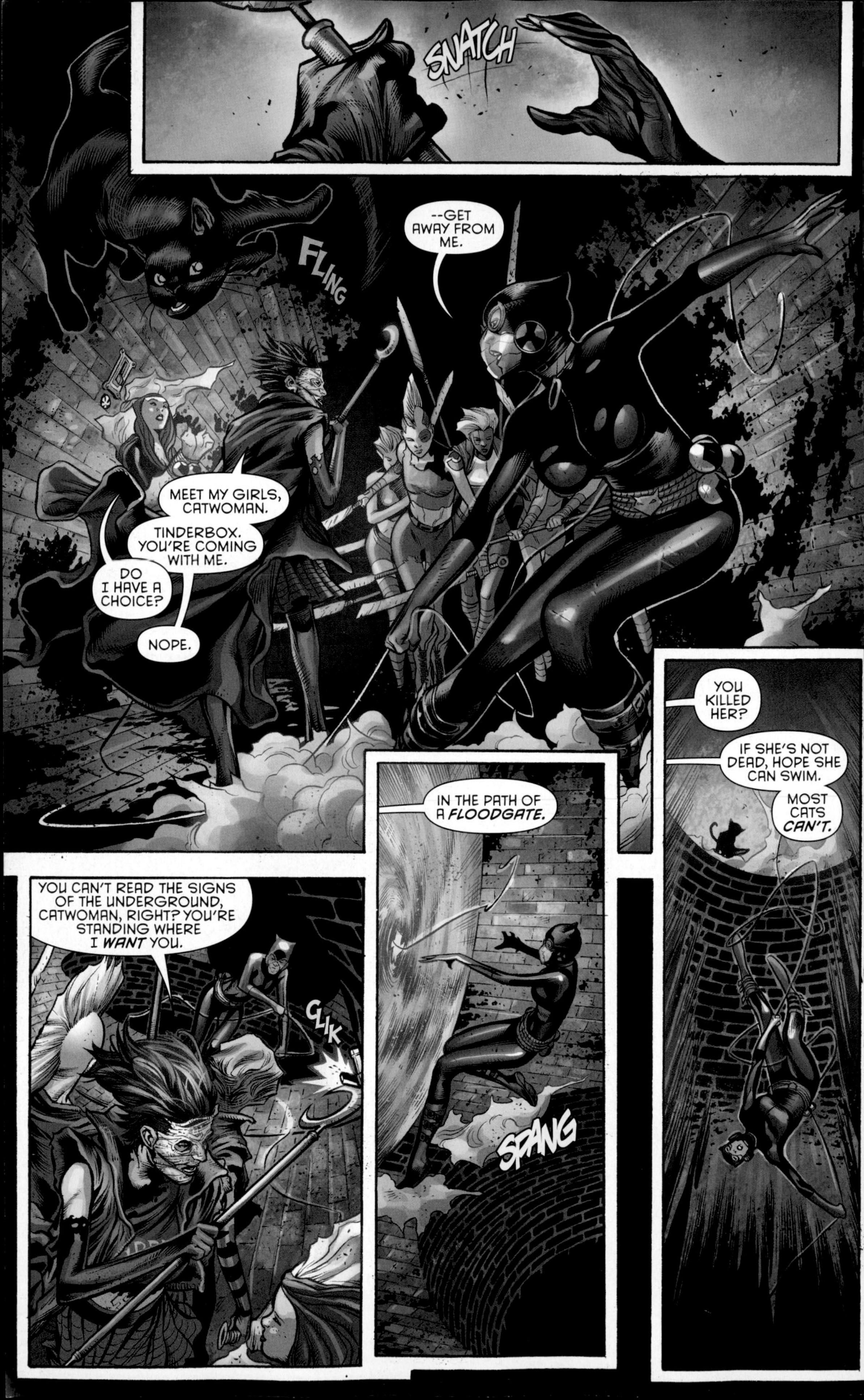
SNATCH
FLING
--GET AWAY FROM ME.
MEET MY GIRLS, CATWOMAN.
TINDERBOX. YOU'RE COMING WITH ME.
DO I HAVE A CHOICE?
NOPE.
YOU CAN'T READ THE SIGNS OF THE UNDERGROUND, CATWOMAN, RIGHT? YOU'RE STANDING WHERE I *WANT* YOU.
GLIK
IN THE PATH OF A *FLOODGATE.*
SPANG
YOU KILLED HER?
IF SHE'S NOT DEAD, HOPE SHE CAN SWIM.
MOST CATS *CAN'T.*

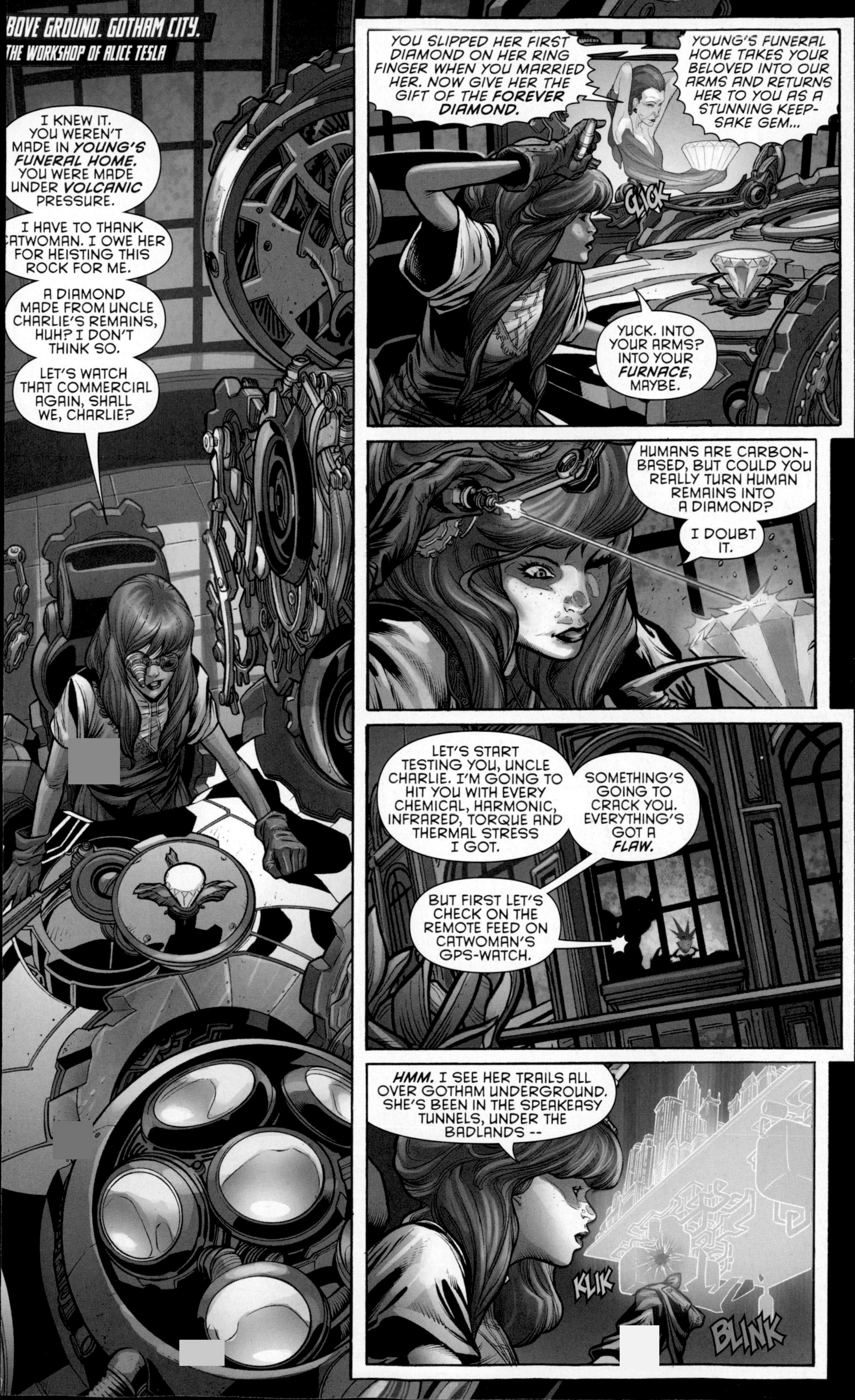
BOVE GROUND. GOTHAM CITY.
THE WORKSHOP OF ALICE TESLA
I KNEW IT. YOU WEREN'T MADE IN YOUNG'S FUNERAL HOME. YOU WERE MADE UNDER VOLCANIC PRESSURE.
I HAVE TO THANK CATWOMAN. I OWE HER FOR HEISTING THIS ROCK FOR ME.
A DIAMOND MADE FROM UNCLE CHARLIE'S REMAINS, HUH? I DON'T THINK SO.
LET'S WATCH THAT COMMERCIAL AGAIN, SHALL WE, CHARLIE?
YOU SLIPPED HER FIRST DIAMOND ON HER RING FINGER WHEN YOU MARRIED HER. NOW GIVE HER THE GIFT OF THE FOREVER DIAMOND.
YOUNG'S FUNERAL HOME TAKES YOUR BELOVED INTO OUR ARMS AND RETURNS HER TO YOU AS A STUNNING KEEP-SAKE GEM...
CLICK
YUCK. INTO YOUR ARMS? INTO YOUR FURNACE, MAYBE.
HUMANS ARE CARBON-BASED, BUT COULD YOU REALLY TURN HUMAN REMAINS INTO A DIAMOND?
I DOUBT IT.
LET'S START TESTING YOU, UNCLE CHARLIE. I'M GOING TO HIT YOU WITH EVERY CHEMICAL, HARMONIC, INFRARED, TORQUE AND THERMAL STRESS I GOT.
SOMETHING'S GOING TO CRACK YOU. EVERYTHING'S GOT A FLAW.
BUT FIRST LET'S CHECK ON THE REMOTE FEED ON CATWOMAN'S GPS-WATCH.
HMM. I SEE HER TRAILS ALL OVER GOTHAM UNDERGROUND. SHE'S BEEN IN THE SPEAKEASY TUNNELS, UNDER THE BADLANDS --
KLIK
BLINK

"--RIGHT NOW SHE'S SOMEWHERE VERY *DARK.*"

KLINK

OH, THANK *GOD!*

Get high up and out of their light--*phew..*

SWIIIP

That blind toss grabbed something. Now what?

Footsteps. Sounds like five or six big men.

They're breaking step, they must be crossing a bridge. What's my angle here?

Warhogs! Don't want to tussle with those grunts again.

Carrying a body. A *burnt* body. Must have come from charneltow

OH. GOD. NO! THOSE CLOTHES... THAT'S *RAT-TAIL.*

YOU DIDN'T MAKE IT.

THE LEAST I CAN DO IS TAKE YOU BACK AND BURY YOU ABOVE GROUND IN THE BADLANDS.

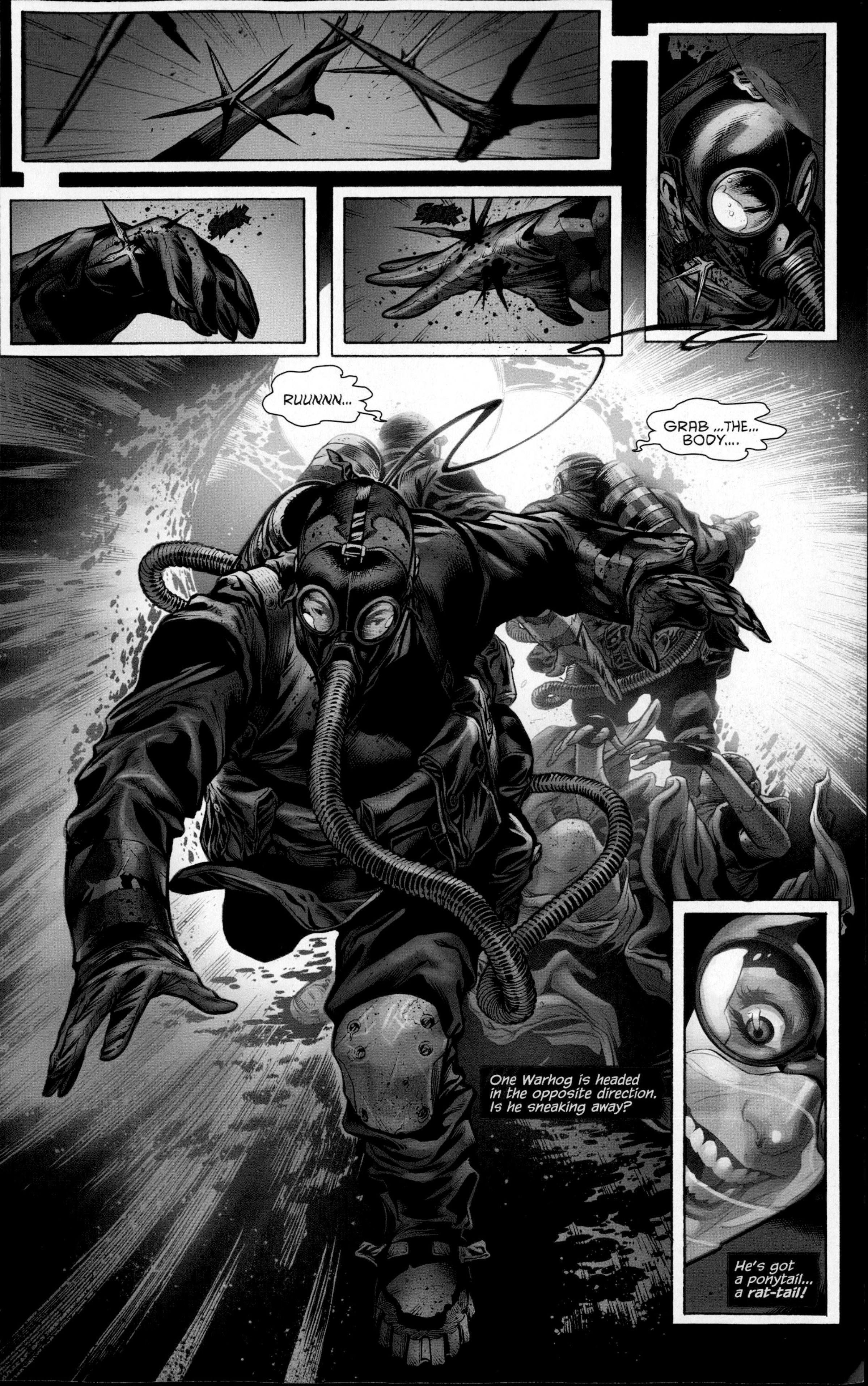
RUUNNN...
GRAB ...THE... BODY....
One Warhog is headed in the opposite direction. Is he sneaking away?
He's got a ponytail... a rat-tail!

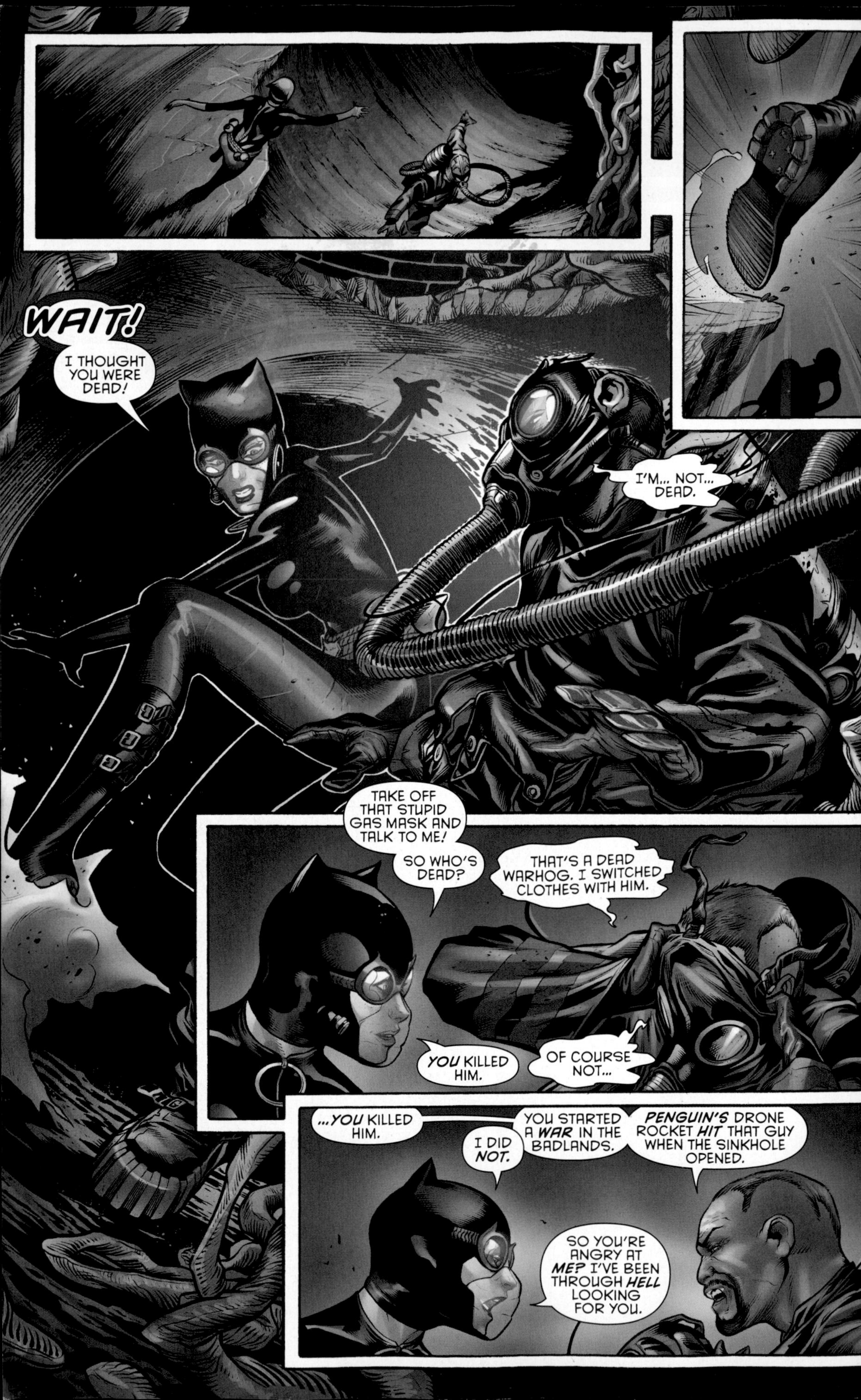
WAIT!
I THOUGHT YOU WERE DEAD!
I'M... NOT... DEAD.
TAKE OFF THAT STUPID GAS MASK AND TALK TO ME!
SO WHO'S DEAD?
THAT'S A DEAD WARHOG. I SWITCHED CLOTHES WITH HIM.
YOU KILLED HIM.
OF COURSE NOT...
...YOU KILLED HIM.
I DID NOT.
YOU STARTED A WAR IN THE BADLANDS.
PENGUIN'S DRONE ROCKET HIT THAT GUY WHEN THE SINKHOLE OPENED.
SO YOU'RE ANGRY AT ME? I'VE BEEN THROUGH HELL LOOKING FOR YOU.

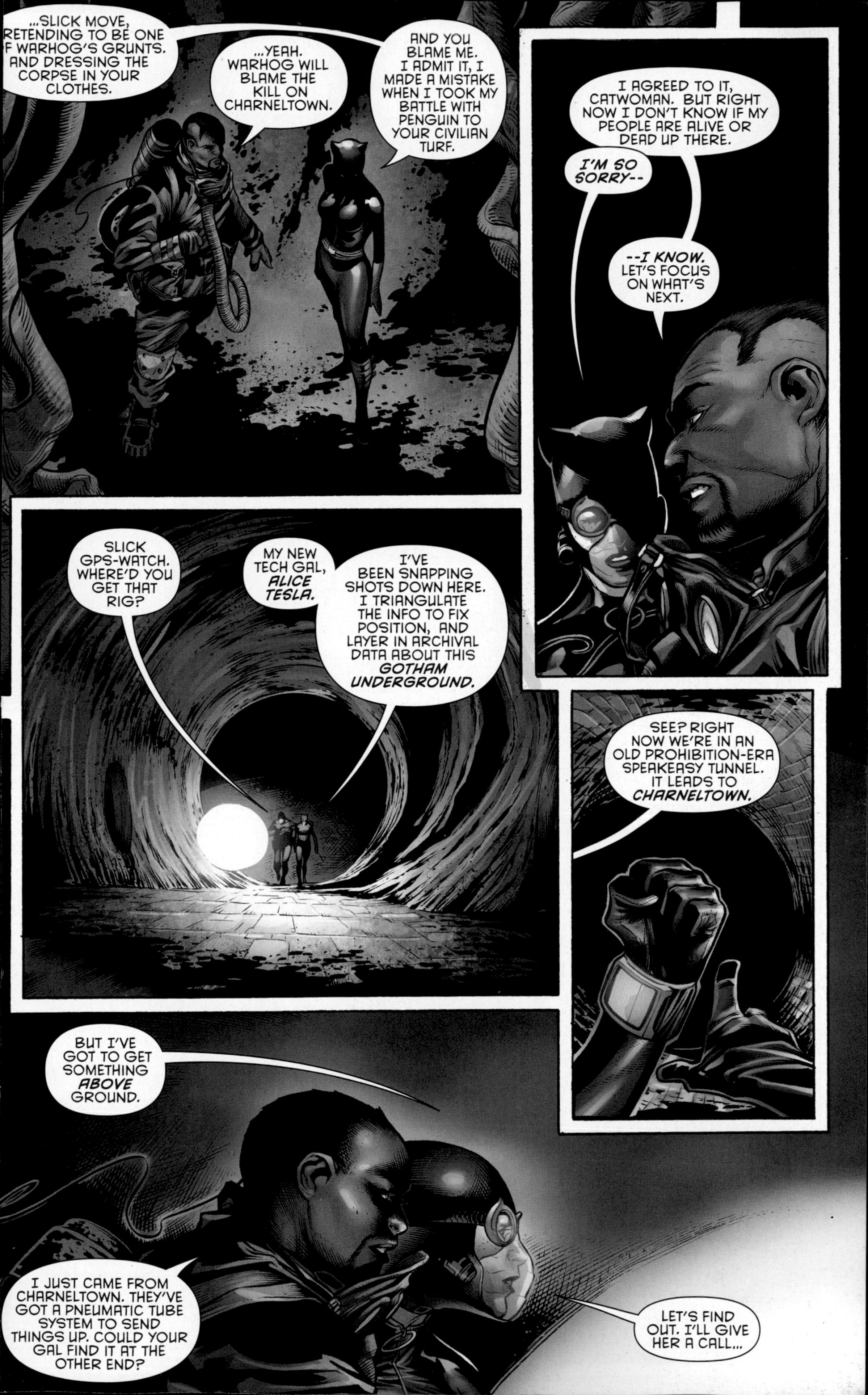
...SLICK MOVE, RETENDING TO BE ONE F WARHOG'S GRUNTS. AND DRESSING THE CORPSE IN YOUR CLOTHES.
...YEAH. WARHOG WILL BLAME THE KILL ON CHARNELTOWN.
AND YOU BLAME ME. I ADMIT IT, I MADE A MISTAKE WHEN I TOOK MY BATTLE WITH PENGUIN TO YOUR CIVILIAN TURF.
I AGREED TO IT, CATWOMAN. BUT RIGHT NOW I DON'T KNOW IF MY PEOPLE ARE ALIVE OR DEAD UP THERE.
I'M SO SORRY--
--I KNOW. LET'S FOCUS ON WHAT'S NEXT.
SLICK GPS-WATCH. WHERE'D YOU GET THAT RIG?
MY NEW TECH GAL, ALICE TESLA.
I'VE BEEN SNAPPING SHOTS DOWN HERE. I TRIANGULATE THE INFO TO FIX POSITION, AND LAYER IN ARCHIVAL DATA ABOUT THIS GOTHAM UNDERGROUND.
SEE? RIGHT NOW WE'RE IN AN OLD PROHIBITION-ERA SPEAKEASY TUNNEL. IT LEADS TO CHARNELTOWN.
BUT I'VE GOT TO GET SOMETHING ABOVE GROUND.
I JUST CAME FROM CHARNELTOWN. THEY'VE GOT A PNEUMATIC TUBE SYSTEM TO SEND THINGS UP. COULD YOUR GAL FIND IT AT THE OTHER END?
LET'S FIND OUT. I'LL GIVE HER A CALL...

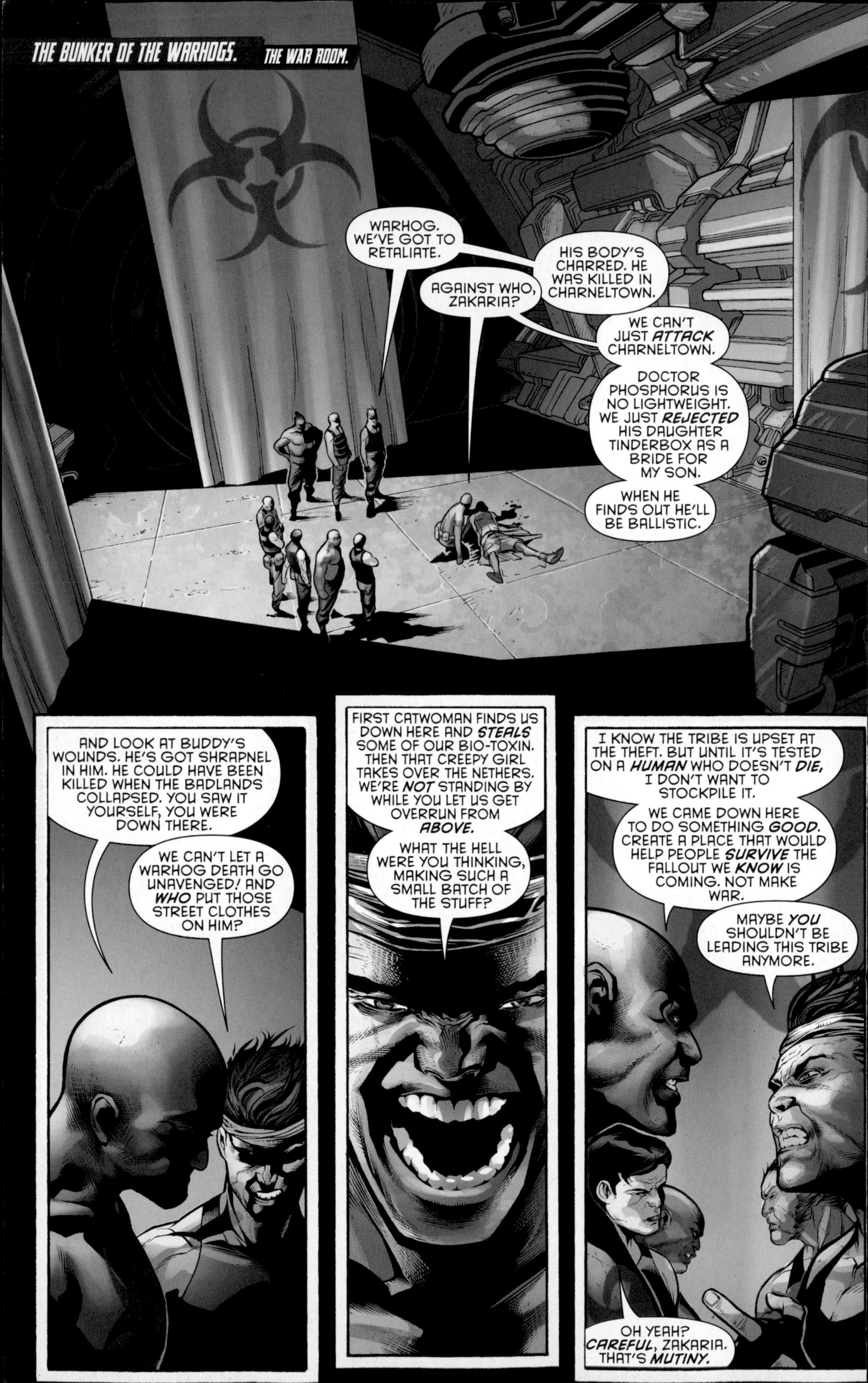
THE BUNKER OF THE WARHOGS.
THE WAR ROOM.
WARHOG. WE'VE GOT TO RETALIATE.
HIS BODY'S CHARRED. HE WAS KILLED IN CHARNELTOWN.
AGAINST WHO, ZAKARIA?
WE CAN'T JUST ATTACK CHARNELTOWN.
DOCTOR PHOSPHORUS IS NO LIGHTWEIGHT. WE JUST REJECTED HIS DAUGHTER TINDERBOX AS A BRIDE FOR MY SON.
WHEN HE FINDS OUT HE'LL BE BALLISTIC.
AND LOOK AT BUDDY'S WOUNDS. HE'S GOT SHRAPNEL IN HIM. HE COULD HAVE BEEN KILLED WHEN THE BADLANDS COLLAPSED. YOU SAW IT YOURSELF, YOU WERE DOWN THERE.
WE CAN'T LET A WARHOG DEATH GO UNAVENGED! AND WHO PUT THOSE STREET CLOTHES ON HIM?
FIRST CATWOMAN FINDS US DOWN HERE AND STEALS SOME OF OUR BIO-TOXIN. THEN THAT CREEPY GIRL TAKES OVER THE NETHERS. WE'RE NOT STANDING BY WHILE YOU LET US GET OVERRUN FROM ABOVE.
WHAT THE HELL WERE YOU THINKING, MAKING SUCH A SMALL BATCH OF THE STUFF?
I KNOW THE TRIBE IS UPSET AT THE THEFT. BUT UNTIL IT'S TESTED ON A HUMAN WHO DOESN'T DIE, I DON'T WANT TO STOCKPILE IT.
WE CAME DOWN HERE TO DO SOMETHING GOOD. CREATE A PLACE THAT WOULD HELP PEOPLE SURVIVE THE FALLOUT WE KNOW IS COMING. NOT MAKE WAR.
MAYBE YOU SHOULDN'T BE LEADING THIS TRIBE ANYMORE.
OH YEAH? CAREFUL, ZAKARIA. THAT'S MUTINY.

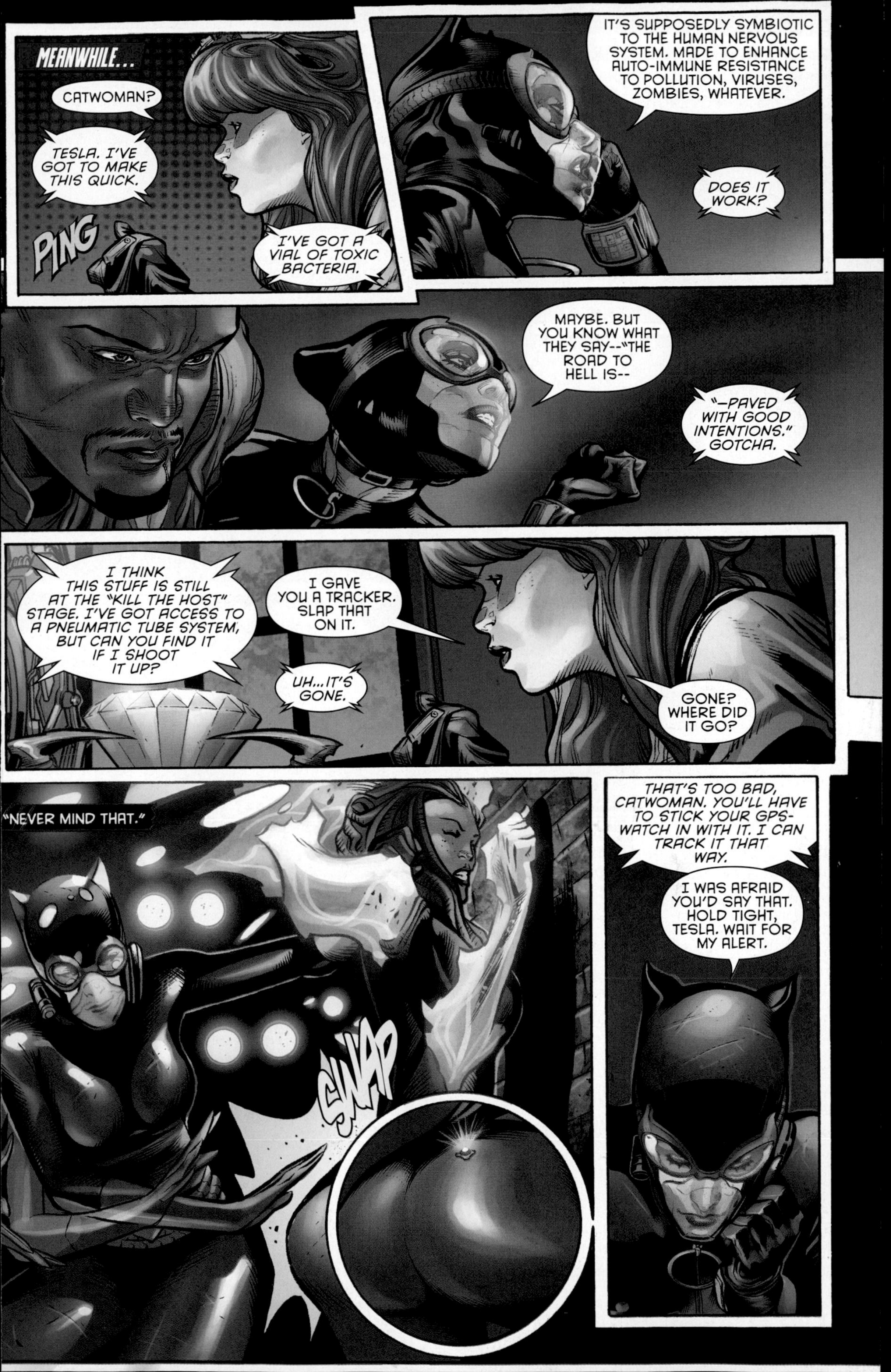
MEANWHILE...
CATWOMAN?
TESLA. I'VE GOT TO MAKE THIS QUICK.
PING
I'VE GOT A VIAL OF TOXIC BACTERIA.
IT'S SUPPOSEDLY SYMBIOTIC TO THE HUMAN NERVOUS SYSTEM. MADE TO ENHANCE AUTO-IMMUNE RESISTANCE TO POLLUTION, VIRUSES, ZOMBIES, WHATEVER.
DOES IT WORK?
MAYBE. BUT YOU KNOW WHAT THEY SAY--"THE ROAD TO HELL IS--
"--PAVED WITH GOOD INTENTIONS." GOTCHA.
I THINK THIS STUFF IS STILL AT THE "KILL THE HOST" STAGE. I'VE GOT ACCESS TO A PNEUMATIC TUBE SYSTEM, BUT CAN YOU FIND IT IF I SHOOT IT UP?
I GAVE YOU A TRACKER. SLAP THAT ON IT.
UH...IT'S GONE.
GONE? WHERE DID IT GO?
"NEVER MIND THAT."
SWAP
THAT'S TOO BAD, CATWOMAN. YOU'LL HAVE TO STICK YOUR GPS-WATCH IN WITH IT. I CAN TRACK IT THAT WAY.
I WAS AFRAID YOU'D SAY THAT. HOLD TIGHT, TESLA. WAIT FOR MY ALERT.

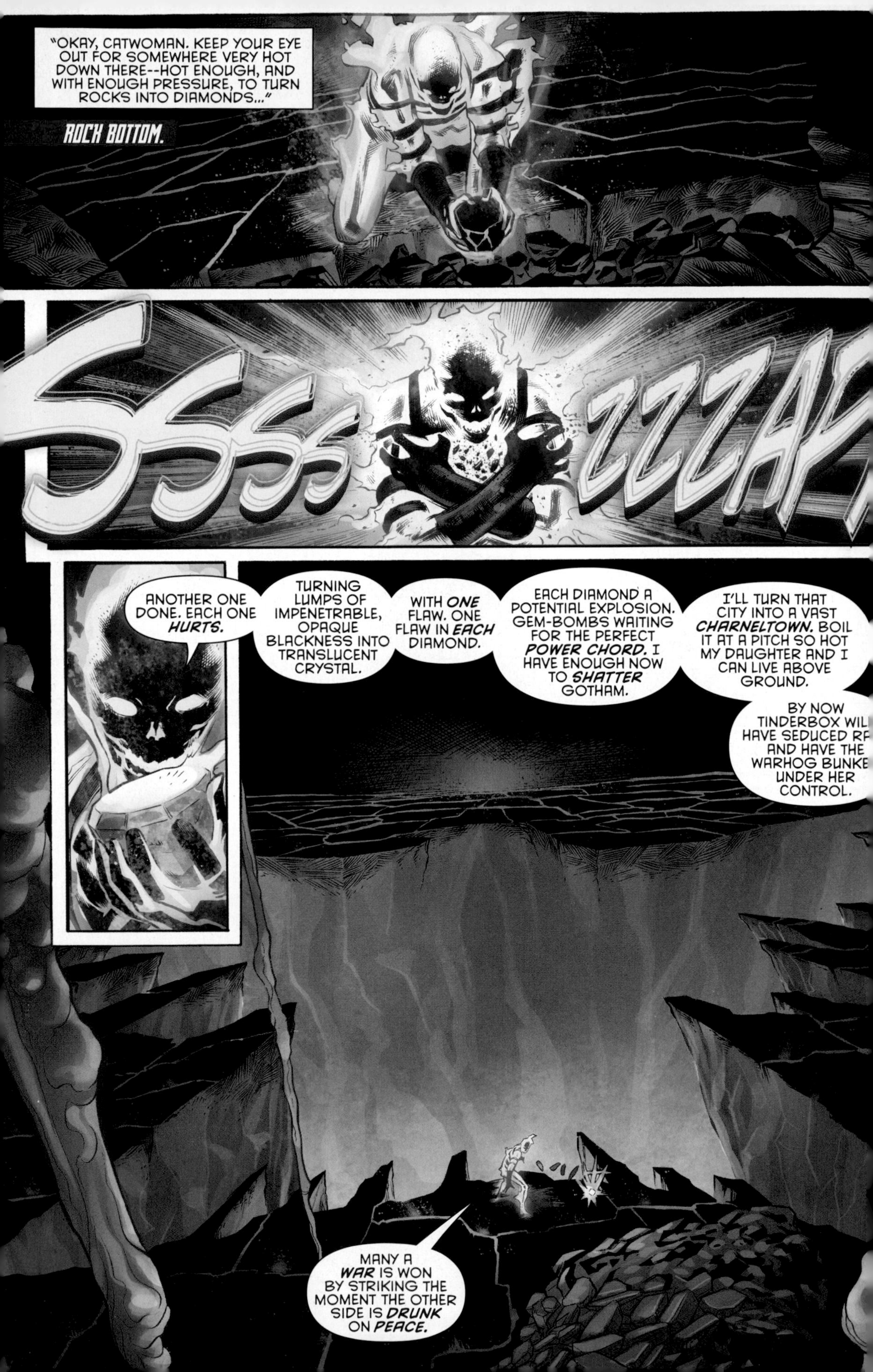
"OKAY, CATWOMAN. KEEP YOUR EYE OUT FOR SOMEWHERE VERY HOT DOWN THERE--HOT ENOUGH, AND WITH ENOUGH PRESSURE, TO TURN ROCKS INTO DIAMONDS..."
ROCK BOTTOM.
SSSSSZZZZAP
ANOTHER ONE DONE. EACH ONE *HURTS.*
TURNING LUMPS OF IMPENETRABLE, OPAQUE BLACKNESS INTO TRANSLUCENT CRYSTAL.
WITH *ONE* FLAW. ONE FLAW IN *EACH* DIAMOND.
EACH DIAMOND A POTENTIAL EXPLOSION. GEM-BOMBS WAITING FOR THE PERFECT *POWER CHORD.* I HAVE ENOUGH NOW TO *SHATTER* GOTHAM.
I'LL TURN THAT CITY INTO A VAST *CHARNELTOWN.* BOIL IT AT A PITCH SO HOT MY DAUGHTER AND I CAN LIVE ABOVE GROUND.
BY NOW TINDERBOX WIL HAVE SEDUCED RA AND HAVE THE WARHOG BUNKE UNDER HER CONTROL.
MANY A *WAR* IS WON BY STRIKING THE MOMENT THE OTHER SIDE IS *DRUNK* ON *PEACE.*

DOCTOR PHOSPHORUS!

HMMM. WHAT NOW?

SPIT IT OUT, MAN.

OUR SPIES SENT SOME INTEL.

THE WARHOGS, SIR. THEY BROKE INTO THE PNEUMATIC TUBES IN SECTOR FIVE, STOLE SOME GEMS. AND...

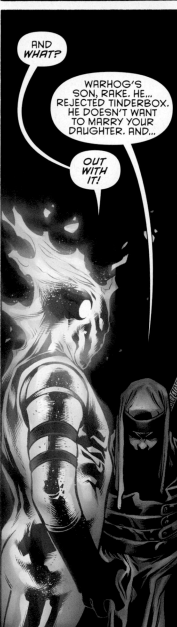

AND WHAT?

WARHOG'S SON, RAKE. HE... REJECTED TINDERBOX. HE DOESN'T WANT TO MARRY YOUR DAUGHTER. AND...

OUT WITH IT!

THE NEW GIRL, SIR. THE ONE THAT TOOK OVER THE NETHERS. THE ONE WITH THE STRANGE FACE. SHE TOOK TINDERBOX HOSTAGE.

THAT HORROR HAS MY DAUGHTER?

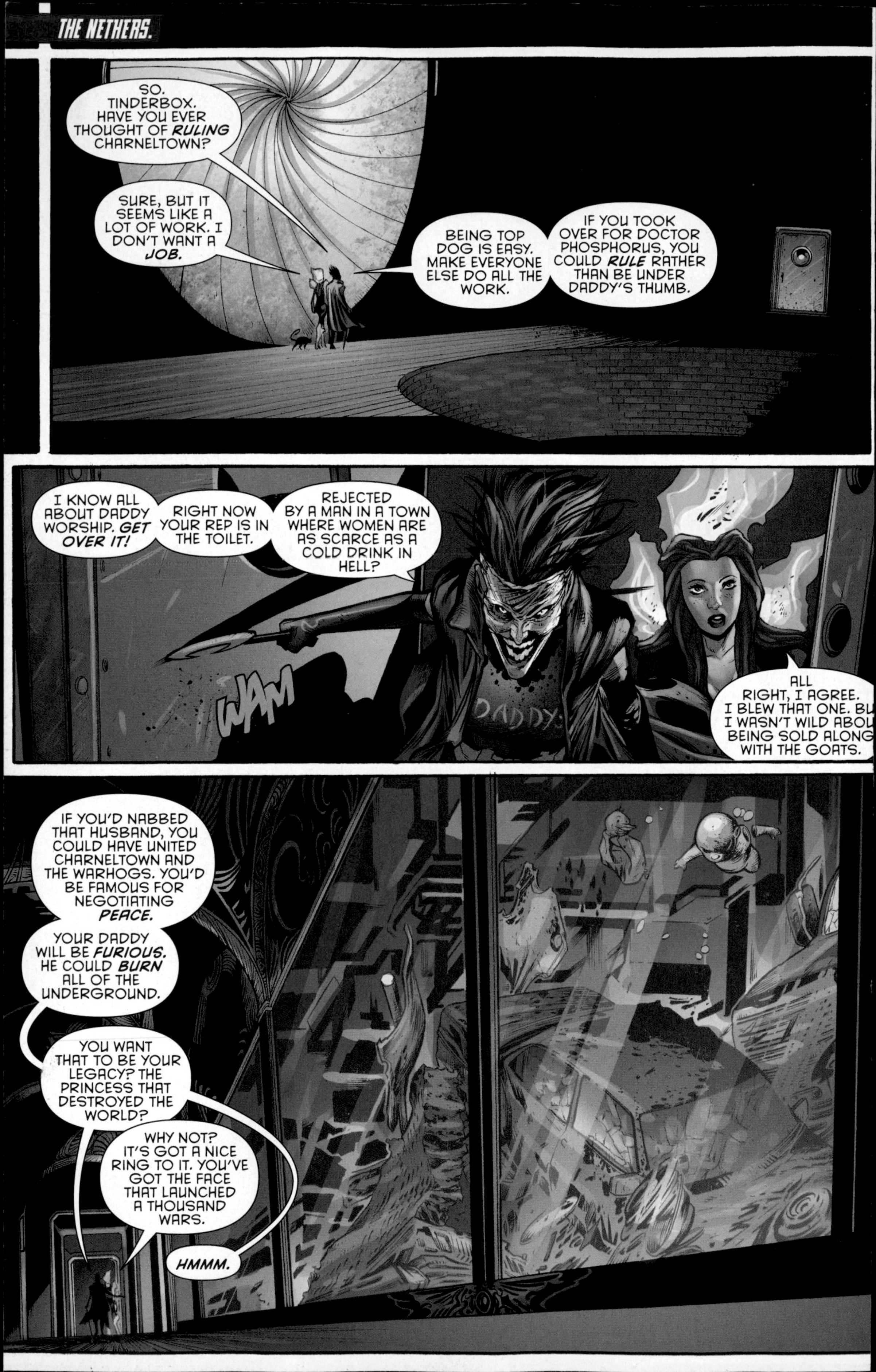
THE NETHERS.
SO. TINDERBOX. HAVE YOU EVER THOUGHT OF RULING CHARNELTOWN?
SURE, BUT IT SEEMS LIKE A LOT OF WORK. I DON'T WANT A JOB.
BEING TOP DOG IS EASY. MAKE EVERYONE ELSE DO ALL THE WORK.
IF YOU TOOK OVER FOR DOCTOR PHOSPHORUS, YOU COULD RULE RATHER THAN BE UNDER DADDY'S THUMB.
I KNOW ALL ABOUT DADDY WORSHIP. GET OVER IT!
RIGHT NOW YOUR REP IS IN THE TOILET.
REJECTED BY A MAN IN A TOWN WHERE WOMEN ARE AS SCARCE AS A COLD DRINK IN HELL?
WAM
DADDY
ALL RIGHT, I AGREE. I BLEW THAT ONE. BU I WASN'T WILD ABOU BEING SOLD ALONG WITH THE GOATS.
IF YOU'D NABBED THAT HUSBAND, YOU COULD HAVE UNITED CHARNELTOWN AND THE WARHOGS. YOU'D BE FAMOUS FOR NEGOTIATING PEACE.
YOUR DADDY WILL BE FURIOUS. HE COULD BURN ALL OF THE UNDERGROUND.
YOU WANT THAT TO BE YOUR LEGACY? THE PRINCESS THAT DESTROYED THE WORLD?
WHY NOT? IT'S GOT A NICE RING TO IT. YOU'VE GOT THE FACE THAT LAUNCHED A THOUSAND WARS.
HMMM.

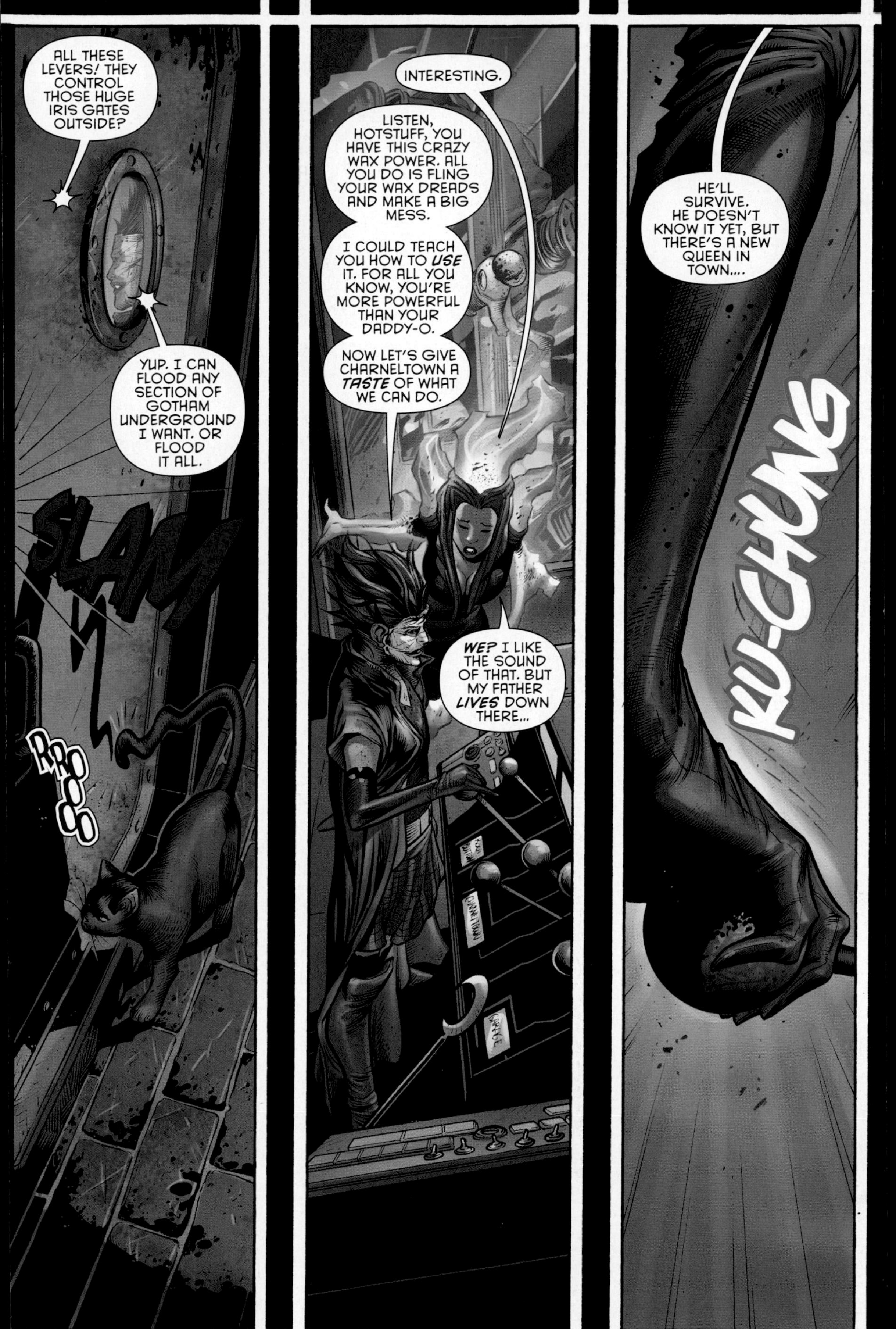
ALL THESE LEVERS! THEY CONTROL THOSE HUGE IRIS GATES OUTSIDE?
YUP. I CAN FLOOD ANY SECTION OF GOTHAM UNDERGROUND I WANT. OR FLOOD IT ALL.
SLAM
RROOOO
INTERESTING.
LISTEN, HOTSTUFF, YOU HAVE THIS CRAZY WAX POWER. ALL YOU DO IS FLING YOUR WAX DREADS AND MAKE A BIG MESS.
I COULD TEACH YOU HOW TO USE IT. FOR ALL YOU KNOW, YOU'RE MORE POWERFUL THAN YOUR DADDY-O.
NOW LET'S GIVE CHARNELTOWN A TASTE OF WHAT WE CAN DO.
WE? I LIKE THE SOUND OF THAT. BUT MY FATHER LIVES DOWN THERE...
CHARNELTOWN
HE'LL SURVIVE. HE DOESN'T KNOW IT YET, BUT THERE'S A NEW QUEEN IN TOWN....
KU-CHUNG

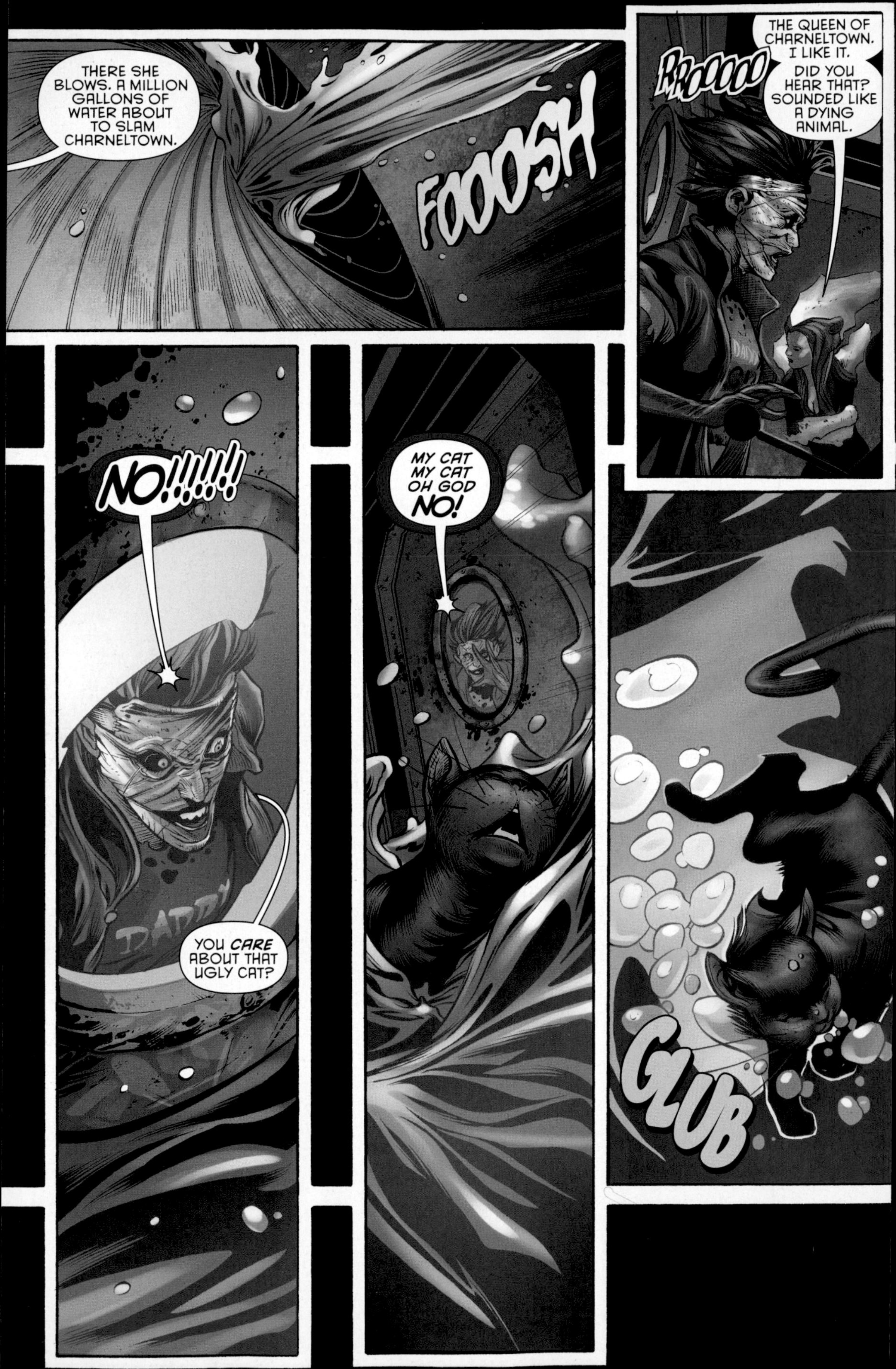
THERE SHE BLOWS. A MILLION GALLONS OF WATER ABOUT TO SLAM CHARNELTOWN.
FOOOSH
RROOOOO
THE QUEEN OF CHARNELTOWN. I LIKE IT.
DID YOU HEAR THAT? SOUNDED LIKE A DYING ANIMAL.
NO!!!!!!!
YOU CARE ABOUT THAT UGLY CAT?
MY CAT MY CAT OH GOD NO!
GLUB

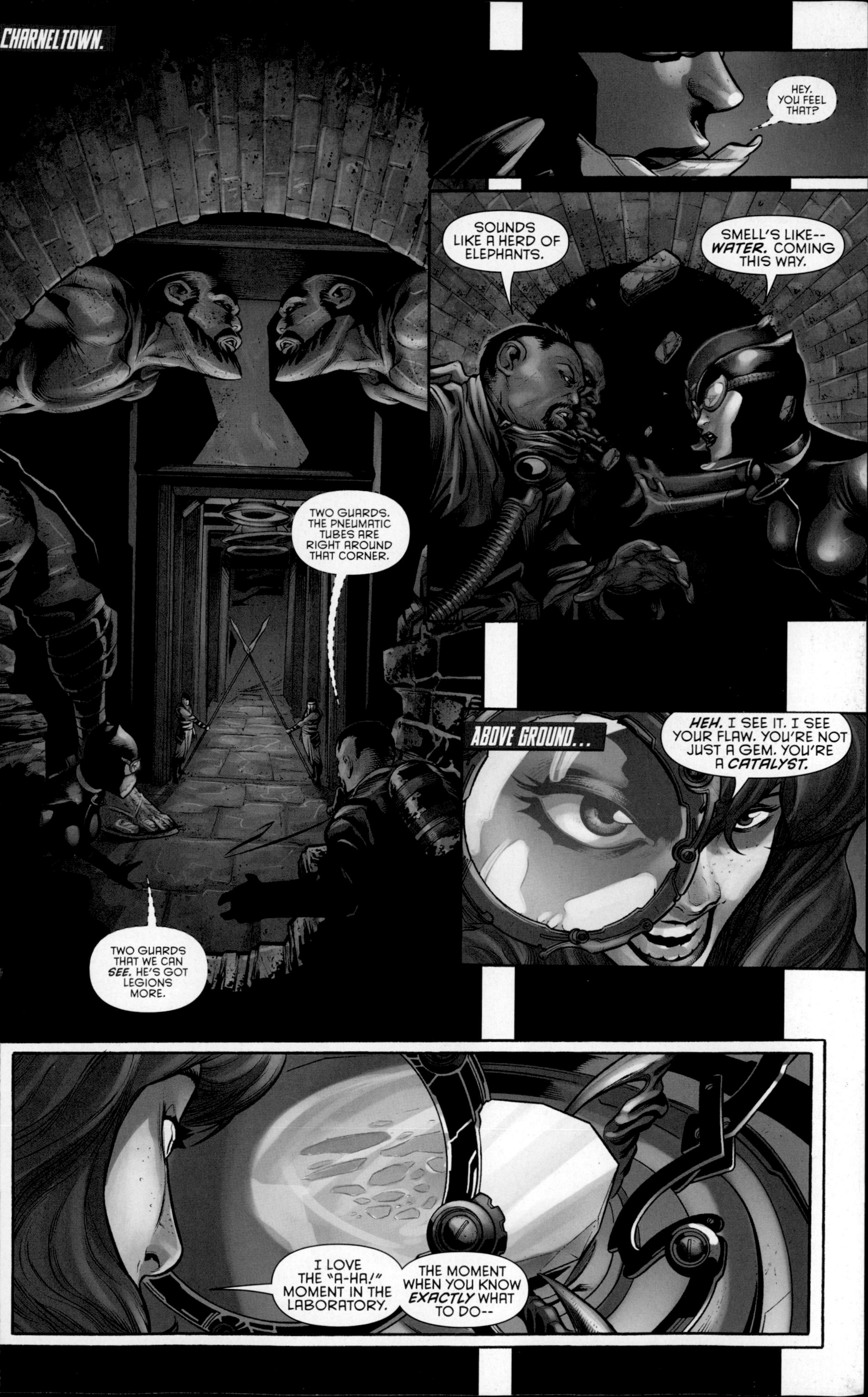
CHARNELTOWN.
HEY. YOU FEEL THAT?
SOUNDS LIKE A HERD OF ELEPHANTS.
SMELL'S LIKE-- WATER. COMING THIS WAY.
TWO GUARDS. THE PNEUMATIC TUBES ARE RIGHT AROUND THAT CORNER.
TWO GUARDS THAT WE CAN SEE. HE'S GOT LEGIONS MORE.
ABOVE GROUND...
HEH. I SEE IT. I SEE YOUR FLAW. YOU'RE NOT JUST A GEM. YOU'RE A CATALYST.
I LOVE THE "A-HA!" MOMENT IN THE LABORATORY.
THE MOMENT WHEN YOU KNOW EXACTLY WHAT TO DO--

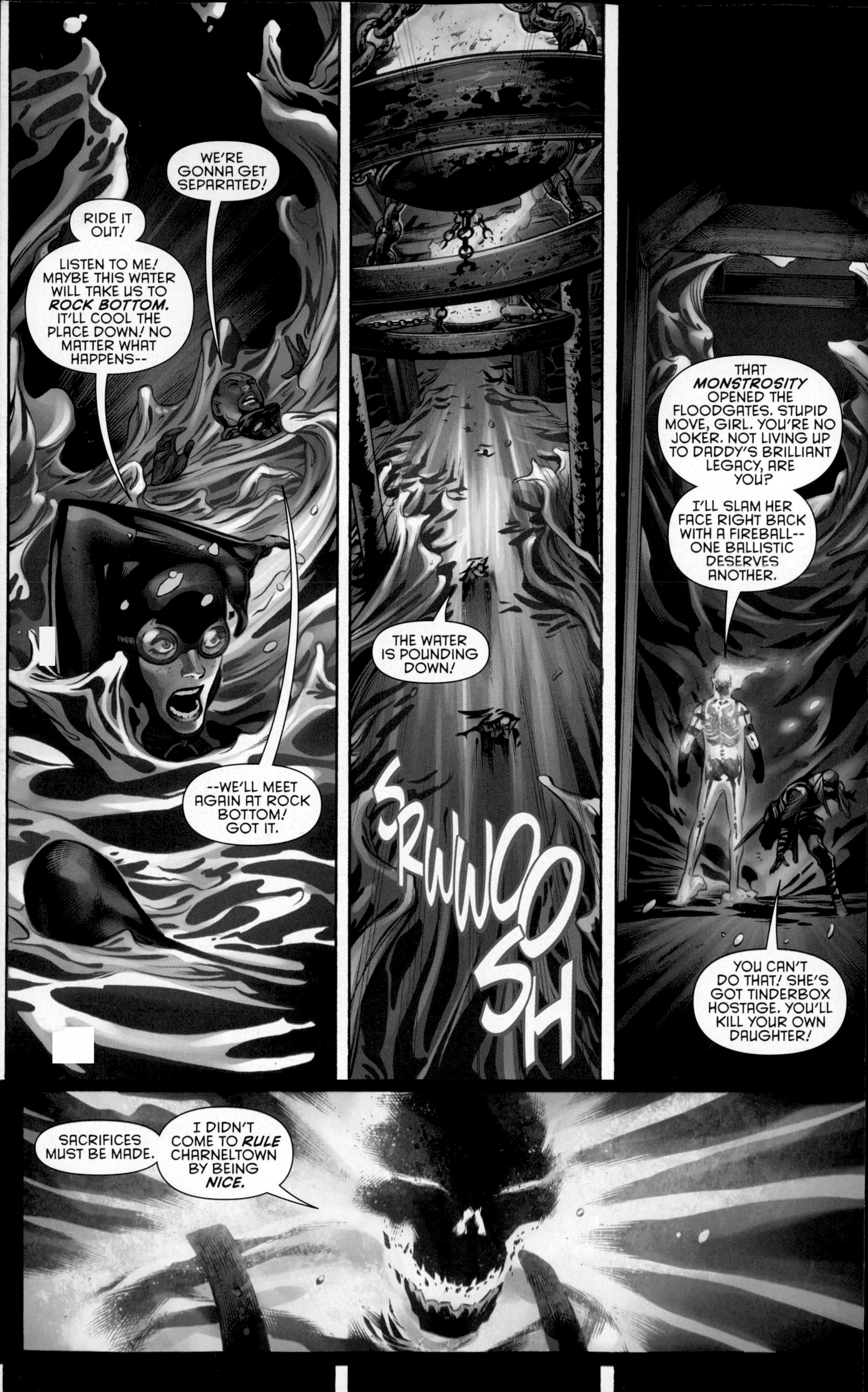
WE'RE GONNA GET SEPARATED!
RIDE IT OUT!
LISTEN TO ME! MAYBE THIS WATER WILL TAKE US TO ROCK BOTTOM. IT'LL COOL THE PLACE DOWN! NO MATTER WHAT HAPPENS--
--WE'LL MEET AGAIN AT ROCK BOTTOM! GOT IT.
THE WATER IS POUNDING DOWN!
SRWWOOSH
THAT MONSTROSITY OPENED THE FLOODGATES. STUPID MOVE, GIRL. YOU'RE NO JOKER. NOT LIVING UP TO DADDY'S BRILLIANT LEGACY, ARE YOU?
I'LL SLAM HER FACE RIGHT BACK WITH A FIREBALL-- ONE BALLISTIC DESERVES ANOTHER.
YOU CAN'T DO THAT! SHE'S GOT TINDERBOX HOSTAGE. YOU'LL KILL YOUR OWN DAUGHTER!
SACRIFICES MUST BE MADE.
I DIDN'T COME TO RULE CHARNELTOWN BY BEING NICE.

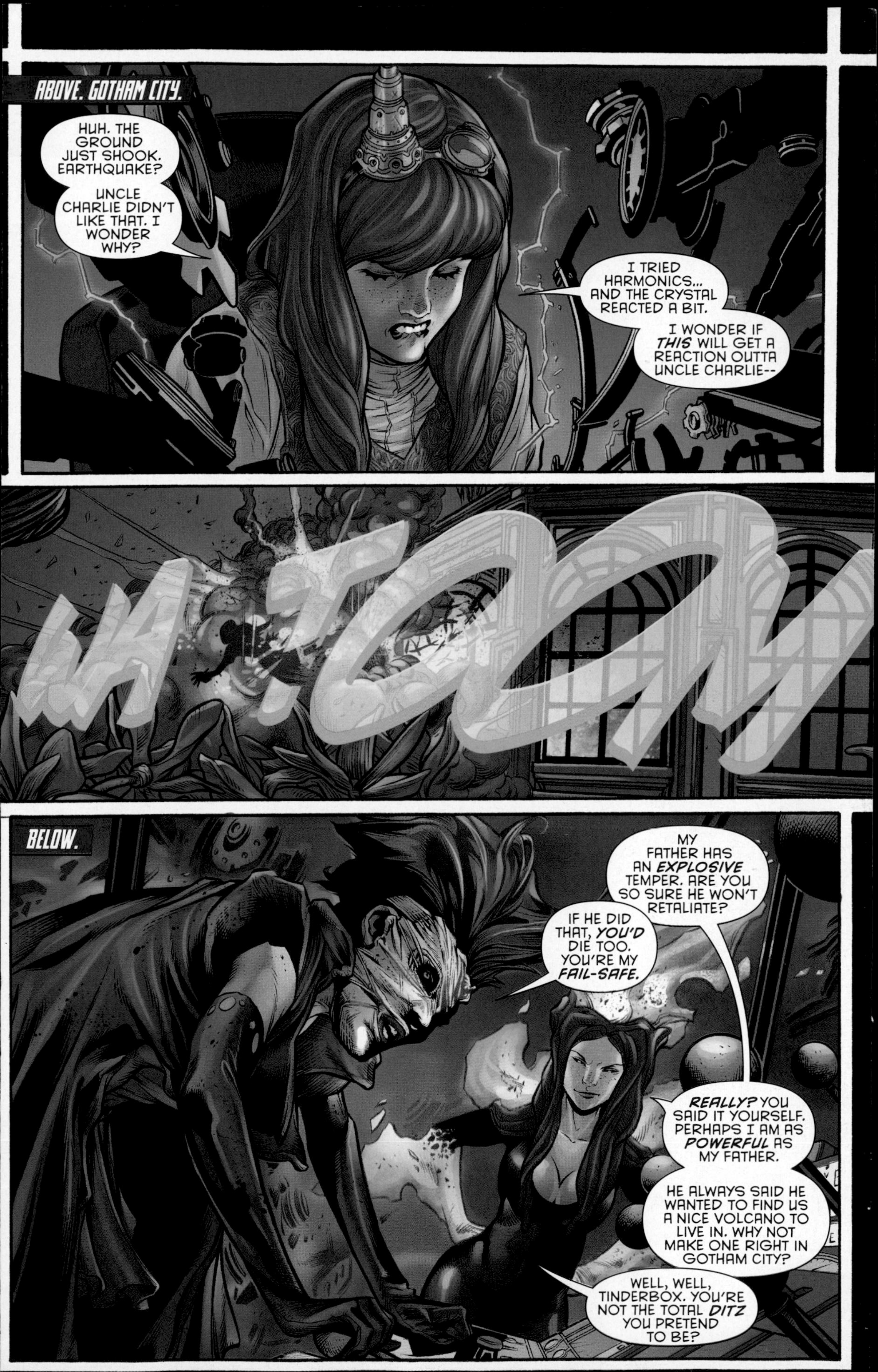
ABOVE. GOTHAM CITY.
HUH. THE GROUND JUST SHOOK. EARTHQUAKE?
UNCLE CHARLIE DIDN'T LIKE THAT. I WONDER WHY?
I TRIED HARMONICS... AND THE CRYSTAL REACTED A BIT.
I WONDER IF *THIS* WILL GET A REACTION OUTTA UNCLE CHARLIE--
BELOW.
MY FATHER HAS AN *EXPLOSIVE* TEMPER. ARE YOU SO SURE HE WON'T RETALIATE?
IF HE DID THAT, *YOU'D* DIE TOO. YOU'RE MY *FAIL-SAFE.*
REALLY? YOU SAID IT YOURSELF. PERHAPS I AM AS *POWERFUL* AS MY FATHER.
HE ALWAYS SAID HE WANTED TO FIND US A NICE VOLCANO TO LIVE IN. WHY NOT MAKE ONE RIGHT IN GOTHAM CITY?
WELL, WELL, TINDERBOX. YOU'RE NOT THE TOTAL *DITZ* YOU PRETEND TO BE?

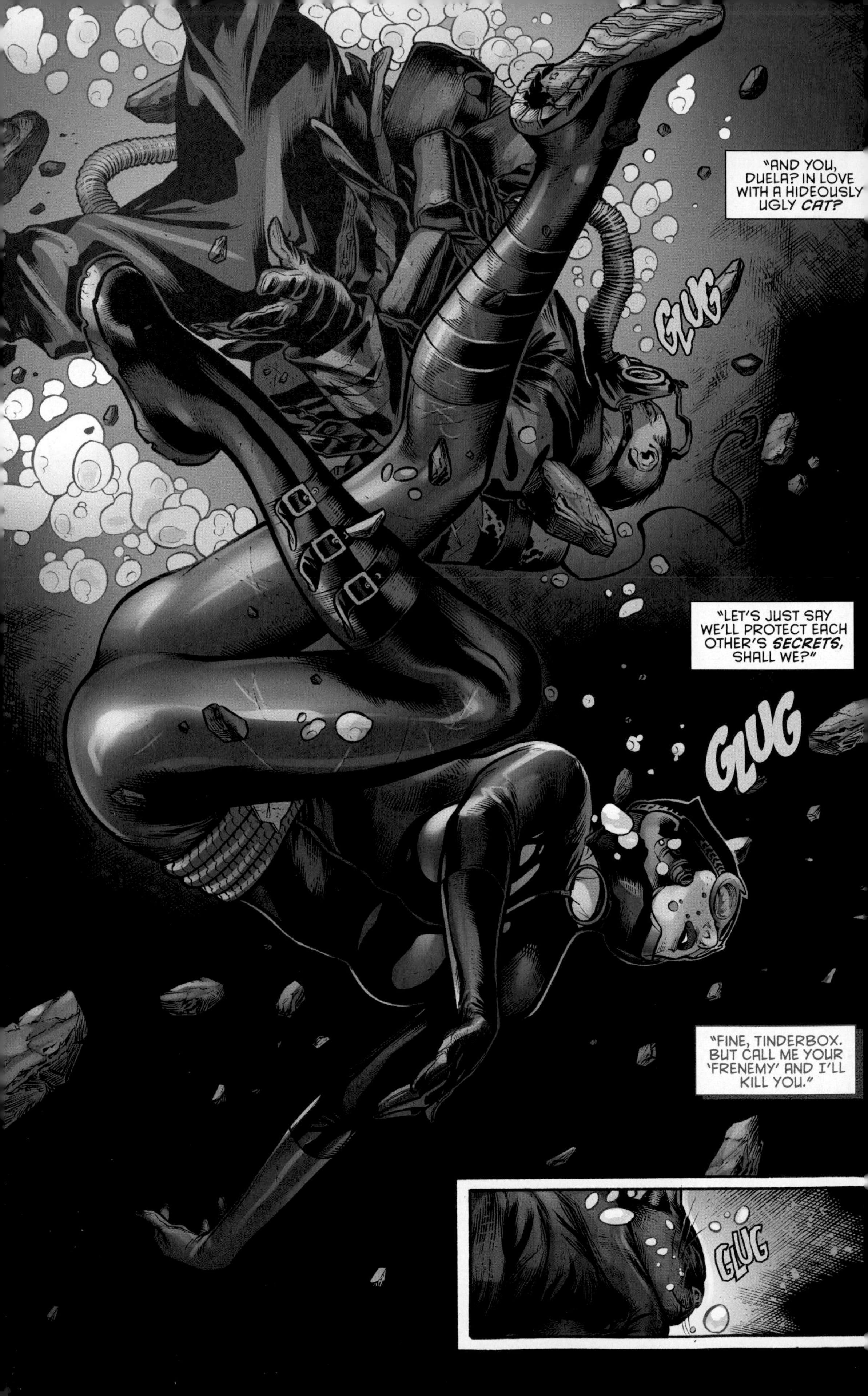
"AND YOU, DUELA? IN LOVE WITH A HIDEOUSLY UGLY CAT?
GLUG
"LET'S JUST SAY WE'LL PROTECT EACH OTHER'S SECRETS, SHALL WE?"
GLUG
"FINE, TINDERBOX. BUT CALL ME YOUR 'FRENEMY' AND I'LL KILL YOU."
GLUG

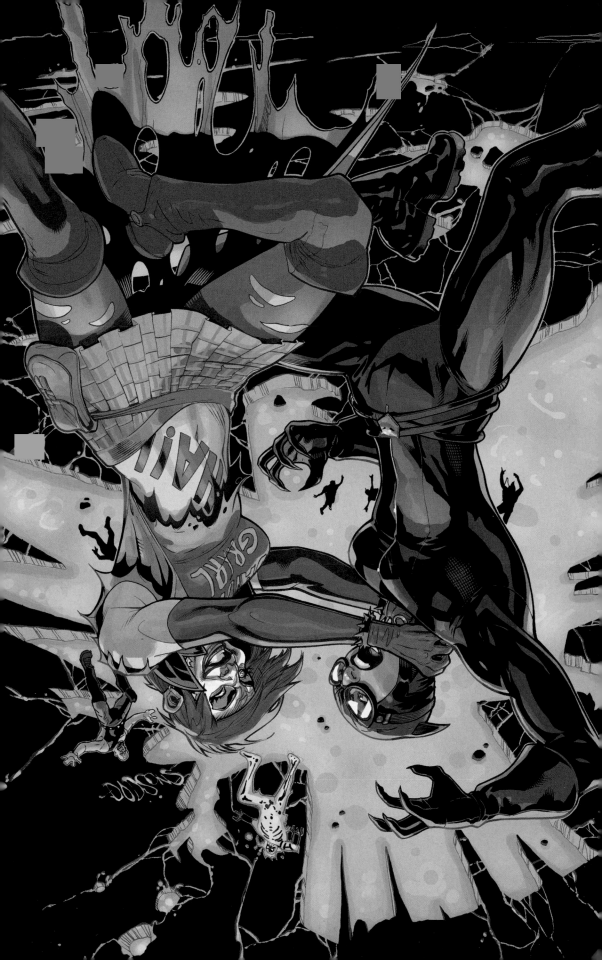

ANN NOCENTI
writer

RAFA SANDOVAL
penciller

JORDI TARRAGONA
inker

SONIA OBACK
colorist

TERRY & RACHEL DODSON
cover artists

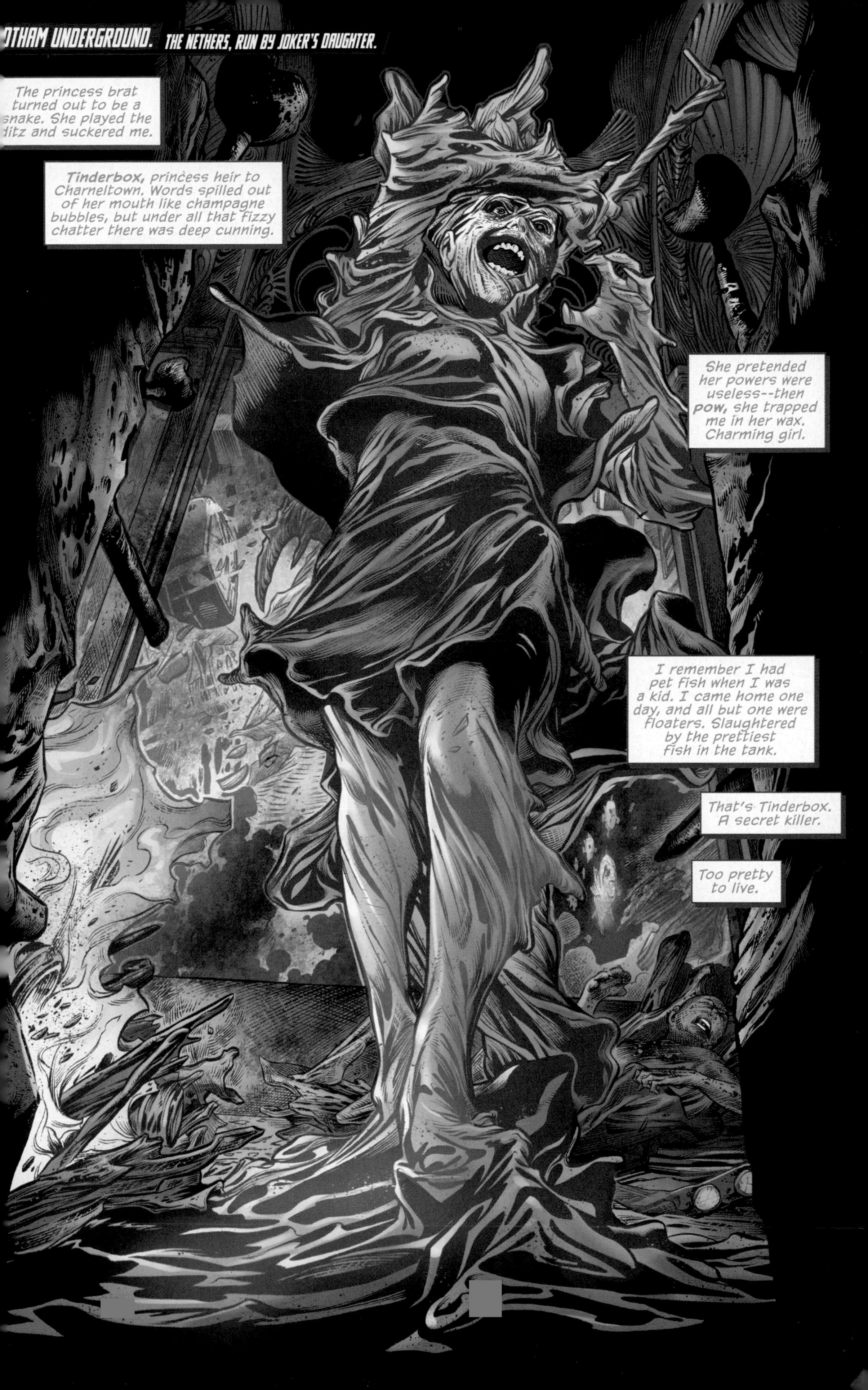
OTHAM UNDERGROUND. THE NETHERS, RUN BY JOKER'S DAUGHTER.
The princess brat turned out to be a snake. She played the ditz and suckered me.
Tinderbox, princess heir to Charneltown. Words spilled out of her mouth like champagne bubbles, but under all that fizzy chatter there was deep cunning.
She pretended her powers were useless--then pow, she trapped me in her wax. Charming girl.
I remember I had pet fish when I was a kid. I came home one day, and all but one were floaters. Slaughtered by the prettiest fish in the tank.
That's Tinderbox. A secret killer.
Too pretty to live.

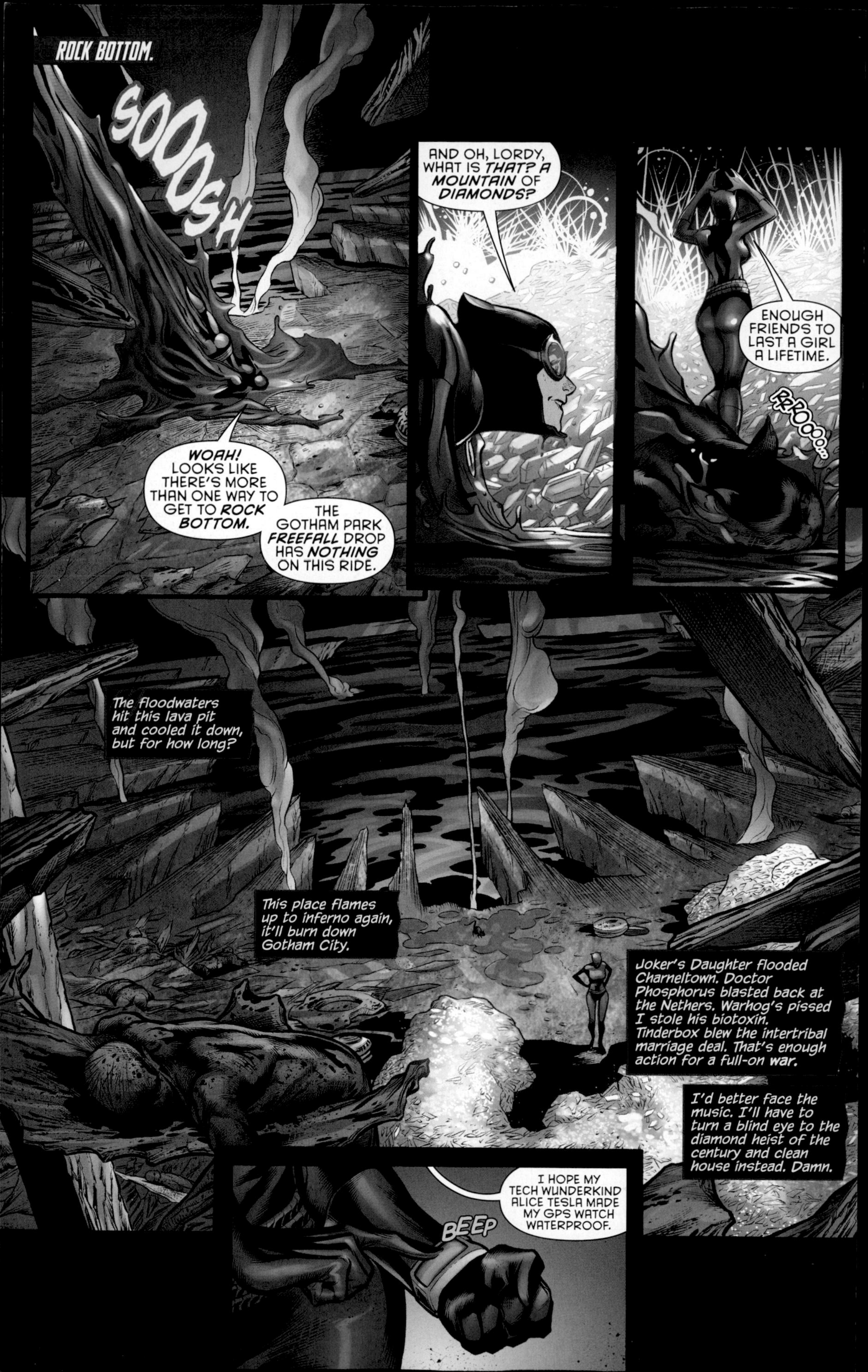

ROCK BOTTOM.
SOOOSH
WOAH! LOOKS LIKE THERE'S MORE THAN ONE WAY TO GET TO ROCK BOTTOM.
THE GOTHAM PARK FREEFALL DROP HAS NOTHING ON THIS RIDE.
AND OH, LORDY, WHAT IS THAT? A MOUNTAIN OF DIAMONDS?
ENOUGH FRIENDS TO LAST A GIRL A LIFETIME.
RRROOOO...
The floodwaters hit this lava pit and cooled it down, but for how long?
This place flames up to inferno again, it'll burn down Gotham City.
Joker's Daughter flooded Charneltown. Doctor Phosphorus blasted back at the Nethers. Warhog's pissed I stole his biotoxin. Tinderbox blew the intertribal marriage deal. That's enough action for a full-on war.
I'd better face the music. I'll have to turn a blind eye to the diamond heist of the century and clean house instead. Damn.
I HOPE MY TECH WUNDERKIND ALICE TESLA MADE MY GPS WATCH WATERPROOF.
BEEP

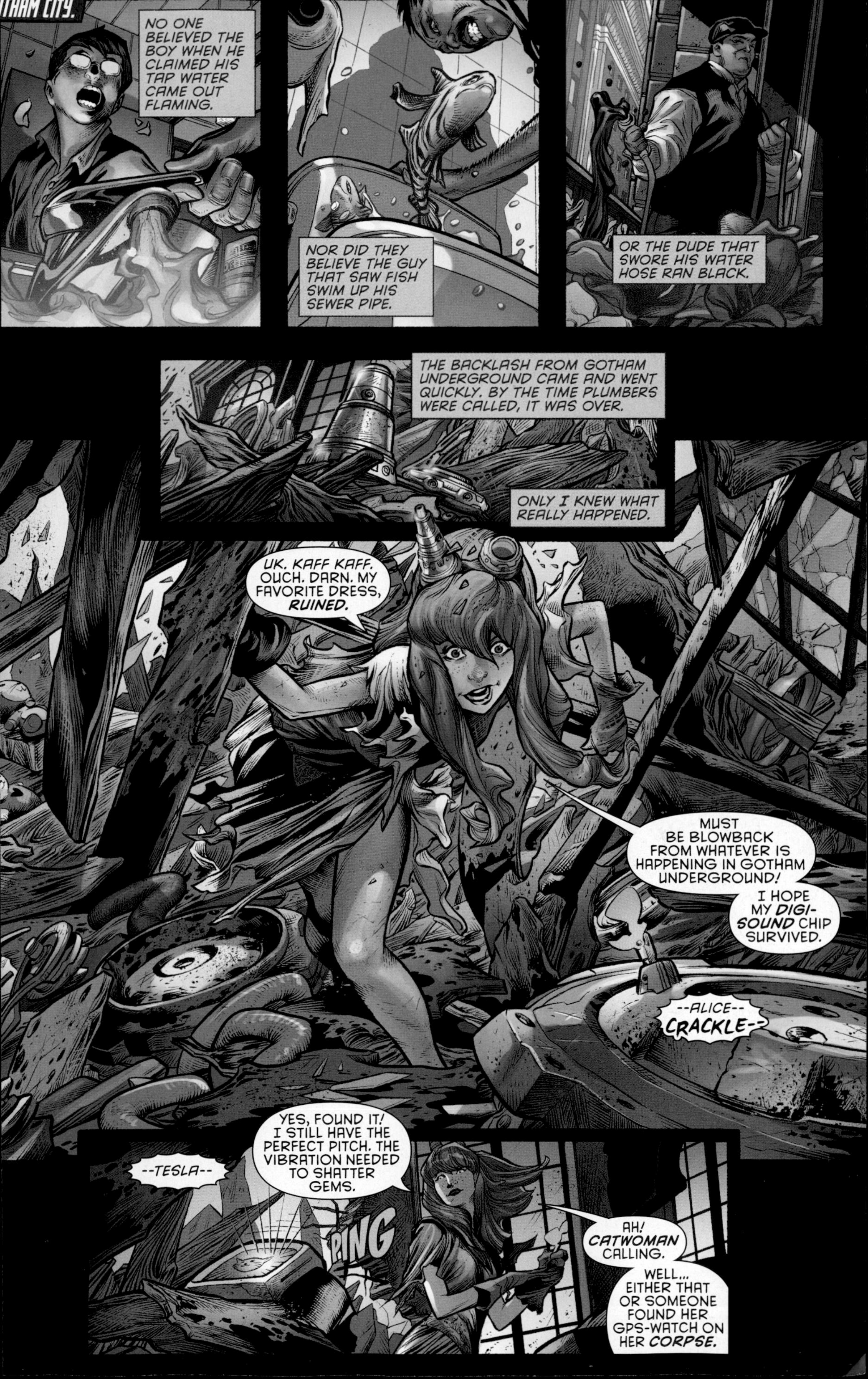

...THAM CITY.
NO ONE BELIEVED THE BOY WHEN HE CLAIMED HIS TAP WATER CAME OUT FLAMING.
NOR DID THEY BELIEVE THE GUY THAT SAW FISH SWIM UP HIS SEWER PIPE.
OR THE DUDE THAT SWORE HIS WATER HOSE RAN BLACK.
THE BACKLASH FROM GOTHAM UNDERGROUND CAME AND WENT QUICKLY. BY THE TIME PLUMBERS WERE CALLED, IT WAS OVER.
ONLY I KNEW WHAT REALLY HAPPENED.
UK. KAFF KAFF. OUCH. DARN. MY FAVORITE DRESS, RUINED.
MUST BE BLOWBACK FROM WHATEVER IS HAPPENING IN GOTHAM UNDERGROUND!
I HOPE MY DIGI-SOUND CHIP SURVIVED.
--ALICE--
CRACKLE--
--TESLA--
YES, FOUND IT! I STILL HAVE THE PERFECT PITCH. THE VIBRATION NEEDED TO SHATTER GEMS.
PING
AH! CATWOMAN CALLING.
WELL... EITHER THAT OR SOMEONE FOUND HER GPS-WATCH ON HER CORPSE.

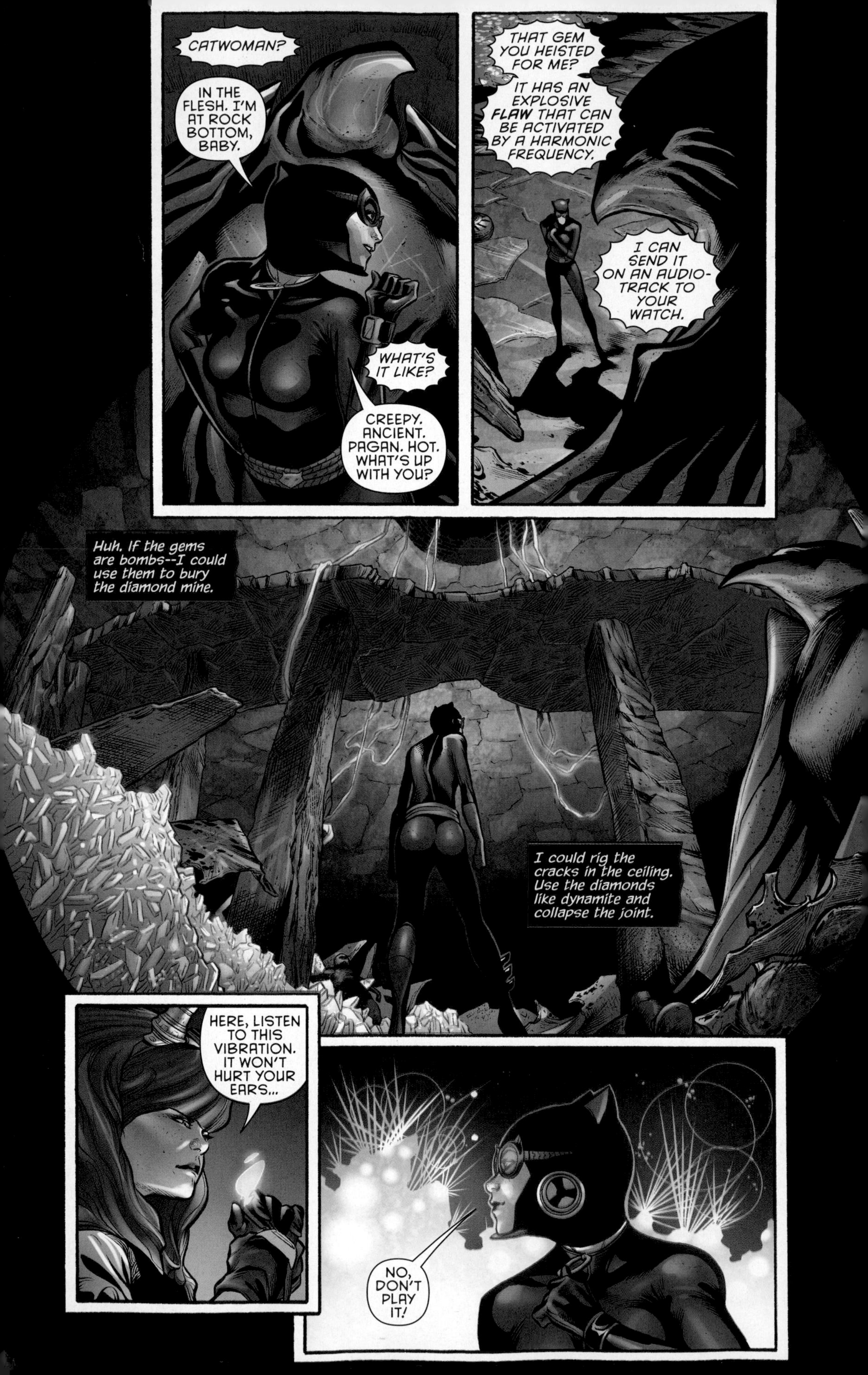
CATWOMAN?
IN THE FLESH. I'M AT ROCK BOTTOM, BABY.
WHAT'S IT LIKE?
CREEPY. ANCIENT. PAGAN. HOT. WHAT'S UP WITH YOU?
THAT GEM YOU HEISTED FOR ME?
IT HAS AN EXPLOSIVE FLAW THAT CAN BE ACTIVATED BY A HARMONIC FREQUENCY.
I CAN SEND IT ON AN AUDIO-TRACK TO YOUR WATCH.
Huh. If the gems are bombs--I could use them to bury the diamond mine.
I could rig the cracks in the ceiling. Use the diamonds like dynamite and collapse the joint.
HERE, LISTEN TO THIS VIBRATION. IT WON'T HURT YOUR EARS...
NO, DON'T PLAY IT!

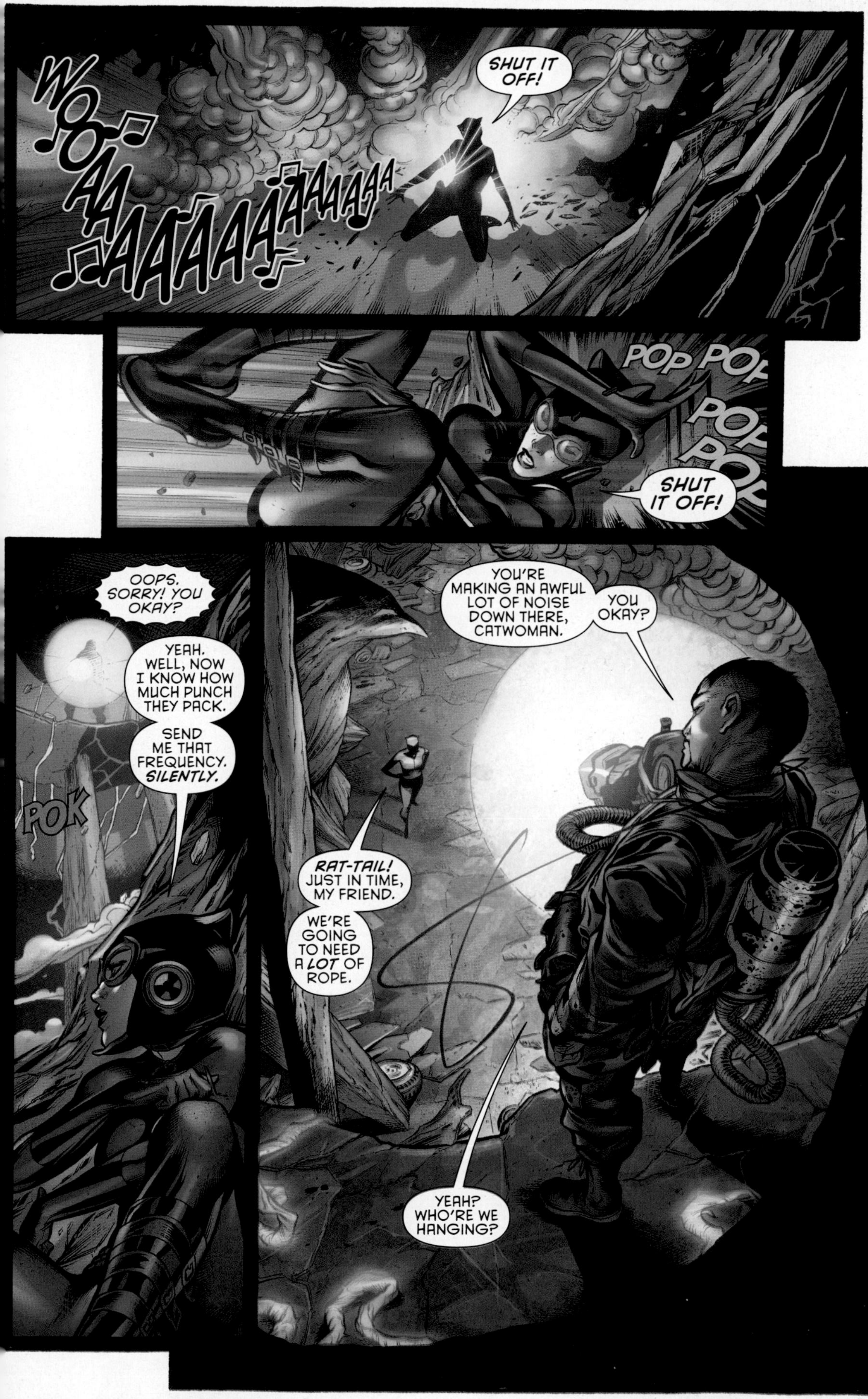
WOOAAAAAAAAAAAAAA
SHUT IT OFF!
POP POP
POP POP
SHUT IT OFF!
OOPS. SORRY! YOU OKAY?
YEAH. WELL, NOW I KNOW HOW MUCH PUNCH THEY PACK.
SEND ME THAT FREQUENCY. *SILENTLY.*
POK
YOU'RE MAKING AN AWFUL LOT OF NOISE DOWN THERE, CATWOMAN.
YOU OKAY?
RAT-TAIL! JUST IN TIME, MY FRIEND.
WE'RE GOING TO NEED A *LOT* OF ROPE.
YEAH? WHO'RE WE HANGING?

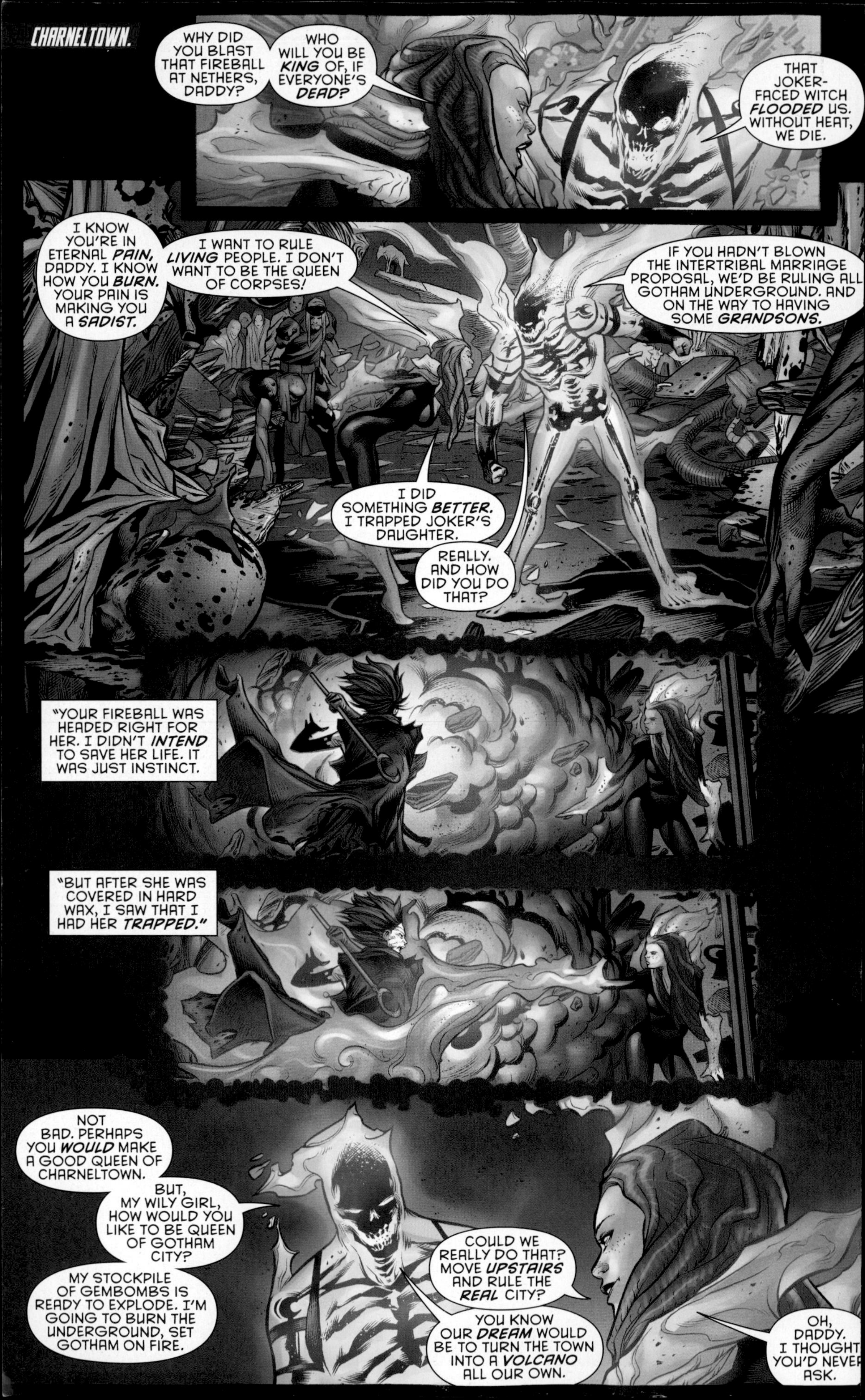
CHARNELTOWN.
WHY DID YOU BLAST THAT FIREBALL AT NETHERS, DADDY?
WHO WILL YOU BE KING OF, IF EVERYONE'S DEAD?
THAT JOKER-FACED WITCH FLOODED US. WITHOUT HEAT, WE DIE.
I KNOW YOU'RE IN ETERNAL PAIN, DADDY. I KNOW HOW YOU BURN. YOUR PAIN IS MAKING YOU A SADIST.
I WANT TO RULE LIVING PEOPLE. I DON'T WANT TO BE THE QUEEN OF CORPSES!
IF YOU HADN'T BLOWN THE INTERTRIBAL MARRIAGE PROPOSAL, WE'D BE RULING ALL GOTHAM UNDERGROUND. AND ON THE WAY TO HAVING SOME GRANDSONS.
I DID SOMETHING BETTER. I TRAPPED JOKER'S DAUGHTER.
REALLY. AND HOW DID YOU DO THAT?
"YOUR FIREBALL WAS HEADED RIGHT FOR HER. I DIDN'T INTEND TO SAVE HER LIFE. IT WAS JUST INSTINCT.
"BUT AFTER SHE WAS COVERED IN HARD WAX, I SAW THAT I HAD HER TRAPPED."
NOT BAD. PERHAPS YOU WOULD MAKE A GOOD QUEEN OF CHARNELTOWN.
BUT, MY WILY GIRL, HOW WOULD YOU LIKE TO BE QUEEN OF GOTHAM CITY?
MY STOCKPILE OF GEMBOMBS IS READY TO EXPLODE. I'M GOING TO BURN THE UNDERGROUND, SET GOTHAM ON FIRE.
COULD WE REALLY DO THAT? MOVE UPSTAIRS AND RULE THE REAL CITY?
YOU KNOW OUR DREAM WOULD BE TO TURN THE TOWN INTO A VOLCANO ALL OUR OWN.
OH, DADDY. I THOUGHT YOU'D NEVER ASK.

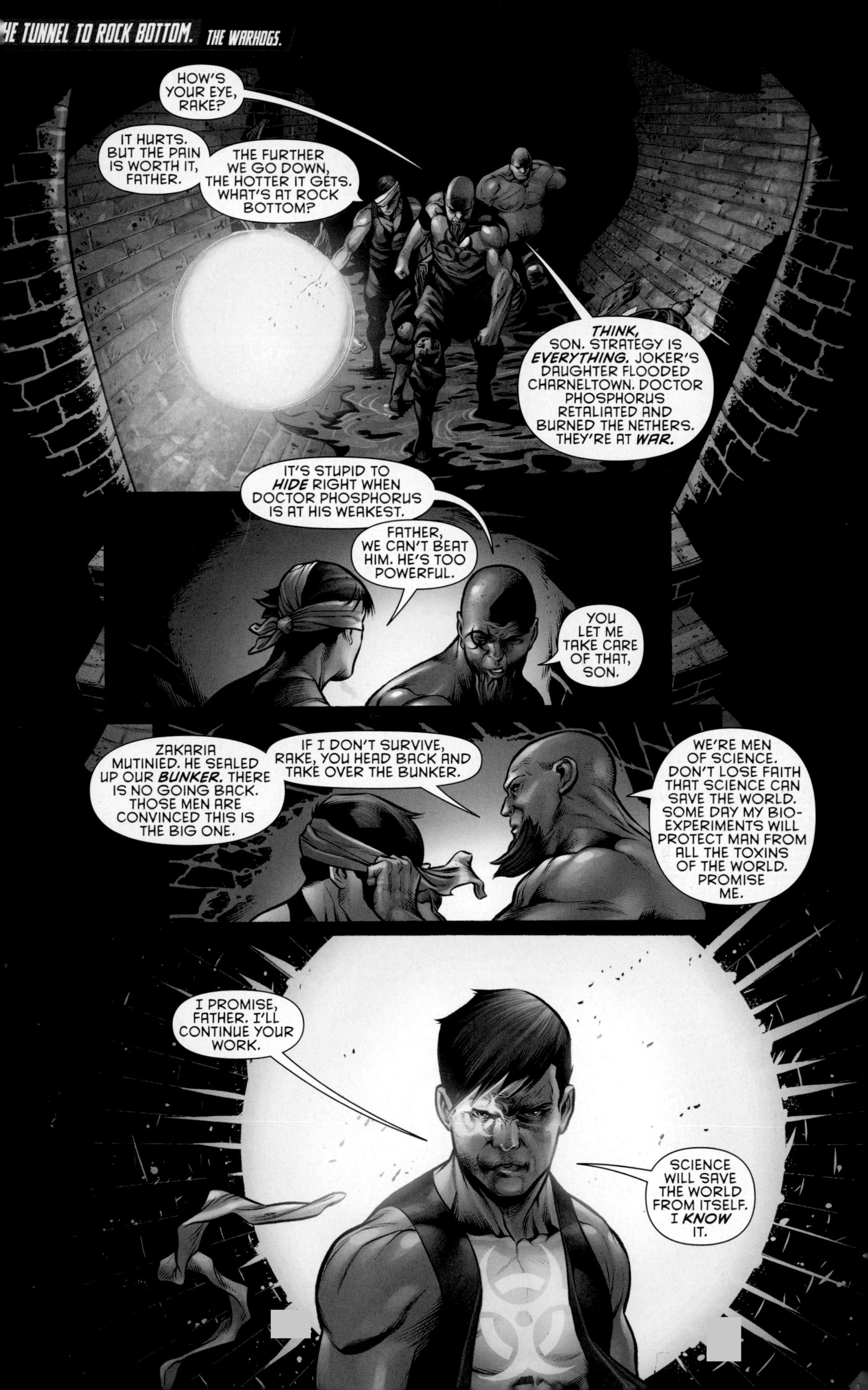
HE TUNNEL TO ROCK BOTTOM. THE WARHOGS.
HOW'S YOUR EYE, RAKE?
IT HURTS. BUT THE PAIN IS WORTH IT, FATHER.
THE FURTHER WE GO DOWN, THE HOTTER IT GETS. WHAT'S AT ROCK BOTTOM?
THINK, SON. STRATEGY IS EVERYTHING. JOKER'S DAUGHTER FLOODED CHARNELTOWN. DOCTOR PHOSPHORUS RETALIATED AND BURNED THE NETHERS. THEY'RE AT WAR.
IT'S STUPID TO HIDE RIGHT WHEN DOCTOR PHOSPHORUS IS AT HIS WEAKEST.
FATHER, WE CAN'T BEAT HIM. HE'S TOO POWERFUL.
YOU LET ME TAKE CARE OF THAT, SON.
ZAKARIA MUTINIED. HE SEALED UP OUR BUNKER. THERE IS NO GOING BACK. THOSE MEN ARE CONVINCED THIS IS THE BIG ONE.
IF I DON'T SURVIVE, RAKE, YOU HEAD BACK AND TAKE OVER THE BUNKER.
WE'RE MEN OF SCIENCE. DON'T LOSE FAITH THAT SCIENCE CAN SAVE THE WORLD. SOME DAY MY BIO-EXPERIMENTS WILL PROTECT MAN FROM ALL THE TOXINS OF THE WORLD. PROMISE ME.
I PROMISE, FATHER. I'LL CONTINUE YOUR WORK.
SCIENCE WILL SAVE THE WORLD FROM ITSELF. I KNOW IT.

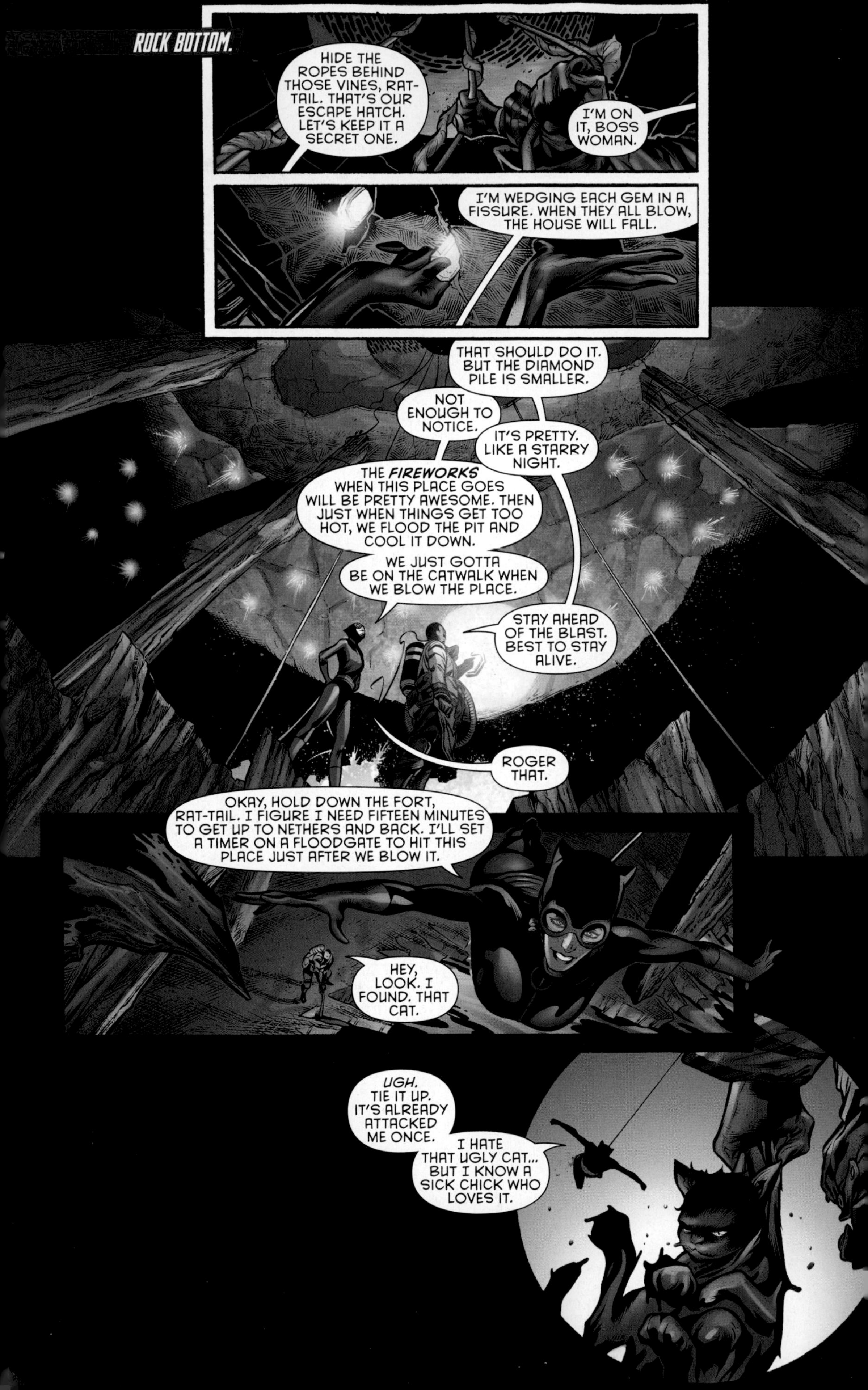
ROCK BOTTOM.
HIDE THE ROPES BEHIND THOSE VINES, RAT-TAIL. THAT'S OUR ESCAPE HATCH. LET'S KEEP IT A SECRET ONE.
I'M ON IT, BOSS WOMAN.
I'M WEDGING EACH GEM IN A FISSURE. WHEN THEY ALL BLOW, THE HOUSE WILL FALL.
THAT SHOULD DO IT. BUT THE DIAMOND PILE IS SMALLER.
NOT ENOUGH TO NOTICE.
IT'S PRETTY. LIKE A STARRY NIGHT.
THE *FIREWORKS* WHEN THIS PLACE GOES WILL BE PRETTY AWESOME. THEN JUST WHEN THINGS GET TOO HOT, WE FLOOD THE PIT AND COOL IT DOWN.
WE JUST GOTTA BE ON THE CATWALK WHEN WE BLOW THE PLACE.
STAY AHEAD OF THE BLAST. BEST TO STAY ALIVE.
ROGER THAT.
OKAY, HOLD DOWN THE FORT, RAT-TAIL. I FIGURE I NEED FIFTEEN MINUTES TO GET UP TO NETHERS AND BACK. I'LL SET A TIMER ON A FLOODGATE TO HIT THIS PLACE JUST AFTER WE BLOW IT.
HEY, LOOK. I FOUND. THAT CAT.
UGH. TIE IT UP. IT'S ALREADY ATTACKED ME ONCE.
I HATE THAT UGLY CAT... BUT I KNOW A SICK CHICK WHO LOVES IT.

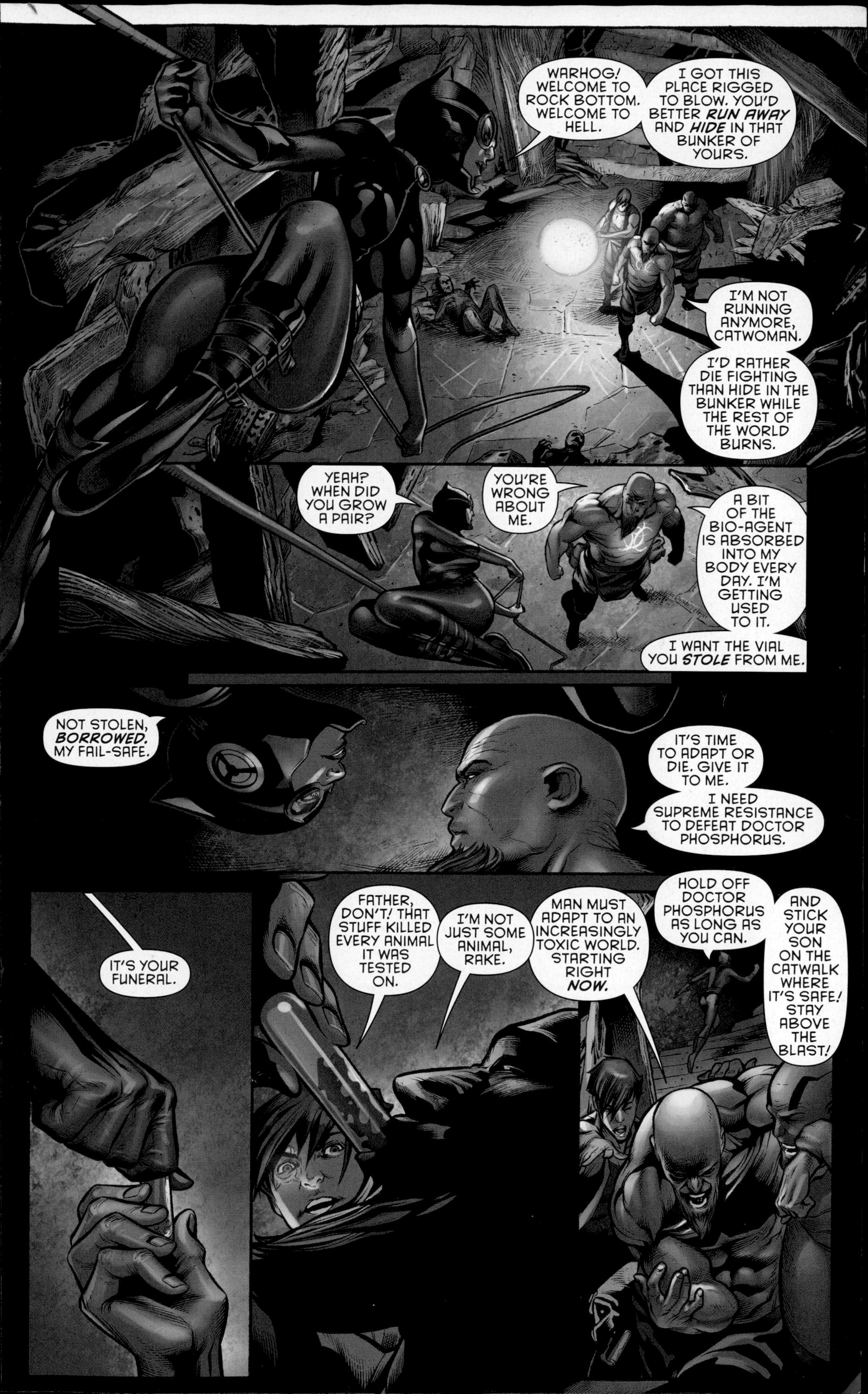
WARHOG! WELCOME TO ROCK BOTTOM. WELCOME TO HELL.
I GOT THIS PLACE RIGGED TO BLOW. YOU'D BETTER RUN AWAY AND HIDE IN THAT BUNKER OF YOURS.
I'M NOT RUNNING ANYMORE, CATWOMAN.
I'D RATHER DIE FIGHTING THAN HIDE IN THE BUNKER WHILE THE REST OF THE WORLD BURNS.
YEAH? WHEN DID YOU GROW A PAIR?
YOU'RE WRONG ABOUT ME.
A BIT OF THE BIO-AGENT IS ABSORBED INTO MY BODY EVERY DAY. I'M GETTING USED TO IT.
I WANT THE VIAL YOU STOLE FROM ME.
NOT STOLEN, BORROWED. MY FAIL-SAFE.
IT'S TIME TO ADAPT OR DIE. GIVE IT TO ME.
I NEED SUPREME RESISTANCE TO DEFEAT DOCTOR PHOSPHORUS.
IT'S YOUR FUNERAL.
FATHER, DON'T! THAT STUFF KILLED EVERY ANIMAL IT WAS TESTED ON.
I'M NOT JUST SOME ANIMAL, RAKE.
MAN MUST ADAPT TO AN INCREASINGLY TOXIC WORLD. STARTING RIGHT NOW.
HOLD OFF DOCTOR PHOSPHORUS AS LONG AS YOU CAN.
AND STICK YOUR SON ON THE CATWALK WHERE IT'S SAFE! STAY ABOVE THE BLAST!

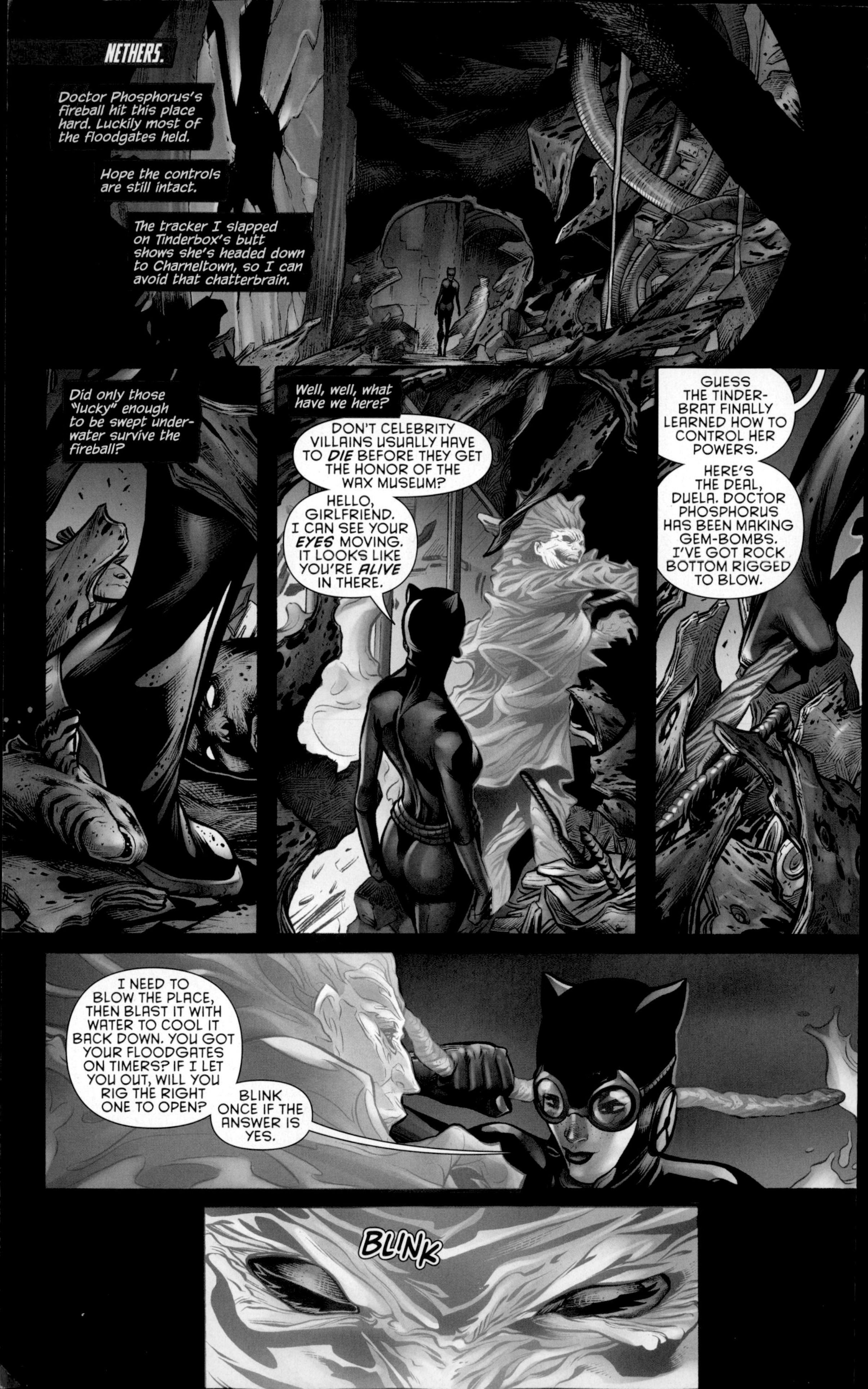
NETHERS.
Doctor Phosphorus's fireball hit this place hard. Luckily most of the floodgates held.
Hope the controls are still intact.
The tracker I slapped on Tinderbox's butt shows she's headed down to Charneltown, so I can avoid that chatterbrain.
Did only those "lucky" enough to be swept underwater survive the fireball?
Well, well, what have we here?
DON'T CELEBRITY VILLAINS USUALLY HAVE TO DIE BEFORE THEY GET THE HONOR OF THE WAX MUSEUM?
HELLO, GIRLFRIEND. I CAN SEE YOUR EYES MOVING. IT LOOKS LIKE YOU'RE ALIVE IN THERE.
GUESS THE TINDERBRAT FINALLY LEARNED HOW TO CONTROL HER POWERS.
HERE'S THE DEAL, DUELA. DOCTOR PHOSPHORUS HAS BEEN MAKING GEM-BOMBS. I'VE GOT ROCK BOTTOM RIGGED TO BLOW.
I NEED TO BLOW THE PLACE, THEN BLAST IT WITH WATER TO COOL IT BACK DOWN. YOU GOT YOUR FLOODGATES ON TIMERS? IF I LET YOU OUT, WILL YOU RIG THE RIGHT ONE TO OPEN?
BLINK ONCE IF THE ANSWER IS YES.
BLINK

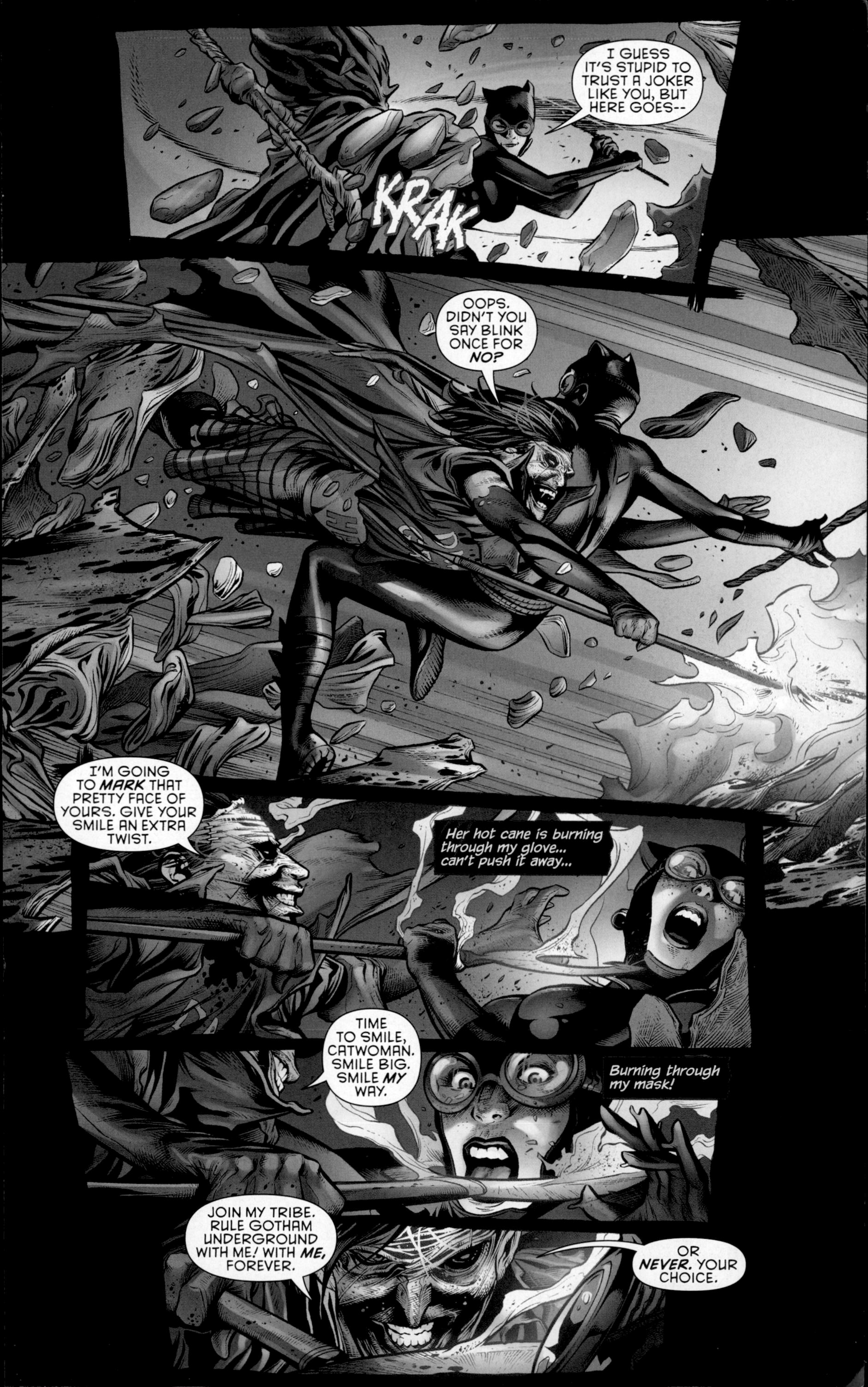
I GUESS IT'S STUPID TO TRUST A JOKER LIKE YOU, BUT HERE GOES--
KRAK
OOPS. DIDN'T YOU SAY BLINK ONCE FOR NO?
I'M GOING TO MARK THAT PRETTY FACE OF YOURS. GIVE YOUR SMILE AN EXTRA TWIST.
Her hot cane is burning through my glove... can't push it away...
TIME TO SMILE, CATWOMAN. SMILE BIG. SMILE MY WAY.
Burning through my mask!
JOIN MY TRIBE. RULE GOTHAM UNDERGROUND WITH ME! WITH ME, FOREVER.
OR NEVER. YOUR CHOICE.

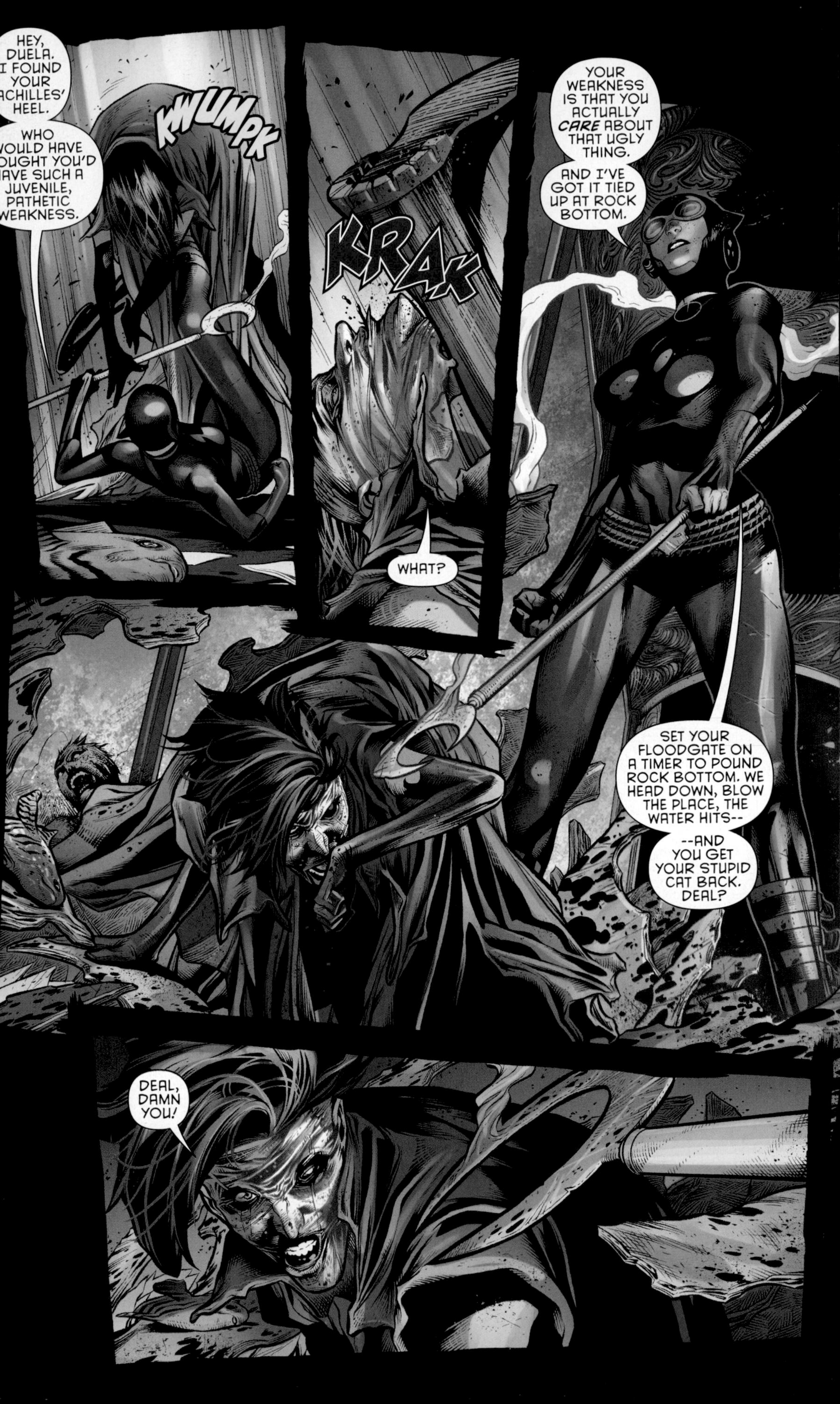
HEY, DUELA. I FOUND YOUR ACHILLES' HEEL.
WHO WOULD HAVE THOUGHT YOU'D HAVE SUCH A JUVENILE, PATHETIC WEAKNESS.
KWUMPK
KRAK
WHAT?
YOUR WEAKNESS IS THAT YOU ACTUALLY CARE ABOUT THAT UGLY THING.
AND I'VE GOT IT TIED UP AT ROCK BOTTOM.
SET YOUR FLOODGATE ON A TIMER TO POUND ROCK BOTTOM. WE HEAD DOWN, BLOW THE PLACE, THE WATER HITS--
--AND YOU GET YOUR STUPID CAT BACK. DEAL?
DEAL, DAMN YOU!

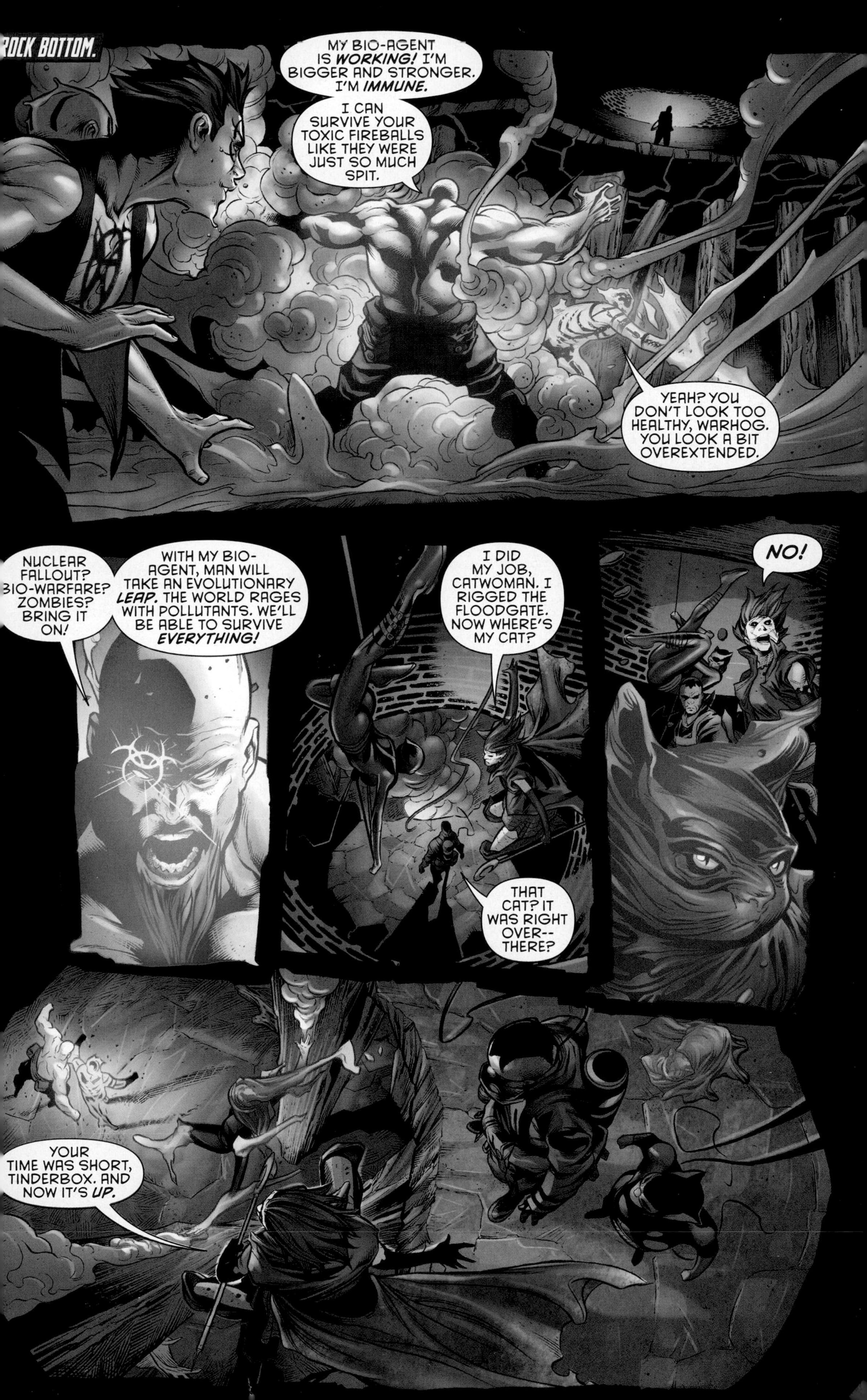
ROCK BOTTOM.
MY BIO-AGENT IS WORKING! I'M BIGGER AND STRONGER. I'M IMMUNE.
I CAN SURVIVE YOUR TOXIC FIREBALLS LIKE THEY WERE JUST SO MUCH SPIT.
YEAH? YOU DON'T LOOK TOO HEALTHY, WARHOG. YOU LOOK A BIT OVEREXTENDED.
NUCLEAR FALLOUT? BIO-WARFARE? ZOMBIES? BRING IT ON!
WITH MY BIO-AGENT, MAN WILL TAKE AN EVOLUTIONARY LEAP. THE WORLD RAGES WITH POLLUTANTS. WE'LL BE ABLE TO SURVIVE EVERYTHING!
I DID MY JOB, CATWOMAN. I RIGGED THE FLOODGATE. NOW WHERE'S MY CAT?
THAT CAT? IT WAS RIGHT OVER-- THERE?
NO!
YOUR TIME WAS SHORT, TINDERBOX. AND NOW IT'S UP.

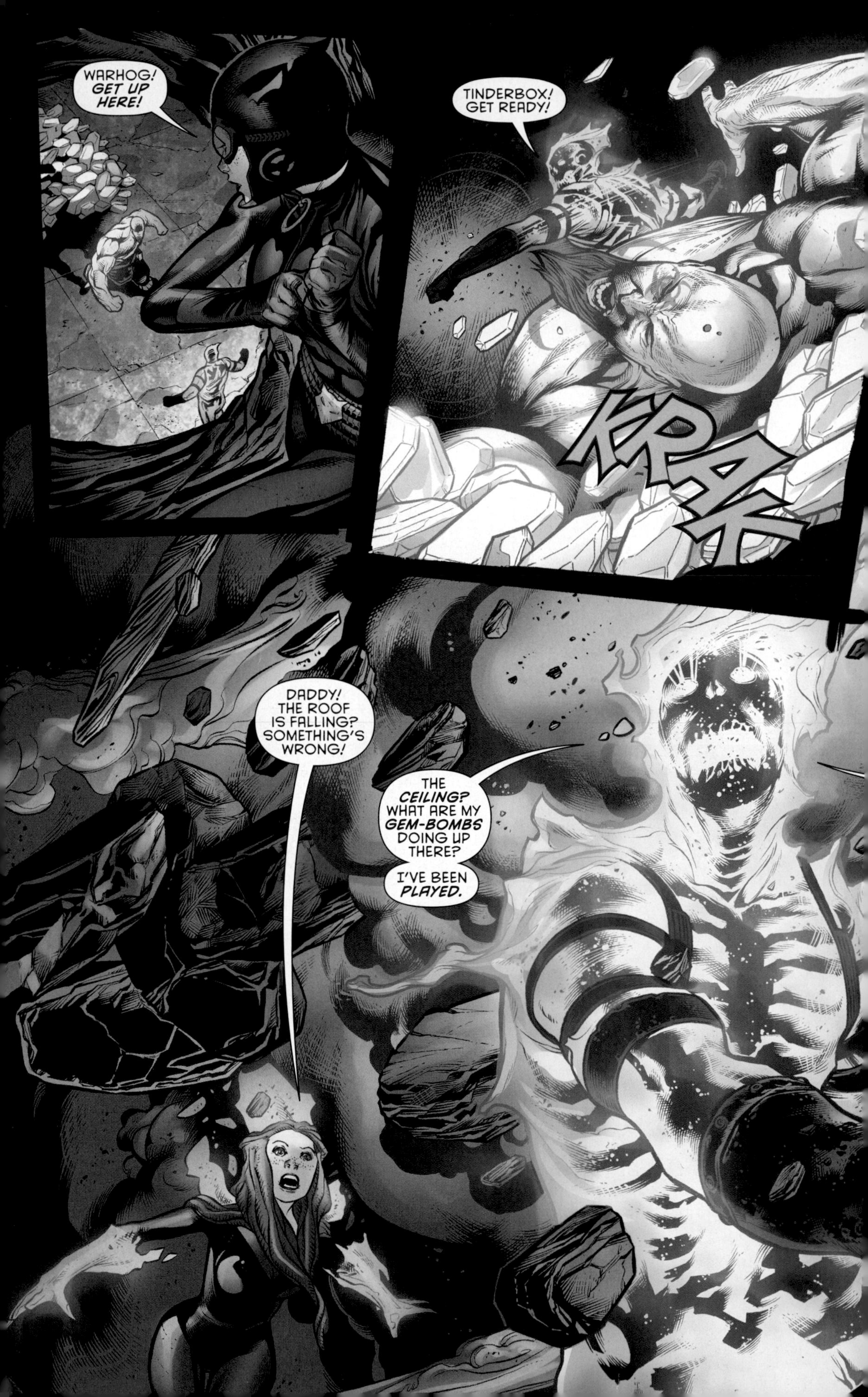
WARHOG! GET UP HERE!
TINDERBOX! GET READY!
KRAK
DADDY! THE ROOF IS FALLING? SOMETHING'S WRONG!
THE CEILING? WHAT ARE MY GEM-BOMBS DOING UP THERE?
I'VE BEEN PLAYED.

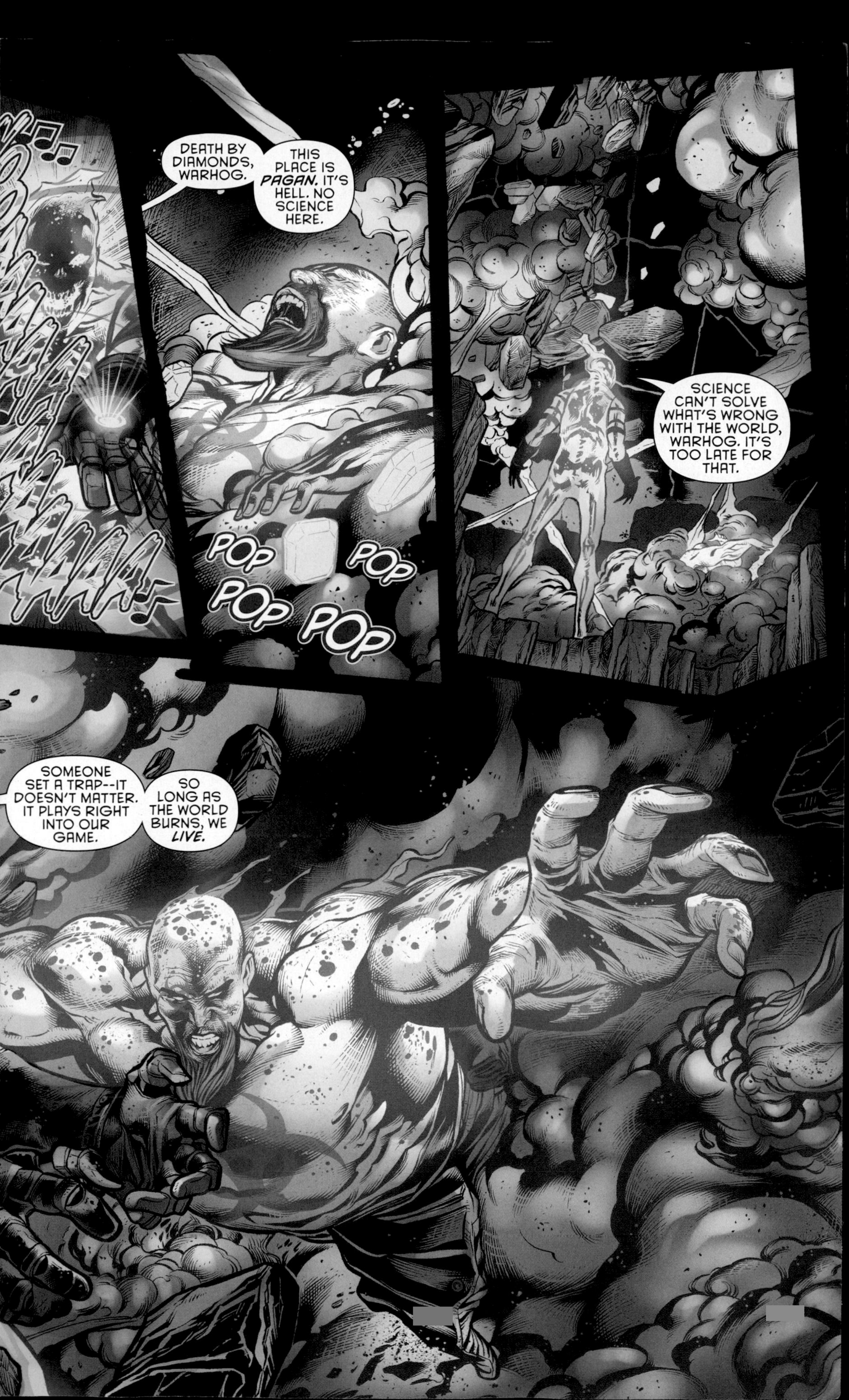
DEATH BY DIAMONDS, WARHOG.
THIS PLACE IS PAGAN. IT'S HELL. NO SCIENCE HERE.
POP POP POP POP
SCIENCE CAN'T SOLVE WHAT'S WRONG WITH THE WORLD, WARHOG. IT'S TOO LATE FOR THAT.
SOMEONE SET A TRAP--IT DOESN'T MATTER. IT PLAYS RIGHT INTO OUR GAME.
SO LONG AS THE WORLD BURNS, WE LIVE.

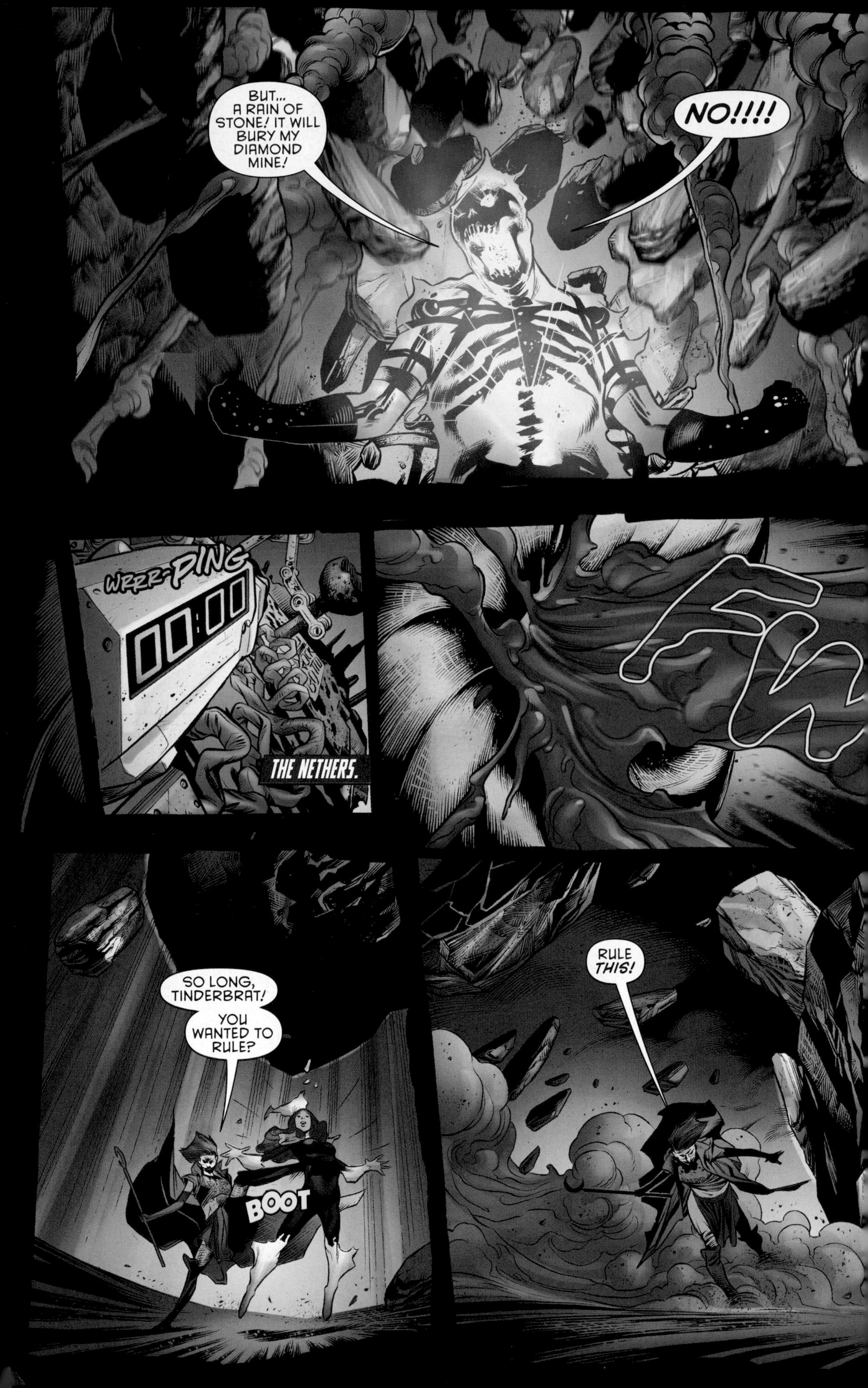
BUT... A RAIN OF STONE! IT WILL BURY MY DIAMOND MINE!
NO!!!!
WRRR-PING
00:00
THE NETHERS.
SO LONG, TINDERBRAT!
YOU WANTED TO RULE?
BOOT
RULE THIS!

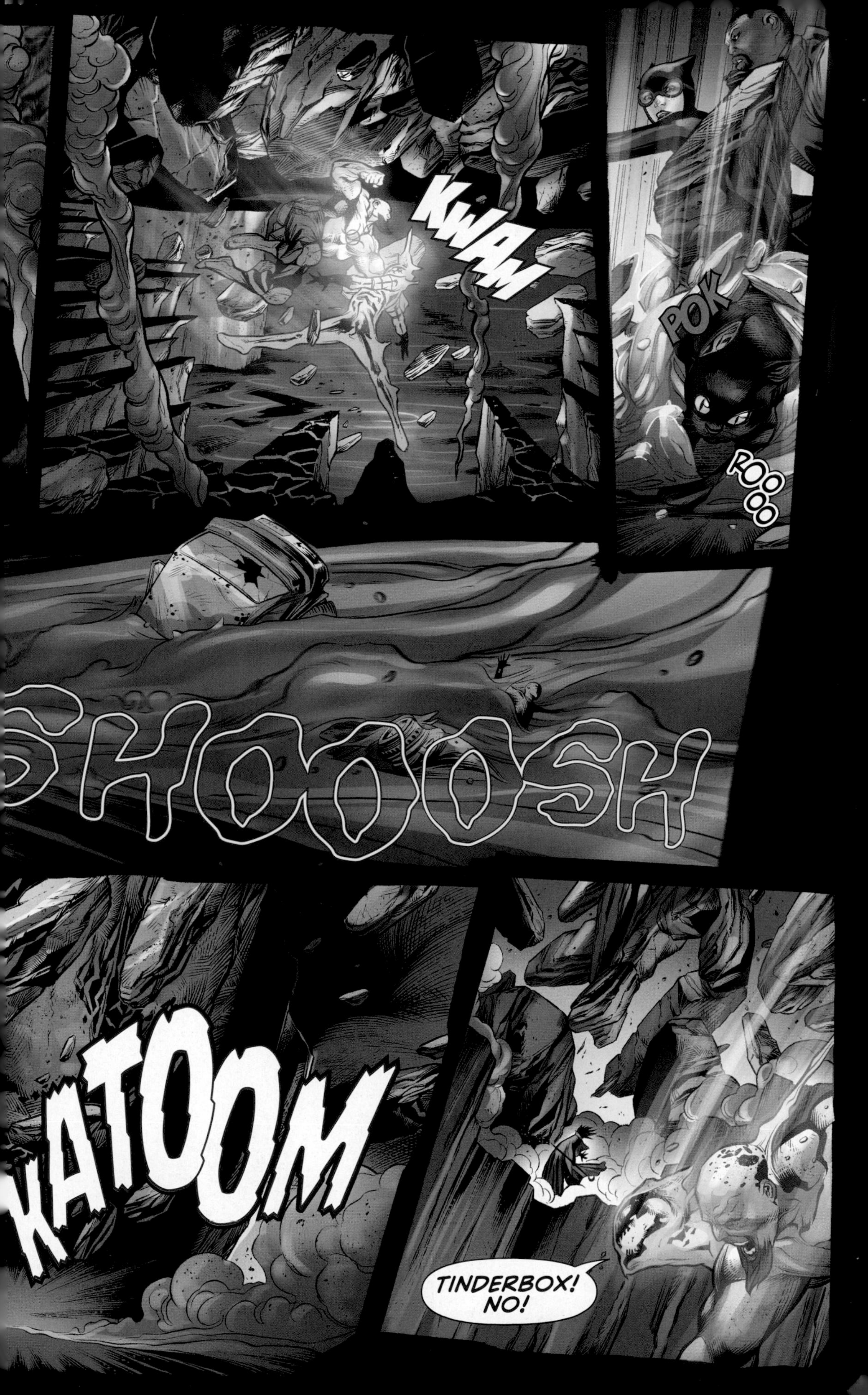
KWAM
POK
ROOOO
SHOOOSH
KATOOM
TINDERBOX! NO!

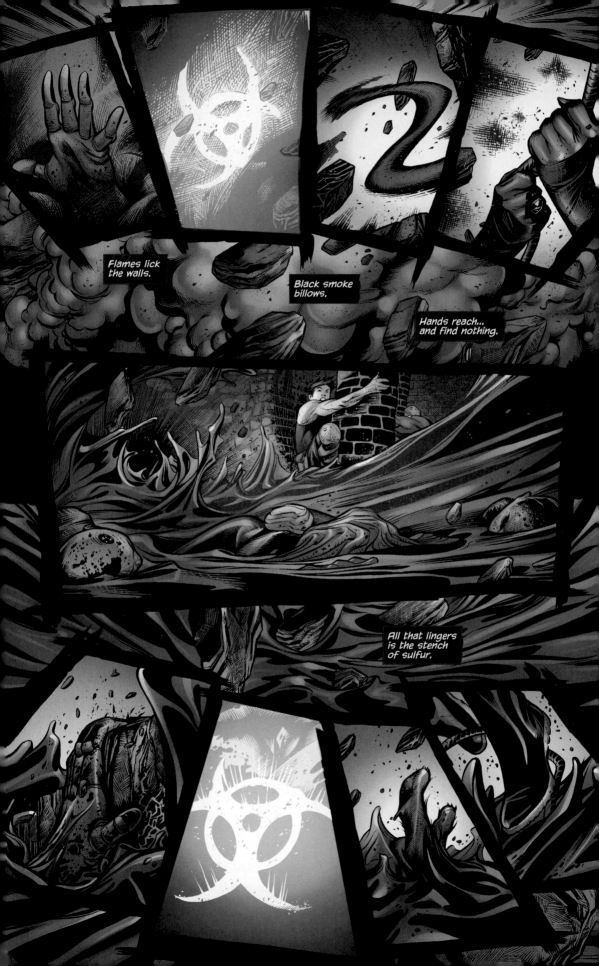

Flames lick the walls.

Black smoke billows.

Hands reach... and find nothing.

All that lingers is the stench of sulfur.

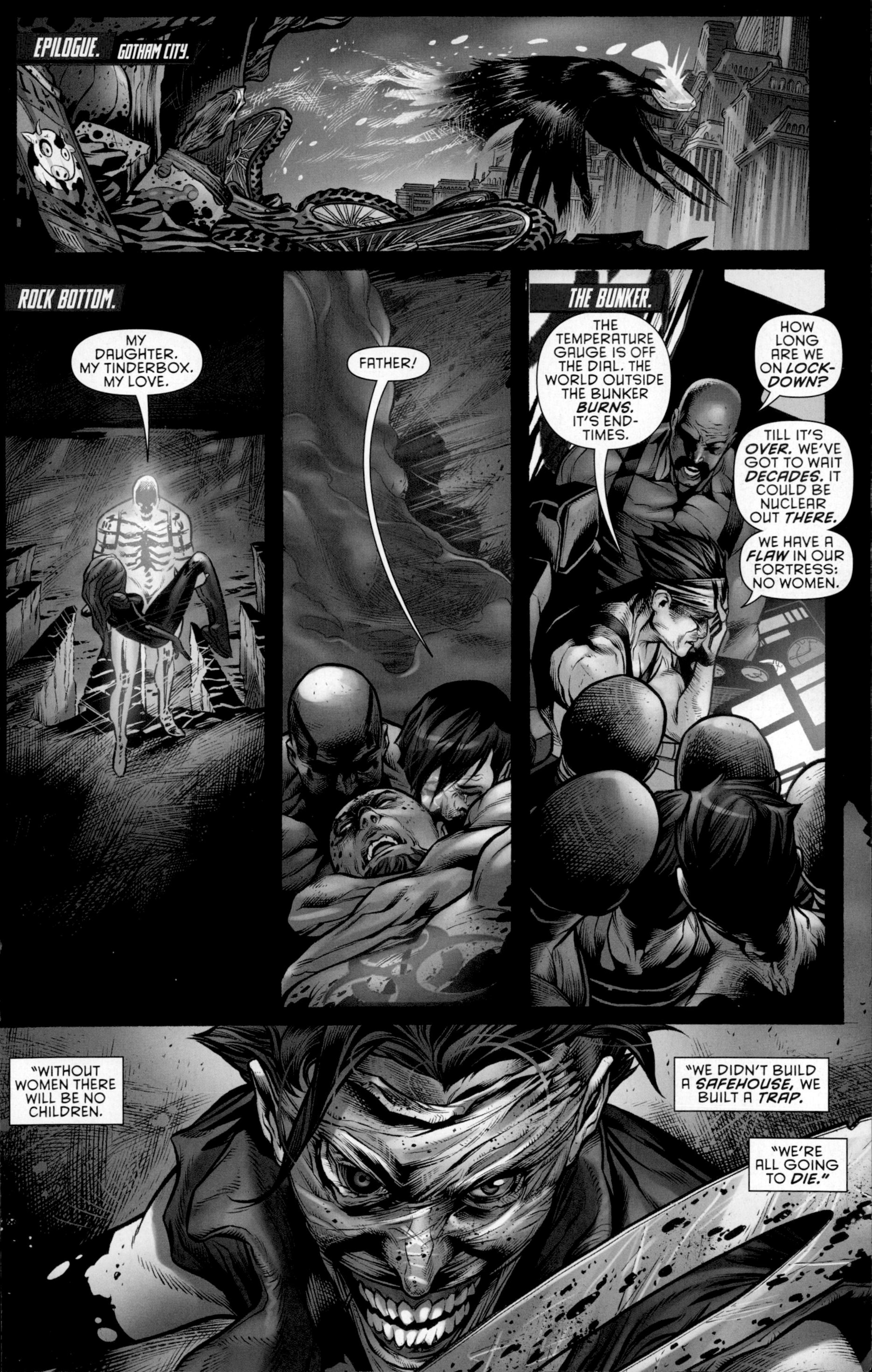
EPILOGUE.
GOTHAM CITY.
ROCK BOTTOM.
MY DAUGHTER. MY TINDERBOX. MY LOVE.
FATHER!
THE BUNKER.
THE TEMPERATURE GAUGE IS OFF THE DIAL. THE WORLD OUTSIDE THE BUNKER BURNS. IT'S END-TIMES.
HOW LONG ARE WE ON LOCK-DOWN?
TILL IT'S OVER. WE'VE GOT TO WAIT DECADES. IT COULD BE NUCLEAR OUT THERE.
WE HAVE A FLAW IN OUR FORTRESS: NO WOMEN.
"WITHOUT WOMEN THERE WILL BE NO CHILDREN.
"WE DIDN'T BUILD A SAFEHOUSE, WE BUILT A TRAP.
"WE'RE ALL GOING TO DIE."

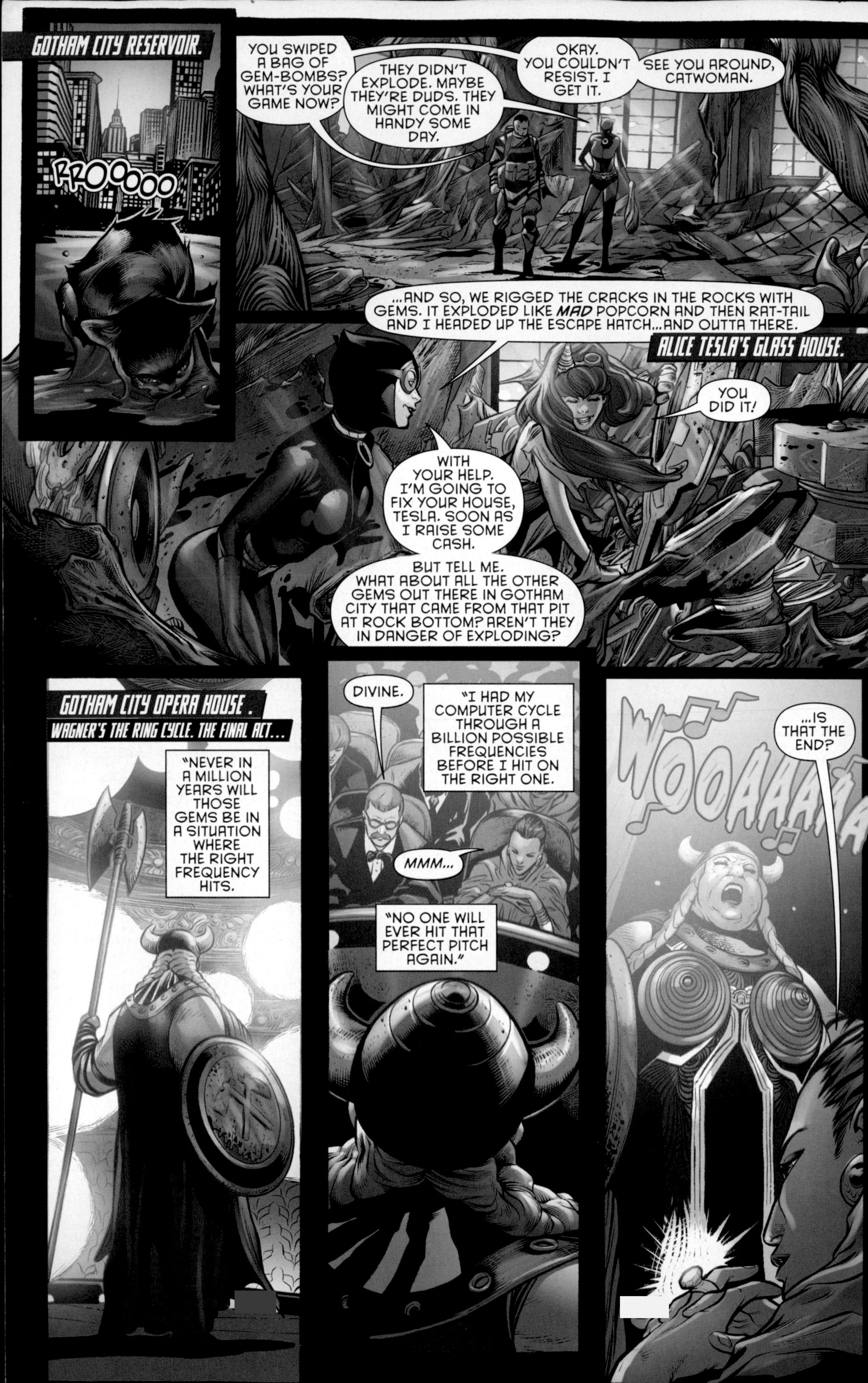
GOTHAM CITY RESERVOIR.
RROOOOOO
YOU SWIPED A BAG OF GEM-BOMBS? WHAT'S YOUR GAME NOW?
THEY DIDN'T EXPLODE. MAYBE THEY'RE DUDS. THEY MIGHT COME IN HANDY SOME DAY.
OKAY. YOU COULDN'T RESIST. I GET IT.
SEE YOU AROUND, CATWOMAN.
...AND SO, WE RIGGED THE CRACKS IN THE ROCKS WITH GEMS. IT EXPLODED LIKE MAD POPCORN AND THEN RAT-TAIL AND I HEADED UP THE ESCAPE HATCH...AND OUTTA THERE.
ALICE TESLA'S GLASS HOUSE.
YOU DID IT!
WITH YOUR HELP. I'M GOING TO FIX YOUR HOUSE, TESLA. SOON AS I RAISE SOME CASH.
BUT TELL ME. WHAT ABOUT ALL THE OTHER GEMS OUT THERE IN GOTHAM CITY THAT CAME FROM THAT PIT AT ROCK BOTTOM? AREN'T THEY IN DANGER OF EXPLODING?
GOTHAM CITY OPERA HOUSE .
WAGNER'S THE RING CYCLE. THE FINAL ACT...
"NEVER IN A MILLION YEARS WILL THOSE GEMS BE IN A SITUATION WHERE THE RIGHT FREQUENCY HITS.
DIVINE.
"I HAD MY COMPUTER CYCLE THROUGH A BILLION POSSIBLE FREQUENCIES BEFORE I HIT ON THE RIGHT ONE.
MMM...
"NO ONE WILL EVER HIT THAT PERFECT PITCH AGAIN."
WOOAAAAA
...IS THAT THE END?

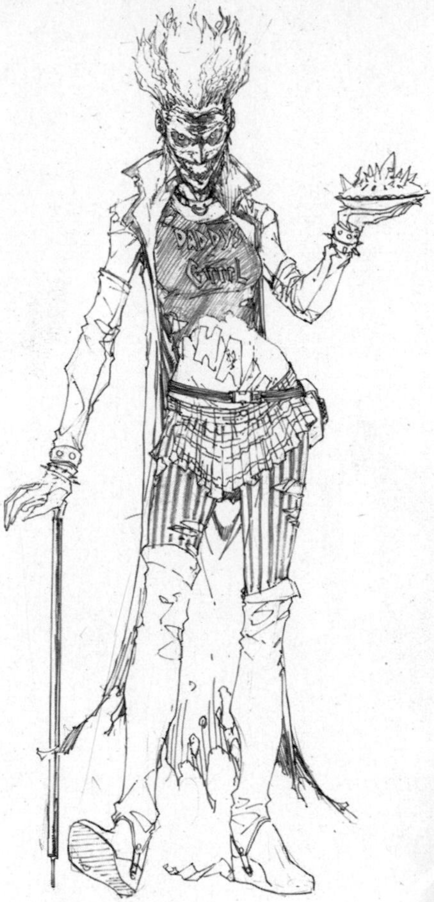
DADDYS
GIRL
HA

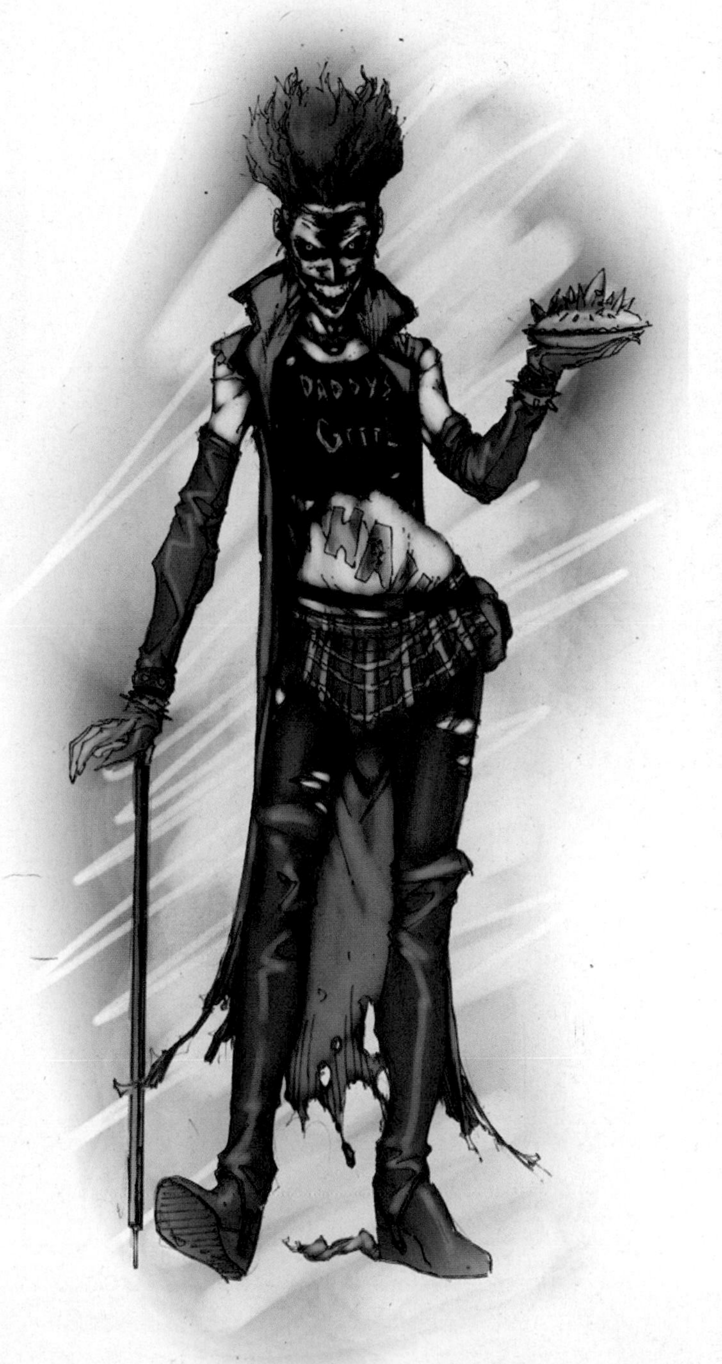
DADDYS
GIRL
HA

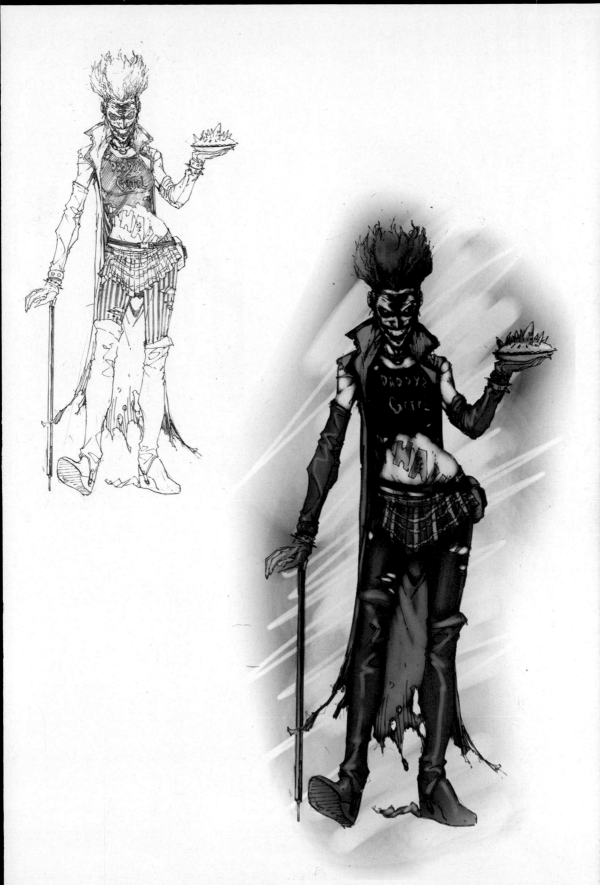

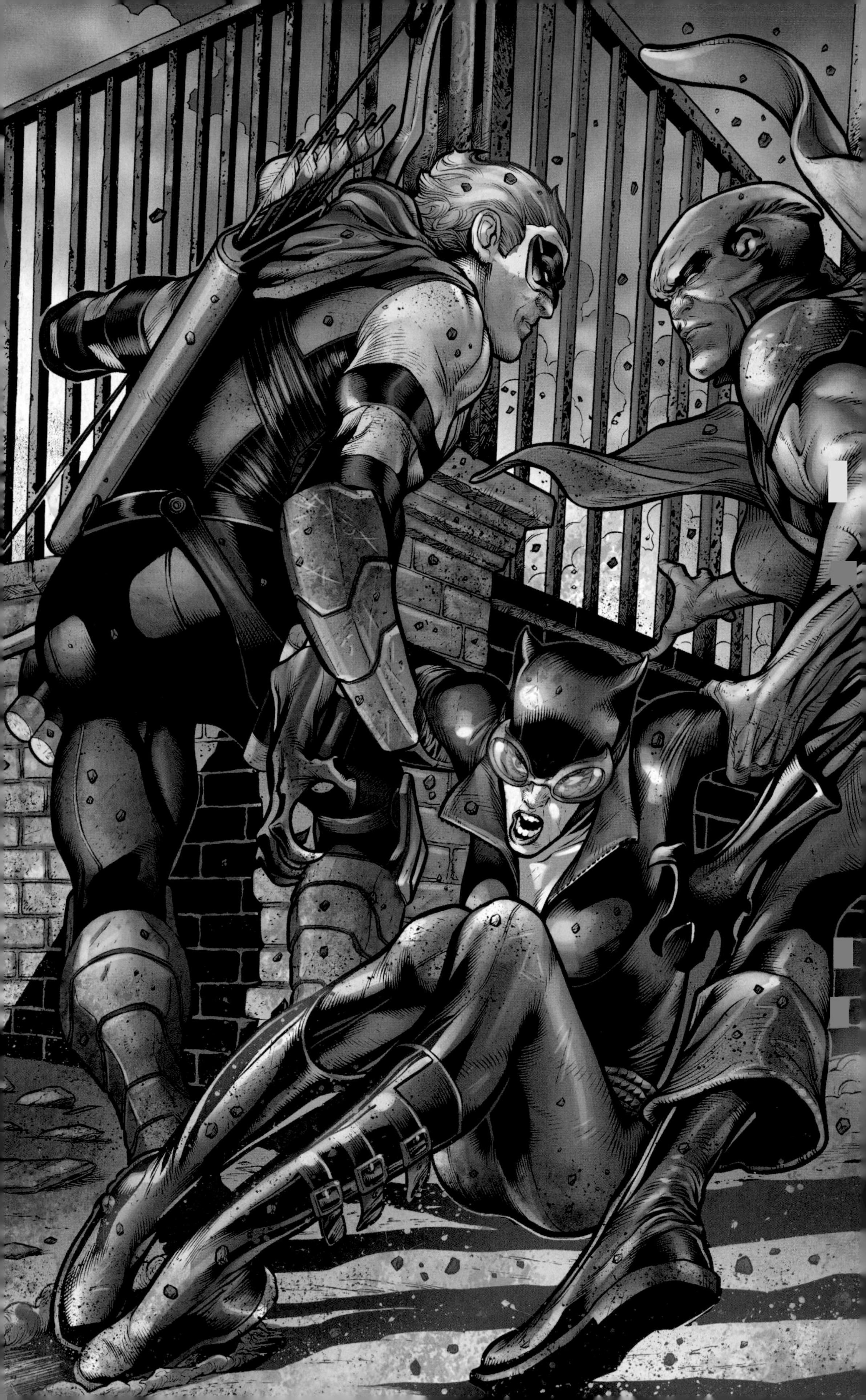

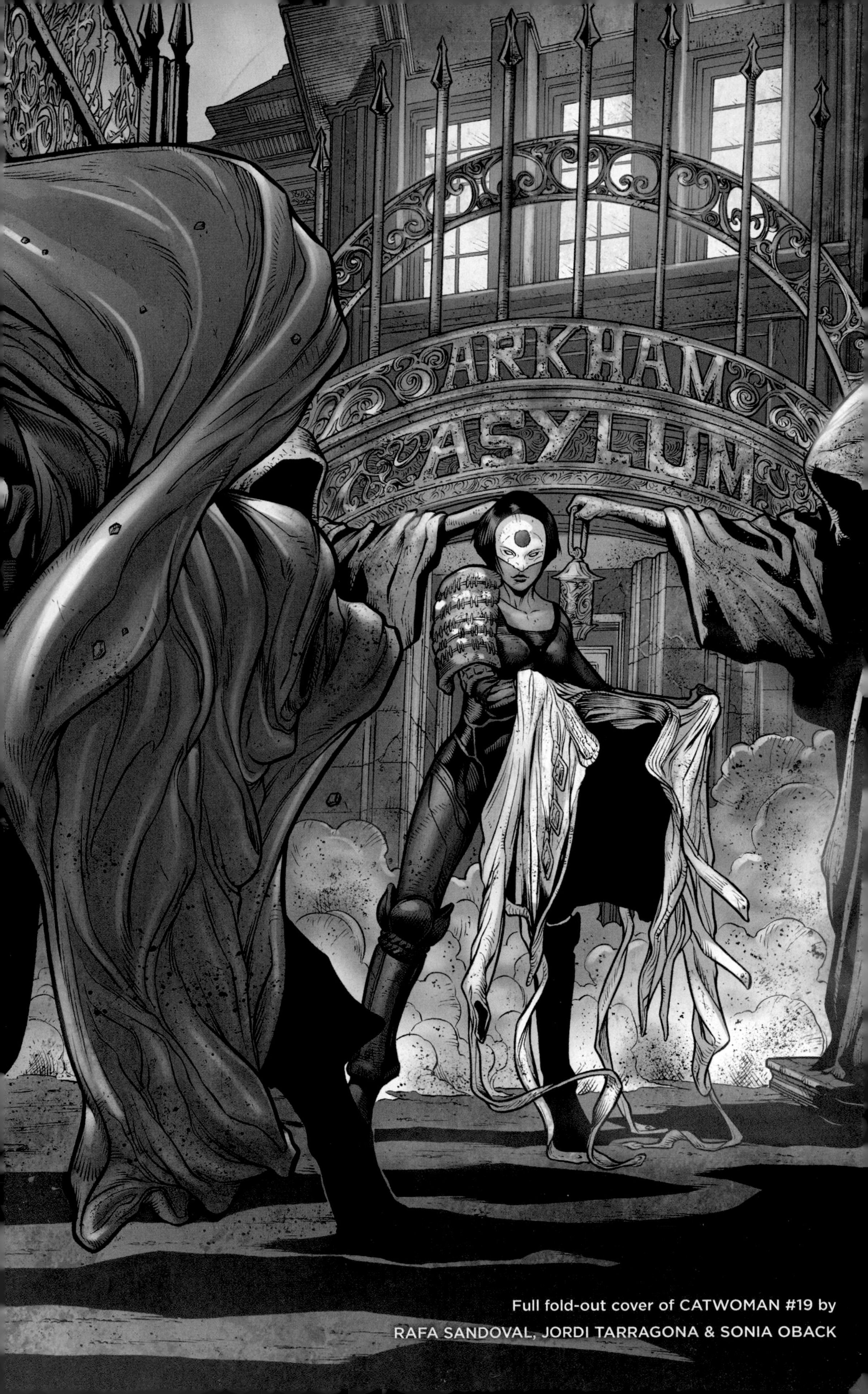
ARKHAM ASYLUM

Full fold-out cover of CATWOMAN #19 by
RAFA SANDOVAL, JORDI TARRAGONA & SONIA OBACK

DC
COMICS™

FROM THE PAGES OF *BATMAN*

CATWOMAN VOL. 1: TRAIL OF THE CATWOMAN

ED BRUBAKER & DARWYN COOKE

CATWOMAN VOL. 2:
NO EASY WAY DOWN

GOTHAM CITY SIRENS:
STRANGE FRUIT

GOTHAM CITY SIRENS:
UNION

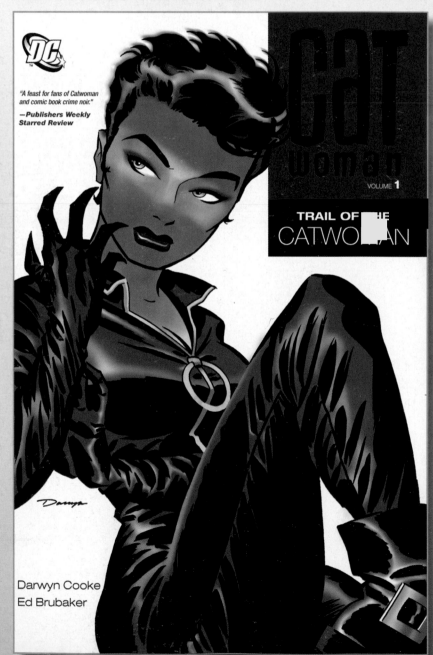